9-23-06

Happy 6

Sorry i

late. Love Sharon

Bedford Goes to War

The Heroic Story
of a Small Virginia Community
in World War II

James W. Morrison

For copies of this book or to share information on
Bedford County in World War II, please contact the author:

James W. Morrison
80 Chickadee Circle
Moneta, Virginia 24121-2342
Phone: 540-721-1991
E-mail: EZWriter@att.net

Cover photo: Company A, 116th Infantry Regiment, 29th Infantry
Division, originally from Bedford, Virginia, marching
in Ivybridge, England, circa 1943-1944. Photo by unknown photographer provided courtesy of Allen M. Huddleston.

Cover design, maps, and formatting of photos by Melinda Williams,
Melinda's Computer Graphics, Rocky Mount, VA

Library of Congress Catalog Card Number: 2004102448
ISBN: 1890306657

WARWICK HOUSE PUBLISHING
720 Court Street
Lynchburg, Virginia 24504

Dedication

This book is dedicated
to the men and women of Bedford County, Virginia,
who aided their country during World War II,
and especially to those who served
in the Armed Forces of the United States
and those who gave their lives
so others could live in freedom.

Contents

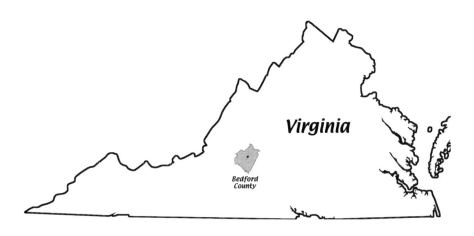

Virginia

Bedford
County

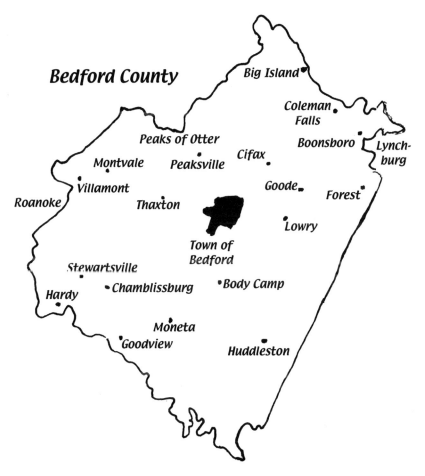

Bedford County

Big Island

Coleman
Falls

Peaks of Otter   Cifax   Boonsboro   Lynch-
                                                     burg
Montvale   Peaksville

Villamont   Goode   Forest

Roanoke   Thaxton

                                    Lowry

                 Town of
                 Bedford

Stewartsville

Hardy   Chamblissburg   Body Camp

              Moneta
           Goodview   Huddleston

Top: Peaks of Otter beyond future town of Bedford, circa 1855.

Center: A view of Peaks of Otter today.

Bottom: Town of Bedford, looking north, probably 1930s-1950s. Rail line runs east and west in center of town. Main Street is two blocks south, parallel to tracks. Bridge Street runs north and south in the center of photo, crossing over the rail tracks. Main business district is at intersection of Main and Bridge Streets. At top center is Bedford High School. Several factories lie along rail tracks at far right center.

(*Bedford Bulletin-Democrat,* June 23, 1962, provided by Eleanor Yowell.)

Bedford Firemen's Band leading Company A down Main Street, probably 1930s-1941. (Photo courtesy of the Bedford City/County Museum)

Bedford business district, looking north along Bridge Street. Jones (Green's) Drug Store was located in the corner building on the right.
(Photographer unidentified. Copy provided by Eleanor Yowell.)

Hampton Looms, the "woolen mill," now closed.

Piedmont Label Company, still in operation.

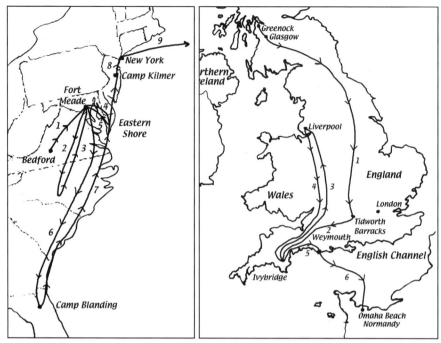

Top left: Company A's areas of deployment in the U.S., 1941-1942.
Top right: Company A's deployment in Europe, 1942-June 1944.
(Maps by Melinda Williams, Melinda's Computer Graphics, 2004)

Bedford's Company A of the Virginia National Guard, 1940.
(National Guard Yearbook for 1940)

Company A, expanded, at Fort Meade, MD, August 1941.

Men of Company A who had worked at Rubatex/Salta Corp. Photo was taken on February 10, 1941, after Bedford's National Guard Company A had been called to active federal service, and before the company departed on February 21 for Fort Meade. (Copy of photo from the archives of the Bedford City/County Museum)

Right: Men of Company A believed to have worked at Hampton Looms, the woolen mill. Photo may have been taken after Company A was mobilized but before it left Bedford. From left to right: Billy Mann, Clyde Powers, Frank Draper, Cedrick Broughman, Clifton Lee, and William Craghead. Draper and Lee were killed on D-Day. (Photo courtesy Gamiel Draper)

Ray Stevens and Grant Yopp at Fort Meade, Maryland, 1942.

Grant Yopp and his wife Elsie visiting in Washington, D.C., while Grant was stationed at Fort Meade, 1942. (Both photographs of Grant Yopp courtesy of Virginia Pizzati)

Top: Men of Company A in England, probably 1943. From left to right, front row: possibly Weldon Rosazza, unidentified soldier, then probably Richard Swift of Alexandria, VA, Bob Edwards, Alex Reynolds, Sherman Watson, Roy Stevens, and Earl Newcomb. Back row: Gordon White, unidentified, Jack Powers, Andrew Coleman, and John Wilkes. Rosazza, White, Powers, and Wilkes, were killed on D-Day, and Coleman died of illness soon thereafter.

(Photo provided to the Bedford newspapers by Mr. and Mrs. Earl Newcomb)

Bottom: Bedford men in England, probably 1943. Left to right, front row: Elmere Wright, possibly Bob Edwards, possibly Gordon White, last unidentified. Back row: first unidentified, Boyd Wilson, John Wilkes, unidentified, and Ray Stevens.

Top left: Four Bedford baseball players in London, probably May 1943. From left to right: Elmere Wright, Tony Marsico, Pride Wingfield, and Frank Draper. Wright, Marsico, and Draper were on the team that won the European Theater of Operations championship.

Top right: John Schenk and Pride Wingfield with their bicycles in front of a Nissen hut in England, 1943.

Left: Wedding picture from England of Meade Hite Baker and his English bride. Baker was a member of Company A and was from Southwest Virginia but not Bedford County. On the left was best man Frank Draper, from Bedford. Both Baker and Draper were killed on D-Day.

The Baker wedding party.

Seven Dean Brothers In The Armed Service

Floyd Dean   Mr. and Mrs. J. F. Dean   Orien Dean

Lester Dean   Halsey Dean   Ward Dean   John Dean   Bernard Dean

Top: Mr. and Mrs. J. F. Dean and their seven sons serving in the military, a number probably not exceeded in Virginia. John Dean was killed in Normandy on June 17, 1944. (Courtesy of Ward and Mary Dean)

Bottom: Five sons and one daughter of Mr. and Mrs. H. B. Powers served in the armed forces. Jack Powers, of Company A, was killed on D-Day.
(The Bedford newspapers often featured photos and captions of multiple brothers and sisters serving in the military.)

Eloise Powers   William Powers   Henry Powers   Archie Powers   Jack Powers

POWERS IN SERVICE—Mr. and Mrs. H. B. Powers of Bedford, have three sons and one daughter in the service. One son lost his life in the Normandy invasion. Their oldest son, Auville T. Powers, 36, registered and passed the physical examination but has not been called on account of his age.

Cadet Nurse Eloise Powers, 20, is stationed at Grace Hospital, Richmond.

Pvt. William E. Powers, 28, has served overseas 10 months, has suffered two wounds and has been awarded the Purple Heart. He is expected home soon.

T. Sgt. Henry C. Powers, 30, entered service with the 116th infantry and has been overseas for 31 months.

Cpl. Archie R. Powers, 22, in service for more than two years, served with Patton's army.

Sgt. Jack Powers, 25, entered the service with the 116th infantry and was killed on D-Day.

Left:
Public-service
advertisement on
rationing.
(*Bedford Bulletin*,
February 18, 1943)

Below: Ration Books
and Stamps.
(Courtesy Edie Morrison)

Left:
Public-service advertisement for
salvaging tin cans.
(*Bedford Democrat*, March 11, 1943)

Top left: William Yowell and his bomber flight crew and ground crew, England, 1944. Yowell is in the back row, third from the right.

Top right: William and Eleanor Yowell, far right, relax in the desert with bomber crew members and wives on a break from training at Alamogordo, New Mexico, in early 1944. (Photo courtesy of Eleanor Yowell)

Left: The 10-man, B-17 bomber crew, with which Joe Goode served. Goode is on the far left of the back row. (Photo courtesy of Joe Goode)

Right: Joseph Danner, a B-26 pilot killed in a crash in England after 50 missions over enemy territory. (Photo courtesy Mrs. Margaret Simpkins)

Above: Joseph Danner's grave following the return of his remains to Bedford in 1948. Bomber-shaped floral arrangement by florist and former bombardier Harold Jarvis.
(Photo courtesy Mrs. Margaret Simpkins)

Right: Joseph Danner's headstone in Bedford's Greenwood Cemetery, 2000. Standing to the left is Harold Jarvis's son, Rob, who narrated the historical drama, *Bedford Goes to War*.

Below: Henry Chappelle, standing by a model and photos of the Navy ocean-going tugboat, USS *Montcalm*, on which he served.

Right: Destroyer USS *Picking*, on which Woodrow Hubbard served. *Bottom left: Picking's* officers and crew. Hubbard is on upper right side. (Photos of Hubbard and *Picking* provided by David Hubbard, some of which were obtained over the internet.)

Right:
Woodrow Hubbard.

NEWS OF OUR MEN and WOMEN IN UNIFORM

A/c William D. Goode, who has been stationed at Selma Field, Monroe, La., has been transferred to Plant Park, Fla.

Private Nelson P. Brooks, who has been located at Shreveport, La. for several months, is now stationed at Camp Stewart, Ga.

Second Lieutenant Ashford Chappelle, of Bedford, has been called to active duty, according to an announcement issued by the War Department recently.

Mitchell Parrish, seaman second class, USNR, has been transferred from Camp Peary to Shoemaker, California.

Rodney Saunders, of Bedford, is a 17-year-old recruit in the U. S. Navy. He is a son of Charles Saunders.

Pvt. Garland Humphreys, of Big Island, who entered U. S. service early in the Spring, is now located at Fort McClellan, Ala.

Sam A. Wilson, hospital attendant 1/c, stationed in Philadelphia, has been transfered to Norma, Okla. He entered the service about a year ago.

Mrs. Robert Watson, of Vinton, is spending a couple of weeks in Boston, Mass., with her husband, who is stationed at the Boston Naval Training School.

Pvt. Leonard Siler, in training at Camp Edwards, Mass., returned to his station last Saturday evening, after a 3-day pass. His wife is residing near him at Onset, Mass.

Warrant Officer Fred O. Broyles has recently been transfered from Jacksonville Army Air Base, Jacksonville, Fla., to Flora, S. C., Ord. Plant, Flora, Miss. He is a son-in-law of Mr. M. T. Gray, of Blue Ridge.

Robert Lynch, son of Mr. and Mrs. Sexter F. Lynch, of Moneta, left on June 14th for duty in the U. S. Navy. He was a popular boy and his family and friends wish him the best of luck.

Cpl. S. C. Rockecharlie, son of Mr. and Mrs. W. S. Rockecharlie, now stationed in England, writes he is well and also met an old friend from Bedford, John Thompson, whom he was very glad to see.

George C. Dooley, Jr., son of Mr. and Mrs. George C. Dooley, of Vinton, was among a class of fourteen aviation cadets appointed cadet officers within their ranks at Foster Field, Texas. Cadet Dooley was appointed flight lieutenant.

Sgt. Hylton Cobb has returned to Fort Riley, Kans., after a furlough He was accompanied home by his wife and daughter, Pamela, who have been near him at Junction City, Kans. En roue home they met St.-Sgt. W. B. Cobb in Cincinnati, Ohio.

Private Annie L. Arthur, daughter of Mrs. Harry C. Arthur, Rte. 1, Bedford, who has been stationed at the Third Training Center of the Women's Army Corps at Fort Oglethorpe, Ga., has been assigned to WAC Detachment, 1227 SU, Station Complement, at Fort Story, Va.

Sgt. Payton M. Otey, now with the U. S. Army in England shown with his wife who was with him both in California and New York, where he was stationed before embarking.

Top left: Sample of *Bedford Bulletin's* "News of Our Men and Women in Uniform," featuring a photo of Sgt. and Mrs. Payton Otey.

Top right: Samuel Moses Jackson, first Black from Bedford County to be killed in action in the war. (Photo courtesy of Annie Pollard and the Bedford City/County Museum)

Bottom right: Russell Otey, while serving in the U.S. Army Air Forces. In 1978, Otey became the first Black to be elected mayor of the City of Bedford. (Photo courtesy of Mrs. Russell Otey)

Bottom left: James Rucker, Guantanamo Bay, Cuba. (Photo courtesy of Mrs. Russell Otey—Marie Rucker Otey— sister of James Rucker)

Top left: Taylor N. Fellers, captain and commander of Company A. He was killed on D-Day.

Top right: Front page of *Bedford Democrat*, July 20, 1944, reporting first, belated news of the death of Bedford men on D-Day.

Bottom left: Clarence Higgenbotham places flowers on the fresh grave of his brother-in-law, Taylor Fellers, in Normandy in June 1944. (Photo courtesy of Bertie Higgenbotham Woodford, sister of Taylor Fellers.)

Bottom right: Taylor Fellers' grave in Bedford's Greenwood Cemetery.

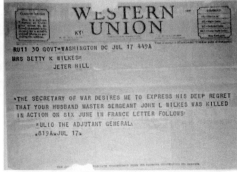

Top left: John and Bettie Wilkes. *Top right:* Western Union telegram from the War Department, dated July 17, informing Bettie Wilkes of the death of her husband, John, on D-Day, June 6, 1944. (Courtesy Bettie Wilkes Hooper)

Above: Rubye Wilkes-Archer is buried next to her brother, John Wilkes, in Bedford's Greenwood Cemetery. She joined the Army as a nurse after her brother's unit was activated. She served in the Army for 28 years, saw service in Korea and Vietnam, and retired as a lieutenant colonel.

Above: Brothers Bedford Hoback, left, and Raymond Hoback both served in Company A and were killed on D-Day.

Left: Rubye Wilkes-Archer

Top left: Ivylyn and John Schenk on their wedding day in August 1942.
Top right: Ivylyn Schenk signaling "V for Victory" in her Victory Garden.
(Two photos courtesy of Ivylyn Schenk Hardy.)

Bottom: Envelope containing a letter written by Ivylyn Schenk to her husband, John, on June 5, 1944, postmarked June 6, returned to sender unopened and stamped "Deceased." John Schenk was killed on June 6, D-Day.

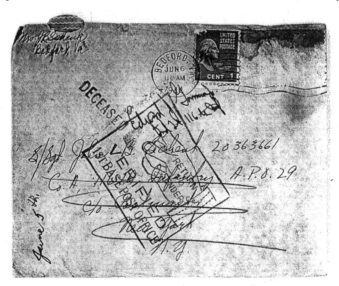

Top left: Frank Draper, of Company A, was killed on D-Day and buried initially in England.

Top right: Draper's casket is removed from the train upon return of his remains to Bedford in July 1948.

Below right: Pallbearers remove the casket after funeral services.

Above: Headstone.

Below: Services in Greenwood Cemetery for Frank Draper.

(Photos courtesy of Carder Tharp Funeral Home and Crematory)

Twin brothers Roy & Ray Stevens, age six.

Above:
Helen and Roy Stevens at home.

Above: Ray Stevens, left, was killed on D-Day. Roy Stevens was later wounded. (Photos courtesy of Roy Stevens)

Left:
Roy Stevens'
World War II
Memorabilia.

Top: Memorabilia of Bernard Saunders, who was a prisoner of war of the Japanese for three-and-a-half years.

Bottom left: William "Billy" Parker, who was a prisoner of war of the Germans and in later years a bear hunter.

Bottom right: Charlie Sneed, who was killed in the Anzio Invasion with four other men from Bedford County.

Top left: William Merriken, a survivor of the Malmedy Massacre in the Battle of the Bulge.

Top right: Pfc. Richard B. Walker (left) and Pfc. Warren Davis were killed in the Malmedy Massacre. (Photos provided courtesy of William Merriken)

Right: Richard Walker is buried in Morgan's Baptist Church cemetery in southern Bedford County. Warren Davis is buried in the Henri-Chapelle American Cemetery in Belgium.

Left: Charlie M. Sneed, Jr. (opposite page) is buried in Bedford's Oakwood Cemetery. Of the other four Bedford men killed near Anzio, one is buried in Italy and three were missing in action.

Left: Bedford County Courthouse honor roll plaque memorializing Bedford County men lost in World War I and II.

Below: Memorials outside the Bedford County Courthouse, honoring Bedford County men who died in all wars (flag pole), served in all foreign wars (stone on the left), died in the Normandy Invasion and later battles of World War II (stone on the right), and died in the Civil War (obelisk).

Below: Company A veterans at the stone and plaque memorializing Bedford County men in the 116th Infantry who gave their lives in preparation for and participation in the Normandy Invasion and later battles of World War II. Men believed to be, from left to right: Howard Faribault, Glenwood "Dickie" Overstreet, Pride Wingfield, Roy Stevens, unidentified, unidentified, Elisha Ray Nance, Herbert Jones, unidentified, Harry Hargis, Carl Danner, and Allen Huddleston.

Top left: Former Bedford High School (now Middle School), with stone and plaque honoring all former Bedford High School students who served in the war and especially the nineteen who lost their lives in the war.

Top right: Close-up of Bedford High School plaque.

Bottom left: World War II honor roll mounted inside the entrance of the Bedford Baptist Church. Names of men who died in the war are followed with a star.

Bottom right: Plaque at the Bedford Baptist Church indicating the dedication of the church's tower bells.

Top photos: Main Street Methodist Church display case and honor roll for those serving in World War II and those who died.

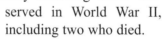

Middle: Bedford Christian Church memorials—on the left a stained glass window memorializing Frank Draper; in the center the church's honor roll; and on the right a stained glass window memorializing John Dean.

Bottom left: Banner at the Salem United Methodist Church in Bedford County honoring those who served in World War II, including two who died.

Bottom right: Banner at the Center Point Methodist Church in Bedford County honoring six men from that church who served, including two gold stars for the Hoback brothers.

Left:
Aerial view of the
National D-Day Memorial.
(Photo courtesy of Loyd Woodford,
Lynchburg Detachment of the
Marine Corps League, and
the National D-Day Memorial
Foundation)

Right:
The National D-Day
Memorial filled with
21,000 people
at June 6, 2001,
dedication, at which
President George W. Bush
spoke.
(*Bedford Bulletin*)

Bottom: View of memorial's Victory Arch. "Overlord" was the code name for the Normandy Invasion. (Courtesy of National D-Day Memorial Foundation)

Top left: The National D-Day Memorial Arch.
Top right: "Across the Beach" sculpture at the National D-Day Memorial.

Left: Tribute to the fallen, with a Ranger scaling the cliff in the background.
Right: Gravesite of Elmere Wright, Company A, at the Normandy American Cemetery in France.

Left: Lucille Hoback Boggess, Roy Stevens, and Helen Stevens at a presentation on D-Day at Bedford Central Public Library, September 2001.

Prologue

The Book

This book is a story of Bedford, Virginia—both Bedford County and the town of Bedford—during the World War II years of 1940-1945. The story tells what happened on the home front and to Bedford's young men and women when they left home to serve in America's armed forces. It focuses on Bedford's role in the broad scope of the war, while giving appropriate attention to Bedford's special tragedy—the D-Day Invasion of Normandy.

The book has two parts. Part I tells the general story of what happened in Bedford and to its service personnel during the war. Part II illustrates in detail the personal experiences of over forty individuals from Bedford County.

Bedford's experience in World War II is unique. In many ways, however, it may be typical of the experiences of thousands of communities across America. The book attempts to relate what was happening nationally and internationally before specifying what happened in Bedford. The author hopes that readers everywhere, not just in Bedford, will be stimulated to look into the experiences of their own families, friends, and communities during World War II.

Bedford

Bedford County has long been a place of beauty, history, and patriotism. The county lies in scenic, rural, southwest Virginia. Its long and distinguished history dates back 250 years to 1754 when, during the British colonial period, the county was formed by an act of the Virginia Assembly. It was named for the Fourth Duke of Bedford, John Russell, who was then Secretary of State for Great Britain.[1] Throughout the county's history, the people of Bedford have been patriotic in peacetime and in war. Bedford men have fought and died in nearly every major war of America.

A Place of Beauty

The county lies at the eastern edge of the Blue Ridge Mountains, part of the Appalachian chain. A range of the Blue Ridge runs along the northern and western edges of the county, and the ridgeline delineates part of the county's boundaries. Just below the ridgeline runs a segment of the Blue Ridge Parkway. This scenic road offers spectacular views of Bedford County from 2,500-3,200 feet above sea level. (The parkway was built to promote tourism in the area and as an economic relief project during the Great Depression. Construction began in the mid-1930s and provided work for many in the Bedford area through the federal government's Works Projects Administration and Civilian Conservation Corps.)

Dominating the Bedford County horizon are the Peaks of Otter, part of the Blue Ridge. The twin peaks, Sharp Top and Flat Top, rise to heights of about 4,000 feet above sea level and can be seen from most of Bedford County and beyond. A third peak, Harkening Hill, lies to the northwest and is not as visible from the county.

To the east and south of these mountains lie rolling hills covered with trees, broad pastures, and crop land. The rolling hills account for the majority of the county's terrain.

With an area of over 760 square miles, the county is the fifth largest in size among Virginia's ninety-five counties.[2] Its shape roughly resembles a trapezoid, taller than wide, and tilted northeast to southwest. Through its center, the county measures about thirty miles east-to-west and about forty miles north-to-south.

Two bodies of water help form the county's boundaries—the historic James River in the north and, in the south, the Roanoke River, which was dammed up in the 1960s to form Smith Mountain Lake.

With its blue-haze mountains, verdant rolling hills, and green and blue rivers and lakes, Bedford County is beautiful country.

The quaint City of Bedford adds to the charm of the area. This municipality, located in the center of the county, was established in 1782 as the Town of Liberty. It became the new county seat, replacing New London to the east. The town was incorporated in 1839. In 1890, it was renamed "Bedford City." In 1912, the word "City" was dropped, and the town was referred to as "Bedford." In 1968,

Bedford became an independent city and is now officially the "City of Bedford." Throughout the periods of the two World Wars and into the 1960s, however, it was the "town of Bedford."[3]

The relatively large cities of Roanoke and Lynchburg lie just across the boundaries in adjacent counties to the west and east, respectively. The population of each of these cities has exceeded the entire population of Bedford County since at least 1930.[4] A major Virginia state highway and a railway pass through the center of Bedford County, each connecting to Roanoke and Lynchburg. Two other rail lines run generally east-west through the northern and southern parts of the county.[5]

The People

Just prior to World War II, the 1940 Census recorded the population of Bedford County at 29,687 and the town of Bedford at 3,973. The county's population had remained stable at about 30,000 since 1900. (The population would remain at about 30,000 until 1980, when the county began to grow. In the 2000 Census, the county's population numbered 61,082, and the City of Bedford had grown to 6,359.)[6]

The great majority of Bedford County's population has always lived in rural areas of the county. In 1940, 87 percent lived in rural areas, and only 13 percent lived in the town of Bedford. (By 2000, most of the county's population still lived in rural areas. Just over 10 percent lived in the City of Bedford and another sizeable percentage lived in suburban areas of the county adjacent to Lynchburg and Roanoke and in subdivisions such as those at Smith Mountain Lake.)

The economy of the county in 1940 was a mixture of farming, industry, and commerce, and so it remains today.

Military Patriotism

Bedford County's patriotism has been evident for two and a half centuries. Nearly 300 men from Bedford served in the colonial militia in the 1750s. During the French and Indian Wars from 1758-1774, a company of fifty-two men from Bedford fought with the American colonial and British forces. At the Battle of Point Pleasant on October

10, 1774, the company commander, Capt. Thomas Buford, was killed in action.[7] In the Revolutionary War, nearly 500 men from Bedford may have served in the militia or Continental Army, and Bedford citizens provided food supplies to American units.[8]

A volunteer company from Bedford fought in the War of 1812; all but four died or suffered severely from disease.[9] In the Civil War, according to one account, some 3,500 men from Bedford County fought for the Confederacy. There seem to be no authoritative records on how many of these men died.[10] In the Spanish-American War, sixteen men from Bedford served.[11]

In World War I, some 2,100 Bedford County men registered for the draft, and 796 actually ended up serving. Of these, thirty-nine were killed or died in the service of their country.[12] In the Korean War, according to unofficial accounts, at least 172 Bedford County men served; three were killed or died in service, twenty-one were wounded, and two were prisoners of war.[13] In the Vietnam War, nineteen men from the county were killed or died in service.[14] Individual Bedford men served in the Gulf War in the early 1990s and in the war with Iraq in 2003, and Bedford men served as an active-duty Army unit in support of Operation Enduring Freedom and the war against terrorism beginning in 2004.[15]

With the possible—even likely—exception of the Civil War, World War II had a greater impact on the Bedford community than any other war. Aside from the Civil War, more men from the Bedford community served in the military and more died while in military service during World War II than in any prior or subsequent war, and the relative impact on the home front was similar.

Bedford's Company A

Beginning in the early 1920s and continuing into the 1940s, Bedford County and the town of Bedford were home to a National Guard infantry company, Company A. The company met in the basement of the Bedford County Courthouse.

Company A was an element of the 116th Infantry Regiment of the Virginia National Guard, a regiment that had earned itself a distinguished place in American history. Some have said that the lineage of the 116th Infantry can be traced back to 1741 and the formation of a militia regiment in Augusta County in the Colony of Virginia, and then to a unit that served under none other than George Washington around the time of the French and Indian War.[16] Others trace the lineage back at least to the Civil War and the "Stonewall Brigade," formally known as the 1st Brigade, Army of the Shenandoah, Confederate States of America, commanded by Thomas J. "Stonewall" Jackson.[17] In a publication of the Virginia National Guard, the following accolade is written:

> While the numerals of the 116th Infantry are comparatively young, its military ancestry and service to the Commonwealth ante-date the founding of the Republic. Through the Colonial Wars, the Revolutionary War, and down through the years, volunteers, ancestors of this regiment, were to be found in the great legions which made the United States of America a reality.[18]

Continuing with this lineage, in March 1917, during World War I, some Virginia National Guard units, including the 2[d] Virginia Infantry Regiment, were mustered into Federal service. In October 1917, at Camp McClellan, Alabama, the 2[d], along with elements of the 1st and 4th Virginia Infantry Regiments, were reorganized and designated the 116th Infantry Regiment of the 29th Division.

The 116th became part of a newly organized 29th ("Blue and Gray") Division, which comprised men from Virginia, as well as New Jersey, Maryland, and the District of Columbia. The 29th, including its 116th Infantry Regiment, was deployed to France in June 1918 and fought in two campaigns, including the Meuse-Argonne offensive in September 1918, where the division sustained 4,781 casualties.[19]

During World War I, the 116th Infantry had a Company A, but it consisted of men mostly from the Staunton, Virginia, area, with others from Richmond and Alexandria. This Company A lost twenty-one men killed or missing in action and fifty-six wounded in action during that war.[20]

The 29th Division returned to the United States in May 1919. The units were demobilized, and the men mustered out.

More than two years later, in September 1921, the Virginia National Guard formed the first National Guard company to be based in Bedford. That company was designated Headquarters Company, 2^d Virginia Infantry Regiment. A month later, in October, the Virginia National Guard reorganized the 2^d Regiment and, in March 1922, redesignated it the 116th Infantry Regiment. At that point, the name of Bedford's company was changed to Rifle Company, Company A, 116th Infantry, a name that would survive through World War II and into the twenty-first century.[21]

Company A's service in World War II became legend. At the end of the war, Company A was deactivated. By July 1946, however, it was reorganized and Bedford men again enlisted, including six men who had served with the company during World War II.[22]

Company A served as a National Guard unit throughout the post-World War II period, and a new armory was built on East Main Street in Bedford to accommodate the unit. In early March 2004, soldiers in Company A were called up for an eighteen-month tour of active duty with the U.S. Army as part of Operation Enduring Freedom. While Company A was an element of the 1st Battalion of the 116th Infantry Regiment, it deployed in 2004 as part of the 3^d Battalion of the 116th Infantry. This was the first time Company A had been called up for active-duty federal service since February 1941.

Part I

Bedford's Story

Chapter 1

Bedford Before the War

In 1940 Bedford was a small, predominantly agricultural community. In the county there were more than 4,000 individual farms; about twenty small, rural communities; and the sole town of Bedford. Farming was the main occupation. Commerce, industry, and social activities were generally concentrated in town. Company A of the Virginia National Guard was based in the town but drew men from throughout the county.

The People

The nearly 30,000 residents in the county comprised about 6,900 families, with 87 percent living in rural areas. Nearly four out of every five residents were White, and the rest were Black. Only sixty-three people were foreign-born, and they were all White and lived in town. The racial mix among the nearly 4,000 people in the town of Bedford was about the same as the county—77 percent White and 23 percent Black.[1]

Communities and Schools

The twenty small, rural communities included Big Island, Body Camp, Boonsboro, Chamblissburg, Cifax, Coleman Falls, Cool Spring, Goode, Goodview, Forest, Hardy, Huddleston, Lowry, Moneta, Montvale, Peaksville, Stewartsville, Thaxton, and Villamont. Many had their own churches, small stores, and schools.

Schools in the county numbered about 100. Most were small, elementary schools located in the countryside. Schools were segregated racially. Of the nine accredited high schools in the county, one was for black students.[2]

Farms

On the more than 4,100 farms in the county in 1940, farm families operated dairy farms, raised cattle and poultry, ran apple and peach orchards, and grew tobacco, tomatoes, corn, hay, and various grains.[3] Harvesting pulpwood was an important source of income for some. Much of the pulpwood was taken to the Bedford Pulp and Paper Mill, located in the Big Island community on the James River in the north-central part of the county, where it was processed to make paper products. Families from the farms and rural communities often came to the town of Bedford to do business and shop, especially on Saturdays.

Town of Bedford

The town of Bedford lay in the center of the county, near the foot of the Peaks of Otter. In addition to its scenic location between the mountains and the rolling countryside, Bedford had a reputation for quaintness, cleanliness, industriousness, and civic pride. The towns-people adopted the title "World's Best Little Town."

Bedford was divided into a downtown business section, indus-trial areas, and residential neighborhoods. Tracks of the Norfolk and Western railroad cut nearly through the center of the town, running east and west, and a train station was located only a few blocks from the courthouse.

The heart of downtown was the intersection of Main Street and Bridge Street, the latter of which ran north and south and bridged the railroad tracks. Within a few blocks of this intersection were the courthouse, public library, churches, banks, professional offices, stores (including at least two drug stores with soda fountains where people congregated over five-cent cups of coffee), two movie theaters, and the Masonic Lodge.

Several factories were located along the rail line running through the center of town. The Piedmont Label Company, on the western edge of downtown, made labels for canned foods and other products. East of the center of town and along the rail line were three factories, each making civilian-consumer products in 1940. The Rubatex plant made a variety of rubber products, including padding for football uniforms used across America.⁴ Hampton Looms of Virginia, often called the "woolen mill," made fabrics, and Belding Heminway, often called the "silk mill," made synthetic fiber products. The most notable industry elsewhere in the county was the Bedford Pulp and Paper Company in Big Island.

Further away from the center of town were residential areas and social facilities, such as schools, parks, the Elks National Home, and cemeteries.

News and Communications

The community was served by two newspapers, the Bedford Bulletin and the Bedford Democrat, each of which published the news once a week, in mid-week.⁵ The radio provided up-to-date news. Newsreels at the two theaters in town furnished slightly-dated, visual news. There was, of course, U.S. mail service. A Western Union telegraph office was located in Jones Drug Store on the northeast corner of Main and Bridge Streets, and people met at the store for coffee, conversation, and news about the community.

(In post-war stories of Bedford, this store would gain fame as "Green's Drug Store," where the telegrams arrived announcing casualties. In 1941, before he was due to enter the Navy, proprietor James Jones sold the drugstore to Charles E. Green from Chatham, Virginia. Throughout the war, perhaps because of a desire to retain Jones's customers, some sensitivity over Jones's departure, or some other reason related to the war, Green continued to use the name "Jones Drug Store" as the official name of the store, and advertisements in the newspapers read "Jones Drug Store, Charles E. Green, Owner and Manager" or "Proprietor." Many people, nevertheless, informally referred to it as "Green's Drug Store" or "Charlie Green's drug store." Not until after the war, in October 1945, did Green change the name to "Green's Drug Store," explaining in part that he was tired of customers not familiar with him calling him "Mr. Jones.")⁶

Social Groups

Bedford was a socially active community. In the racially-segregated society, there were more organizations for Whites than for Blacks. White men belonged to such groups as Rotary, Lions, Masons, American Legion, and Veterans of Foreign Wars. For white women, there were auxiliaries of the men's groups; church groups; garden, literary, and home demonstration clubs; Daughters of the American Revolution; United Daughters of the Confederacy; Business and Professional Women's Club; the American Association of University Women; and the Red Cross volunteer program.

The Bedford Firemen's Band, which had been organized in 1925 by a man identified with the local volunteer fire company, was active and retained an affiliation with the fire company. The band included some fifty white, male and female, amateur musicians, few of whom were firemen and few of whom had musical training. The band played and marched at many civic events in Bedford, as well as at events as far away as Washington, D.C., and New York City. The band played in President Franklin D. Roosevelt's first inaugural parade in 1933.[7]

Blacks attended their own churches and formed at least three civic bodies—the Negro Organization Society of Virginia, the County-wide Civic League, and a Youth and Young Peoples League.[8]

Bedford's National Guard Unit—Company A

In 1940 there were at least eighty-five men serving in Company A.[9] Some members lived in the town of Bedford, and others lived elsewhere in the county.

Men joined for a variety of reasons—social, financial, and patriotic. Many saw their friends and relatives join and thought joining would be "the thing to do." They enjoyed the camaraderie, and they got to wear uniforms, fire weapons, and travel for training and maneuvers. Some enjoyed the challenge of assuming leadership positions within the organization. The pay—generally $1 for an evening drill session once a week and more for the two-week summer drill—was significant for many of the men, who experienced the Great Depression. As Roy Stevens, a Company A and D-Day veteran, has said, "The uniform looked good and you got a dollar a day, and that was four times a month, and you went camping two weeks in the summer, playing soldier."[10] Serving their community, state, and country was another motivation, probably more felt than stated by those who served.

Coming from a small community, some of the men were related. There were at least four sets of brothers in Company A—George and James Crouch, Bedford and Raymond Hoback, Clyde and Jack Powers, and twin brothers Ray and Roy Stevens.

Company A met on Monday evenings in the armory in the basement of the courthouse on Main Street. In good weather, the men engaged in tactical training outdoors. In bad weather, they had classes in the armory. They practiced close-order drills and sometimes went to a firing range to practice their marksmanship. In the summer, usually August, they deployed for two weeks of training, usually to military facilities at Ogdensburg, New York, or A. P. Hill Military Reservation north of Richmond, Virginia.

Company A was one of the top-ranked companies in the National Guard. In competition with all the National Guard units across the country, it twice won first place for skill in rifle-target practice. In competition with other companies within the 116th Infantry Regiment alone, Company A won the trophy for best all-around rifle company six out of ten years and won kitchen banners each of the five years there was competition.[11]

The Approach of War

As time passed in the year 1940 and crisis loomed ever larger in Europe and Asia, life in Bedford would change, not only for the men in Company A, but, indeed, for the entire Bedford community. America began in earnest to strengthen its defenses, while still hoping to avoid war.

Chapter 2

Preparing for War, 1940-1941

Storm Clouds on the Far Horizon

In the late 1930s and into 1940, the Bedford community enjoyed the peace and quiet of rural and small-town living. The newspapers reported the standard local social gatherings, meetings of the county board of supervisors, and even some arrests.

As the 1930s had progressed, however, the newspapers had increasingly reported ominous events from overseas. Particularly troubling were campaigns of aggression launched by Japan, Italy, Germany, and, in late 1939, the Soviet Union.

In 1931 Japan invaded Manchuria. In 1935 Italy invaded Ethiopia, and Germany began building up its forces, in violation of the Versailles Treaty ending World War I. In 1936 Germany reoccupied the Rhineland, and the Spanish Civil War broke out. In 1937-1938 the Japanese defeated Chinese forces in eastern China and seized most of China's major industrial and transportation centers. Also in 1938 Germany occupied Austria and, through the Munich Agreement with Britain and France, gained Sudetenland from Czechoslovakia.

In spring 1939 German forces seized the remainder of Czechoslovakia, and Italy conquered Albania. On September 1, 1939, Germany invaded Poland, leading Britain and France to declare war on Germany. Later in September, the Soviet Union, having secretly agreed with Germany a month earlier to divide Poland, invaded eastern Poland. The Soviet Union also invaded Finland.

American Views on the War

When war began in Europe in September 1939, the U.S. Neutrality Act of 1937 became operative, prohibiting any American sales of armaments to belligerents. Opinions about possible American roles were divided. Most Americans appeared opposed to German, Italian, and Japanese aggression but did not want America to enter the war. Some wanted to avoid anything that might draw the United States into the war, while others wanted at least to provide material support to Britain and France.

A majority view began to develop that the United States should at least sell armaments to Britain and France and increase America's military preparedness. President Roosevelt persuaded Congress in November 1939 to pass a new Neutrality Act, which had the effect of permitting sales of American arms to Britain and France so long as the arms were not transported on American ships, which would be vulnerable to attack. Those in Congress advocating American intervention pressed for the strengthening of America's military forces.[1]

The News in Bedford

In Bedford, in the first week of September 1939, the front pages of the two local newspapers were still devoted to local news, featuring articles on auto accidents, a lightning strike, a school group, and liquor profits. The *Bedford Bulletin* carried two, short, front-page articles on the war in Europe, one a summary of developments in the war and the other a report about how the war was causing American food prices to increase. The newspaper also ran an editorial on page six expressing opinions on the war under a title of "Folly and Ambition." A week later, in addition to local news, the front page contained a major article on the war and the brave defense by the Poles, and there were two editorials on the war-related increase in food prices and the need to prepare for a lengthy war.[2]

1940—The War Intensifies

The news of the war became even worse in 1940. In the spring, German forces invaded Denmark, Norway, Luxembourg, the Netherlands, and Belgium. When Belgium surrendered in late May, more than a third of a million British, French, and Belgian troops escaped by sea from Dunkerque, France, to Britain. In early June, the Germans launched an offensive against France. Italy then declared war on Britain and France and invaded a small area of southern France. The

French government surrendered to the Germans on June 22. In July German planes began what would be a prolonged bombing of Britain. Italian forces in Africa invaded British and French Somaliland in August, and in September they invaded Egypt. On September 27 the German, Italian, and Japanese governments announced their agreement to form an alliance—the Axis. In October Italy invaded Greece, and in December the British engaged the Italians in North Africa.

First Peacetime American Draft

When the war in Europe began in September 1939, there were only 190,000 men in the active U.S. Army. This number grew to 270,000 in 1940. The active Army was backed by 200,000 men in the National Guard.[3]

In early September 1940, the U.S. Congress passed the Selective Training and Service Act, which President Roosevelt signed into law on September 16. The United States had instituted military drafts during the Civil War and World War I, but this was the first draft instituted while the United States was not at war.

The new law would increase the number of men on active duty with the Army to over one million. It required that men between the ages of twenty-one and forty-five register for a draft and authorized calling as many as 900,000 men to active duty for a year's training.[4] Only those men who had reached age twenty-one and had not yet reached the age of thirty-six were actually liable for service initially. Young men would be drafted into the Army to undergo active duty training for a year and then would pass into the reserves for ten years or until they reached age forty-five, after which they would be subject to recall in an emergency. Draftees would be paid $21 a month for the first four months and $30 a month thereafter, with opportunities for raises.[5] By the end of October more than sixteen million men across America had registered for the draft through 6,500 local draft boards.[6]

Bedford's Draft Board

By October 1940 a draft board was established in Bedford County, comprising members named by President Roosevelt, upon the recom-

mendation of Governor Price of Virginia. The draft board was responsible for registering all men in Bedford County of designated ages,
classifying them as to fitness and availability for service, and delivering
those in the appropriate classification groups to an induction center in
Roanoke for examination and possible induction into the military.

The draft board set up an office on the third floor of the courthouse.[7] The national Selective Service System estimated that the
county would register 4,800 men. On October 16, 3,269 young men
actually registered at the Bedford High School and nine other locations in the county.[8] Although many men had to register, authorities
in Bedford expected that the county, to meet its quota, would have to
furnish only between 100-200 men for actual military service.[9]

Before the end of October, the draft board posted in front of the
courthouse a list of all the men who had registered. Each registrant
was assigned one of 7,836 numbers. The national Selective Service
System would subsequently use a lottery to draw numbers for those
to be drafted. Young men from the Bedford community went to the
courthouse to learn their draft lottery numbers, and they often stopped
to talk to others doing likewise.[10]

The draft board asked each registrant to fill out a questionnaire,
which the board would use to determine whether or not the registrant
should be made available for military service. The board was to assign
each registrant to one of thirteen classifications of availability for
military service. Classification I-A was for those fit for general military
service. Other classifications were for those to be deferred from military
service for one reason or another, such as a physical condition making
them fit for only limited military service; student status; involvement in
needed war or agricultural production; provider for dependents; prior
military service; and status as a minister, alien, or conscientious objector. Classification IV-F was assigned to those physically, mentally, or
morally unfit for service.[11] Questions included marital status and the
nature of occupation. Prominent citizens volunteered to help the young
men fill out the forms. Those classified I-A would be subject to being
called up first.[12] Many men from the county were expected to be able
to claim an agricultural exemption. Those with dependents were also
expected to be deferred in at least this initial stage.[13]

The first lottery was held on October 29 in the War Department auditorium in Washington, D.C. President Roosevelt had indicated that 800,000 men would be drafted for one year's training. With the President presiding over the ceremonies, a blindfolded Secretary of War Henry L. Stimson drew the first of 9,000 capsules containing numbers for those to be drafted. (Only 7,836 of the 9,000 numbers had been assigned to young men, and the remainder would be held for future registrants.) Stimson handed the capsule to the President, who opened it and read the number—158—into microphones that were being used to broadcast the event over the various radio networks. Cabinet members then took turns drawing a number, followed by Congressmen, veterans, and other officials. After the dignitaries left and for several hours more, clerical staff members continued to draw capsules and record numbers in the order drawn, until all 9,000 numbers had been recorded.[14]

Twelve men in Bedford County had been assigned the first number drawn, 158.[15] Having this number did not necessarily mean that a man would enter military service. If he had been classified in one of the deferred or unfit for service categories, he would not have to serve. If he had been classified I-A, available for service, he would still be subject to pre-induction examinations.

To pass the physical examination, a man had to be at least five feet tall, weigh at least 105 pounds, have correctable vision, have at least half his natural teeth, and not have flat feet, a hernia, or venereal disease. Throughout the country, about half the men examined failed the test, primarily because of bad eyes and teeth.[16]

Whether a Bedford County man was drafted also depended upon the quota for draftees that the Selective Service System gave to the Bedford County draft board. By the end of October, the draft board estimated that the county's quota for providing servicemen would be about 400. As over 300 county men were already serving in the armed services and the National Guard and others were volunteering for service, the board expected that less than 100 additional men would have to be drafted, and probably not until springtime.[17] The Army began to suggest that young men enlist so that they could get in on the ground floor and move up through the ranks faster than those drafted.[18]

By mid-November the local draft board revised upwards its count of the number of Bedford County men already serving—ninety men in National Guard Company A, 248 others serving elsewhere in the armed forces, and twenty-four recent volunteers—and estimated that only thirty-eight men might need to be drafted.[19]

Company A Prepares for Active Duty

In the fall of 1940, many National Guard units had been alerted that they would be called to federal active duty in early 1941 for one year of training. Bedford's Company A and its parent unit, the 116th Infantry Regiment, were among those alerted. The *Bedford Bulletin* reported on September 12, 1940, that Company A expected to be called up within the next few months.[20] Other units of the 116th Infantry were also alerted, including those based nearby in Roanoke, Lynchburg, Chase City, South Boston, Farmville, Martinsville, and Charlottesville.

Company A leaders expected that about twenty men in the unit who were married would be excused from the call-up and that the company would have to replace these men with recruits. The leaders began recruiting replacements for these married men, suggesting to potential recruits that they would get to serve with their friends and neighbors rather than be drafted and placed into units with strangers.[21]

On or about January 20, 1941, the U.S. War Department ordered Company A to assemble at the armory in Bedford on February 3 for ten days of mobilization before deploying by train to Fort George G. Meade, located in Maryland between Baltimore and Washington, D.C. At Fort Meade, Company A, would join other units of the 116th Infantry Regiment and its parent unit, the 29th Infantry Division, for a year of intensive training.[22]

Company A Expands and Is Inducted into the Active Army

Company A's roster grew in size during the final days of January and the early days of February. Some men who had become inactive in the National Guard returned to active status, and the company welcomed additional recruits.

On January 23 the *Bedford Democrat* listed the names of sixty-eight officers and men in Company A, four of whom were said to be inactive.[23] By January 30 the newspaper reported that there were four officers and eighty-six men on the active and inactive rosters and that the company was "anxious to recruit to the full peacetime requirements of 114 men." The company commander, Capt. James L. Patterson, expressed the view that the company's recruiting was an exceptional opportunity for young Bedford County men, who were subject to the draft, to join a home unit.[24]

On February 3 Company A assembled at the armory in Bedford and was inducted into the active U.S. Army.[25] (The planned one-year tour of active duty would, after the attack on Pearl Harbor and America's entry into the war, be extended to the duration of the war.) On the day of induction, there were ninety-two names on the company's roster.[26]

By February 6 the company roster totaled ninety-eight, including four officers, two "assigned second lieutenants," and ninety-two men.[27] On February 8 Army medical personnel gave physical exams to the enlisted men at the armory. Six failed the examinations, and the number of enlisted men in the company fell from ninety-two to eighty-six, leaving the company with a total of ninety-two officers and men.[28]

Thus, between January 23 and February 8, the number of officers and men in Company A grew from sixty-eight to ninety-two, but, despite all the recruiting efforts, the company never reached the desired peacetime level of 114 while remaining in Bedford.

From February 3 until the unit left Bedford on February 21, Company A was in a mobilized status at the armory in the courthouse. The men slept in the armory, went on marches of eight to ten miles with full packs and equipment, engaged in maneuvers and combat drills, and ate their meals at various restaurants in Bedford. The *Bedford Democrat* reported that:

> The men speak in high praise of the courtesies shown them by the people of the town, and in particular the courtesies and consideration shown them by their former employers. And the people of

the town likewise speak in high praise of its own Company "A" and the credit it reflects upon the community.[29]

Farewell Party for Company A

The Bedford community prepared a parade, farewell party, and dance for Company A for Saturday night, February 8. The parade and party were organized by the local chapter of the Veterans of Foreign Wars, the Bedford Firemen's Band, and the Bedford Volunteer Fire Company. The party was paid for by contributions from local manufacturing plants and merchants. The evening began at 7:30 with the parade, consisting of Company A, led by the Firemen's Band and Fire Company, departing from the courthouse and proceeding down Bedford's main streets before ending at the Bedford High School gymnasium, where the party and dance were held.[30] Several community leaders addressed the men of Company A as they stood in formation in the gymnasium. The following summary of the leaders' remarks was reported in the *Bedford Democrat*:

> We are behind you, every one of us….We send you out with confidence that you will add lustre to the history of Bedford….this town and its citizens are proud of you….You will take up where some of us have left off….we know you will acquit yourselves well as you fulfill the task assigned to you by your country….You've left good jobs, many of you, but they will be waiting for you on your return—after a year of training which you will enjoy….We wish you a safe return in your homes and firesides….God bless you and the best of luck as you start out upon your great adventure….[31]

At the party, the management of the local theaters presented movie passes to all the men of Company A. As part of the dance, there was a grand march led by Company A's officers and their wives, ending with a shower of red, white, and blue balloons. Dancing was said to have continued until early morning. During the ceremonies, Captain Patterson thanked those assembled and said that the send-off was one "we shall long remember."[32] (Over sixty years later, some of the veterans could not remember the parade, party, and dance.)

Company A Leaves Bedford

After all of this fanfare, Company A's actual departure from Bedford on February 21 must have seemed anti-climatic. The *Bedford Democrat* reported:

> The order from Army headquarters came a few days ago and in the early hours of today, without fanfare, without the blast of trumpets or ceremony, the men quietly slipped through the dawn before the town was astir and embarked for service in the United States Army. The number of the train and the exact hour of departure was not disclosed....[33]

Captain Patterson, who left for Fort Meade a day earlier, was reported to have expressed, before departing, not only Company A's appreciation to the community for their support and cooperation but also his confidence that "the pride and confidence which the 'home people' feel in Company 'A' will never be cause for regret."[34]

The *Bedford Bulletin* reported that the train with most of the men of Company A departed Bedford at approximately 6 a.m. It also reported that many townspeople had commented on the splendid appearance of the soldiers and that none of the soldiers had been heard grousing or complaining. (Over sixty years later, some veterans and townspeople recalled that relatives came to the train station to see the men off and that the departure was in daylight, not before dawn.)

The *Bedford Bulletin* concluded by saying that, with the departure of Company A, "The town feels strangely empty."[35]

Company A at Fort Meade

The train took the men to Laurel, Maryland. From there they were trucked to nearby Fort Meade, where they were to be based for most of the next one-and-a-half years. (At least two of the men drove a car belonging to one of the officers.)

At Fort Meade, Company A met up with other elements of its parent units, the 116[36] Infantry Regiment and the 29[36] Infantry Division, the latter of which comprised primarily units from Virginia, Maryland, the District of Columbia, and part of Pennsylvania.[36] With units from both the north and south, it was called the "Blue-Gray" Division, and its shoulder patch was a two-toned, blue and gray, yin and yang symbol.

At Fort Meade, Company A began to expand in manpower. By the middle of June, it had received its full number of selectees, most of whom were from Virginia but some of whom were from Baltimore and Washington. Some men were discharged from the Army because their term of service had expired, but they were given the opportunity to re-enlist. Some men from Bedford left the company for reassignment to other units or returned to civilian life because of their physical condition. A photograph of the company taken at Fort Meade in July shows 136 men; at least one other man, S/Sgt. Earl R. Newcomb from Bedford, was not present for the photo.[37] By August 21, the company had expanded to 167 men—six officers and 161 men.[38]

Although based at Fort Meade, the company traveled to other bases for training. At one point, the entire company and its sister units marched south 125 miles from Fort Meade to A. P. Hill Military Reservation for training.[39] The men also trained at Camp Pickett, southwest of Richmond, in the summer of 1941. In the late fall of that year, they participated in maneuvers in the Carolinas.

While stationed at Fort Meade, the men could get passes on the weekends, and some returned to Bedford to visit and see loved ones. At least one, S/Sgt. Newcomb, obtained a week's furlough and returned to get married. Some wives and girl friends were able to visit the men at Fort Meade, staying at a guesthouse on the base.

Some of the men turned to local sights, particularly after payday. An article on Company A in one of the Bedford newspapers reported that "Washington and Baltimore are familiar sights while the money lasts."[40]

Expansion of the War, the Draft, and Enlistments

Throughout 1941, as more Bedford men were drafted and Company A continued its active training, the war situation intensified.

In March, with Britain under attack, the U.S. Government enacted the Lend-Lease Act, authorizing the President to make available defense articles, services, and information to any country whose defense was vital to America's defense, i.e., Great Britain in the first instance.[41] In April, Germany invaded Yugoslavia and Greece, and in June, Germany invaded the Soviet Union. Italy and Romania then declared war on the Soviet Union. In July, the United States suspended all financial and trading relations with Japan.

In September 1941, the U.S. Navy, which was not part of the draft program, began a recruiting campaign to encourage young men to enlist in the Navy and the Marine Corps. The Navy sought the support of newspapers across the country, including those in Bedford. Following a Navy-hosted meeting and luncheon for the media at the Hotel Roanoke in nearby Roanoke, the *Bedford Democrat* ran two consecutive front-page articles encouraging enlistment and advising young men to watch the newspaper for a series of advertisements. The articles included such statements as:

> The pay offered is good and with regular increases a youth can earn up to $126.00 per month, food, clothing and medical care free.

> Young men caught in the recent draft for Army service would do well to watch this paper for details of Navy life, and the advantages in vocational training which the Navy offers.

> ...in addition there are free sports and entertainment, even the latest Hollywood pictures. On top of this, Naval men get free travel and adventure in colorful places—a thing few civilians can afford.

> The Navy is composed of hand-picked men. Candidates for volunteer service must be men of more than average intelligence, of fine moral character....[42]

Conflict in the North Atlantic

American assistance to Great Britain in 1941 brought U.S. forces in the Atlantic closer to conflict with the German Navy. In addition to providing assistance through the Lend-Lease Act, President Roosevelt had negotiated an exchange of American destroyers for British bases in the Atlantic, and he deployed U.S. forces to relieve British forces defending Iceland. Even more directly, the President negotiated an arrangement with the British to divide responsibility for providing armed escorts for merchant ship convoys crossing the Atlantic. The U.S. Navy was ordered to escort convoys of friendly ships sailing between North America and a line generally to the east of Iceland, with the British escorting convoys east of this line.[43]

In the summer of 1941, a German U-boat (submarine) sank the American merchant ship *Robin Moor*. In the fall, German submarines and U.S. Navy escorts escalated the conflict. On September 4, the American destroyer USS *Greer* and a German U-boat fired on each other. Neither was hit. President Roosevelt then ordered the Navy to fire on any ship trying to interfere with American shipping. On October 17, a German U-boat torpedoed the destroyer USS *Kearny*, which lost eleven men but was able to reach port under her own power. On October 30, a German submarine torpedoed a U.S. Navy oiler, the *Salinas*, which managed to make port with no loss of life.[44]

In the midst of all this, President Roosevelt designated October 27 as Navy Day. Supporting this initiative, the *Bedford Bulletin* on October 23 devoted its entire front page to promoting the Navy and encouraging enlistment.[45] In a Navy Day address at a hotel in Washington, the President referred to the naval conflict in the North Atlantic:

> We have wished to avoid shooting but the shooting has started. And history has recorded who fired the first shot. In the long run, however, all that will matter is who fired the last shot.[46]

Then on October 31, German U-boat U-562 torpedoed and sank the destroyer USS *Reuben James*. Nearly three-fourths of her crew perished, a loss of 115 officers and men. The *Reuben James* was the first U.S. Navy ship to be lost in World War II to action that was undeniably hostile. All of this occurred more than a month before the Japanese attack on Pearl Harbor and the subsequent declarations of war against each other by Germany and the United States.[47]

Folk singer Woodie Guthrie would memorialize the incident in his song *"Reuben James"*—"Tell me what were their names....Did you have a friend on the good *Reuben James*?" As it turned out, some people in Bedford County did.

Bedford's First Casualty of the War

The *Bedford Bulletin* reported the sinking of the *Reuben James* on its front page on November 6. In the last paragraph, the paper reported that a young man from the Villamont area of Bedford County, William H. Newton, had been a member of the crew and that his name had not been on the list of those rescued, yet neither had his name appeared on the list of known dead.[48]

In its next edition on November 13, the *Bedford Bulletin* reported—on page ten—that Seaman Third Class Newton's father had been informed that his son had been aboard the ship and was presumed to be among the missing. His father was quoted as saying, "I have one consolation. He volunteered to give his life for his country."[49]

Seaman Third Class Newton had enlisted in the Navy in June 1938, at age seventeen, and had previously served aboard the destroyer USS *Roan*. His parents later recorded that their son had "participated in an engagement with German submarines on convoy duty going to the rescue of the USS *Solinas* (sic)."[50]

Newton was the first man from Bedford County to be killed in action in World War II, even before America declared war. He was twenty years old when he died.

Why the *Bedford Bulletin* mentioned Newton only in the last paragraph of the original article and reported the presumption of his death only on page ten of the second article is open to speculation. It may have had something to do with the undeclared nature of these hostilities, the uncertainties surrounding his loss, the newspaper's commitment to promoting Navy recruitment, or some other reason. Whatever the reason, henceforth, the *Bedford Bulletin* would announce on its front page any reports that Bedford County men had been killed or were missing in action.

By early December, America was officially at war, and its military preparations began to expand exponentially.

Chapter 3

Entering the War, 1941-1942

Japan Attacks and America Enters the War

On Sunday, December 7, 1941, "a date which will live in infamy," in the words of President Roosevelt, Japan attacked American forces at Pearl Harbor in Hawaii and subsequently attacked American and other forces in the Philippines and elsewhere in the Pacific. The United States declared war on Japan on December 8. Germany and Italy declared war on the United States on December 11, and the United States then declared war on Germany and Italy in return.

In its weekly edition on December 11, the *Bedford Bulletin*, perhaps understanding that the community had heard from the radio and other sources about the Japanese attack and America's entry into the war, allocated only the upper-right corner of its front page to the story. The story carried the headline "America Joins the Allied Nations in World-Wide War" and a sub-headline "Action Precipitated by Japanese Attack." The headlines on other articles printed at the top of the front page and given only slightly less prominence read, "Large Crowd Greets Christmas Opening," "Local Legion Post Pledges Support (for the war)," and "Farmer Loses Life When Home Burns."[1]

An editorial in that edition of the newspaper spoke to the gravity of the war situation. Under the title "The Nations Line Up," the editorial called for resolve and sacrifice for what "will, in all probability, be a long war," reasoning that:

> ...On the one side is liberty, freedom and all the blessings they bestow. On the other is slavery....
>
> This is to be a war to the death....because we do face a long, grim struggle, we must prepare ourselves, not only to work and produce, but to make sacrifices such as the American people have not known since the Revolutionary period. Everything we have,

even our lives, must be thrown into this fight if the forces which have gained such headway in their ambition to conquer and rule are to be finally defeated. It would be suicidal for the government or the people to operate on the assumption that the United States can amble through this war on a "business as usual" policy. The situation calls for subordination of everything, including a great many of the liberties for the preservation of which we are at war, to the national effort to win this war in the most decisive manner and in the shortest time possible. Less than full unity, full determination to win, and the utmost in sacrifice and labor, may place final victory in doubt.[2]

America Mobilizes

In the weeks after the Pearl Harbor attack, the U.S. Government began announcing plans for a major mobilization. The Roosevelt Administration planned to raise, train, and equip a force of eight to ten million men. Men who had already volunteered for service, had been drafted, or were serving in the National Guard were to be retained on active duty until the emergency was ended. Congress repealed the act prohibiting sending American troops outside the Western Hemisphere or U.S. possessions, but offensive operations were not expected before 1943.[3]

At the time of the attack on Pearl Harbor, more than 500 young men from Bedford County were already serving in the armed forces. The number had steadily increased over the preceding months. When the draft law became effective in late 1940, over 200 men had been serving. In the months before Pearl Harbor, the local draft board had sent 205 men to serve in the Army—about 75 percent White and 25 percent Black. Company A accounted for nearly 100 men entering the service, and at least thirty-eight more had enlisted as volunteers.[4] After Pearl Harbor, this number of volunteer enlistees increased. Some fifteen young men volunteered within three weeks after the Japanese attack.[5]

In mid-December, local draft boards across the country were instructed by Washington not to give out further news or quotas on the number of men sent to induction centers. Hence, the Bedford newspapers stopped publishing this type of information.[6]

By late January 1942, Congress passed a new draft law authorizing the Army to expand to as many as seven million men. The Navy, which had depended solely on enlistments, was authorized to increase to half a million men, although it was recognized that the Navy might eventually need up to one million men. Authorization was given to require men between the ages of eighteen and sixty-four to register for the draft, but only those who were between the ages of twenty and forty-four were actually eligible for call-up. Men twenty-eight years old and older, who had been deferred, were to be reclassified and made eligible for service, and a warning was issued that married men with self-supporting wives might no longer be exempt from service.[7]

Bedford and the Expanded Draft

In February the *Bedford Democrat* on page one announced the names of four men from Bedford County said by the local draft board to be delinquent with respect to their selective service responsibilities. Three had failed to fill out their questionnaires and gave no change of address, and the fourth failed to return for a physical exam. The board expressed the belief that the men had been negligent rather than intentionally trying to evade the draft. At the same time, the board called the offenses serious, said that they would be dealt with by law, and asked that anyone knowing anything about the men report the information to the draft board.[8]

Ivylyn Jordan, an elementary school teacher in the Moneta community of Bedford County, was called upon to help register men for the draft at her school building. In her diary or journal on Monday, February 16, 1942, she wrote with patriotic enthusiasm:

A new job today! Up at 6 Eastern War Time in order to be at school at 7 E.W.T. to register our community's men between the ages of 20 and 45! In all we registered 110 men....[9]

By April, older men between the ages of forty-five and sixty-four were directed to register for the draft. On April 27, the day designated for registration, 2,456 men from Bedford County registered at eleven selected schools.[10]

In July the Selective Service System announced that men in categories previously deferred from active duty would soon be called up. The local draft board reported that it had been directed to furnish twelve white men in the I-B category (slight physical problem, fit for limited military service). These men would be assigned to "limited duty" corps area service and would free up physically-fit soldiers to be reassigned to combat units.[11]

The head of the Virginia Selective Service System announced that married men would soon begin to be drafted. He also announced that those rejected previously for failing to pass a fourth-grade literacy test would be reclassified and possibly drafted.[12] Also in July, the Women's Army Auxiliary Corps appealed for women to join the service.[13]

America's Draft Expands Further

By September there was news of further expansion of the draft. Major General Lewis B. Hershey, head of the national Selective Service System, announced plans to induct by the end of the year men who were married but had no children. He said that those with children would probably be inducted soon thereafter. The Bedford draft board reported that it was starting to call men twenty years of age.[14]

In October an Army recruiting officer for the southwestern area of Virginia announced that the Army was now open to volunteers who were eighteen and nineteen years old. He also announced that volunteers now had a much wider selection for the branch of the Army in which to serve. Previously, volunteers could choose only among the combat branches—infantry, cavalry, coast artillery, field artillery, engineer, signal corps, air force, and armored force. Now, they could also select among the support branches, such as quartermaster, ordinance, chemical warfare, medical corps, and military police.[15]

In November President Roosevelt lowered the draft registration age to eighteen, ordering men who had turned eighteen since July to register for the draft. The Bedford draft board ordered young men eighteen and nineteen years old to register beginning December 11. These men could register at the draft board office in the Bedford

County Courthouse, or, if it was more convenient, they could register at the draft board offices in Roanoke or Lynchburg, with these offices then sending the records to Bedford.[16]

In December President Roosevelt directed the Army and Navy to stop accepting voluntary enlistments (except for a few specialists) and to obtain new recruits solely through the Selective Service System's draft program. Additionally, men between thirty-eight and forty-four were reclassified as 4-H and deferred from induction.[17] The directive on ending enlistments was later amended to allow enlistments in the Navy, Marine Corps, and Coast Guard until February 1, 1943. Voluntary enlistments in these three services were precluded for men who had been ordered to report for induction in the Army and men holding occupational deferments as necessary workers in agriculture and the aircraft and ship-building industries.[18]

Company A Deploys to Protect the Eastern Shore

When the Japanese attacked Pearl Harbor on December 7, 1941, Company A and its parent 29th Infantry Division were on maneuvers in Virginia. The division was moving in two columns on its way back from North Carolina. Company A and its sister units were in bivouac in the South Boston area in south central Virginia. Units in the other column were bivouacked at A. P. Hill Military Reservation north of Richmond. Some of the men in Company A were watching a movie in the South Boston area on December 7 when the Japanese attack was announced. The division returned to Fort Meade on December 8.[19]

The War Department soon deployed elements of the 29th from Fort Meade to the Eastern Shore. These elements were made part of the Chesapeake Bay Frontier Defense Command, based at Fort Monroe in Norfolk, Virginia. The units patrolled the beaches along the eastern coast of the United States from Atlantic City, New Jersey, to the Outer Banks of North Carolina.[20] As part of this operation, Company A deployed in late December to Camp Somerset, Maryland, near Nassawadox on the southern tip of the Delaware-Maryland-Virginia Peninsula. There the men patrolled the shore areas by vehicle and boat. John B. Schenk, a sergeant in Company A, wrote his girl friend on December 28 that he had gone on a twenty-five-mile boat patrol in the ocean off Accomac County.[21]

The deployment to the East Coast of elements of the 29th Infantry Division, including Company A, lasted about a month. In late January 1942, these units were replaced by a coast artillery unit and local home guards.[22]

The Eastern Shore residents were reportedly extremely hospitable to the men of Company A while they patrolled the coast. Sergeant Schenk wrote that in his first two days in the area he ate all his meals not with his unit but with local families. When patrolling prevented the men from joining the family for dinner, the families sent dinner to the men. In late January 1942, Schenk wrote:

> I have never been anywhere and been treated so nice. When we left the whole community were there to bid us goodby....A Regiment of Dam Yankees are taking our place and the folks on the Peninsula are really mad.[23]

Company A Moves South

From Nassawadox, Company A returned to Fort Meade. At some point in December 1941 or early 1942, Taylor N. Fellers was promoted from first lieutenant to captain and placed in command of Company A.[24]

In mid-April 1942, the 29th Infantry Division, including Company A, left Fort Meade for good. The division deployed to A. P. Hill Military Reservation for two months of training and war games and then deployed to the Carolinas for maneuvers. On August 17, the division was pulled out of the Carolina maneuvers and ordered to Camp Blanding, Florida, about halfway between Jacksonville and Gainsville.[25]

When word reached Bedford that the men might soon be sent overseas, at least six wives and girl friends of men in Company A traveled to Florida to see their loved ones.

On September 6 the division received orders to prepare for immediate overseas deployment. The men were not told their destination.[26]

When they were issued cold weather gear, Sergeant Schenk speculated that there was a slim chance that they might be sent to Alaska.[27]

Company A Deploys to England

Company A and its parent 29th Infantry Division traveled north by train from Florida to Camp Kilmer, New Jersey, arriving on September 18. Camp Kilmer was a holding area for troops being shipped abroad. On September 26, the 116th Infantry Regiment, including Company A, left Camp Kilmer by train and traveled to Hoboken, New Jersey, where they took ferries to New York City. They boarded the ocean liner *Queen Mary*, which had been converted into a troop transport ship, and sailed for Europe on September 27. The rest of the division sailed aboard the sister ship, *Queen Elizabeth,* a week later.[28]

The *Queen Mary* could transport 15,000 troops from New York to Europe in five days. Once fully under way, she traveled at such a speed that neither friendly escorts nor enemy submarines and surface ships could keep up. Her cruising speed was twenty-eight knots. German U-boats could move at only twelve knots on the surface and seven knots submerged. Being unescorted for most of the Atlantic crossing, the *Queen Mary* sought to protect herself from enemy submarines by zig-zagging, changing course every eight minutes. She ferried some 570,000 Allied troops across the Atlantic during World War II, making ten eastward trips in 1942 and twenty more eastward trips in the first half of 1943 in preparation for the Allied invasion of the European Continent.)[29]

On October 2, as the *Queen Mary* neared the European land mass where German naval and air forces presented a greater danger, she was met off the northern Irish coast by seven British Royal Navy ships sent to escort her the final 160 miles to her destination in Scotland. While the six destroyers in the group positioned themselves around the *Queen Mary* at a distance of a couple miles to guard against submarines, the seventh ship, the cruiser HMS *Curacao*, crisscrossed back and forth in front of the *Queen Mary* to provide air defense.[30]

Shortly after 2 p.m., the *Curacao*, which was starboard (right) of the *Queen Mary*, turned to port (left) and into the ocean liner's course. The *Queen Mary* also turned to port to try to avoid a collision, but the

Curacao made a similar move. The *Queen Mary* ran over the smaller ship, cutting it into two pieces, both of which sank.[31]

Some Company A men aboard the *Queen Mary* saw the British ship sink and still remember the incident.[32] The *Queen Mary*, under orders not to stop, as stopping would have made it vulnerable to enemy attack, sailed on. Other ships rescued ninety-seven of the British sailors, but some 300 were lost. The *Queen Mary's* captain called together the officers of the 29th Infantry Division and instructed them to tell their men not to mention the incident for the rest of the war, so as to help keep the enemy from learning the details of Allied operations.[33]

On October 3 the *Queen Mary* safely reached its destination, Greenock, Scotland, a small port some twenty miles from Glascow.[34]

From Scotland, the men of Company A were moved by rail to southern England, where they were to live and train for twenty months, until they embarked for the Normandy Invasion. Members of the Bedford community received letters from their loved ones in Company A saying that their unit was in England. For reasons of military security, the men were enjoined from saying exactly where they were.[35]

Enlisting Civilian Support in the War Effort

The years 1941-1942 also saw the beginning of government programs to enlist civilians in civil defense preparedness and the beginning of rationing and other restrictions on certain consumer goods. Industries began making products for the military. Volunteers began salvaging materials useful for the war effort and preparing surgical dressings for the military. Citizens began buying war bonds, contributing to the Red Cross and United Services Organization, and growing Victory Gardens. In the ensuing years, civilian support for the war effort would expand significantly. (These activities on the home front are covered in detail in Chapters 6-11.)

Chapter 4

Serving Their Country, 1942-1945

A total of more than sixteen million American men and women served in the armed forces at some time during World War II.[1] By the end of the war in 1945, there were more than twelve million American men and women still in active service, with approximately 8,300,000 in the Army—including the Army Air Forces, 3,400,000 in the Navy, 484,000 in the Marines, and 170,000 in the Coast Guard.[2]

In Bedford County, as the war progressed through the early 1940s, more and more young men voluntarily enlisted or were drafted into military service. Young women also began to enlist. By the end of the war, more than 3,000 men and women from the county—just over 10 percent of the population—had served in the armed forces during the conflict.[3] Most were white males. The number of black males was roughly proportional to the minority black population in the county. Some fifty women from Bedford volunteered for service, including at least one black woman.[4] Many individual families in the Bedford area had more than one of their offspring serving in the military. One family had seven sons serving.

As throughout America, the majority of men joined the Army. Most of these served in the ground forces, but many served in the U.S. Army Air Corps, or, after June 1941 when the name was changed, the U.S. Army Air Forces.[5] The next largest number joined the Navy, the second largest service. Others joined the Marine Corps and the Coast Guard. Many of the women served as military nurses.

Men and women from Bedford served within the United States and in all overseas theaters to which the United States deployed forces. They wrote home about their experiences, although they were limited by government censorship rules.

Many Bedford men were wounded in action. At least twenty-one men were captured and held as prisoners of war by the Japanese and Germans. Many, paying the ultimate sacrifice, were killed in action, died as a result of wounds received in combat, or died as a result of accidents or illness while serving their country.

Increase in Enlistees and Draftees

As the war progressed and as the draft was expanded to encompass both younger and older men and men who were fathers, an increasing number of young Bedford men entered the armed forces.

By July 1943 the local draft board reported that an estimated 2,108 men from the Bedford community were serving in the U.S. armed services. This included not only those who had been drafted but also volunteers and those who had entered the service with National Guard Company A when it was activated. A total of 5,046 men in Bedford County between the ages of eighteen and thirty-eight had registered for the draft—3,890 Whites and 1,156 Blacks. The clerk of the draft board expressed the belief that all men between eighteen and thirty-eight had been registered and that the only new registrants in the future would be young men turning eighteen. By the end of July, a total of 1,541 men, including 1,253 Whites and 288 Blacks, had been sent by the local board for examination at the induction center in Roanoke and had passed the examinations and been accepted for military service.[6]

When the board sent men to the Roanoke induction center, they would, if they passed the examinations, be inducted there. On March 5, 1943, for example, the board sent sixty-one white men to the induction center. By this time, the Navy and Marine Corps, not just the Army, were accepting draftees. Of the sixty-one sent that day, forty-eight were accepted for service—forty-three for service in the Army, four for the Navy, and one for the Marines. The names of those accepted were published in the local newspapers, the names of those rejected were not.[7] On July 14, seventy-four white men were sent to Roanoke; twenty-seven were accepted for the Army and fifteen for the Navy, but thirty-two—or 43 percent—were rejected.[8]

A large percentage of the men rejected at the induction center in Roanoke were rejected because of illiteracy. Others were rejected for physical reasons. With the need for more servicemen in the armed forces, the Selective Service System in July was prepared to accept about 5 percent of those who failed the literacy test and some who failed the physical exam.[9]

In August the U.S. Selective Service System authorized local draft boards after October 1 to call up for service men who had been fathers since before Pearl Harbor, but only if these men were "absolutely required" to meet monthly quotas.[10]

In April 1944, with needs for servicemen increasing, Selective Service Director Hershey asked American farmers to make available for military service every possible man among the 350,000-400,000 men under age twenty-six still remaining on the farms. Hershey declared that deferments for young farmers should not be continued except where they met the strictest requirements for exemption.[11]

That same month, Eleanor Yowell wrote her husband in England about the impact of the draft:

> It seems about every man under age 38 has been drafted from here except a favored few, and there has been a lot of talk about them. My former boss is still being deferred and at this point is vacationing in Florida—and drove down there to boot! Several men who were busted out of the Army are now being drafted.[12]

Financial Compensation for Service Personnel and Spouses

In addition to other hardships, serving in the military often involved financial sacrifice. Enlisted men and non-commissioned officers earned between $50 and $138 a month in basic pay. The scale for those in the Army and their Navy and Marine equivalents was: private, $50; private-first-class, $54; corporal, $66; sergeant, $78; staff sergeant, $96; technical sergeant/first sergeant, $114; and master sergeant, $138. Basic pay was increased by $10 a month after twelve months of service and by 5 percent for each three years of service. Pay was increased by 20 percent for foreign service and sea duty. Officers were paid more.[13]

Women in the Women's Army Auxiliary Corps (WAACs) initially were paid less than the men. "Auxiliaries" (privates) received $21 a month for the first four months and $30 a month thereafter, compared to the $50 a male private earned. Specialists would receive $5-$15 more per month. "Leaders" (non-commissioned officers) would receive $54-$72 per month (male non-coms earned $66-$138).[14]

In October 1942 Congress increased the starting pay for WAACs from $21 a month to $50 a month, matching the pay for Army privates and Navy recruits.[15]

Wives of servicemen also received compensation from the U.S. Government. For example, the wife of a private with no other dependents received $50 a month. Of this $50, $22 came out of her husband's $50 basic pay (he, thus, personally received $28 a month), and the government provided her the other $28. Wives with children received additional compensation from the government—$12 for the first child and $10 for each additional child.[16]

Wives of many Bedford servicemen worked during the war years and lived independently, while others moved in with parents or other loved ones in order to make ends meet.

Blacks in the Service

In the World War II era, national policy regarding Blacks in the military, particularly at first, reflected significant prejudices against Blacks and reluctance to accept them into the armed forces and place them in combat units. One scholar has written:

> Because the leadership of the armed forces was prejudiced against Blacks, the mobilization plan of 1940 called for only about half as many Blacks as Whites to be drafted in proportion to their respective populations. Blacks were to be confined largely to service rather than combat units and be excluded entirely from the Army Air Corps and Marines, and from the Navy except as waiters.[17]

Indeed, in 1941, Blacks accounted for about 10 percent of the American population but less than 6 percent of the Army. By 1945, however, the black percentage of the Army had risen to over 8.5 percent.[18]

Discrimination in the military became a political issue early in the war. The Army soon responded to the pressure by increasing the number of Blacks as a percentage of the Army's total manpower. The Army also agreed to create black combat units, having previously assigned many Blacks to the Quartermaster Corps and Corps of Engineers.[19] The Army created two black infantry divisions (which had some white officers), but only one of these, the 92d Infantry (Buffalo) Division, saw serious combat.[20] The Army also created some smaller black combat units in both the Army and the Army Air Corps/Army Air Forces, such as the 366th Infantry Regiment and the 99th Pursuit Squadron (Tuskeegee Airmen). Most black squadrons in the Army Air Forces, nevertheless, were used for airfield maintenance.[21]

The Navy was forced to enlist Blacks for general service and eventually assigned some Blacks to labor units and integrated a few non-combat ships. Still, some 95 percent of Blacks in the Navy were stewards, responsible for preparing and serving food.[22]

(In 1948 President Harry S. Truman ordered equal treatment and opportunity for black servicemen, and the practice of segregating units by race was ended.)[23]

The Military Experience of Blacks from Bedford

About 490 black men from Bedford County enlisted or were drafted into the armed forces. They accounted for just over 16 percent of the total of some 3,000 men from the county who joined the military. (As a percentage of the county's overall population in 1940, Blacks accounted for about 21 percent—6,357 Blacks in a population of slightly less than 30,000.)[24] Of the some fifty women from Bedford County who served in the armed services or Red Cross overseas, only one, Doris H. Reid, is known to have been black.[25]

The Bedford newspapers, in reporting on men sent by the draft board for pre-induction physicals, sometimes emphasized the failure of Blacks to pass physical examinations, while not emphasizing the failures of Whites. In July 1942, for example, the *Bedford Democrat,* reporting on test results for one group of men sent to the Army induction center in Roanoke, gave its page-one story the title "Colored Conscripts Fail in Health Test." Actually, as the story related, only half the men sent to the induction center—nine of eighteen—failed the

test, and one-third (or six) passed. As for others, two were transferred
to other boards, and one failed to report. The names of those accepted
and transferred were reported, the names of those failing were not.
The reasons for the rejections were not stated.[26]

Most of the black servicemen from Bedford served in the Army.
Sizeable numbers also served in the Army Air Forces and the Navy.
Fewer served in the Marines and the Coast Guard.[27]

Many of the black servicemen from the Bedford community
served in support units. Those joining the Army usually were assigned
to support or combat service support units, including quartermaster
and transportation units. Many joining the Navy became stewards.
An article in the *Bedford Bulletin* on October 14, 1943, announced
unlimited opportunities for "Negro boys between 17 and 18 years of
age to enter Naval Service as Steward Mates," in which capacity they
would prepare and serve "chow for the fighting man."[28]

Some, however, were assigned to combat units. At least five men
from the Bedford community were assigned to the 366th Infantry
Regiment. This regiment was attached to the 92[d] Infantry (Buffalo)
Division during combat operations in Italy, and the men in the regiment saw action elsewhere other than Italy. (See the profile in Part II
of this book of Willie J. Hobson, a veteran of combat with the 366th.)
Some were assigned to other Army infantry units, as well as Navy
and Marine combat organizations. At least one Bedford man was
assigned as an airplane mechanic at the Tuskeegee Army Airfield in
Alabama.[29]

The prejudices of the 1940s are reflected in the following extract
from "The Military History of Bedford County," specifically a chapter
on World War I and II written probably in 1950-1951 by Gates R.
Richardson, who taught school in Bedford before going into the men's
clothing business:

> As in World War I, there were few casualties among our negro
> soldiers. So far as I have been able to learn only three Bedford
> negroes lost their lives. The American negro has not yet proved
> himself a dependable fighter. An effort was made to build one
> negro air squadron which served in Africa but this group failed to

live up to its press notices. As in World War I our negroes were generally assigned to work battalions in the rear areas and the real fighting was left to the white soldiers.[30]

(Richardson's commentary seems to deprecate the combat contributions of black soldiers without acknowledging fully the government's policy from the outset of generally assigning Blacks to non-combat, support units or acknowledging the contributions made by Blacks serving in both support and combat units.)

In his history, Richardson alluded to fears early in the war of racial strife but did express appreciation for the contribution black civilian and military personnel made to the war effort:

The Virginia State Guard was organized to protect the common-wealth from trouble within. Many of our people feared efforts to sabotage our industries and our war preparation by stirring up strife between labor and management. Not the least of our fears was that of trouble from our rather large negro population. Many thought our negroes would offer a splendid target for foreign agents intent upon disrupting the American war effort by stirring up racial strife. Happily our negroes co-operated heartily in our war work. Many of them were inducted into the armed services and on the whole they made a valuable contribution to Bedford's war effort.[31]

At least four Blacks from the Bedford Community paid the ultimate sacrifice and were killed or died while serving in the armed forces during the war.

Women in the Service

Women served during the war in several military or military-related roles. Many joined as nurses, assigned to the Army Nurse Corps or the Naval Nurse Corps. Some became nurses through the Cadet Nurse Corps program, in which the government paid for the cadet nurse's tuition and the cadet nurse agreed to serve in the military for the duration of the war plus six months.[32] Other women served as clerks and administrative and logistical assistants. Some women flew aircraft. Others served in the American Red Cross overseas field hospital program and the United Service Organization.

In 1942 the Army expanded the opportunities for women to serve in positions other than nursing. In July of that year the Army recruiting and induction officer for Virginia announced that his offices were ready to take applications from women wishing to join the Women's Army Auxiliary Corps (WAACS). The name was later changed to Women's Army Corps (WACS). The recruiting officer indicated that women could receive a specialist's rating if they had experience in positions such as accountants, bakers, cashiers, clerks, cooks, drivers, messengers, motion picture projectionists, pharmacists, printers, radio and telephone operators, secretaries, and typists. Each WAAC member was to have equal opportunity to be selected for officers' training school. Benefits of being a WAAC were said to include attractive uniforms, comfortable and congenial living quarters, wholesome food, health services, and thirty days of leave per year.[33]

This Army recruiting publicity did not mention pay, which at the time was far less for women than for men. Not until October 1942 did Congress equalize the pay between women and men in the armed forces.[34]

By March 1943 the U.S. Government had authorized enrollment of 150,000 WAACS. To join, women had to be between twenty-one and forty-four, have no dependents or children under the age of fourteen, and be mentally and physically fit. The Army expanded its recruitment, and a woman lieutenant from the WAACS recruiting station in Roanoke visited the Bedford post office for two days in March to hand out applications and answer questions.[35]

Women pilots served in the Women's Auxiliary Ferrying Squadron (WAFS) and as Women Air Force Service Pilots (WASP).[36]

The Navy resisted accepting women until the end of 1942 but eventually recruited women for the Naval Nurse Corps and the Women Accepted for Voluntary Emergency Service (WAVES).[37]

The Coast Guard initiated a program for women called "SPARS," and the Marine Corps began enrolling Women Marines in early 1943.[38]

By the end of the war, more than 300,000 women had served in the military during the war.[39]

Another three-and-a-half million women volunteered to assist the American Red Cross during the war, working on many projects related to the war.[40]

Bedford Women in the Service

Over the course of the war, about fifty women from the Bedford community volunteered for service with the armed forces.[41] Many appear to have taken the initiative themselves. Others may have been influenced by military recruiters.

Recruiters came to Bedford on several occasions seeking women recruits. On at least one occasion, local women's groups assisted. In late April 1944, a "Women-in-War" forum was held in the Bedford County Courthouse to help recruit for the Women's Army Corps. The meeting, featuring a woman lieutenant from the Lynchburg recruiting office as the main speaker, was sponsored by the Bedford branches of the American Association of University Women and the Business and Professional Woman's Club.[42]

Of the some fifty who served, approximately twenty-eight joined the Women's Army Corps. About ten of these served as Army nurses with the rank of lieutenant. Some served with the Army Air Forces. About thirteen served with the Navy. Four joined the Coast Guard, two joined the Marine Corps, two enrolled in the Cadet Nurse program, and at least two served with the American Red Cross overseas.[43]

The first woman from the Bedford community to volunteer for duty with the armed services appears to have been Rubye V. Wilkes, who joined the Army Nurse Corps in 1941 as a second lieutenant. She entered the service on February 14, 1941, less than two weeks after her brother, John L. Wilkes, a master sergeant in Company A, was ordered to active duty. After marrying Howard Archer, a lieutenant she met while in the service, she used the last name "Wilkes-Archer." She spent thirty-eight months in the Pacific area and returned to the United States on June 6, 1945. (She went on to make a career of the military, serving for twenty-eight years, including in Korea and Vietnam during those wars, and retiring in 1967 as a lieutenant colonel.)[44]

The second woman to join the military appears to have been Doris L. Agee, who joined the Army Nurse Corps in June 1941. The first Bedford woman to enter the Navy appears to have been Betty J. Brydges, who joined in December 1942 and became an ensign and communications officer. The first to join the Coast Guard was Edith V. Booth (later Murchison), who joined in late December 1942.

Two Bedford women joined the Marine Corps; it is not clear who joined first—Mary L. Biggs or Marguerite A. Terry.

Doris H. Reid, the only black woman from Bedford known to have volunteered for the armed services, entered the Army in September 1944, serving as a private.

Mary Witt served as a Red Cross field hospital supervisor in Europe. She served first in England, beginning in July 1942, and soon after D-Day she oversaw field hospitals in France serving troops fighting the Germans. By 1946 she was supervising hospitals in Japan. Eileen Brent served with the Red Cross as a recreation director in India.

Families with Multiple Members Serving

Many families in the Bedford community, especially large farm families with many sons, had more than one family member serving in the armed services. Many families had multiple sons serving. There were other cases where those serving included sons and daughters, brothers and sisters, husbands and wives, and even a father and son.[45]

The *Bedford Bulletin* and *Bedford Democrat* frequently printed photographs of those serving, with short captions giving the individual's name, a few details about his or her service, and the parents' names. There were many single photos and a lesser number of photos of two or more family members in the service.

Those listed below represent some of the families with multiple members serving. There may well have been other families with multiple members serving, especially families with two members serving. Black families are so identified; others are presumed to be White.

Seven Sons

Mr. and Mrs. J. F. Dean appear to have had the most sons serving—seven in total. They were Floyd, Orien, Lester, Halsey, Ward, John, and Bernard. The first four served in the Navy, and the last three served in the Army. John Dean was killed in action in France; the others survived the war. An eighth and younger son, Herman, was also drafted, but probably after the cessation of hostilities. Mrs. Dean received an award at a ceremony at the Hotel Roanoke, in nearby Roanoke, in recognition of her family's contribution to the war effort.[46]

Six Sons

Mr. and Mrs. B. F. Chappelle had six sons serving—Henry, Alphonso, John, Thomas, James, and Wilhelm.

Five Sons/Daughters

Mrs. M. Caudill had five sons serving—Frank, William, Charles, Daris, and Robert.

Mr. and Mrs. R. L. Johnson had five sons serving—Garland, Jason, Nelson, Morris, and Jack. A sixth son, Robert, served in the Virginia State Guard.

Mr. and Mrs. A. C. Karnes had five sons serving—Dean, Eugene, Albert, Clyde, and Claude Karnes.

Mr. and Mrs. O. R. Graves had five sons serving—Harlan, Ovid, Frank, Clark, and Lowell.

Mr. and Mrs. F. M. Otey, a black family, had five sons serving—Clark, Frank, Payton, Russell, and William. In the 1970s, Russell became the first Black to be elected mayor of Bedford.

Mr. and Mrs. H. B. Powers had four sons and one daughter serving—Henry (Clyde), William, Jack, Archie, and Eloise. Jack was killed on D-Day. Another son, Auville, registered and passed the physical examination but was not called because he was thirty-six years old.

Mr. H. V. Simkins had five sons and one son-in-law serving—L. Vernon, Troy, Hugh, Cleo, and Curtis Simkins, and Samuel Edwards.

Mr. and Mrs. R. S. Tanner had five sons serving—Charles, Frank, James, Rufus, and Frederick.

Four Sons/Daughters

Mr. and Mrs. J. Carey, a black family, had four sons serving—Henry, Herbert, Jackson, and Lon.

Mr. and Mrs. P. H. Craig had four sons and two sons-in-law serving—Robert, Garrett, Lewis, and William, and Charles Reid and Claude Johnson.

Mr. and Mrs. T. G. Daniel had four sons serving—Orie, Gerald, Floyd, and Herbert. Herbert was killed in action on Iwo Jima, and Gerald was a prisoner of war in Germany.

Mrs. H. Hubbard (last name presumably Poindexter previously) had three sons, one daughter, and two sons-in-law, a brother, and a brother-in-law serving—sons William, Robert, and Albert Poindexter; daughter Wilda Poindexter Murphy; sons-in-law Luther Murphy and George Fell; brother William Seay; and brother-in-law Charles Evans.

Mr. and Mrs. F. A. Karnes had four sons serving—Carl, Lewis, James, and Eddie.

Mr. and Mrs. H. G. Nance had four sons serving—Francis, Hubert, Glen, and Henry. Francis was killed in Italy in October 1944.

Mr. and Mrs. O. S. Overstreet had four sons serving—Luther, Winston, Mahlon, and Woodie.

Three Sons/Daughters

Mr. and Mrs. H. Booth had two daughters, one son, and a son-in-law serving—Edith Virginia Booth Murchison, Margaret Booth Waldron, Harry (Billy) Booth, and Arthur Murchison.

Mr. and Mrs. E. F. Burford had three sons serving—Macon, Rucker, and Landon.

Mr. and Mrs. J. E. Cocks had three sons serving—James, Odell, and Eugene.

Mr. and Mrs. J. S. Craighead had three sons serving—Nelson, William, and Ray.

Mr. and Mrs. J. W. Davis had three sons serving—Warren, Howard, and John. Warren was killed in the Malmedy Massacre in Belgium.

Mr. and Mrs. F. P. Draper had three sons serving—Frank, Warren Gamiel, and David. Frank was killed on D-Day.

Mrs. A. B. and the late R. B. Gibbs had three sons serving—Paul, June, and Marshall.

Mr. and Mrs. W. H. Graham had two sons and one daughter serving—Henry, Wilson, and Viola.

Mrs. M. D. and the late J. E. Jackson, a black family, had three sons serving—John, Joseph, and Thomas. John was killed in action in the South Pacific in October 1944.

Mr. and Mrs. Johnson had three sons serving—Albert, Hubert, and Thomas.

Mr. and Mrs. M. B. Karnes had three sons serving—Edward, Raymond, and Frank.

Mr. and Mrs. E. L. Kirby had three sons serving—Howard, Kyle, and Coy.

Mr. and Mrs. J. W. Payne had three sons serving—George, Hoyt, and Kermit.

Mr. and Mrs. W. L. McManaway had three sons serving—Charlie, Edwin, and Stewart.

Mr. and Mrs. J. E. Parker had three sons serving—Earl, Joseph, and William. Earl was killed on D-Day, Joseph was killed later in France, and William (Billy) was a prisoner of war.

Mr. and Mrs. W. E. Stevens had three sons serving—Ray, Roy, and Warren. Ray was killed on D-Day in the Normandy Invasion, and Roy was seriously wounded in the fighting near St. Lo.

Mr. and Mrs. A. W. Waldron had three sons, one daughter-in-law, and one grandson serving—Willis, Sherman, and Wesley, Wesley's wife Margaret H. Waldron, and grandson Hubert Waldron.

Mr. and Mrs. L. Wilkes had two sons, one daughter, and one son-in-law serving—John and Henry Wilkes, Rubye Wilkes-Archer, and Howard Archer. John was killed on D-Day.

Mr. and Mrs. R. Williamson had two sons and a daughter serving—Andrew, Ishmael (Pete), and Ruth.

Two Sons/Daughters

Mr. and Mrs. H. C. Arthur had a son and daughter serving—Harry and Annie.

Mr. and Mrs. J. W. Allen had a son and daughter serving—John and Helen. John was killed in action in France.

Mr. and Mrs. W. H. Booth had a son and daughter serving—Henry and Virginia.

Mr. and Mrs. J. Catlin had two sons serving—John (Jack) and R. W. (Bill), both combat pilots.

Mr. and Mrs. J. Hoback had two sons serving—Bedford and Raymond, both of whom were in Company A and were killed in the D-Day Invasion of Normandy.

The late Dr. and Mrs. S. Rucker had two daughters serving in the Army Nurse Corps—Frances and Margaret.

Husband-Wife, Father-Son

E. Ray Nance and Alpha Mae Watson were married in November 1944, while both served in the Army as lieutenants. Ray Nance is a Company A survivor of the D-Day Invasion.

Warner Wheeler and his son, Lynwood (Jack) Wheeler, were a rare combination of father and son serving in the military at the same time.

Aviators

Aviators in World War II faced significant risks, both in training and in battle. While aviators in the U.S. Army Air Corps and, after June 1941, the U.S. Army Air Forces, accounted for a relatively small portion of total Army manpower, they represented 43 percent of Army personnel killed accidentally (35,946 airmen) and 18 percent of total Army battle deaths (52,173 airmen of 291,557 total Army battle deaths). Two of the worst days for battle losses of American airmen occurred in August and October 1943. On each of these two days, the U.S. Eighth Air Force sent about 300 American bombers based in England on bombing missions against targets in south-central Germany. On each day, sixty aircraft—many with ten men aboard—failed to return.[47]

Many men from the Bedford community served as aviators—pilots, navigators, and other air crew members. At least nine were killed in airplane accidents, five were killed in action, and one was executed by a German after safely parachuting from his plane.

(Peter Viemeister, a retired aviation executive and writer living in Bedford County, has written a book, *A History of Aviation: They Were There*, [Hamilton's, Bedford, 1990], which devotes several chapters to World War II. In those chapters, he, in part, recounts the personal experiences of many of the aviators and airmen from the Bedford area. Viemeister interviewed many of these men, most of whom are now deceased. The following summary, prepared by the author of this book, draws, with permission, on material in the Viemeister book, supplemented with information from other sources. The aviators were members of the U.S. Army Air Forces, unless identified as Naval or Marine Corps aviators.)

Joseph Danner, Joseph Goode, Teaford Hatcher, Harold Jarvis, and William Yowell are profiled in detail in Part II of this book and are not further mentioned in this chapter.

Brown A. Brally, a staff sergeant from the Evington area of either Bedford or neighboring Campbell County, served as a waist gunner on a B-17 Flying Fortress bomber. He received the Distinguished Flying Cross.

Randolph Stith Brent II, a lieutenant, flew as a P-47 Thunderbolt pilot. He flew some 500 hours and was involved in eight missions attacking Japanese bridges and aircraft carriers. After the war, he worked in radio and television and as director of the Bedford Chamber of Commerce.

Hubert B. Burkholder served as a staff sergeant and tail gunner on the B-17 Flying Fortress "Up'n At'm." He was awarded the Distinguished Flying Cross for action against targets in Germany and in support of Allied troops in France.

John E. "Jack" Catlin, Jr., a 1939 graduate of Bedford High School, enlisted in 1943 during his fourth year at the Virginia Military Institute. He became a P-51 Mustang fighter pilot and flew a number of missions in Europe escorting bomber aircraft. A back injury led to his being grounded. Later in life he worked for the Central Intelligence Agency.

R. W. "Bill" Catlin, brother of Jack Catlin and a 1940 graduate of Bedford High School, joined the Marine Corps and became an F-4U Corsair fighter-attack pilot. He flew about 100 combat missions, including missions in support of American amphibious landings at Mindoro Island and Luzon in the Philippines, with a total of 305 combat hours. For his service, he was awarded the Air Medal with a Gold Star. After V-J Day, celebrating the victory over Japan, Catlin buzzed Bedford in a Corsair. He had plans to study aeronautical engineering.

Joseph Craighead, a sergeant, was a gunner on a B-24 Liberator bomber.

Gordon Deacon, a 1937 graduate of Bedford High School, served as a transport pilot. He ferried aircraft across the Atlantic to destinations in Europe and North Africa and flew cargo to Burma, destined for China. After the war, he worked in air traffic control in Tennessee and Florida.

Thomas Dooley, a native of the Kelso area northwest of the town of Bedford, served as a master sergeant. He flew as a liaison pilot in the China-Burma-India Theater. Part of an air commando group, he flew a L-5B Stinson liaison aircraft, informally called a "grasshopper" or "flying Jeep." He and his unit evacuated wounded and carried passengers and cargo. For his service in Burma, he was awarded the Distinguished Flying Cross and Air Medal with Oak Leaf Cluster. After the war, he ran the Northside Supply and General Merchandise Company in Bedford with Dean Wilkerson, his brother-in-law and fellow-veteran.

Oscar Watt Gills, a 1940 graduate of Bedford High School, served as a lieutenant and pilot of a B-17 Flying Fortress bomber. On his 24th mission, his plane was shot down over Germany. He bailed out, was captured, and spent over eight months as a prisoner of war before being liberated. After the war, he became a banker.

Tom Jennings became a navigator on a R5D Navy transport aircraft. Based on Guam, he flew missions to various Pacific islands, the Asian mainland, and the west coast of the United States, transporting passengers, wounded, and cargo, and often flying ten to fourteen hours at a stretch. After the war, he went to medical school and became a family doctor.

Bobby G. Johnson graduated from Montvale High School in 1943 and volunteered for service following his graduation. He entered the air cadet program in the summer of 1944, hoping to become a pilot. As the U.S. Army Air Forces at that time needed gunners more than pilots, he became a gunner on a B-29 Superfortress bomber. After the war, he went into the construction business with fellow airman Joe Laughon.

Raymond W. Karnes, a staff sergeant serving as a nose gunner on a B-24 Liberator bomber based in England, flew twenty missions, including ones over Berlin, earning the Air Medal with two Oak Leaf Clusters and the Distinguished Flying Cross.

C. J. "Joe" Laughon, a graduate of Moneta High School, became a gunner on a B-24 Liberator bomber. On his fourth mission, his plane was hit by flak but was able to land in Yugoslavia, where the crew was rescued by partisans. Laughon went on to fly twenty-four more missions. He became a business partner with fellow aviator veteran Bobby G. Johnson after the war.

Lloyd O. Laughon, a farmer turned staff sergeant, flew as a tail gunner on the B-17 Flying Fortresses "Sugar" and "Sweet Patootie." He flew thirty combat missions, including ones against targets at Schweinfurt, Frankfurt, Augsburg, and Munich. On a mission over the heart of Berlin, the planes in his unit were met by some sixty German fighter aircraft. Laughon's plane had one engine shot away and two others damaged, and the crew had to jettison guns, ammunition, and armor plate to lighten the load. Laughon thought at one point the vibration would tear the wings off. The crew was fortunate and was able to complete its mission and return to base safely. Laughon was awarded the Distinguished Flying Cross and the Air Medal with three Oak Leaf Clusters.

R. Bernard Overstreet, a first lieutenant, flew thirty missions in Europe and was awarded the Distinguished Flying Cross and the Air Medal with four Oak Leaf Clusters. Later in the war he flew in the United States, helping to ferry aircraft.

William Overstreet, served as a P-51 fighter pilot in the 357th Fighter Group based in England. On D-Day, he spent eighteen hours in the cockpit and flew three missions over France, attacking ground targets with bombs when there were no German fighters present. He downed ten German fighters during the war. On one occasion, his plane was downed by antiaircraft fire over France, and he was captured. With the help of a pipe wrench, he was able to knock out his German military captors. He escaped from France with the help of the French resistance. Another time he got too close to a German ammunition train he was attacking, and it blew up and downed his plane. He escaped from France again with the help of the resistance.[48]

Don Thurston Parker enlisted in October 1940. He became a glider pilot, flying and landing a glider in France on D-Day. After the war he opened a precision machine shop in Bedford.

Laron Deferris Shannon, Jr., a graduate of New London Academy in eastern Bedford County, flew the "Hump" in the Burma-China-India Theater.

William W. Shields, a staff sergeant, flew as a tail gunner on a B-17 Flying Fortress in the Mediterranean Theater. He flew fifty combat missions, including ones against the Polesti oil fields in Romania. He had worked at the Rubatex plant before the war. After the war, he was a game warden in Bedford for thirty-seven years.

Macon Witt, a sergeant, served as a gunner on a B-24 Liberator bomber. He flew on thirty-one missions against enemy targets. Before the thirty-second mission, he came down with a cold and was ordered not to fly. The plane and the other crew members were lost on the mission.

First Reports of Bedford Men Missing and Killed in Action

On August 13, 1942, the *Bedford Bulletin* reported that Pvt. Bernard W. Saunders had been officially reported as missing in action. Private Saunders had been stationed in the Philippine Islands when Japanese forces attacked in December 1941.[49] Not until April 1943—a year after American forces in the Philippines surrendered—would Private Saunders' parents receive word that the Japanese government was holding their son as a prisoner of war.[50] Private Saunders miraculously survived more than three years of harsh treatment by the Japanese. (See details in Part II of this book.)

On October 29, 1942, the *Bedford Bulletin* reported on page one that Morris E. Canaday, a private first class, who had lived in the Goode area of the county, had been killed in combat at age twenty-one while serving with the Marine Corps.[51] The article stated correctly that Private First Class Canaday was "the first man from Bedford County whose death has been reported since the entry of the United States into war." The headline for the story—"First Man Reported Killed in Action From Bedford Co."—was misleading, however, in that Seaman Second Class Newton of Bedford County previously had been killed in action when a German submarine sank the USS *Reuben James* on October 31, 1941, prior to America's declaration of war. The story did not mention Newton.

Private First Class Canaday had enlisted in January 1942 and was believed to have sailed in April of that year for the South Pacific. His mother later recorded that he was killed on September 24, 1942, in the fighting on Guadalcanal.[52] (Guadalcanal, one of the Solomon Islands northeast of Australia, had been taken by Japanese forces early in the war. After months of intense fighting, it was recaptured by American forces in February 1943.)[53]

The first combat casualty from the town of Bedford was reported on April 22, 1943. The *Bedford Bulletin* informed its readers that Sgt. Robert Francis Nance was missing in action. He was a crewman on a U.S. Army Air Forces bomber presumed to have been shot down in the Mediterranean.[54] In May 1944, after a year of hearing nothing further of Sergeant Nance, the U.S. Government, as was standard practice, declared him to have been killed in action. His aircraft had been on a bombing mission against targets in Sicily and was shot down off the coast and crashed into the sea. Sergeant Nance had worked at the Piedmont Label Company in Bedford before enlisting in the Army in July 1942. He was twenty-nine when he was killed.[55]

Prisoners of War

During World War II, the Germans captured and held as prisoners of war (POWs) about 1,700,000 Allied soldiers, including about 90,000

Americans. The Japanese captured and held as POWs approximately 145,000 Allied soldiers, including about 15,000 Americans.[56] In general, POWs suffered worse under the Japanese than under the Germans. Close to 37 percent of Allied POWs held by the Japanese died in captivity, while about 1 percent of those held by the Germans died.[57]

Beginning in 1942, the Bedford newspapers ran several articles on two local men captured in April of that year in the Philippines by Japanese forces—Pvt. Bernard Saunders and Lt. Col. John R. Boatwright.

At least twenty-one men from Bedford County were among those captured and held as POWs. (The experiences of two of these men, Private Saunders, who was captured and held by the Japanese for over three years, and Pvt. William "Billy" Parker, who was captured by the Germans and held for seven-and-a-half months are related in some detail in Part II of this book.)

Three other Bedford men in a unit captured by the Germans during the Battle of the Bulge were herded into a field and shot, rather than being moved to a prison camp in the rear. One, wounded, managed to escape. (See the Malmedy Massacre in Chapter 14.)

In early February 1944, the Bedford press reported that the War and Navy Departments had revealed that 5,200 American servicemen had been tortured, starved to death, and wantonly murdered since their surrender in April 1942 to the Japanese on the Bataan Peninsula in the Philippines. The U.S. Government had known of these atrocities for months but had not released the information until it determined there was no hope of getting aid to the prisoners. The U.S. Government had sent 3,000 tons of foodstuffs and medical supplies to the Soviet port of Vladivostok after the Japanese had indicated a willingness to distribute the supplies to American POWs, but the White House subsequently concluded and announced that the Japanese government would not allow the aid to reach the American POWs.[58]

The very same month of this announcement of Japanese atrocities, the Red Cross sponsored a presentation in Bedford which, by comparison, portrayed the Germans as being more humane in their treatment of POWs. As part of a fund-raising campaign and tour of Virginia, the Red Cross brought to Bedford a former American POW, a sergeant from Oklahoma, who had been held by the Germans.[59] The sergeant told a capacity audience at the courthouse of his experiences fighting in Tunisia, being wounded and captured in the campaign in Sicily, and then being held in a German POW camp in Austria for three-and-a-half months before being swapped in a prisoner exchange. He told how once a week the POWs received Red Cross food packages, which were used to supplement the rations of black bread and potatoes, which the Germans fed to the POWs and German guards alike. The packages, he said, were somehow kept under lock and key, and dual keys—one kept by a guard and one by a prisoner—had to be used to access the contents.[60]

As part of this Red Cross campaign, a POW package, packed by volunteer Red Cross workers, was displayed at Jones (Green's) Drug Store, and Bedford Mayor J. W. Gillaspie proclaimed March 1944 as American Red Cross Month.[61]

Later in 1944 officials appeared to have been somewhat more optimistic with respect to the ability of loved ones to communicate with POWs held by the Japanese. In November the Bedford Red Cross chapter notified families of men captured in the Philippines that they could come to the Red Cross office and fill out a special Red Cross message form to be sent to their loved ones. The Red Cross would not guarantee delivery but said it would make every effort to reach the addressee "so that they may establish contact with their families as soon as possible after the islands are liberated." Families were also encouraged to continuing writing the POWs by regular mail.[62]

After the war, returning POWs would corroborate reports of their harsh treatment. Lt. Col. John Boatwright, a native of Lynchburg, whose wife lived in Bedford County, had been a POW of the Japanese for over three years. He was commanding a regiment of the 51st Division in the Philippines when captured in spring 1942 as American forces on the Bataan Peninsula surrendered. He was transported to a prison on the island of Formosa and then moved to Manchuria, where he was eventually liberated at the end of the war. In a letter to his wife shortly after the Japanese surrender, he wrote: "I have been a prisoner for so long and have looked forward to freedom so much, I can hardly realize I am a free man. I have been systematically starved by these savages since captured, so I am lucky to still be alive." He had been allowed only twelve letters from his wife during his more than three years of captivity.[63]

Pfc. William ("Billy") Parker, speaking of his seven-and-a-half months as a POW of the Germans, would later give a less favorable account of life in a German POW camp than the sergeant who visited Bedford on behalf of the Red Cross (see the Parker story in Part II of this book).

Lt. William D. Anderson, who served in the 101st Airborne Division, was captured by the Germans in December 1944, during the major German counteroffensive known as the "Battle of the Bulge." Wounded in the leg and without having his wounds treated, Lieutenant Anderson was forced by the Germans to march some thirty-five miles. Another American soldier shared some of his bandages. Although Lieutenant Anderson was suffering greatly, not until ten days after his capture would the Germans give him a shot of morphine, and not until forty days after capture did they allow a French doctor to remove the shrapnel from his leg. In the POW camp, each day he was fed only three slices of bread, six small potatoes, and a small portion of "grass" soup. Occasionally, the Germans gave him a bowl of barley mush. He once traded another prisoner two days rations of bread for a second- or third-hand toothbrush. He was eventually liberated by Soviet forces moving against Berlin.[64]

Pvt. Cavitt K. Bartley, who lived near the Irving community and had been a pre-medical student at Roanoke College before entering the service, was captured on November 29, 1944. The U.S. Third Army liberated him in the Munich area on April 30, 1945.[65]

T/Sgt. John Chappelle, who lived in Lowry before his family moved to Roanoke, was held as a POW of the Germans for eighteen months. A gunner on a B-25 bomber in Europe, he was reported missing in action over Germany on February 25, 1944. A telegram to his parents announcing his liberation was the first word they had of him since he was reported missing.[66]

Pvt. William R. (Jack) Dooley, who had first fought in North Africa, served with the 36th Division and was captured in the fighting near Naples, Italy, in September 1943 and imprisoned in German

POW camps for twenty months. He was held in a camp near Danzig, where he worked on a farm. The Germans marched him and others 600 miles to the Hanover area as Soviet forces advanced into Germany. Eventually he was liberated by an American tank unit. He reported that he and his fellow POWs had the pleasure of disarming and guarding their own German guards. Private Dooley reportedly was the first POW from Bedford County to return home.[67]

Marvin B. Padgett, who had served in the U.S. Army in the Philippines and then in 1938 gone to work as a civilian for an oil company in Manila, was taken prisoner by the Japanese when they invaded the Philippines in 1941. According to information from the Japanese government, relayed through the International Red Cross and the U.S. War Department, he and 1,775 other prisoners of war were being moved in October 1944 by ship from the Philippines to another location, when the ship was sunk unwittingly by an Allied submarine in the South China Sea 200 miles from the coast of China. The War Department indicated that Mr. Padgett was presumed to have been killed and would be carried on the department's records as killed in action. He was thirty-five at the time of his death.[68]

Other Bedford men who were prisoners of war of the Germans include Sgt. James M. Ayres, Pvt. Elmer N. Branch, Pvt. Fletcher B. Burks, Pvt. Gerald W. Daniel, Pvt. Aubrey B. English, Pfc. Otha B. Eubank, Lt. Watts Gills, Sgt. Willie W. Howell, Pvt. Glen Knighton, Sgt. Albert H. Massey, T/5 Guy O. Mayhew, Lt. Ernest R. Shelton, and Pfc. Robert Wicks.[69] Other POWs who were either from the Bedford County area near Vinton or from Vinton, itself, were Pfc. Carl R. Austin, Sgt. Jesse H. Burton, and Pvt. Dennis T. Johnson. Another POW, Arthur W. Burkholder, seaman, first class, mentioned in the Bedford newspapers, previously lived in Arcadia before moving to Lynchburg.[70]

New Absentee Voting Procedures for Service Personnel

In its 1944 session, the Virginia General Assembly passed an act providing procedures for Virginia service personnel to be able to apply for absentee ballots to vote in elections. Requirements for registration and payment of poll taxes were waived.[71]

Servicemen Arrested and Convicted of Manslaughter in Roanoke

In December 1944, two brothers from Thaxton, Pvts. Roy and Ernest Holdren, were arrested and charged with the murder of a man during a fight outside a restaurant in Roanoke. A third brother, James Holdren, who had recently been honorably discharged from the Navy, was held as a material witness.[72] Roy and Ernest Holdren were first sentenced to six months in jail for assault, and later their case was sent to a grand jury for possible murder.[73] In January 1945, the two brothers were convicted of voluntary manslaughter and sentenced to five years in the penitentiary.[74]

Discharges

During the war, some men were discharged on an individual basis for medical or personal reasons. As the war began to wind down in 1945, however, the government began planning for a more general discharge of service personnel. In mid-May, the Army announced a partial demobilization plan. (This plan did not apply to Navy and Marine Corps personnel.)

The Army's plan was formulated to discharge over 1,300,000 men over a twelve-month period. It was based on a point system, in which soldiers received points for length of service, overseas and combat duty, decorations, wounds, and parenthood. The plan applied to men in all theaters but did not automatically apply to all men. Men whose work was vital to the war against Japan were to be retained in service.[75]

In late May the Bedford County draft board announced that six men had been discharged under the new point-demobilization system. The first man to be discharged under this system was John Ralph Sligh, who had been inducted on July 2, 1941. He had served nearly four years. Robert Lee Goode was one of the first men from the original National Guard Company A to be discharged under the point system, after having served on active duty nearly four years and four months.[76]

For several months after the surrender of Germany and then after the surrender of Japan, the local newspapers reported the names of Bedford County men whom the local draft board said had been discharged or, in the case of officers, placed on inactive status. For example, on September 6, 1945, less than a month after the Japanese surrender, the *Bedford Democrat* listed the names of 305 white men and fifty black men who had been discharged as of September 1 and the names of four officers who had been placed on inactive status.[77]

Bedford's servicemen and servicewomen were beginning to come home.

Chapter 5

Life in the Military

In letters to loved ones in Bedford, many servicemen and servicewomen wrote short accounts of some of their experiences in the military. The recipients in Bedford—often the mothers of those writing—sometimes shared these accounts with the *Bedford Bulletin*, which, in turn, shared them with the public. Many of the following accounts are excerpted from this newspaper. In addition to publishing excerpts of letters, the *Bedford Bulletin* featured short reports on the service of young men and women in the military, under a series of evolving titles, "News of Soldier Boys at Home and in Camp," "News of Boys in the Armed Forces," "News of Men in the Armed Services," and, finally, "News of Our Men and Women in Uniform." After the war, at least one veteran wrote about his experiences and made the manuscript available to the public.

Company A Trains in England

For twenty months, from October 1942 to June 1944, the men of Company A trained in England for the invasion of the European mainland. During this time, the unit was based mainly in two locations—Tidworth Barracks and Ivybridge. It deployed for short periods to at least three other areas.

After landing in Scotland, the 29th Infantry Division, including Company A, was transported south and based at Tidworth Barracks, an old British-cavalry camp located approximately eighty miles west of the center of London. Seven months later, in May 1943, the division and Company A vacated Tidworth Barracks in order to make room for other American troops being deployed to England. Elements of the 29th were scattered to various locations in Cornwall and Devon Counties, both located at the end of the southwestern peninsula of England.[1]

Company A and its parent unit, the 1st Battalion of the 116th Infantry Regiment, moved to an encampment adjacent to the small town of Ivybridge, located in Devon County about ten miles east of Plymouth and six miles north of the English Channel.[2]

In early 1944, Company A deployed temporarily for four or five weeks to Liverpool, on the west coast of central England, where the men patrolled the docks to prevent pillage of supplies arriving for American forces.[3]

Company A also left Ivybridge temporarily to participate in landing exercises in the coastal area of Slapton Sands, located east of Ivybridge and on the English Channel. Military planners thought the tidal flats of Slapton Sands resembled the Normandy coast. The 29th Infantry Division conducted exercises at Slapton Sands in December 1943-January 1944 and again in April 1944.[4]

The village of Slapton and six other neighboring villages, with a total of 3,000 residents, had been evacuated in December 1943 to provide an area for Allied military training.[5] In April 1944, shortly after the 29th Division completed its exercise, German naval forces attacked Allied ships during an exercise in the Slapton Sands area involving soldiers of the U.S. 4th Division. German E-boats—high-speed craft equipped with torpedo tubes and torpedoes, similar to American PT Boats—sank two transport ships, killing over 700 American soldiers.[6] According to a Company A veteran, Allied authorities kept news of this tragedy secret, and neither Company A nor the public heard about it until more than thirty years later.[7]

Finally, in mid-May, in preparation for the invasion, the elements of the 29th Division, including Company A, were moved from their scattered encampments to assembly areas near Plymouth and Falmouth on the coast of the English Channel.[8]

Living in England with Company A

During their first months in England, at Tidworth Barracks, the men of Company A lived in the old British barracks there. When they moved to the Ivybridge area, they lived in Nissen huts. These huts, named after a Canadian engineer officer who invented them in World War I, were prefabricated buildings made of curved, corrugated steel sheets bolted to wooden frames.[9] Inside the huts, the men slept on blankets on beds without mattresses. On maneuvers, they slept in two-man pup tents.

There were complaints about the cool, rainy weather in England. S/Sgt. John Schenk wrote:

> The weather here is terrible, one minute we have light rain and the next minute it is heavy rain. Anyway you look at it there is always rain. Here it is the middle of July and I am sitting by a fire wearing my long handle underware (sic). If it gets (any) damn colder I may have to go to bed to keep warm. I could get up and run around the block but that takes energy and I am a little short at present....[10]

Life for American soldiers in Britain did not consist entirely of military training. In the evenings when they were not on maneuvers, the men often listened to the radio, went to see motion pictures, or played cards or Ping-Pong. Occasionally, they had a beer party in the mess hall. Some went in search of women.

The ground troops listened to American radio shows and music, presumably, the same radio shows to which William Yowell, a bomber pilot from Bedford stationed at Lavenham, England, listened. Yowell wrote the following to his wife in mid-May 1944:

> At night we sit around the barracks listening to the radio. U.S. Armed Forces have good programs and no advertising. The music really gets to me. So many songs remind me of things we used to do and places we have been....[11]

> We are sitting here in the barracks listening to the radio. Just heard the Jack Benny program. The Armed Forces network gets transcriptions of all the big programs. The German stations are making all these cracks about the (future) Invasion. One was that General Eisenhower was going to be awarded the Nobel Peace Prize. They say that their forces are withdrawing according to plan. If you can get any addresses of the boys in the National

Guard Co. from home, please send them to me, as some might
just be near here.[12]

One of Company A's beer parties was notable enough for John
Schenk to mention it in a letter to his wife:

The beer party that I told you about was a big success. There was
only one black eye in the whole brawl. Plenty of headaches but
they are doing better....[13]

In the evenings and on weekends, the men often visited nearby
towns, where they ate fish or Canadian bacon and chips (fried potatoes) off newspapers, visited bars for a drink, went to movies and
dances, played billiards, and snacked on hamburgers and other food at
the British equivalent of the USO or Red Cross. They were sometimes
given furloughs and often used these breaks to visit London and other
English cities and towns, where, among other things, they went to
shows and movies.

Toward the end of their stay, the men of Company A and other
units may have been restricted from visiting Ivybridge. One soldier in
Company A would later write:

The nearby village of Ivybridge was "off limits" for passes since
there had been too many fights in the pubs with locals or black
American troops and the white boys.[14]

Most of the company leaders were Southerners from Bedford.
Many of the men who came into the company to augment its strength
and replace those from Bedford who went on to new assignments
were Northerners. Company Commander Captain Fellers, who had
served with the men from Bedford since before the war, wrote home
from England in April 1943:

The boys in the company are doing well. Most of the Bedford
boys I have left are my key non-coms. I am beginning to think it is
hard to beat a Bedford boy as a soldier. Out of less than a hundred
we left there with I would say about a dozen have made officers

and several more will be soon. They are good practical officers, too, with a year or more of regular non-commission service behind them. I am truly proud to be commanding my old home town outfit and just hope I can carry them right on through and bring all of them home. The replacements we have got from time to time have been northerners. Mostly New Englanders but I think most of them have developed a southern drawl by now. I still find the battle of Bull Run and Gettysburg going on in quarters when I go in for bed check at night. They sit around and smoke their pipes and fight it all over again. Among them are Diplomats, Statesmen, Politicians, and Guard house lawyers. It is really interesting just to listen. And when one of them gets back from pass and starts telling about a girl he met, from his description, you would wonder how Heddy Lamar and Lana Turner ever got so popular....

We are all O.K. so don't worry about us. Plenty of hard training but plenty of food and a little time off to relax....[15]

One of the Northerners, John Barnes, a soldier from Utica, New York, who joined Company A in February 1944 as an individual replacement, has written the perspective of a Northern newcomer to Company A:

At first we felt like outsiders. To us, mostly Northerners or from the Midwest, these Southerners seemed like real rubes, but we never said that out loud. In fact, when I had to say I was from New York, I immediately added, "but not from New York City."[16]

For their relaxation time, some Bedford men found transportation. John Schenk and Pride Wingfield acquired bicycles so they could ride out into the countryside, partly to visit local farmers to purchase fresh eggs, so they would not have to eat powdered ones.[17]

William Yowell, who had served in Company A for three years before the war, had similar experiences while serving as a bomber pilot at the base at Lavenham. He, too, lived in a hut and had a bicycle which he used to travel a few miles off base. On one bicycle ride, he and a fellow officer visited a pub for some beer and then bought fish and chips to take back to the men at the base. His squadron once had a beer party with sandwiches, cookies, and ice cream. He reported visiting London twice, and once he visited Cambridge, where he ran into Joseph Danner, a B-26 pilot from Bedford. He also related that he and most of the members of his bomber crew went to church together almost every Sunday.[18]

M/Sgt. John Wilkes sent home photos showing some of the men enjoying themselves at a swimming facility. John Schenk swam in the English Channel in August 1943, ten months before D-Day. He wrote his wife:

> Just got back from a two-day pass….I really had a grand time, went in swimming in the channel which was cold as the dickens….[19]

In the summer of 1943, four men from Company A—Frank Draper, Anthony Marsico, Elmere Wright, and Pride Wingfield—played on a regimental baseball team while in England. The team, minus Wingfield who had returned to America for training, went on to win the European Theater of Operations championship in 1943.[20]

Captain Fellers and a fellow officer from Lynchburg made friends with a British family. Staff Sergeant Draper served as best man at a large wedding of a fellow soldier from southern Virginia, Meade Hite Baker, who married a young British woman in December 1943.[21]

As the men of Company A continued to train, they watched for news of the war. John Schenk wrote his wife at the end of January 1944:

> The war news is looking very good today. Maybe this mess will be over before we know it. Some say it is a matter of a few months. The Russians are really causing Jerry a few headaches and the Air Force is causing a few sleepless nights so it shouldn't be too long. It couldn't be too soon for me….[22]

Some Personal Experiences Worldwide

Some men from Bedford served together in units deployed both in America and abroad. More than ninety Bedford County men served in Company A when it left Bedford for Fort Meade, and at least thirty-nine were still in the company as late as June 6, 1944, when nineteen were killed during the D-Day Invasion. The 83[d] Chemical Mortar Battalion had at least five Bedford County men in it when it participated in the Invasion of Anzio, Italy, in January 1944, all five losing their lives. A U.S. Army Air Forces company which served in the Pacific and fought in the Solomon Islands had five Bedford men in it. At least five Bedford County men served in the 366th Infantry Regiment, a unit manned with Blacks. Battery B of the 285th Field Artillery Observation Battalion had three Bedford men in it, two losing their lives and the other severely wounded in the Malmedy Massacre in Belgium during the Battle of the Bulge.[23]

Beyond this, there were several instances in which servicemen from Bedford sought out or came across other men from Bedford and had short reunions. Sometimes brothers were able to seek out one another and meet for a short visit. On other occasions, men who had not known each other in Bedford had chance meetings.

Two brothers, Pfc. Floyd R. Daniel and Pvt. Orie H. Daniel, who were serving in Europe and had not seen one another in twenty-one months, were able to spend a furlough together in England.[24]

Cpl. Warren Stevens, serving in action in Germany, was able to get a weekend pass to travel to Paris to see his brother T/Sgt. Roy O. Stevens, who had been wounded and was in rehabilitation. Their brother, Ray, had been killed in the D-Day Invasion.[25]

Lt. Thomas Chappelle, with the aid of the Red Cross, was able to locate and visit his brother-in-law Pfc. Morris Johnson on Tinian Island in the Pacific.[26]

Sgt. Luther Overstreet met Pvt. Linston Patterson in far away New Guinea when Patterson was a patient in Overstreet's medical unit.[27]

Lloyd O. Laughon, staff sergeant and tail gunner on a B-17 bomber based in England, wrote home about some of his flying experiences and about meeting Cpls. Carlton Stevens and Drewry Woodford and talking about "growing up in dear old Bedford County."[28]

Many of the Bedford service personnel found new friends in the military from across the country. Hettie Hopkins, an Army nurse from Goode with the rank of lieutenant, wrote in the summer of 1943 about arriving in San Francisco with forty-three other nurses after sixteen months with the troops in the South Pacific, where the nurses lived in Army tents. She reported:

> ...(the tents) weren't bad. One of the boys built a little white picket fence around the tents and it was real homey. We had to bathe in pairs in a sheltered place up the river. One of us would take some leaves and fan the other to keep from getting eaten up with mosquitoes.

One fellow nurse thought that the soldiers spoiled her and the other nurses:

> We felt like revered characters. Not a one ever, at any time, showed us disrespect.

The nurses were said to be pleased to be back in civilization, staying in a hotel with electric lights and bathtubs and being able to shop. Lieutenant Hopkins wrote:

> It's the first time in months and months we've been able to walk on genuine rugs or sit in real sophisticated chairs. Boy, this is simply wonderful.

All the nurses were said to desire to return to the front after a brief rest.[29]

Woodrow Hubbard, a seaman first class in the Navy, sent his wife in Moneta the following account of the Battle of Leyte Gulf in the Philippines in October 1944:

> For once I can surprise you by telling you something of what I have been doing the past several weeks. We have been permitted to write, without evading censorship rules, of our participation in the invasion of Leyte in the Philippines....it was an exciting chance to be a part of the largest invasion fleet ever to set sail in the Pacific and to see at first hand what happens when our troops hit an enemy beachhead....we could watch battleships and

cruisers steaming back and forth shelling the beach, landing craft moving in and pouring troops out over their ramps, and planes flying in low to strafe enemy defenses. In the distance we could see an occasional puff showing where the front lines were.

I am glad to report that I am well and that our ship and everyone on it came through unscathed even though we saw some action against enemy planes. We were not involved in the great surface battle that took place around Leyte, but we were on the fringe of it and several times we thought we were headed for some hot action. Ours was only one of many destroyers taking part in the invasion. Our job was to convoy the troop ships to Leyte and then to protect them while the men landed and established beach defenses. Though some of us might have preferred a more violent assignment, we cannot complain because every job counts, and ours was successfully accomplished.[30]

Kenneth Dooley, a private in the Army, wrote his mother two letters in June 1944, saying he was in France, had been in "plenty of action," and had not received a scratch, adding:

I guess that you are kind of surprised at getting letters from me while I am in combat. I am still all right and having a hell of a time. The going isn't too tough yet. There isn't much I can tell you but I can say I rode a German bicycle this morning. The French people are right good to us. They give us milk and eggs and sometimes wine or other drinks. We sure have had a time understanding them....I will close with my love. Go read the papers and you will find where I am and what I am doing.[31]

John V. (Jack) Harris, Jr., a private in the military police, wrote in the summer of 1944 from a hospital in England where he was recuperating:

Just a few lines to let you know I am O.K. I gave my Purple Heart to a lady at the Red Cross and asked her to send it to you....I don't want anymore or anything that looks like it—they are too hard to get, but I want to keep this one. I would like to tell you more, but you will have to wait until I get home. About all I want now is another German Lugar pistol to match the one I already have.

What do you think of the war and the way us boys have got these super-men on the run?...

In your next letter, let me know how many boys in old Company A were lost in the landing and since. That outfit sure made a name for itself during the invasion. I saw a number of boys from my old outfit not long ago, but lost touch when I had to return to England.

Please grease my rifle and pistol with good oil every month or so and take good care of my car and dogs. As ever, the old "hell raiser," the M.P. Rebel, Jack.[32]

Raymond Archer Noell, who left Bedford with Company A and later became a lieutenant in another unit fighting in France, wrote his sister of his experiences in France:

I believe I've told you in my letters the way the French people treat us and the way we eat over here. I spend mostly money that I get off of Germans....I found a Jerry the other day who had $28 on him in French money. That will buy me lots of eggs and chickens. It certainly is touching when we take one of these French towns. All the townspeople come out and give us cider and flowers and start ringing the church bells the first time for four years. That makes a big lump come up in our throats and makes us realize what we are fighting for.

I saw a good USO show several nights ago. It certainly was nice to see American girls once more....[33]

Warren Woodford, a corporal in the Army, was in the first group of American soldiers to reach Africa early in the war. In October 1944 he wrote his family that he had been in the thick of things ever since. He had been wounded on D-Day, kept at a base hospital for six weeks, and then returned to the battlefront. He also had been awarded a Bronze Star, his seventh medal, but his mind seemed more on food and home:

If you send me a box, please let it be filled with smokes and candy, as we are not getting many cigarettes now and candy is a thing of the past. I only hope I can come home for that long rest you wrote about and some of the good food you are saving for me. I could sure use some good food right now, for it has been many long months since I have lived like folks.[34]

Mary Witt, a field supervisor for American Red Cross hospitals in England and France, described her life in post D-Day France:

Life is rather rugged, tents, cots, a helmet for a bath, mud that is glue, yellow-jacket bees that nearly drive everyone crazy, crickets in your bed, battle dress at all times, and a complexion like alligator skin. But we are all well, and seem to be thriving on it.

We travel all the time. I have my own Jeep and do my own driving. We get into some tight spots at times but so far no Germans have taken a shot at us.

Just now the sky is full of our big bombers going and returning from a mission. The sight is really something with the vapor fumes spreading out behind each plane.[35]

(For more information about Miss Witt, see the profile on her in Part II of this book.)

Paul Thomasson, an Army private first class from Goodview, was wounded in the Invasion of Anzio and was hospitalized for three months before rejoining his unit in France, where he was wounded a second time. As a patient at the Army's Walter Reed Hospital in Washington, D.C., he described in a printed interview some of the action in Italy before the Allies marched on Rome:

The Germans began an all-out counter-attack....Our losses were heavy. My company commander was killed at my feet, and I was all alone in a field....Germans came up on both sides and had me surrounded. One wounded German saw me trying to hide and he came up and insisted on surrendering to me. I sent him on up the road toward our lines. I lay there until dark and finally an American infantry company came up, chased the Germans out, and I was safe.

We wore new, dark combat suits and the rain had soaked into the clothing making it all the darker. One day I was moving along minding my own business back of our lines when several American soldiers saw me, took my dark combat suit for a German uniform and let me have it. I had to crawl through mud and ditches, jump walls, and even scoot underneath a tank before I got away from their shots.[36]

S/Sgt. William D. Poindexter sent his mother the following note shortly after Christmas Day, December 25, 1944:

Thanks so much for the nice box I received from you today and on Christmas Day, too; it made Christmas seem more real....We had a grand dinner today. There was all you wanted of turkey, gravy, Irish potatoes, cranberry sauce, sweet potatoes, peas, slaw, apple pie, apples, raisins, hard candy, biscuits, sugar, milk, coffee, and wine....

I guess everyone at home is standing on their heads about the news. I'm now in Belgium and there is nothing to worry about for we can control anything over here. It makes no difference where we fight, just so we kill all the Germans who want to fight, so it might as well be here as Germany.

You may wonder how I got way down here, but I can't tell you anything yet.

Hope all of you had a nice Christmas, and I'm sure I will be there for the next one. Remember I love you. Your son, Bill.[37]

William Powers, an Army private, notified his parents in January 1945 that he was in a hospital in France recovering from frozen feet and hands. (Powers had two brothers also serving in France, a sister was a cadet nurse, and another brother, Sgt. Jack Powers, was killed in France on D-Day.) Powers reported:

It shore is cold over here now with snow knee deep and some places it is over our heads, and boy it is hard going, too. I am back with the cooks for two days now for my feet nearly froze and they swelled up and broke my shoe strings, and my fingers got so cold they cracked open on the ends.

I am getting along fine and have a little feeling in my feet so I will soon be O.K. and back with my company again, so don't worry about me for I could stay in this hospital from now on. Boy this nice, soft, white bed feels good, for it has been so long since I slept in one. Good, hot food served in bed! Boy, this is O.K. with me....[38]

Esther Overstreet, a corporal in the Women's Army Corps serving as a driver in the Miami area, was commended to her commanding officer by an Army Air Forces colonel who had occasion to be her passenger. In the commendation, published in the *Bedford Bulletin*, the colonel wrote:

The undersigned recently had occasion to be a passenger in a government sedan driven by Corporal Esther F. Overstreet.... (Her) driving...was so above average and her attitude so military it is desired to commend her highly and to state the qualifications...(a) Smoothness of starting, shifting gears and acceleration to driving speeds both in and out of traffic; (b) smoothness in slowing up for necessary stops; (c) alertness in looking ahead to anticipate changes in traffic lights or other conditions requiring prompt and proper handling of vehicle; (d) observance of safe and proper speeds at all times; (e) knowledge of city and most logical and economical routes; (f) pleasant manner and military bearing and neatness....In view of the fact that the majority of our government drivers in the Army are grossly negligent in following the above principles of good driving and as a result needlessly and prematurely wear out equipment as well as waste much needed gasoline, Corporal Overstreet's example of proper driving is outstanding and deserves recognition....[39]

Walker L. Ayres, a lieutenant serving in Belgium, sent a letter to the *Bedford Bulletin* in October, relating the fame in Europe of the 29th Infantry Division. He was responding to an article he had seen in an August edition of the *Bedford Bulletin* reporting on the 29th Infantry Division's ceremony for those lost in the invasion:

> May I say that the fame and glory of this outfit is known far and wide over here and I am sure their gallantry will not be soon forgotten. This is scant help to those who lost their loved ones, but at least they can be proud of their men. I am….The people of this country and France are, as a whole, very grateful that we have run the Germans back to Germany. I have never been as royally treated in my life as these past few months. Honestly, I believe they would go hungry for a week to see us sit down and eat one good meal. It makes the whole struggle seem so much more worthwhile to know that it's appreciated by someone.[40]

Harold C. Crouch, a machinist's mate, first class, served in the Navy for four years, in many theaters of operations, and on several types of naval craft. He spent time on a Navy cruiser. He was with the First Marine Division Reinforced when that unit made assaults on a number of Japanese-held islands in the Pacific, including Guadacanal. He served on a patrol torpedo (PT) boat and was listed in 1943 on *Yachting Magazine*'s honor roll of PT heroes. He worked in the engine room of the aircraft carrier *Hornet* when Lt. Col. (later Gen.) Jimmy Doolittle and his men flew their B-25 bombers off that ship to bomb Tokyo and other Japanese cities.

While he was in a hospital in Corona, California, the *Los Angeles Times* interviewed him, and someone sent the article to Bedford, where it was summarized in the *Bedford Bulletin*. In the interview, Crouch indicated that after all the excitement of his life in the Navy, he would face a post-war problem:

> How am I going back to a quiet life in Bedford, Va., after we win the war? I can't imagine sitting on a stool in my favorite drugstore sipping a chocolate soda.[41]

Chapter 6

Home Front:
Overview and Civil Defense

Overview of the Bedford Home Front

Life on the Bedford home front became increasingly active as the war progressed. Bedford's citizens continued to work or go to school, do their usual chores, worship at their churches, shop, and socialize, but they found themselves presented with new challenges to everyday living as well as opportunities for service to their community and country.

People tried to keep up with developments in the war by listening to the radio and reading the local newspapers and national magazines. They corresponded with loved ones serving in the armed forces. Both in the work place and at home, people stepped forward to fill jobs or assume chores and other responsibilities previously performed by young men and women who had entered the military.

A whole new dimension was added to people's lives with the creation of volunteer organizations and activities designed specifically to contribute to the war effort. The volunteer programs at the local level were modeled on similar ones being established at the federal and state levels; the higher authorities provided guidance and, in some case, quotas for the local entities.

The volunteer programs gave the people who remained in Bedford opportunities to become directly and concretely involved with the war effort. Some citizens volunteered to serve on local boards and committees. Many others contributed their time and resources as workers, without taking leadership positions. A few of the boards and committees hired small staffs to deal with day-to-day operations.

Many leaders of the community volunteered to serve on the local Selective Service Board, the War Price and Rationing Board, the War Finance Committee, the Civil Defense Council, and the Salvaging

Committee. A number of older men and those deferred from military service joined the Virginia Protective Force (later called the Virginia State Guard). Others served as airplane spotters and air raid wardens.

On a broader scale, many people in the Bedford community did their best to see that the military received top priority for resources. Workers at local plants such as Rubatex, Hampton Looms of Virginia, Belding Heminway, Bedford Paper and Pulp Company, and Piedmont Label contributed by producing material needed for the war effort and by helping to keep the American economy running. Some workers from Bedford moved to other areas of the country to work in defense industries.

Many people in the county promoted and bought war bonds. They raised money for the Red Cross and other organizations providing relief for American service personnel and people in war-torn areas. Many grew Victory Gardens to help feed their families so that other food stocks could go to those in the military and Allies in need. Nearly all conserved on the consumption of food, gasoline, and other rationed items, and many contributed to the effort to salvage materials needed for the war effort.

A few women were added to leadership positions in the long-established, local American Red Cross chapter. Many other women volunteered to assist as workers to help the Red Cross prepare surgical dressings and other items needed by the military and those in war-torn areas.

Several women stepped forward to organize campaigns to salvage recyclable materials needed for the war. Others helped teach adults how to grow and preserve vegetables, and still others helped monitor prices charged by local merchants.

A few historically-minded citizens formed the Bedford County World War II History Committee and submitted regular reports to a Virginia history commission in Richmond.

The *Bedford Bulletin* and *Bedford Democrat* increased their reporting on the war as American involvement escalated. They ran reports on the fighting around the world and reported on the activities of Bedford men and women in the service. The editors wrote lengthy editorials on the war, and both newspapers published public service notices and ran war-related advertisements paid for by coalitions of local businesses. They encouraged and sometimes chided the citizens of Bedford to do more to support the war effort.

Through all of this, the people of Bedford continued to socialize and tried to maintain a degree of humor, some of which was reflected in the newspapers and in letters.

Organizing the Home Front for War

One scholar has described how American citizens responded in the immediate aftermath of the attack on Pearl Harbor:

> As the government struggled to mobilize, many civilians took matters into their own hands, forming a huge variety of volunteer organizations....Volunteerism became a big part of U.S. life, which helped somewhat to offset the government's failure to plan ahead....Far more than any other warring nation, the United States would depend on volunteers, and especially women, to organize the home front.[1]

In Bedford, volunteers played an extremely important role in organizing the home front activity. They did not, however, take matters into their own hands, nor were they out ahead of the government's efforts, with the possible exception of the formation of the Bedford County Defense Council shortly after the attack on Pearl Harbor.

In almost all cases, Bedford volunteers stepped forward in response to requests from Virginia authorities, who, in turn, were responding to initiatives from the federal level. This is true for organizations from the Federal Selective Service System to the volunteer Red Cross.

Bedford, for the most part, followed national and state plans and bureaucracies in organizing itself to assist the war effort. Before the war, at least two local organizations existed in Bedford with responsibilities to authorities at state and federal levels—Company A of National Guard and the local American Red Cross Chapter. Other local organizations reporting to state or federal authorities were established shortly before America entered the war or during the war.

Women played important roles, particularly in Red Cross programs and salvaging, but for most other volunteer activities, consistent with the times, men were placed in charge.

In October 1940 a local draft board, the Bedford County Selective Service Board, was established to support the U.S. Selective Service System and its mission of providing men for military service.[2] Members of the board were appointed by President Roosevelt upon the recommendation of the governor of Virginia. The first appointed chairman of the three-man board was J. Moorman Johnson. (J. W. Gillaspie, the mayor of Bedford, later served as chairman.) The board opened an office on the third floor of the courthouse.[3] Without compensation, Bedford men served on the draft board and as advisors to young men filling out selective service questionnaires. Local doctors examined selectees in the early months of the war until the examinations began to be done at the induction centers in Roanoke and Lynchburg.[4]

In January 1941 industrial classes were offered at Bedford High School as part of a nationwide training program designed to produce more trained workers. The program, funded with National Defense funds, offered classes in metal work, electrical wiring, and carpentry.[5]

In February 1941 Bedford mustered a company of the statewide Virginia Protective Force to help replace the National Guard unit which had been called to active duty.[6] In June, veterans groups in Bedford began organizing aircraft warning volunteers.[7]

In mid-1941 the U.S. Department of Agriculture (USDA) established defense boards in each county of America to coordinate local agriculture activity as it related to national defense. Bedford County's USDA Defense Board held its first meeting in September in the USDA county agent's office.[8] In October, the local defense board announced agricultural production goals for the county, ranging from a 1-3 percent increase in meat production to a 23 percent increase in production of rye.[9]

In December 1941, after the attack on Pearl Harbor, a Bedford County Defense Council, patterned after the Virginia Defense Council, was organized to plan and supervise civil defense efforts. This became the central, guiding body for many defense-related activities in the county.

On February 9, 1942, America shifted to "War Time," turning clocks back an hour in an effort to conserve energy.[10] (Not quite a year later, Lyle's Drug Store would announce that it would begin closing at 8 p.m. to help save coal and electricity.)[11]

In 1942 or early 1943, a local War Price and Rationing Board was established under the auspices of the Federal Office of Price Administration to help monitor price controls on the sale of goods, to issue rationing coupons on a wide variety of consumer products, and to oversee implementation of the rationing process. Dan Weinberg was appointed chairman of this board.[12] Several women served on the rationing board without compensation, and other women monitored prices charged by local merchants. There was a small, paid staff.[13]

While a national Civilian Defense Corps was established nationally in mid-1942 to help protect the home front by using volunteers as air-raid wardens, plane spotters, and auxiliary firemen and policemen, Bedford appears not to have participated in this organization per se, and local newspapers made no reference to it. Instead, the Bedford County civil defense program appears to have been organized locally as part of a statewide program. After the threat of an invasion dissipated by late 1943, the national organization was disbanded. Occasional blackouts and air-raid drills, however, continued, as did Bedford's civil defense establishment.[14]

Civil Defense

Mustering the Virginia Protective Force

In early 1941, shortly before Virginia National Guard units were called to active Army duty, the Commonwealth established the Virginia Protective Force, with a primary mission of local defense. In Bedford, on January 31, prior to the departure of Bedford's Company A for Fort Meade, an organizational and recruiting meeting was held at the courthouse in an effort to form a company of at least two officers and forty men of the Virginia Protective Force. The organizers were soon successful in mustering Company 73 of the Virginia Protective Force, with three officers and fifty-nine enlisted men. The men were volunteers and were not subject to the draft because of their age, physical condition, or occupational deferment.

Company 73 became part of the 7th Battalion, which was commanded by an officer from Lynchburg and included elements from not only Lynchburg but also Farmville. The Bedford company, minus uniforms and guns, held its first drill on February 17 in the Bedford County Courthouse, where Company A had its armory. Capt. Owen Keeler, who worked at the Bedford post office, became the first company commander. (W. Earl Johnson would later rise to become captain and company commander in 1944.)[15]

Men served in the Virginia Protective Force without pay for regular drills. They drilled in defending against enemy paratroopers, dealing with civil disturbances, and guarding transportation, industrial, and utility facilities. Units could be called into the service of the state for up to sixty days at a time for riot, strike, or other such duty. The Commonwealth of Virginia designed the uniforms and prescribed the color of gray but provided no funds to buy the uniforms, apparently hoping that local communities or individuals would find funds to buy the uniforms.[16]

The company made progress on a number of issues. By April 7, 1941, it reportedly received a consignment of Enfield rifles. (Another source reported that the men were armed only with shotguns, as the rifles were shipped to the British.) By the end of May the company had enough donations to obtain uniforms.[17] In December 1941, just days after the attack on Pearl Harbor, the company announced that it had arranged with the town of Bedford for an emergency signal system to alert the men of the company to assemble. A continuous blowing of the fire siren and the ringing of the courthouse bell would signal the men to report at once to the armory, in uniform and ready for duty.[18]

Some industrial and transportation sites were guarded during the war, perhaps with the assistance of the Virginia Protective Force and hired guards. Railroad bridges across the James River at Lowry and Snowden were reportedly guarded by armed men, and the Rubatex plant in Bedford and the paper mill at Big Island were also said to be guarded.[19]

In 1944, at the recommendation of the governor of Virginia, the Virginia General Assembly changed the name of the Virginia Protective Force to the Virginia State Guard. The force had grown to some 4,000 officers and men, comprising fifty companies, organized into twelve battalions. The men in the organization had recommended the name change to eliminate public confusion about the organization and to bring the name in line with the state guards in thirty-nine of the forty-four states with similar organizations.[20]

As late as February 1945, the Bedford company of the Virginia State Guard was seeking recruits to fill the ranks of men who had joined the regular armed forces. It made an appeal for enlistment by men over draft age, those exempted from active service because of an occupational exemption, and those who had been discharged from active military service.[21]

Aircraft Warning Volunteers

In June 1941, under instructions of the aircraft warning service of the Virginia Defense Council, the commander of Bedford's American Legion post, assisted by the commander of the Veterans of Foreign Wars, began organizing aircraft observation posts throughout Bedford County. About ten posts were established. If the warning system were activated, two volunteers, from a list of sixteen rotating volunteers, were to man each post. The volunteers were to come from those ineligible for Selective Service but with good eyesight and hearing. Following an improved model of the British aircraft warning system, any warnings of threatening aircraft were to be telephoned to a filtering station in Roanoke and subsequently to Richmond and Norfolk. Fortunately, the system never needed to be activated, and by June 1944 those citizens who had volunteered to be airplane spotters were released from their duties.[22]

Bedford County Defense Council

The Bedford County Defense Council, established in December 1941, shortly after the Pearl Harbor attack, opened an office in the courthouse in January 1942.[23] Mr. duVal Radford led the council and served as county defense coordinator.[24] The Defense Council called for volunteers. The immediate response from the community must have been disappointing, as the council met in mid-January to discuss the insufficient number of volunteers stepping forward.[25]

By February, however, several committees, led by volunteer workers, had been organized. The county was divided into zones according to centers of population. The town of Bedford was divided into six zones, which in turn were divided into posts. In addition to the various zone organizations, functional committees were organized for air raid wardens, fire wardens, police, public works, and public utilities protection.[26]

Also in February the council organized at least three defense nursing classes, taught by local registered nurses.[27]

By May, the Defense Council had established committees or departments for salvage, home nursing, first aid/Red Cross, farm programs, defense savings, nutrition, and the rationing board.[28]

Chairmen or representatives of the various committees or departments held meetings throughout the county to inform citizens about their organizations. In addition, several Bedford citizens completed first aid instructor classes so they could teach first aid to members of the defense council committees and departments and later to other citizens of the county.[29]

Blackout Exercises

Bedford participated in the national blackout program. This program was designed to counter any possible enemy bomber attacks by darkening lights in homes and businesses and on motor vehicles, thereby making it more difficult for the enemy to identify population centers.

At least five blackout exercises were conducted in the Bedford community in 1942 and 1943. With headquarters in the courthouse, the town was divided into zones, under the control of chief wardens. The wardens and some volunteers were given training in fire prevention and fire fighting, especially against incendiary bombs, and in how to recognize and respond to a poison-gas attack. They patrolled the zones during the exercises.[30]

On June 17, 1942, Bedford participated in the first Virginia-wide blackout exercise. All buildings except defense industries were to be darkened, either by turning off lights or covering windows and doors to prevent any light from escaping. For a short period, even defense industries had to be blackened. Sometime during the exercise, a test for air raid warning of approaching bombers was to be conducted. During this test, emergency vehicles were to turn on their sirens to simulate both the beginning and end of the air raid. Only officials were to be allowed on the streets. County air raid wardens were to be at their posts, and citizens were requested to leave the telephone lines free for official use. Vehicular traffic was permitted during the blackout, provided only parking or dim lights were used, except during the test air raid when vehicles had to pull to the side of the road, stop, and turn off all lights.

Civil defense volunteers from the Defense Council organizations, the police, and the Virginia Protective Force helped monitor the exercise. Officials were given authority to enter buildings and extinguish lights or otherwise enforce compliance with the blackout. Persons not cooperating were subject to fines and imprisonment.[31]

The *Bedford Democrat* reported that officials called the June 17 blackout a complete success, observing:

> As dusk covered the town, lights went out, neighbors gathered in groups and over all there was a hushed feeling unnatural for those accustomed to the American way of life....The fire flies were the only apparent unpatriotic citizens here.[32]

Later, during a forty-five-minute blackout exercise in August, several merchants had to be reminded to turn out their lights, and many people sat on their porches in the dark.[33]

In late September, the newspapers announced that another blackout would be held sometime between October 5 and 12.[34] By the time of yet another exercise on March 17, 1943, an improved system of blackouts and signaling of approaching and departing enemy aircraft was in place. All lights had to be extinguished but only for a reduced period of time when enemy aircraft might be in the vicinity.[35]

Eleanor Payne wrote to her husband-to-be how this exercise on March 17 interrupted her evening:

> Last night Bertie, Sara, and Mary Jane came over to play bridge. No sooner had we started before the blackout siren started blowing, and we had to put out the lights for a half-hour.[36]

Another statewide blackout test was conducted a month later in April.[37] By January 1944, however, Washington announced that blackouts and air raid alerts would be terminated entirely, except in coastal areas where they would be held only once every three months and only on Sunday.[38] Concern over enemy air attacks, at least in the American hinterland, had abated.

Chapter 7

Home Front: Restrictions on Consumers

Rationing and Price Controls

During the war, the U.S. Government restricted the production and sale of many items for the civilian economy. This was done to ensure that the military received the resources it needed, to prevent hoarding within the civilian economy, and to facilitate a fair distribution of scarce goods among the public. Given the likelihood of inflated prices for scarce goods, the government also instituted price controls on many items.

Over time, Washington established several bureaucracies, policies, and regulations to implement these restrictions. The War Production Board directed American industries to terminate production of such items as civilian passenger cars and to produce military equipment instead. The Office of Price Administration directed the rationing of restricted consumer items and set price controls on these items. It used 5,500 local War Price and Rationing boards, with a total of some 60,000 full-time workers plus volunteers, to provide information to the public and administer the rationing and price control systems.[1] One of these boards was located in Bedford County.

The system for controlling production, rationing goods, and limiting prices became extensive and complicated. Rubber and then sugar were the first consumer items to be rationed. Eventually the government rationed a wide variety of items and banned the production of over 300 consumer products, including bicycles, waffle irons, beer cans, toothpaste tubes, coat hangers, and metal caskets.[2]

National Rationing System

The Office of Price Administration used its nationwide system to control consumption. It used three types of rationing during the war—simple stamp or coupon, certificate, and point stamp rationing.[3]

In simple stamp or coupon rationing, a consumer first had to obtain a book of stamps or a coupon card from the local rationing board and then present the stamps or coupons, along with cash, to merchants in order to acquire rationed items. Stamps were used for most items. Cards with tear off coupons were used for gasoline. To prevent hoarding, the stamps were coded so that they could be used for only one given month. One person in a household could gather all the ration books of household members and use them for purchases.

Ration books had sheets of stamps in them, perforated for easy removal of individual stamps. Each sheet contained stamps numbered from one to forty-eight and featuring a symbol of a piece of military equipment, e.g. a tank, cannon, airplane, or ship. Sheets differed in the type of military equipment featured.

Ration stamps were eventually required for the purchase of sugar, meat, canned and frozen foods, dairy products, bottled juices, and other items. Stamps were color-coded. Red stamps were used to acquire meat, fish, and dairy items. Blue stamps were used to obtain canned or bottled fruits, vegetables, juices, and soups; frozen fruits and vegetables; and dried fruits.

In certificate rationing, one first obtained a certificate from the rationing board for a controlled item, such as a new vehicle tire, and then presented the certificate and money to the merchant.

In point rationing, as used with War Ration Book Four, the stamps were marked with both a letter and a number. The numbers, ranging from one to eight, when added up, represented a point allowance for each month. Stores marked the products to indicate the price plus the number of point stamps needed to procure the product. A resident then had to decide how to spend his or her points and cash among the variety of goods, some of which might be in abundant supply and thus relatively cheap in points and price, while others were relatively scarce and expensive in points and price. [4]

During the course of the war, four separate War Ration Books were made available to each American. War Ration Book 1 was distributed in spring 1942. It initially was used only for rationing sugar but later was used also for rationing coffee and other items. Book 2 was issued in February 1943, and Book 3 was issued in May-June 1943. The last book, Book 4, was designed to last two years and was distributed in late October 1943.[5]

Rationing and Price Control in Bedford County

Locally in Bedford, the burden of implementing the federal rationing system was initially imposed upon the Bedford County Clerk of the Circuit Court. (Price control was mandated later.) With the first restrictions in 1942 falling on the sale of vehicle tires and tubes, a tire rationing board was established. The process became more complicated when rationing was next imposed on sugar. While the clerk of the court was said to have received instructions on how to administer the sugar rationing, the actual process of rationing sugar was initially administered by the tire rationing board through the public schools. A. G. Cummings, superintendent of schools, was designated as chief sugar rationing registrar. The school system was called upon to register people wanting to sell and buy rationed items. Cummings's responsibilities for administering rationing would continue to grow.

With this confusing process probably manifested across the nation, the federal Office of Price Administration soon established local war price and rationing boards in each county across the country. The Bedford County War Price and Rationing Board was established to manage the overall system and was given an office in the Bedford County Courthouse.

This board and its staff, with the help of others, assumed the responsibility for administering the entire rationing and price control process. It notified the public, via the newspapers and handouts, of the details of the rationing system and distributed ration stamps, coupons, certificates, and point stamps. It publicized information on price controls and monitored compliance with retail price ceilings. It also conducted hearings to deal with abuses of the system. Over the war years, three men served as chairman—J. T. Richardson, Jr., Dan Weinberg (who owned the two theaters in Bedford), and G. F. McKee.[6]

Several other organizations continued to be involved, however, in helping to administer the system. For example, on February 11, 1943, a meeting was held in Bedford to discuss distribution of War Ration Book 2. Present were not only members and clerks of the War Price and Rationing Board but also all Bedford Town and County school principals and many teachers, and officials from the Roanoke District Office of the federal government's Office of Price Administration. It was announced that A. G. Cummings, superintendent of Bedford Schools, would serve as supervisor of registration for the county, assisted by field supervisors from designated high schools and elementary schools.[7]

The Evolution of Restrictions

Rubber, Cars, and Trucks

The Japanese attacks in the Pacific cut off 98 percent of America's crude rubber supply. Some 75 percent of the rubber imported by the United States had been used in manufacturing tires and tubes. Thus, on December 11, 1941, just days after the initial Japanese attacks, the Federal Office of Price Administration froze the sale of tires to civilians. By January 5, 1942, the government lifted the freeze but began rationing the sale of tires. The government also restricted production and sale of rubber products for a wide number of civilian uses.[8]

In Bedford, rationing meant no tires and tubes for most people for the duration of the war. Only those with an essential need to use their cars or trucks were allowed to buy new tires and tubes. For the month of January 1942, the entire quota for all the cars in Bedford County was a total of sixteen tires and thirteen tubes, and the quota for trucks was about three times these numbers. There were no special provisions for those living in remote sections of the county. When individuals were allowed to make a purchase, their names were published in the newspapers.[9]

The media anticipated how life at home would be affected by the rubber restrictions: "…for women…no more elastic girdles and foundation garments, for children no more teething rings, rubber rattles, bathtub toys…no more rubber balloons….(play vehicles) will

no longer be rubber-tired…no more pencil erasers…rubber bands…
garters…elastic waist bands…boots…bathing caps…bathing suits…
rubber balls (for tennis)…." *Time Magazine* wrote that:

> The American male, his pants and socks dragging, his sports
> ruined, his wife bulging in the wrong places, his balloonless chil-
> dren teething on wood, his car tireless in the garage, riding off to
> work on a hard-benched bus or subway, unable to erase mistakes,
> or snap a rubber band around them, could now get down to really
> hating Japan and the Axis.[10]

As for cars and trucks, the government, in January 1942, first
prohibited the purchase, sale, and delivery of new passenger cars
and trucks, pending establishment of a rationing system. In March,
the government announced a rationing system for automobiles but
also announced that production of new automobiles and light trucks
would be stopped entirely within a matter of weeks so that the plants
could be converted to production of planes, guns, tanks, and other war
materials.[11]

Sugar Rationing

The next product to be restricted, in spring 1942, was sugar. There
were several reasons for rationing this product. Sugar cane was used
to make molasses, which in turn was used to make industrial alcohol,
which was needed to make explosives.[12] Much of the sugar supply
lay overseas, and shipping was scarce and risky militarily. Americans,
moreover, had begun to hoard sugar, which was needed by the armed
forces. Government controls were intended to ensure that war needs
were met first and that remaining supplies were fairly allocated among
civilians.[13]

Bedford newspapers in March 1942 announced that people needed
to register to sell and buy sugar and that the school system would be
helping to administer the registration. The newspapers also published
federal government instructions for using war ration books to buy this
product.

Both merchants wishing to sell sugar and commercial users of sugar, such as bakeries, canneries, and restaurants, had to register at their nearest high school. Those wanting to make a purchase for home use had to register at their nearest elementary school. Stamps in War Ration Book 1 were to be used for actual purchases and those who already possessed sugar were to have an appropriate number of additional stamps torn from their war ration book when they first went to buy the staple.[14]

Gasoline and Heating Oil Rationing

In May 1942, the government began to require people in the eastern part of the United States, where there was a gasoline shortage, to register to buy gasoline. Thus, gasoline ration cards came to Bedford that month.

There were several categories of cards. Category A cards, permitting the purchase of twenty-one gallons of gasoline between mid-May and July 1 (less than four gallons a week), were issued to 1,100 drivers in the county whose driving was not essential for the war. Other categories permitted gasoline purchases at levels between thirty-three and fifty-seven gallons for the period. Class "X" cards permitted unlimited purchases of gasoline and were issued to drivers of ambulances, taxis, and hearses, and to practicing doctors and ministers. Each card was marked in the upper right corner with the letter that represented the owner's assigned category of need. The card had to be filled out with the vehicle owner's name and address, the make and style of vehicle, and the state vehicle registration number.[15]

School superintendents and teachers were asked to handle the gasoline registration, as they had the sugar registration.[16] For a second registration period in early July, volunteers were asked to substitute for teachers, who were on vacation.[17]

In November, gasoline rationing was applied nationwide.[18] Also in 1942 the government began to ration heating oil.

Price Ceilings

In the summer of 1942, the government's Office of Price Administration established ceilings on the prices of many goods, as a way to help control inflation.[19] Controls were also imposed on prices charged by many service industries and trades. These price controls covered sixty-one groups of services and thousands of individual services, such as the repair of automobiles, trucks, farm machinery, small electrical appliances, store and kitchen equipment, and shoes; developing and printing of photographs; and dry cleaning and laundering.

In Bedford, people providing these services had to file papers with the local War Price and Rationing Board and post in their establishments statements of the highest prices they had charged for these services in March 1942, which became the maximum they could charge in the immediate future. The local board appointed three men to serve as merchant counselors to assist merchants and individuals in understanding and applying the regulations.[20] The board was also assisted by county residents who served as Price Panel Assistants. These assistants visited local stores to provide assistance on price control problems.[21] Many price ceilings were temporary.[22]

Any merchant who violated the rationing and price control regulations could be deprived of the right to sell the rationed or price-controlled goods. At a hearing in Roanoke in February 1944, a commissioner of the Office of Price Administration levied penalties on four merchants from a broad area of southwest Virginia (none from Bedford) for violating the regulations. Two were restricted from selling rationed goods for several months, one was placed on probation, and the other received a six-month suspension.[23]

Controls on Food Production and Allocation

In June 1942, the government took control of food production and allocation. The War Production Board delegated authority to the Food Requirements Committee, chaired by the secretary of agriculture, which was given authority to determine what food might or might not be produced, what food might be imported and exported, and how food supplies were to be allocated.[24]

Meat and Coffee Restrictions

In September 1942, meat began to be rationed. In November, coffee was rationed.[25] Coffee had become short in supply after ships used to import the coffee from South America were diverted to the war effort.[26]

In June 1943, in addition to the rationing of meat, price ceilings were established on pork, beef, veal, and lamb. Newspaper articles informed customers that they could ask merchants to show them a list of top prices and advised them to report any violations to the War Price and Rationing Board.[27]

Reduced Speed Limit and Ban on Pleasure Driving

In fall 1942 the government imposed a thirty-five-miles-per-hour speed limit on the nation to help conserve gasoline and rubber.[28]

In January 1943 it banned pleasure driving (non-necessity driving) in seventeen eastern states during an emergency period of gasoline and fuel oil shortage. Gasoline rations could be used only for occupational driving and family and personal necessities, the latter defined as shopping, medical care, occupational meetings, religious services, and driving to an emergency. The rations could not be used for pleasure driving, such as going to places of amusement, sightseeing, touring, vacationing, and making social calls (service personnel on furlough, however, were permitted to use cars for social calls). Color-coded windshield stickers were issued to indicate an individual's need to drive, e.g., work commuter, delivery person, emergency driver, and pleasure driver.[29] Those caught driving for pleasure faced the cancellation of all or part of their gasoline ration.

In February 1943 several people in the Bedford community were charged with violating the ban on pleasure driving. Hearings were held by the War Price and Rationing Board, aided by local attorneys. In the first hearing, charges were dropped against five of the six charged, and one was to be continued.[30]

The government dropped the ban on pleasure driving in March 1943, but limited holders of class "A" gasoline ration cards to one-

and-a-half gallons of gasoline a week.[31] Two months later, the government restored the ban.[32]

After the restoration of the ban, the War Price and Rationing Board in June summoned eleven people to appear before the board to answer charges of having violated the ban. Six were exonerated, but five were found guilty and had their gasoline rations revoked for a thirty-day period.[33]

By July, in order to prevent people from transferring their coupons to others, authorities required that those buying gasoline had to write their license numbers on the top of their coupons.[34]

In September 1943 the Office of Price Administration again lifted the ban on pleasure driving. Implying that the ban was lifted because drivers had protested and the ban was difficult to enforce, the government indicated it would rely on the patriotism of drivers to use no more gasoline than was absolutely necessary to meet their essential needs.[35]

Shoes

On February 9, 1943, shoes were added to the items rationed. Unlike previous rationing announcements, the White House gave no advance notice of the rationing of shoes and made the restrictions effective a half hour after the announcement. Each individual was limited to purchasing no more than three pairs of shoes a year, although families were permitted to pool their coupons. To illustrate how confusing all the rationing could be, in order to buy a pair of shoes, one had to use the No. 17 stamp of the sugar-coffee ration book.[36]

Preserved Foods, Cheese, and Fats

In mid-February 1943, the local newspapers announced that a wide variety of foods were to be rationed, including canned and bottled fruits and juices; frozen, dried, and dehydrated fruits; canned and potted vegetables and vegetable juices; frozen vegetables; canned soups; and all types of baby food. Excluded from rationing were such items as fruit cakes, jams and jellies, frozen fruits and vegetables in containers weighing over ten pounds, and condiments.[37]

Also in 1943, cheese and fats were rationed.[38]

Liquor

Liquor was also rationed. Eleanor Payne, in a letter to her future husband who was training to become a pilot, reported an incident she had heard:

> Let me tell you a funny story. Bill Cowlbeck loaned his whiskey ration book to Bill Thomas, who in turn loaned it to Charlie Green. Charlie accidentally threw it into a trash container which was hauled away. Bill C. is most unhappy I hear![39]

Following and Not Following the Rules

Bedford may have had its share of grousing over rationing, as well as some black market activity and loaning of coupon books, but Mary Dean, who worked at the local War Price and Rationing Board office, in later years expressed the personal belief that in the Bedford community "99 percent of people followed the rules."[40]

Some, however, broke not only the rationing rules but also the law against theft of property. In August 1943 two Bedford men and a man from Roanoke, all identified as Negroes, were arrested for stealing gasoline ration coupons and selling them on the black market. Pete Barlow of Bedford, described as "janitor assistant at the courthouse in Bedford," appears to have stolen the coupons a few at a time from a locked cabinet in the War Price and Rationing Board office located in the courthouse. John Hubert Hurt, a Bedford taxi driver, and James W. Beatty, who resided in Roanoke and worked for the Norfolk and Western Railroad, engaged in selling the coupons on the black market in Bedford, Roanoke, and elsewhere in southwest Virginia.

Prior to this, the men were said not to have been in trouble with the law.

When Hurt was arrested, he was found to possess 828 coupons which could be used to purchase 31,040 gallons of gasoline. One report indicated that the men were accused of stealing coupons for 65,000 gallons of gasoline and that this was a "drop in the bucket" compared to what they had actually stolen.[41]

In January 1944, in the U.S. District Court in Roanoke, Hurt pled guilty to charges of illegal possession and transferring of ration coupons and was sentenced to eight months in prison. Barlow was tried in federal court in Lynchburg and was sentenced to prison for one year and a day. It is not clear what happened to Beatty, who had, when confronted, cooperated with authorities by using marked bills to purchase coupons from Hurt.[42]

Lifting of Restrictions

By the summer of 1944, many of the restrictions began to be lifted. In June, frozen fruits, vegetables, shortening, and salad and cooking oils were freed from rationing. In July, rubber inner tubes for tires were removed from rationing.[43] In August, the War Production Board lifted the ban that had been placed almost a year earlier on the sale of ammunition to hunters.[44]

By June 1945 the consumer situation had eased, and the government authorized industries to produce 200,000 passenger cars beginning July 1, provided they could find the materials on the free market.[45]

Chapter 8

Home Front: Volunteer Activities

Volunteering

The people on the Bedford home front willingly volunteered their services for many war-related activities. A few served on the local Selective Service Board, while others helped young men fill out the paperwork required by the draft. Some volunteered to assist the county's Defense Council, its Salvage Committee, the War Price and Rationing Board, and the committees that promoted the sale of war bonds. Many served voluntarily in the local unit of the Virginia Protective Force, and others stood ready to warn of the approach of enemy aircraft and serve as air raid wardens and assistants.

Some citizens early in the war established a local committee of the British War Relief Society. Many volunteered to help the Red Cross prepare surgical dressings for the military. Others organized fund-raising campaigns for the Red Cross and the United Service Organization. Some collected books and playing cards for servicemen.

Many aided the war effort by salvaging needed materials and planting Victory Gardens.

Civic Organizations and their War-related Projects

Civic organizations in Bedford were creative in thinking of ways to be helpful. Several conducted campaigns to aid civilians in war-torn areas. In 1941 the Bedford County Committee of the British War Relief Society collected and shipped to England one case of firearms and helmets for home defense; five cases totaling 1,000 items of warm, cleaned, and mended pieces of clothing; four boxes of knitted sweaters and socks; twenty-five locally-knitted Afghans; and $2,000 in cash contributions. The committee raised some of its funds by presenting a "black-faced minstrel," with a thirty-person chorus, at eight high schools during the month of May, charging twenty-five cents admission for adults and fifteen cents for children. It had planned a performance of the *HMS Pinafore* operetta in mid-December 1941 but had to cancel it after the Japanese attack on Pearl Harbor.[1]

In April 1945 the Bedford County home demonstration agent, assisted by several clubs, schools, and churches, made an appeal for the collection of clothing for the liberated people of Europe.[2] Later that month, a committee, led by the chairman of the Bedford Chamber of Commerce, was established to collect used clothing for people in war-torn countries. This committee sought to collect five pounds of clothing per capita in the Bedford community.[3]

The Bedford 4-H Club county council set several defense-related goals for each member. In 1942, for example, the council listed the following as goals: to assist in planting a Victory Garden at home and report on the number of neighbors who planted gardens in 1942 but had not in 1941; to collect scrap iron and paper; to report on the number of war bonds and stamps purchased; and to report on the number of poultry houses remodeled or improved to increase eggs for defense.[4]

To encourage and assist young men interested in becoming Aviation Cadets, the Veterans of Foreign Wars chapter offered to help the young men prepare for the required physical and mental tests.[5] The local Lions Club agreed to write Christmas letters to Lions serving in the armed forces.[6]

The American Legion post and local dairy companies in the summer of 1942 promoted a "Records for the Soldiers" campaign, in which they collected phonograph records. People were asked to leave records beside their empty milk bottles, and the dairy trucks would collect them. The old and broken records would be used for the manufacture of new records for service personnel. In 1943, the Legionnaires held a fund-raising drive to buy cigarettes for servicemen.[7]

The Daughters of the American Revolution chapter purchased war bonds, helped collect rags and hosiery, encouraged members to help the Red Cross prepare surgical dressings, and prepared at least twenty-two "Buddy Bags" containing helpful and entertaining items for Bedford servicemen overseas.[8] A group of men formed a "Victory Pig Club" to produce pork and buy war bonds.[9] The Bedford

Fire Company and Firemen's Band, with an assist from the Virginia Protective Force and Boy Scouts, organized a carnival which raised $2,000 to invest in war bonds; once the bonds were cashed in after the war, the money was to be used to purchase uniforms and equipment for the band.[10]

A chapter of the nationwide Victory Service League was formed in Bedford to promote maintenance and conservation of civilian motor vehicles. The slogan of the League, which was supported by Chevrolet dealers, was "Save the Wheels that Serve America."[11]

Salvaging

Bedford citizens actively participated in nationwide programs to salvage recyclable materials useful for the war effort. Among the materials salvaged were paper, aluminum, tin, scrap iron, other metals, rubber, fats, silk, and nylon. The first collection took place in May 1941. Several salvage campaigns were conducted, some of short duration and others for the duration of the war and even beyond into 1946.

Local civic groups, including the Bedford County Committee of the British War Relief, local Red Cross chapter, Home Demonstration and 4-H Clubs, Girl and Boy Scouts, and Parent Teachers' Association, organized the early campaigns and helped with collections.

A salvage committee was established by early 1942 under the Bedford County Civilian Defense Council to coordinate the salvaging projects. The committee received guidance from not only the local Defense Council but also the national War Production Board and the Virginia State Salvage Committee.

The initial salvaging project, in 1941, was a collection of newspapers and other used paper products, organized by the local Committee of the British War Relief. Assisted by elementary school children, the committee conducted two collections, one in May netting four tons of paper and another in November bringing in six tons. The community was asked to take used newspapers, magazines, and paper boxes to a building opposite the post office on Main Street.[12] Additional paper collections were organized by this committee and others later in the war.

In July 1941 an organizing committee chaired by Virginia State Senator G. E. Heller conducted a campaign to collect aluminum. Through articles in the local newspapers, the committee asked that every household contribute its excess aluminum products, which could be processed and used in the manufacture of airplanes and other items for the military. Trucks picked up items from homes in the town of Bedford, and a collection bin was set up in front of the courthouse. Home Demonstration and 4-H Clubs, as well as the county agricultural board, helped organize collection in the county.[13]

In January 1942, paper collections netted four more tons. The 4-H Clubs announced a campaign to collect both waste paper and scrap iron. Newspaper announcements asked people to collect all kinds of paper—newspapers, magazines, writing and wrapping paper, cartons of all descriptions, and, the most valuable, corrugated paper and boxes. There was said to be a paper shortage, stemming not so much from the scarcity of pulp but from increased demand, especially for packing items for shipment to the military. Incidental proceeds from the sale of the collected items were to go to the local Red Cross chapter and British War Relief chapter.[14]

In February the *Bedford Democrat* ran a front-page article or editorial, likely written by or with the assistance of Mrs. Smith, chairman of the salvage committee, chastising those who were still "pouring" their used paper into garbage trucks, instead of salvaging it for the defense effort. The article listed names of all the people throughout the town who had agreed to serve as neighborhood chairmen and to distribute information about waste paper collection. The article noted that the Virginia Rubatex Corporation, Carlyle's Dairy, and Brooks Transportation Company were, without charge, using their trucks to collect waste paper. For those worried about esthetics, the article opined that, "A bundle of waste paper on the front porch is not nearly so unattractive as a Swastika would be."[15]

By March, collections seemed to be going well, and the list of items to be salvaged had significantly expanded. At least sixteen tons of waste paper had been collected and delivered to the Bedford Pulp and Paper Company. The salvage committee announced a long list of items to be salvaged. All types of rubber (from tires to galoshes), metal (from tools and pots and pans to tooth paste tubes), and paper were said to be the most valuable, but old rags, tin cans, old car license plates, tinfoil, and other household commodities were deemed almost equally important. The committee also announced a long list of stores and residences which were serving as salvage collection centers in the town of Bedford.[16]

In June, after announcing that the collection of waste paper was being discontinued, the committee turned its attention to the collection of rubber.[17] This followed President Roosevelt's order for an intensive two-week drive to collect all types of rubber that had been or could be discarded. The rubber was to be turned in to gasoline stations, which would pay one cent per pound. The rubber would then be collected by petroleum industry trucks and sold to the Rubber Recovery Corporation. Virginians were expected to contribute five pounds per capita. Later in July the federal and state authorities extended the rubber collection campaign for the duration of the war.[18]

In Bedford the salvage committee organized the two-week rubber collection campaign in June, calling for all types of rubber, including tires, rubberized clothing, garden hoses, and even baby bottle nipples. More than fifty-eight tons were collected in Bedford County during this short campaign.[19]

In July the committee ran a campaign to collect waste fats from Bedford kitchens. Fats were being collected throughout America to offset reduced supplies from the Far East and provide glycerin, which was needed to help make explosives for the military. The committee asked housewives to collect fat in wide-mouth cans, in amounts weighing at least one pound, and to take them to the local butcher who would pay for the fat and in turn sell it to renderers.[20]

Later that month authorities announced a six-month campaign to collect scrap iron. The American Legion post in Bedford sponsored a "Victory" scrap parade, led by the Bedford Firemen's Band and the Virginia Protective Force. Everyone was asked to bring scrap metal to deposit in a bin downtown.[21]

In November the salvage committee, in response to military appeals for silk and nylon to make explosive powder bags and other items, appealed to women to donate discarded silk and nylon stockings. The Bedford Parent-Teacher Association organized a rag collection in the schools.[22]

In early 1943 the salvage committee announced the beginning of a campaign to collect tin cans. Cans were to be washed and flattened. Initially, people were asked to drop the cans in a display window at the Bush Grocery Company; later, the town of Bedford began collecting the cans at each home.[23]

In October the committee announced that more than 300 pounds of silk stockings had been collected and shipped to Pennsylvania to be made into parachutes. The committee also announced that national salvage officials were terminating collection of stockings, as domestic production of nylon was going completely to the military and any domestic nylon stockings were now at least two years old and had deteriorated too much to be used for parachutes.[24]

In March 1944 paper and fats were still being collected.[25]

In 1946, after both the war and the salvaging campaigns had ended, the Bedford salvage committee chairman announced that $640.97 had been raised from the sale of salvaged paper, metal, and silk during the war and that this sum had been given to the local Red Cross chapter.[26]

Red Cross Volunteer Activity

The Bedford American Red Cross chapter was active throughout the war period. In addition to raising money for war-related Red Cross programs, the Bedford chapter called on volunteers to donate books for American servicemen, prepare surgical dressings for use in operations on American service personnel, make clothes for needy people in the Far East, and provide kit bags and other items for American service personnel.

Collecting Books

In March 1942 the Junior Red Cross and the Bedford Library Association began a public campaign to collect books to be sent to American servicemen. Collection boxes were placed in Jones (Green's) Drug Store, Lyle's Drug Store, and the library. Within a few weeks, some 100 books had been collected. In April the American Association of University Women organized a "Victory Book Campaign," in which the women collected 550 volumes and playing cards for servicemen.[27]

Preparing Surgical Dressings

The major Red Cross activity in Bedford during the war was the preparation of surgical dressings for the military.

In 1942, when commercial manufacturers were unable to make more than about 10 percent of the surgical dressings needed by the military, the War Department appealed to the American Red Cross for assistance. The Red Cross then marshaled the help of many chapters and thousands of volunteers across the country.

The Bedford County Red Cross Chapter was one of 1,400 chapters asked to make the dressings.[28] The local chapter established a surgical dressings committee. Two Bedford women, Mrs. William F. Kropff and Mrs. Wesley L. Smith, took a training course in Roanoke on how to make surgical dressings and then became the chairman and vice-chairman, respectively, of the Bedford committee. Mrs. Kropff served as chairman throughout the war.

The leaders issued an appeal in the Bedford newspapers for 200 to 300 women and girls to volunteer for as much as two hours a day in the morning, afternoon, or evening. They appealed to housewives, teachers, businesswomen, and schoolgirls over the age of fourteen to volunteer.[29]

The committee began making dressings in September 1942, using a basement room in the new-constructed Bedford Public Library on North Bridge Street. Some 185 women volunteered initially, and the committee said more were needed. All the women were requested to wear "print dresses or smocks and some kind of hair covering." The volunteers could purchase coffee for five cents a cup.[30]

The American Red Cross Headquarters issued a fourteen-page set of specifications for making ten types of surgical dressings. Included were drawings that the local chapters could use in preparing cardboard charts or templates to guide the volunteers in preparing the dressings. The Bedford chapter appears to have been asked to concentrate on preparing two-inch by two-inch surgical sponges used to swab up blood and fluids during surgery. One Bedford participant has described the work as taking square patches of absorbent gauze several inches wide and folding them into two-inch square dressings or absorbent swabs. It took seven folds to prepare a dressing or swab. Those preparing the dressings had to follow directions carefully, leaving no sharp corners or material that could catch on surrounding flesh during the surgery.[31] Some informally referred to the process as "rolling bandages."

The War Department furnished most of the material, but the Red Cross chapters had to provide cartons and wrapping material as well as pay for sending the finished products to Army warehouses.

The number of days and hours a day that the workroom in the library was open depended somewhat on the quota of dressings to be made and the availability of the material. In the first quarter of 1943, the workroom was open for volunteer work three days a week, generally in the mornings, afternoons, and evenings, between 9:30 a.m. and 4 p.m. and 7:30-9:30 p.m. In September 1943 the workroom was open two days a week from 9:30 a.m. to 9:30 p.m., and in June 1944 it was open two-and-a-half days a week. There were weeks during the war when materials were not available and the workroom had to be shut.[32] One woman recalls preparing dressings at the Episcopal Church, across the street from the library, but newspaper articles do not mention use of the church.[33]

Also in 1943 a workroom was opened in the Forest community under the direction of Mrs. Herbert Thomson, and a workroom for Negro workers was opened in the Bedford Training School under the direction of Miss Grace Terry.[34]

On occasion, the Red Cross chapter published in the local newspapers the names of the volunteers and the number of hours they had worked.[35] In August 1944, in an effort to bolster participation and honor those who were participating, the Bedford Firemen's Band surprised about thirty women volunteers at the library one evening by serenading them, and Jones (Green's) Drug Store provided complimentary ice cream.[36]

In March 1945, after more than two years of service and production of 1,001,887 surgical dressings, the Bedford Red Cross chapter closed the three workrooms where, on average, a total of two hundred volunteers had worked each month. According to the War Department, stocks in warehouses were sufficient at that time to fill needs for the next twelve months.[37]

In May 1945 the Bedford Red Cross chapter received a letter of thanks from a U.S. Army Medical Corps officer in the Philippines. The officer wrote that while looking through his supplies he found numerous cartons of surgical dressings made by the Bedford chapter. He related that he had been to Bedford many times, as his mother-in-law had been born and raised in Bedford. He expressed his appreciation for the dressings and gave assurances that they were being employed usefully.[38]

Making Clothes for Needy Civilians in Asia and Kit Bags for American Servicemen

In addition to making surgical dressings, the Bedford Red Cross chapter on at least two occasions during the war made garments for needy civilians in the Far East and kit bags for American servicemen. In March 1942 the chapter reported having made operating gowns, bed shirts, women's and children's bed jackets, and sweats and socks for civilians in the Far East; by war's end, 227 knitted garments had been produced. The chapter supplied the hospital at Camp Pickett, southwest of Richmond, with some 6,000 cookies, 200 utility bags, twenty-six bathrobes, and seven lap covers. In September 1943 the chapter began to make kit bags for American servicemen, each containing a soap box and soap, playing cards, cigarettes or tobacco, a shoe polishing cloth, a small pencil, paper and envelopes, hard candy, shoe laces, razor blades, a small book, and a sewing case. By the end of the war, the chapter had made a total of 864 Army kit bags and 144 Navy kit bags.[39]

Victory Gardens

Origin and Purpose

The U.S. Secretary of Agriculture advocated the idea of Victory Gardens shortly after Pearl Harbor, and his department soon began distributing information for this program.[40] Some claim the department dragged its feet in promoting the program, yet by April 1942 Americans were cultivating six million Victory Gardens.[41] At the program's peak, there were twenty-two million Victory Gardens planted across America, producing over one-third of all vegetables being grown in the country. The program, per se, was voluntary, although by law people who owned farms were required to set aside at least one acre of land to grow vegetables for family consumption or to be sold at low prices locally.[42]

Victory Gardens were promoted to meet the needs of families while freeing up other food stocks for the military and Allies in need. Moreover, using fresh produce from gardens or preserving it at home for later consumption cut back on the demand for metal cans. One local newspaper article estimated that if each housewife in Bedford County gave up buying one can of fruit or vegetables a week, by the end of the year enough metal would have been saved to make 2,406 machine guns.[43]

Mixed Views in Bedford

The Bedford community had mixed views about growing Victory Gardens. Many people, particularly in the countryside, had traditionally planted vegetable and fruit gardens every year and would continue to do so. Some organizations encouraged those who traditionally planted such gardens to continue with their gardens and encouraged others to begin to plant gardens. At least two working wives of men serving in Europe found time in their busy schedules to plant Victory Gardens and to write enthusiastically about them in letters to their husbands. The traditional garden clubs, however, which focused on flower gardens, appear to have been reluctant, at least initially, to encourage their members to plant vegetables.

In February 1942 the Bedford County Board of Agriculture announced plans for a county Victory Garden program. The goal was to have a good vegetable and small fruit garden on every farm in Bedford County. Beyond that, however, the board encouraged everyone who was capable of doing so, including town and non-farm families, to plant a garden. The board expressed the hope that a farm garden could meet a family's needs for the entire year and that orderly succession plantings could produce vegetables and fruits over a long season. Plans were made to hold garden meetings in every community, with professional workers assisting. Leaflets and other information were to be distributed at these meetings by the board's neighborhood committeemen and the county agriculture agent.[44]

The Positions of Garden Clubs in Bedford

Leaders of many of the garden clubs in Bedford appear, at least early in the war, to have been reluctant to encourage members and the public to grow vegetables and fruits. Their reluctance seems to have stemmed from concerns about diminishing the time, effort, and space devoted to growing flowers. Another factor may have been concerns about adversely affecting the livelihoods of local farmers.

The local Rose Society discussed Victory Gardens at its meeting in late January 1942. Mrs. Lela C. Atkinson outlined Virginia's Victory Garden program, but A. G. Cummings, the superintendent of schools, warned against too much emphasis on producing food and the possible neglect of cultivating beautiful flowers. Mr. Cummings saw no possibility of a food shortage and urged members to "let the farmers produce the food—or most of it."[45]

The Board of Agriculture, in encouraging vegetable gardening, did advise those in town against neglecting or destroying lawns and flowers. The Garden Club of Bedford, at its meeting later in February, however, seemed to want to protect flowers more than grow vegetables. Members were advised against digging up flowerbeds to plant vegetables. A report on the meeting stated that, "Many flower gardeners do not know how to raise vegetables…and the loss in beauty and morale would be greater than the gain from vegetables raised…." A further statement that, "Vegetable seeds are scarce…and none must be wasted," seemed to suggest that flower gardeners would likely waste vegetable seeds.[46]

In October 1942 the Liberty Garden Club in Bedford instituted a program of defense activities for the club. The club decided to sell war bond savings stamps at each meeting and to collect medicine bottles, cosmetic jars, and flower containers for Army hospitals. In newspaper reports on this meeting, no reference was made to discussion of vegetable gardening.[47]

At a meeting of the Blue Ridge Garden Club in March 1943, the guest speaker, Bedford County's home demonstration agent, encouraged members to plant vegetable gardens. No reaction was reported. This club reported selling war savings stamps.[48]

By April 1943 the Garden Club of Bedford reported that war activities dominated the club's activities in the previous year. The club had sponsored the sale of war bonds and stamps, selling $15,000 worth in one period. Members had worked as a unit on Wednesdays in preparing surgical dressings for the Red Cross. Members had also made blankets for convalescent soldiers, donated money and empty jars to Camp Pickett for the beautification of the grounds, planted trees in honor of members' sons and daughters serving in the military, and organized a Victory harvest show with proceeds going to Army and Navy relief programs. Again, no mention was made of vegetable gardening.[49]

In May 1943 the *Bedford Democrat* reported that the "colored" people on Longwood Avenue had organized the Longwood Victory Gardening Club. This club seemed to focus on vegetable gardening. The club met once a week in a school building and was sponsored by the Bedford school board. Its activities were part of the gardening program of the Rural War Production Training Program. Mrs. Rosa Schenk, who worked for the school system, was an advisor to the club. There were plans to organize other clubs throughout Bedford County. In addition to studying gardening, the clubs were to study canning and drying of food.[50]

By the summer and fall of 1943, at least one of the older, white-member garden clubs appears to have assumed a greater interest in vegetable and fruit gardening. In July, reports on a meeting of the Liberty Garden Club mentioned Victory Gardens as one of the club's yearly projects, and ten members entered their gardens in a club contest for best Victory Garden. The gardens were judged by a specialist from Virginia Polytechnic Institute in Blacksburg and scored on general appearance, adequate supply of vegetables for family needs, balanced planning, insect and disease control, cultivation, fertilizer, interplanting, and succession of crops.[51]

In October the Liberty Garden Club held a Victory Harvest Fair in downtown Bedford to exhibit "what the garden club members are doing to aid the war effort in the matter of civilian food" and to raise money for the National War Fund, which supported the USO and other organizations. The club raised $25 for the War Fund. Exhibits included garden collections, floral arrangements, breakfast trays, and club projects. Some of the pastries, canned fruits, and vegetables, jams and jellies, and handwork displayed were available for sale. Also in October, club members purchased $2,225 in war bonds.[52]

In May and June 1944 Mrs. N. W. Jarvis, president of the Virginia Federation of Garden Clubs, spoke to two clubs in her home town of Bedford. Meeting with the Bedford Rotary Club in mid-May, she told the Rotarians that garden clubs were not organized just to cultivate flowers and that the clubs had a broader conservation program, aimed, for one thing, at instructing youth about the value and necessity of husbanding America's resources. No reference to Victory Gardens or vegetable gardens was reported. In June, however, at a meeting of the Liberty Garden Club, where there was a discussion of Victory Gardens and vegetables from the standpoint of nutrition, Mrs. Jarvis made a presentation on dehydration of fruits and vegetables and displayed some items she had dehydrated.[53]

Two Gardening Activists

Ivylyn Jordan Schenk (now Ivylyn Hardy) was a strong supporter of Victory Gardens. She was a school teacher in Moneta, daughter-in-law of the before-mentioned Victory Garden-activist Rosa Schenk, and wife of S/Sgt. John Schenk who was in England with Company A. Despite her busy schedule of teaching elementary school, teaching elements of aviation to high school students, teaching black adults in the Moneta area how to produce and preserve food (part of a federal government program), and monitoring consumer prices, she somehow found time to grow and harvest her own Victory Garden. She wrote her husband about her gardening, as well as her other activities. (See her personal story in Part II of this book.)

For Eleanor Yowell, who lived and worked in the town of Bedford, planting a vegetable garden in the spring of 1944 was a new adventure. (See her personal story also in Part II of this book.) She reported enthusiastically on her labor and harvests in letters to her husband, who was serving as a bomber pilot in the Army Air Corps in England (the following extracts are from her book *Flying High*):

(April 26)…Guess what? I'm going to start planting my Victory Garden this afternoon. Bought all the seed yesterday, and everyone at Lyle's (drug store) got a big kick out of it. I didn't know one kind from another, so they would just scoop up a few out of any drawer that struck their eyes….[54]

(April 27) Hi! Whee, am I sore this morning! I'll have you know the garden is all planted, and it is a beautiful job too. Walter Vaughn, who works out here at the (Elks National) Home (where Eleanor also worked), offered to help me. Between us we spaded the upper part of the whole garden down to the alley. Pam (her dog) helped too! Next we raked it and then he laid it off for me and showed me how to plant the seeds. We planted potatoes, onions, squash, radishes, beets, carrots, peas, snaps, lettuce and corn. We worked until 7:30, and at that point I could hardly drag it into the house. Walter said the garden was in good shape, so we should have some nice vegetables. He wouldn't let me pay him, so I'm going to get him a carton of cigarettes or something….[55]

(May 7)…Friday afternoon after work I weeded the garden. All the vegetables are coming up and I am so proud of it!…[56]

(May 16)…You should see the garden! It is really beautiful! Everything is up, and yesterday and today I have been weeding it. Worked 4 hours and just weeded a third of it. Want to get some tomato and cucumber plants this week. Walter said my Great Uncle Oscar used to have one of the best gardens in town….[57]

(May 19)…If you could see me in the garden wielding that hoe, you would get a good laugh I know! The weeds are something else again, and I have to get over the whole garden. Have worked every day this week in it—until 8:30 last night and again tonight....I told them [friends who said they hadn't seen her for a long time] my Victory Garden had top priority....[58]

(June 2)...I've had several people say my garden is one of the nicest Victory Gardens in town. Still look at it in amazement, but sure am tickled with it.[59]

(June 29)...Did I tell you I got some luscious squash and beets out of my garden? Ma says I'm just a dirt farmer.[60]

(July 19)...Have been out in the garden digging potatoes. Evidently I don't know how to dig them because I have sliced so many with the hoe. Got my first tomatoes today, and they are delicious! Also got some squash and beets....[61]

(July 27)...A long dry spell hurt my garden, but did find a bunch of snaps just as I was ready to pull up the vines. Am getting real nice tomatoes and squash. The whole garden needs weeding so badly, but there is a lot of poison oak in it, so I'm not too enthusiastic about getting any more than I already have!...[62]

Continued Encouragement for Planting Victory Gardens

In February 1945 the *Bedford Democrat* ran an article titled "Victory Gardens as Vital as Planes, Tanks, Guns." It reported on a National Victory Garden Conference held in Washington, D.C., to emphasize the need for the nation's families to continue to plant Victory Gardens. In 1944, 40 percent of the nation's supply of fresh vegetables had come from home gardens, and 41 percent of the commercially packed vegetables had been set aside for the armed forces. Also in 1944, however, the government had removed canned goods from the list of items subject to rationing, and only eighteen-and-a-half million Victory Gardens had been planted, compared to twenty-two million in 1943. The Department of Agriculture and the War Food Administration had become concerned that citizens believed the war would soon be over and would not continue planting gardens, and so it asked the public to reverse the downward trend and plant twenty million Victory Gardens in 1945.[63]

Americans would be encouraged to plant Victory Gardens and volunteer for other war-related activities well into 1945, even as the war drew to an end.

Chapter 9

Home Front: Fund Raising

General Overview

During the war, the federal government, the American Red Cross, and a collaboration of the United Service Organization (USO) and twenty-one compatriot organizations launched a series of national fund-raising campaigns to support war-related programs. Each set quotas for communities across the country.

The government conducted seven war bond campaigns between 1942 and 1945. It sold war bonds to raise money to procure military equipment and support military operations.

The American Red Cross conducted an annual "Red Cross War Fund" campaign to pay for its programs, including assistance to American military personnel, people in need in Allied countries, and Americans in need at home.

The USO and the twenty-one compatriot non-governmental organizations conducted annual "National War Fund" campaigns to finance their efforts. All of these organizations raised money to help serve men and women in the armed forces. (The use of the words "War Fund" in the campaigns of both the Red Cross and the USO and its compatriot organizations introduced an element of confusion in newspaper articles and editorials.)

The two Bedford newspapers helped publicize these campaigns, encouraged citizens to contribute, reported on results, and, in editorials, chastised the community when it appeared it was not contributing enough. The *Bedford Democrat*, at least by July 1944, added at the top of page one the words "KEEP ON *Backing the Attack!* WITH WAR BONDS."

People in the Bedford community supported these fund-raising campaigns. Many bought war bonds in response to a variety of war-bond sales campaigns, while others had money regularly withheld from their pay for the purchase of bonds. Many factories and stores flew flags indicating that all the workers in their establishments were regularly purchasing war bonds. Children and others purchased savings stamps at the local post office. Some merchants kept savings stamps in their cash registers and encouraged customers to take those in lieu of change. People donated items for auctions in which the winning bidders committed to buying bonds in the amount that they bid.[1]

Government War Bond Campaigns

The federal government, led by the Department of Treasury, organized a series of nationwide campaigns to sell war bonds to business organizations, individual adults, and even school children. Banks, post offices, and movie theaters served as government issuing agents for the bonds, and women's organizations staffed booths in banks and on the street to help sell bonds.[2] A series of innovations were used in the appeals to the public.

Over the course of the war, the government and volunteers raised about $49 billion through the sale of war bonds to individuals throughout the United States. This accounted for about one-sixth of the revenue used to finance the American war effort, which cost a total of some $300 billion.[3]

War bonds ranged in denomination from $25 and $100 at the lower end of the scale to $10,000 at the upper end. The $25 bond sold for $18.75, and the $100 bond sold for $75, with the bonds becoming redeemable at their full value after a maturity period. Children could buy ten and twenty-five cent stamps at the post office to paste in a booklet which, when full, could be exchanged for a bond. War bonds were also sold to banks, insurance companies, large corporations, and even local governments.[4]

A Bedford County Defense Savings Committee—later called the War Savings Committee and finally the War Finance Committee—was established in February 1942 to organize war bond sales and help the community meet quotas set by the Virginia War Finance Committee. The superintendent of county schools, A. G. Cummings, was appointed chairman, adding to his other volunteer duties as rationing registrar. He would serve as chairman of the War Finance Committee throughout the entire war period.[5] Sixteen other men and women were also appointed to the committee, representing banks, retailers, industry, newspapers, insurance agencies, service clubs, doctors, ministers, the American Legion, and town and county government.[6] By September 1942 the committee had established ten subcommittees to deal with areas such as payroll savings, direct sales, and publicity.[7]

The first war bond campaign began in 1942. The seventh and final campaign would be concluded before the end of the war.[8]

National and state authorities established monthly quotas for the amount of bonds to be sold by lower jurisdictions. Bedford County's first quota in 1942 was $40,000. Its subsequent quotas would increase substantially.[9]

In March 1942 the local Hampton Looms plant announced that 338 of its 344 workers, or over 98 percent, had pledged to make weekly payments to purchase war bonds.[10] A month later, three retail establishments and the office of the county superintendent of schools announced that 100 percent of their employees had agreed to systematic purchase of war stamps and bonds through payroll deduction.[11]

In early May members of the Lions, Rotary, and Business and Professional Women's Clubs conducted door-to-door canvasses, asking each adult and child to pledge to buy war bonds or stamps systematically.[12]

That spring the *Bedford Democrat* began running articles and artistic drawings encouraging people to buy war bonds, often explaining how much individual military items cost and what money from the sale of a single war bond could buy for the armed forces. The *Bedford Bulletin* later did likewise. As examples, the newspapers reported that $100,000 from the sale of bonds could enable the government to buy one fighter aircraft and that money from the sale of a single bond costing $18.75 would let the government pay for thirty-seven miles of cruising by a destroyer or buy one eighty-one-millimeter mortar round or three new bayonets. Some of these articles encouraged people to commit 10 percent of their pay to the purchase of war bonds.[13]

The town of Bedford did its bit. In October 1942 the town announced that it planned to buy bonds with a maturity value of $50,000. Later in the month, the state administrator for war bonds announced that Bedford was the first municipality in Virginia to have 100 percent of its employees regularly invest at least 10 percent of their pay in bonds.[14] The town continued to purchase war bonds, and by the end of 1944 it had bought $105,000 worth. Bedford County also purchased war bonds, beginning with a purchase in October 1943 of bonds with a maturity value of $50,000.[15]

In December 1942 bond promoters announced that at each tobacco warehouse in Bedford a "Tobacco War Bond Row" would soon be established. Tobacco farmers who placed their tobacco to be sold in this row would be willing to accept payment through a bank in the form of war bonds or stamps.[16]

In March 1943 Mrs. Rosa Schenk, the community activist who served as chairman of the Education Committee of the War Finance Committee, announced that six schools had reported that between 40 and 80 percent of the students and 100 percent of the teachers were systematically buying war stamps or bonds.[17] Also in March, nearly forty Bedford business establishments were commended by the secretary of the treasury for sponsoring a war bond advertising campaign in Bedford.[18] By September the number of businesses sponsoring the advertising had grown to seventy-two.[19]

In spring 1943 seven Bedford County high schools sponsored a bond campaign to buy Jeeps for the military. They raised enough funds to pay for thirteen Jeeps.[20]

Local organizations also began campaigns to buy bonds, stipulating that when the bonds were redeemed after the war the proceeds would be used for the organization. The Bedford Volunteer Fire Company and the Firemen's Band, for example, sponsored a carnival, the proceeds from which were to be invested in bonds which, in turn, would be redeemed after the war to buy new equipment and uniforms for the fire company and the band. Everette School near Forest, a black school, sold stamps and bonds that were to be redeemed after the war to make improvements at the school.[21]

In mid-September 1943, on a Friday night, Bedford County held its first war bond rally. There was a parade, featuring American Legion members carrying flags representing the Allies. Some 2,500 people gathered in front of the courthouse for the ceremonies. Awards were given to three businesses for having the best war bond decorations in their store windows. A bond auction was scheduled for the following week. Among the many items donated for the auction by local individuals and businesses were a military saber taken from a German officer, two young bulls, an aged ham, a pig, a milk pail, a box of candy, a box of fifty cigars, a certificate for a $5 permanent wave, a bag of hog meal, and two white rabbits.[22]

The *Bedford Democrat* subsequently reported on the results of the bond auction. A special reporter wrote that "We did pretty good….It was fun, too….There was a good crowd there and everybody seemed to be enjoying it." People bid on the donated items with pledges to buy bonds. The auction resulted in the sale of bonds with a total maturity value of about $50,000. The winning bids often far exceeded the normal value of the donated items, as bidders would eventually get their money back, with interest, once they cashed in the bonds. The bulls raised $21,000 between them, the saber went for $2,000, the box of candy brought $1,500, and the pig went for $750. One woman was overheard at the rally to say, "I went right out to the bank on Salerno Day (the day the Allies invaded Salerno, Italy) and bought another bond. I just couldn't afford it, but I couldn't think of those boys without doing something about it."[23] The auction was so successful that another one was scheduled for the following Saturday.[24]

In late January 1944 the Liberty Theater held two "free movie days." Anyone purchasing an "E" bond of any denomination at the theater received a free pass to see the movie of the day. As part of a nationwide program, the manager posted in the lobby a seating chart for the theater, and whenever someone bought a bond they could have the name of someone in the armed forces inscribed on one of the seats.[25] By February 10, Bedford citizens had purchased bonds in honor of over 200 men and women in the service.[26]

Also in February the Bedford Lions Club organized another Saturday night rally and auction. This auction was held in the Bedford High School auditorium. Musical entertainment was provided. Again, a young Hereford bull led the list of donations. Other donations included a sack of flour, a pair of overalls, nine pairs of nylon hose, another German sword, a dozen light bulbs, four bags of oranges, six boxes of raisins, a wash board, three frying-size chickens, and two chest x-rays.[27] This auction netted $57,050 in bond sales. The bull brought a commitment to purchase $16,500 in bonds, and one pair of nylon hose brought $3,100.[28]

The local American Legion post sponsored another bond auction later that month. To help publicize this auction, an unidentified Legionnaire provided the following poem, which was printed on the front page of the *Bedford Democrat*:

> And if our lines should form, then bend
> Because of things you failed to send
> The extra tank, or ship or plane
> For which we waited all in vain
> And the supplies which never came.
> Will you then come and take the blame?
> For we, not you, will pay the cost
> For battles you, not we, have lost.[29]

A women's committee in Bedford sponsored a third auction. This, plus the auctions sponsored earlier by the Lions Club and the American Legion, raised more than $100,000 in bond sales.[30]

On February 8, 1944, the local school board declared a half-day holiday so that the students in the town and county of Bedford could conduct a house-to-house canvass to sell bonds. The students sold bonds and stamps worth $42,303.[31]

For the campaign that began in June 1944, several events were organized to help sell bonds. On June 20, a parade featuring the Bedford Firemen's Band and the fire company led citizens to a bond rally in front of the courthouse. Other groups participating in the parade were the volunteers who helped prepare Red Cross surgical dressings for the military, the Bedford County nursing unit, the Girl Scouts, the Boy Scouts (both White and Black), the American Legion, the Veterans of Foreign Wars, the Virginia State Guard, and the Bedford Life Saving Crew. Two other events were organized by the Liberty Theater. The first was a children's movie premier, with admission limited to school-age children who purchased a bond or sold one to an adult. The second was a premier of the movie *Sahara*, starring Humphrey Bogart, with admission limited to those purchasing a war bond. The Lions Club also sponsored another Saturday war bond auction.[32]

During the sixth nationwide war bond campaign initiated in November 1944, Bedford newspapers encouraged citizens to continue to buy bonds. A member of the Virginia War Loan Committee spoke at a bond rally in Bedford and was quoted in the press as warning against an attitude that the war was all but won and there was no longer any urgency in buying war bonds.[33] The *Bedford Bulletin* ran an editorial quoting General Eisenhower as having written: "…Here—all of us—count upon you to oversubscribe the war loan and then to transform the money quickly into vital fighting equipment. It is needed NOW." The editorial writer went on to say:

> Hundreds of Bedford County men are fighting on the western front….The Bedford men in that famous division (the 29th Infantry Division) need the assurance that the people in their home county are backing the attack by the purchase of war bonds. When you fail to lend the government use of your money to buy the thousands of things these boys need to carry on, you are leaving them unsupported, turning them out to shift for themselves in the mud and bitter cold among enemy bullets and minefields on the battle front in western Germany.[34]

During the seventh and last war loan drive, begun in May 1945, the Liberty Theater held a movie premiere of a new musical "Hollywood Canteen," with tickets given free to those who purchased war bonds at the theater.[35]

Also in May students were given a half-day holiday to canvass for bond sales. An official at the state level praised Bedford County War Finance Committee Chairman A. G. Cummings for conceiving this "school day" initiative, noting that it had been copied elsewhere in Virginia and that without it at least fifty counties would not make their quotas.[36]

In the final analysis, Bedford County purchased more bonds each year during the war than the quotas given by higher authority. To summarize, the quotas given to Bedford County and the actual sales of bonds were as follows:

	QUOTAS	SALES
1941-42	$385,000	$695,966
1943	$1,122,000	$1,306,920
1944	$1,912,800	$2,982,267
1945	$1,185,000	$2,063,801
grand total	$4,604,800	$7,048,954

Thus, for the entire war period, the Bedford community did more than its duty in purchasing over $7 million in war bonds, exceeding its total wartime quotas of $4.6 million by more than 65 percent.[37]

By early 1946 federal authorities announced that there would be no more war bond drives. The U.S. Treasury did, however, continue to sell Series E, F, and G Bonds. These bonds had previously been called, in succession, Defense Bonds, War Bonds, and Victory Bonds. In the future they would be called U.S. Savings Bonds.[38]

Red Cross War Fund Campaigns

Throughout the war, the American Red Cross also conducted annual campaigns to raise money for its War Fund to help care for Americans in the armed forces and at home and those needing assistance in war-torn areas abroad. The Red Cross had no governmental standing and received no government funding. It depended entirely on voluntary gifts to support its mission.[39]

As a non-governmental organization officially designated to work with American armed forces, the American Red Cross had access to the front lines, base hospitals, and advanced dressing stations. It provided service personnel with surgical dressings, blood transfusions, and hospital nursing. It also assisted those serving in the military with recreation and communications with loved ones back home in case of illness or disaster.

(The International Red Cross was often able to obtain information about American prisoners of war, provide them some assistance, and facilitate correspondence between those held captive and their loved ones.)

The initial Red Cross nationwide War Fund campaign was launched in December 1941 with a goal of raising $50 million. The

Bedford Red Cross chapter's quota in this campaign was $4,000. The chapter issued an appeal in the local newspapers for every person in the county to help make the campaign a success.[40]

Red Cross officials wrote articles for the newspapers, and the newspaper staffs wrote editorials, encouraging citizens to contribute and sometimes chiding them for their lack of response. For example, in January 1942, an article by a Red Cross official and an editorial in the *Bedford Bulletin* chastised the community for raising only a little over half its quota of $4,000 after two weeks of the campaign. The Bedford community was said to have met an identical quota during World War I in only two days, and Richmond and Lynchburg were reported to have already exceeded their quotas.[41] In the 1944 campaign, the *Bedford Democrat* chided the community for dragging its feet in meeting its quota, which had been raised to $14,500.[42] The people of Bedford, perhaps nudged by these newspaper articles and editorials, eventually increased their support.

In March 1943 the *Bedford Democrat* published the names of all the contributors and how much each contributed, ranging from the Piedmont Label Company with a pledge of $500 to individuals giving $20, $15, $10, $6, and even $2 each.[43] The *Bedford Bulletin* in late April of that year published the names of all the contributors to that date but not the amount of their contributions.[44]

In the final analysis, the Bedford community each year of the war exceeded by substantial margins its quotas for contributions to the Red Cross. In 1943 the quota was $8,200, and contributions were $10,800. In 1944, with an increased quota of $14,500, the community donated over $16,800. In 1945 the quota was reduced to $12,000, but the level of giving rose to a new high of almost $20,700.[45] All in all, for the years 1942-1945 inclusive, Bedford County contributed more than $50,000 to the American Red Cross War Fund.

USO and War Fund Campaigns

In addition to the Red Cross War Fund campaign, there were separate campaigns during the war for the National War Fund, which distributed proceeds to twenty-two different service organizations, the largest being the USO.

The USO was established in early 1941 at the request of President Roosevelt and with a grant of $15 million from the federal government. It was to pull together organizations that had worked separately during World War I. The USO, itself, comprised five organizations—the Salvation Army, the Young Men's Christian Association, the Catholic Community Service, Traveler's Aid, and the Jewish Welfare Board. It sought to provide those in the military service a "home away from home" in 1,300 clubs where service personnel could relax, have some entertainment, dance, write letters, and read. The USO also sponsored musical and humor shows at military facilities in the United States and abroad.

In addition to supporting the USO, the National War Fund financed two other large organizations—the War Prisoner's Aid and the United Seaman's Service. The other nineteen service organizations, including ones that provided relief to civilians in war-torn areas, shared less than 50 percent of the fund's proceeds.

The National War Fund was organized hierarchically down to state and county levels. William R. Phelps served as chairman of the Bedford County USO and oversaw raising money in the county for the Virginia War Fund, a component of the National War Fund. Individuals in various parts of the county agreed to direct the campaigns in their areas.

In 1942 Bedford had a quota for the Virginia War Fund of $2,750. When Bedford exceeded this, the quota for 1943 was raised to $8,900. Bedford exceeded this quota by more than $300, and the quota for 1944 was raised to $9,350, which Bedford exceeded by 5 percent. Even in the fall of 1945, after the cessation of hostilities, but while American servicemen were still overseas, Bedford sought to raise another $9,350 for the Virginia War Fund.[46] In all, Bedford County probably contributed more than $30,000 to the War Fund for the USO and other organizations.

In exceeding these quotas, as well as ones established for the county for purchases of war bonds and donations to the American Red Cross, the citizens of Bedford again demonstrated their patriotism during the war.

Chapter 10

Home Front: Bedford's Economy

Bedford County's economy also contributed to the American war effort, and it generally thrived while doing so, as farmers and factories produced goods needed for the military, Allies, and the home front. There were some temporary labor shortages, but Bedford businesses learned to find substitutes and to cope.

Agriculture

Despite the departure of many young farm men to serve in the armed forces or work in defense industries elsewhere, agricultural communities across America and in Bedford County generally managed to increase their levels of production and earnings during the war. In the late 1930s, farmers throughout America earned an annual average of about $8 billion; by 1944 they were earning $20 billion a year.[1]

In Bedford County, production levels of some items declined during the war, but levels for others were sustained or increased significantly. Hog production, for example, declined, but production levels of corn, wheat, oats, and soybeans were either maintained or increased. Production of eggs and chickens increased tremendously, while milk production soared. Gates Richardson, who recorded these developments for his essay on the military history of Bedford County, summed up the situation as follows: "On the whole, we can say that, in spite of the shortage and high price of skilled farm labor, production was maintained at a high level by our hard-pushed farmers throughout the years of World War II."[2]

Bedford County grew large quantities of vegetables and fruits and established canneries to preserve some of its output. Richardson concluded that "Bedford County supplied the nation and its allies with millions of cans of fruit and vegetables in the war years."[3]

In general then, the war seemed to stimulate the agricultural sector of Bedford's economy. Other sectors thrived, too.

Industries

Several Bedford industries produced material used by the military. Probably for security reasons, only few details appear to have been disclosed, particularly before the end of the war. Richardson chronicled these details after the war.[4]

The Rubatex plant, which before the war made padding for football uniforms and other foam rubber products, began focusing on military-related products as early as 1940. By September of that year, the plant began operating twenty-four hours a day, seven days a week, and by January 1941 it had as many as 460 employees. Rubatex produced a light, durable, rubber material used in constructing flotation pontoons and insulating aircraft. It also made outlet valves for gas masks.[5]

Toward the end of the war, in May 1945, the *Bedford Bulletin* ran a front-page article crediting the Rubatex plant with helping Allied forces both to move into the German heartland and bomb Japan. The article, referring to photographs in *Life Magazine* of Allied troops crossing rivers in Germany, reported that materials made by Rubatex helped keep the pontoons from sinking.[6]

The article also reported that when the first B-29 Superfortress bomber was ready for its flight trial at an air base in Ohio, someone discovered that "one essential gadget" was lacking. Without describing this "gadget," the newspaper told how an order was placed with Rubatex and local machinist Tom North stayed in his shop day and night designing and making the machinery to produce the "gadget." When officials at the base called to say they would send a plane to get the part when it was ready, they were informed that it had already been shipped via airmail. The newspaper's concluding paragraph read:

> The Rubatex plant's entire output for the past several years has gone to the Army, Navy and Air Forces, but the company management, the employees and Bedford people generally are especially proud of these two achievements mentioned here. They helped put our armies across European rivers and helped

lift from the ground the giant planes which are now wrecking Japanese cities and war industries."

Another Bedford industry, Hampton Looms, the woolen mill, had government contracts to produce material for military uniforms and coats. It produced 25,000 yards of uniform materials per week throughout the war period, primarily for the Army and Marine Corps.[7] Belding Heminway, the silk mill, made rayon thread, which had military application.[8]

The wood pulp industry was also stimulated by the war. More timber, much of which was pulpwood, was cut in Bedford County during the war than in any period up to that time, despite a manpower shortage.[9] The Bedford Pulp and Paper Company at Big Island processed large quantities of wood pulp, which eventually went to making cardboard and paper for packaging and shipping material to the troops. Pulpwood was also used to make pallets for shipping and powder for firing large guns.[10] In the summer and fall of 1943 there was a drive to cut pulpwood, for which the newspapers used the slogan "Cut-A-Cord for Every Bedford Boy."[11]

Bedford's feldspar mines were said to have operated at capacity during the war, producing minerals used in making such things as paper and glass. The Electro-Metallurgical Company at Holcomb Rock in the northeastern part of the county worked on government contracts.

The Overstreet-Smith Lumber Company produced forty three prefabricated three-room houses which were shipped to Norfolk, Virginia, and other industrial areas to help house the increasing number of defense industry workers. This company also produced 119 moveable lookout towers, which were deployed along American coasts, and 18,500 wooden pallets used for shipping military supplies.[12]

Richardson concluded that: "It is safe to say that Bedford's industrial plant and those who supplied them with their raw materials accounted for 2,500 Bedford County men contributing directly to the war effort." He added that: "Many of Bedford's men were employed in shipyards, aircraft plants and the munitions industries in larger centers throughout the war."[13]

Women in the Labor Force

Many women already worked in Bedford industries and business establishments before America entered the war. After the war began and young men volunteered or were drafted for military service, other women stepped in and filled jobs vacated by these men. Nearly thirty women may have replaced men at the Rubatex plant during the war. At least one woman, Mrs. Rebecca Waldron, took the place of her husband at the Piedmont Label Company when he joined the armed forces.[14]

After the war, many women in Virginia left their wartime jobs. They either voluntarily returned to homemaking, were replaced by returning servicemen reclaiming their jobs, or were let go as companies converted to a civilian-oriented economy. Between May 1945 and May 1946, the number of female production workers in Virginia declined by 18,700 or almost 27 percent, while male employment increased only about 1 percent. In September 1946, however, the Virginia commissioner of labor reported a labor shortage due to women withdrawing from manufacturing industries to remain at home.[15]

This trend applied to at least two factories in Bedford. Rubatex reported that the number of women employees had dropped from thirty during the war to two in September 1946, due to men returning from military service to reclaim their jobs. Hampton Looms reported a decrease in women workers due to men reclaiming their jobs. Belding Heminway, however, reported no change in female employees.[16]

Teachers and Schools

The war had an impact on the school system in the Bedford community. School facilities and their teachers and staffs were used for several war-related programs. The schools helped register young men for the draft, helped with the initial registration of those who wanted to sell and buy rationed goods, and helped promote the sale of war bonds and stamps. Teachers were urged to buy bonds systematically through payroll deductions. Teachers were also invited to help the Red Cross prepare surgical dressings for the military. Students were urged to buy war bonds and stamps and were given time off from school to go house-to-house canvassing to sell war bonds.

Ivylyn Jordan Schenk (now Hardy), an elementary school teacher in Moneta, took on yet additional duties. She taught pre-flight aeronautics to eight high school students, all of whom went on to join the Army Air Forces. She also taught an adult class on how to grow a Victory Garden and how to dry, pressure cook, and can foods. Moreover, she helped monitor retail prices in local stores.[17]

Some teachers left to serve in the armed forces, and others left for better paying jobs with the government or in the wartime economy. The school system responded by asking retired teachers to return to work, and the schools hired people with less training.[18]

Wartime shortages and conservation even affected the Bedford High School yearbook. The yearbooks for 1943 and 1944 were significantly reduced in size and number of pages.[19]

Doctor Shortage

When six doctors in Bedford County were called to active duty by early September 1942, a doctor shortage resulted in the community.[20] For much of the war, the only remaining doctors were located in the town of Bedford. According to Gates Richardson, "During much of the war period, except at (the town of) Bedford, there was no doctor between Lynchburg (to the east) and Roanoke (to the west) and Rocky Mount (to the south) and Buena Vista (to the north)....while the doctors who stayed at home were overworked, the people did not suffer for want of medical care."[21]

Boy Farm Laborers

For the summers of 1943 and 1944, several government agencies worked together to recruit city boys to work on farms as replacements for those farm laborers who had gone off to the military. The agencies were the Farm Extension Service in Blacksburg, Virginia, the Virginia Department of Education, the U.S. Department of Agriculture county agents, and county farm labor offices. Several Roanoke schoolboys between the ages of fourteen and seventeen were placed on Bedford county farms. The host farm families were expected to pay each boy $20-30 a month, provide room and board, and treat the boy as a member of the family.[22]

Impact of Military Service on Retail Stores

When the owners of small retail stores enlisted or were drafted, the stores were often sold or closed. The sale of Jones Drug Store by James Jones, before he entered the Navy, is one example. The owner of the Bedford Jewelry Store discontinued business for the duration of the war when he enlisted in the Navy.[23]

German Prisoners of War

At one point in the war, there were more than 350,000 German prisoners of war (POWs) at more than 100 camps in the United States. (The POWs in the United States were predominantly German; Italians accounted for most of the rest, with a very small number of Japanese.)

Prisoners cleaned and maintained the camps. For this, enlisted prisoners were paid ten cents a day, with which they could purchase items from the stockade canteen (officers were paid, depending on rank, $20-40 dollars a month). Consistent with the Geneva Convention related to prisoners of war, enlisted prisoners could also volunteer for any available labor outside the camp. They were paid eighty cents a day for this outside labor. A prisoner's outside income was deposited into an individual account. He could withdraw up to $10 a month in the form of coupons to be spent at the stockade canteen; the rest accumulated in his account, to be paid upon his release.[24]

In November 1944 a German POW working outside one of the camps in the Roanoke Valley escaped into the countryside. The prisoner, who had been incarcerated at Camp Catawba, escaped while working at picking apples near Coyner Springs, which is across the Bedford County line in Botetourt County. Authorities issued an alert over Roanoke radio stations and called for assistance from the area militia, making many local residents believe that more than one prisoner was involved. Area police, militia, and armed citizens searched for the POW for five days. The prisoner, who became hungry, finally walked up to a home in Webster in Botetourt County and surrendered, and police returned him to Camp Catawba. Strangely, at the same time, the newspapers reported that Roanoke police had picked up a man claiming to be an escaped prisoner hired to commit sabotage by a German-American organization. This may have been a hoax.[25]

In September and October 1945, after hostilities had ceased, a group of thirty German POWs from Sandy Level Camp, located southeast of Bedford in adjacent Pittsylvania County, were trucked into Bedford County to work on local farms. (The last German POWs in America were not shipped back to Germany until July 1946.) The group of POWs trucked to Bedford County worked a total of twenty-seven days at forty-nine farms in seven magisterial districts throughout the county. The prisoners were brought from the camp to the town of Bedford, where farmers picked them up and took them to their farms to work. Late in the afternoon, the farmers took the prisoners back to Bedford, where they were loaded onto vehicles and returned to the POW camp for the night. Averaging seven hours a day each, these prisoners worked a combined total of 798 man-days in Bedford County cutting and shucking corn, filling silos, making hay, and harvesting apples.[26]

The living conditions for the German POWs in Virginia were comfortable compared to the experiences of the young men from Bedford, who suffered as POWs, especially those captured by the Japanese, but also those captured by the Germans.

Thus, with more women in the labor force, supplemental jobs for teachers, recruiting of boy laborers, and occasional work by POWs, the people and businesses of Bedford County found ways to compensate for war-related labor shortages, and the local economy not only did not suffer during the war but actually grew.

Chapter 11

Home Front: Miscellaneous

Resentment Against Those Not Serving

There was a degree of resentment on the Bedford home front and among Bedford servicemen against young men who did not serve in the armed forces.

In May 1943 the chairman of the Bedford History Committee for World War II recorded some of this resentment in a report to a Virginia history commission. She observed that men who were deferred from military service because of their work in agriculture were not happy about constantly having to explain why they were not in the armed forces. One farmer whose son had an agricultural deferment was said to have walked out of his house one morning and found that his fence posts leading to the highway had been painted yellow. The chairman reported that, "There is an increasing sentiment for a uniform, insignia, or some means of identification that would save these (farm) boys such embarrassment." The head of the Virginia commission replied that, "The yellow paint episode goes beyond anything we have had reported to us so far."[1]

The resentment and embarrassment likely increased in April 1944 when Selective Service Director Hershey asked farmers to make available for service all possible men under twenty-six still remaining on the farms.[2]

Pvt. Raymond Atkinson sent his parents the following poem, which was published in a local newspaper in the autumn of 1943.[3] (It is not clear whether Private Atkinson or someone else wrote the poem, although it seems to be attributable to him.)

To The Draft Dodger

I'm writing this short letter,
And every word is true.

Don't look away Draft Dodger,
For it's addressed to you.
You feel at ease and in no danger
Back in the old home town.
You cooked up a pitiful story
So the Draft Board will turn you down.
You never think of the real men,
Who leave there day by day,
You just think of their girl friends,
That you take while they are away.
You sit at home and read your paper
You jump up and yell we'll win,
Just where do you get that we stuff?
This war will be won by men.
Just what do you think, Mr. Slacker,
That this free nation would do?
If all the men were slackers
And scared to fight like you.
I guess that's all Mr. Slacker,
I know your face is red,
America is no place for your kind,
I mean every word I have said.
So I will close this letter, Draft Dodger.
Just remember what I say.
Keep away from my girl friend
For I'm coming home some day.

Conscientious Objectors

During the war years, some 50,000 young men across the United States were classified by the government as conscientious objectors. This classification was recognized by the Selective Training and Service Act of 1940, which authorized the first peacetime draft in the United States. Men claiming conscientious objector status cited religious or philosophical reasons for refusing to serve in the armed forces or refusing to fight. Approximately half of these men were willing to be assigned to positions in the armed forces where they would not have to carry or use weapons, such as the medical corps.

The 1940 act provided that conscientious objectors not willing to serve in the armed forces could be assigned to work of national importance under civilian direction. An Executive Order in 1943 directed establishment of Civilian Public Service Camps, to which some 12,000 conscientious objectors were assigned. They worked on non-military projects at or near the camps. They worked without pay and paid for their own food and clothing. Others were assigned to work at mental hospitals, dairy farms, and other government projects, and some volunteered to be "guinea pigs" for scientific experiments.[4]

In early 1944 the Selective Service System established one of its Civilian Public Service Camps—Camp 121—at a former Civilian Conservation Corps camp at Kelso, located at the foot of the Peaks of Otter, some six miles northwest of the town of Bedford. The National Park Service's Blue Ridge Parkway office in Roanoke was directed to operate the camp. It appointed a superintendent to oversee the work program.

In February, 153 conscientious objectors were moved to the camp from facilities in Augusta County, Virginia. The men ranged in age from eighteen to forty-four, averaging twenty-four. Forty-two were married. Approximately eighty men, or 52 percent, were members of the Church of the Brethren. Some fourteen others were German Baptists, ten were Methodists, and others came from seventeen other religious denominations. Many had been employed in agriculture, and some had professional and managerial backgrounds. They came from twenty-two states in the mid-Atlantic area, the Midwest, and even Florida, Texas, and Oregon.[5]

The Bedford newspapers reported in some detail on the camp and the activities of the men. The men were to work on protection, conservation, and restoration projects for the National Park Service. In February 1944, for example, they worked cutting dead chestnut trees. They were also available for emergency work at farms within fifteen miles of the camp, with services arranged by the county agent. The men were not paid by the government but did receive $2.50 a month from their respective churches to cover items such as soap. Any money paid for farm work was to go not to the men but to the U.S. Treasury for public use after the war. The Brethren Service Committee provided a camp director who supervised the activities of the men when work ended. The newspapers reported:

> Quitting time is at five, after which comes a period for relaxation such as playing games, reading, etc. Supper is at seven....recently a library was added. There is no compulsory hour for bed time, although it is generally understood...that anyone wishing to remain up after eleven p.m. must retire to the library." The men were allowed to return home on furloughs.[6]

Soon after the local newspapers announced the establishment of the camp and the activities of the men assigned there, several Bedford citizens publicly expressed their objections. In the February 24, 1944, edition of the *Bedford Bulletin*, R. L. Johnson, father of three men serving in the armed forces and two more scheduled to be called up, paid for a large advertisement taking issue with conscientious objectors, the program that allowed them recreational time, and having them in Bedford County. Expressing the hope that Bedford servicemen would not see the newspaper stories about the camp, he wrote:

> I wonder what our boys over there (servicemen) think of Bedford and what is at the foot of the good old Peaks of Otter, a place that they hold so dear to their hearts. I wonder, also, if they, too, can stop work at five and relax in a more expansive library and play more diversified games....
>
> If they (the conscientious objectors) do not believe in the freedom others are fighting for, why are they allowed the freedom of the streets of Bedford. I say that if they do not want that freedom badly enough to fight for it, then put them under guard and take that freedom away from them; or put a yellow band on them, or mark them in some way so the children of our town will know them....
>
> What are they (the Johnson sons) fighting for? To whip the yellow devils over there or to protect the yellow ones back here?...
>
> Why should they (the conscientious objectors) mingle at our churches...with the young girls, the sisters and sweethearts of our fighting boys?...

Tell the children the truth and put up a large yellow flag pointing toward the foot of the good old Peaks of Otter.[7]

Other citizens then sent letters to the editor strongly objecting to the camp and supporting Mr. Johnson's opinions. J. J. Saunders, whose son Bernard was a prisoner of war of the Japanese, congratulated Johnson and stated:

My personal opinion of this group (the conscientious objectors) would be unclear to put in print. Their (way) is not the American way of life. Our county government, or whoever is responsible, made a terrible blunder when the camp was permitted to locate here and I hope they will soon move on as unwelcome guests....[8]

H. L. Terry, a World War I veteran, wrote:

At Kelso, close to Bedford, there is a nest of canary birds.... These boys with yellow plumage are hiding behind the skirts of some fanatical religious philosophical doctrine, and when there is a war on and their country is about to be invaded by some other yellow race, then is when they show their true colors which is very saffron....

When the war is over and won, the gang with the yellow plumage should be rounded up and should make a sizeable showing....They should be placed on an isolated island, sufficiently near the equator so as not to necessitate supplying them with heat and shelter like they get at Kelso....

They should depend on the soil and toil for food, they should have no correspondence with their folks.

They ought to be allowed to stew mentally as they think over their past deeds of valor and let's hope they live to be as old as Methuselah.

American soldiers will live always in the hearts of their country, while the conscientious objectors will be buried in the dust of oblivion.[9]

Meda Yoncey opined:

> If they do not think freedom is worth fighting for they should not be allowed to live in a freedom-loving country. They should be deported. Why not establish C.O. camps in the islands of the Pacific? Then they could have much "fun" during their recreation dodging bombs and knowing that each minute may be their last. Let them have at least some taste of it....[10]

Roy E. Ellis wrote that the men at the camp should be called, more appropriately, "conscious cowards." With regard to the men helping farmers, Ellis wrote, "I do not see what they could do to help us as we are all in the war effort and our work would come in conflict with their yellow conscience."[11]

Visitors

Hosting British Sailors

On several occasions, British sailors, whose ships had been sent to Norfolk, Virginia, for repair and resupply, visited Bedford. Norfolk was crowded with military activity, and so the Union Jack Club there arranged to send some of the British sailors inland for a few days or up to a week. Some visited Bedford in September 1941, eighteen visited over two weekends in May 1943, and sixteen visited for a week in July 1943. The sailors were hosted in Bedford homes, and the townspeople dined and entertained them.[12]

Puerto Rican Boy Visitors

In the summer of 1942 the Benevolent and Protective Order of the Elks offered a protective program for chapters located in areas considered to be in danger because of the war. As part of this program, Elks in Puerto Rico sent eight of their sons to live at the Elks National Home in Bedford. The boys attended public school in Bedford during their visit. In 1943, at their annual national convention, the Elks determined that Puerto Rico was no longer likely to be bombed, and most of the boys were subsequently returned home. A couple relocated to other parts of the continental United States.[13]

Touring American Military Heroes

In the spring and summer of 1945, defense-related factories sponsored several tours by heroic American soldiers. In mid-April, a group of soldiers called "Heroes of Bastogne" visited Bedford. Their nickname came from the courage they showed during the fighting in the Bastogne area of Belgium during the Battle of the Bulge. The soldiers spoke to a group of 1,500 citizens at the courthouse, visited the Rubatex and Hampton Looms plants where they urged speedy war production, and were entertained at a dinner at Liberty Academy hosted by plant officials.[14]

In late June, the Radford Ordnance Works in Radford, Virginia, south of Roanoke, organized a tour of combat veterans under the name "Rockets from Radford." Bedford was the sixteenth stop for this troupe, whose purpose was to recruit urgently needed construction workers to complete the Radford plant and increase its production of munitions. The tour included a Congressional Medal of Honor winner from the fighting at Anzio, Italy, as well as battle-scarred American and enemy weapons. The event was held at the Bedford High School athletic field.[15]

Military Aircraft Crashes in Bedford County

Five aircraft on military-related training missions crashed in or near Bedford County during the war. One was a U.S. Army Air Force B-25 bomber; two were light training aircraft which collided; the fourth was a U.S. Navy light, twin-engined Scout bomber; and the fifth was a U.S. Marine Corps Corsair fighter-bomber aircraft.

The B-25 bomber, based in Columbia, South Carolina, crashed into the side of Sharp Top Mountain, outside the town of Bedford, at about 9:15 p.m. on February 2, 1943. Local residents had heard the plane fly over the town at a low altitude headed northwest toward the Peaks. There was an explosion and fire when the aircraft hit the mountain about 1,000 feet below its peak. A group of rescuers climbed two-and-a-half miles up the rugged mountain and reached the site after midnight. Led by Bedford Fire Chief H. F. Turner and town electrician C. O. Updike, and guided by Leonard Stanley who lived nearby, the rescuers found pieces of the plane scattered on the mountain over a 200-square-yard area. They found the bodies of all five members of the crew, burned and mangled so badly that only one could be immediately identified.

A rescue team of thirty men, laboring on the snow and ice-covered mountain, brought the bodies out over the night of February 3. The bodies were shipped to the men's hometowns the next week, accompanied by military escorts. An eighteen-man military team salvaged much of the plane, but many parts were left on the mountain, where they remain today, along with a recent memorial plaque. The exact cause of the crash is still a matter of speculation.[16]

The two light training planes collided in mid-air on April 27, 1943, one mile east of Buford's airport at Montvale. Two instructor pilots and two trainees were killed in the crash. The men were engaged in a regional program to develop Navy flyers, with ground course training given at Roanoke College and flight training conducted at Buford's Airport. D. D. Isenburger of Montvale was one of the instructors killed, and R. A. Wright, a native of Lynchburg but recently of Norfolk, was one of the trainees killed.[17]

The Navy Scout bomber crash-landed on the afternoon of October 24, 1944, near Haydens Bridge in the Huddleston area of southeastern Bedford County. Reports, while not official, indicated the plane was low on fuel. Two of the crew bailed out, while the others crash-landed the plane. No one was injured. Bedford's 73[d] Company of the Virginia State Guard secured the plane until it was removed by truck to the Norfolk Naval Base for repairs.[18]

The Marine Corps Corsair crashed near the Skyline Drive in the National Forest above Big Island in northern Bedford County on April 2, 1945. A pilot in an accompanying aircraft said the Corsair had flown into a cloudbank and failed to emerge. Despite search and rescue efforts, the plane and pilot went missing until mid-September 1945, when Pfc. Claude Humphreys, an Army paratrooper home on furlough in Big Island, went hiking in the area and found the wreckage and the pilot's remains. On September 27, the *Bedford Bulletin* reported that the Marine Corps had found it impossible to salvage the wreckage of the plane and had "granted permission to anyone visiting the scene to take anything they want." The newspaper said that a number of people had visited the site, most carrying away a souvenir of some kind.[19]

Newspaper Coverage of the War

The two newspapers operating in Bedford during World War II—the *Bedford Bulletin* and the *Bedford Democrat*—published once a week (in mid-week) local, national, and international news related to the war and other events.[20]

Both newspapers printed columns or sections reporting news about individual servicemen and servicewomen. The titles of these columns evolved in both newspapers—going from "boys" to "men" and eventually including women. The *Bedford Bulletin's* column evolved from "News of Soldier Boys at Home and in Camp" to "News of Our Men and Women in Uniform." The *Bedford Democrat* used several titles for its column, including "Our Boys in the Armed Services of Their Country," "Service News of Bedford Men, Women" and "Bedford Men and Women in the Armed Forces."

The editors of the two newspapers wrote relatively long editorials on the war. These assessed the political-military situation, urged citizens to support the war effort, and sometimes chided the public to do more.

Both newspapers ran free public-service advertisements and advertisements paid for by coalitions of local businesses supporting the war effort. The *Bulletin* ran snippets of military humor.

Public service advertisements included drawings and text apparently provided by the federal government. These promoted war bond sales and encouraged citizens to salvage needed materials. Some advertisements indicated how many tons of scrap metal were used in making a tank or an antiaircraft gun, and others indicated how many salvaged tin cans it would take to make various weapons.[21]

Paid advertisements were wide-ranging. For example, more than seventy businesses and industries in Bedford joined together to sponsor advertisements promoting the sale of war bonds. The Appalachian Electric Power (AEP) Company proclaimed in one advertisement that the United States had five times the amount of electrical power that it had during World War I.[22] Another AEP advertisement showed a drawing of Hitler with his fingers in his ears and declared that it was "no use, Adolf, you can't shut out that hum" of Americans and machines working twenty-four hours a day.[23] Yet another AEP advertisement urged people to practice preventive maintenance to "keep those electric appliances working."[24]

Esso advertised its contribution to the making of explosives carried by American bombers.[25] General Electric announced that its radio stations were broadcasting to American servicemen and to foreign countries, emphasizing America's determination to achieve victory.[26] The Norfolk and Western Railway urged all workers to work safely and avoid accidents "to speed Victory and Peace."[27]

The Citizens National Bank invited servicemen to mail in deposits to the bank.[28] Greyhound ran an advertisement showing a sailor greeting his family, with a bus in the background. The text indicated that with the war there were more passengers than ever. Citing shortages of bus company resources, it asked people to "travel wisely in wartime."[29] The Bedford Pulp and Paper Company advertised for pulpwood, using war-time phrases, such as "selective service for your trees," trees "to be drafted now," and trees to be "deferred."[30]

Both local newspapers wrote lengthy editorials intended to inform, bolster, and motivate the citizens of the community. As an example, on December 11, 1941, the *Bedford Bulletin* published an editorial titled "The Nations Line Up."

Just days after the infamous Japanese attack on Pearl Harbor, the Philippines, and other points in the Pacific, and the subsequent American declaration of war on Japan, Germany and Italy have now declared war on the United States. And so, the nations line up. On the one side are liberty, freedom, and all the blessings they bestow. On the other side is slavery. This is to be a war to the death. While the Axis powers probably don't plan to invade America immediately, nothing can be clearer than that they plan to conquer Europe, Africa, and Southern and Eastern

Asia. This in all probability will be a long war. America, the British Empire, Russia, and China are vastly superior in wealth, natural resources, and manpower, but the dictator powers have prepared for the struggle and caught the allies unprepared. We must prepare ourselves to work, produce, and make sacrifices. Everything we have, even our lives, must be thrown into this fight. Less than full unity and determination to win may place in doubt final victory.[31]

A week later, the newspaper published two more editorials, one on avoiding hysteria and one on funding the Red Cross War Fund:

In the wake of the attack on Pearl Harbor, the Philippines, and other points in Asia, we must avoid hysteria. It's going to take a lot of courage, infinite patience, and blind faith in our leaders to maintain the morale of the American people on a high level in the face of likely adversities. We must be able to take it when the news is bad, and hold down our optimism when the news is good.[32]

Give Until It "Helps."...(Red Cross) Headquarters in Washington states that a minimum of $50,000,000 is required for needs of the immediate future if the men in camp and those who will go to the front...are to be assured of the attention they may require....Bedford County has been given a quota of $4,000 and should Bedford people fail—which they will not—to meet this call they will, to the extent of their failure, let down the more than 500 young Bedford County men now serving in the various armed services of the nation....This war, involving the nation in the gravest crisis it has ever faced, is going to demand of the American people sacrificial living during the next few years, and it is better that they begin now than later and certainly there can be no other cause more worthy of sacrifice just now than the Red Cross.[33]

On March 12, 1942, the *Bedford Democrat* ran an editorial across the top of the front page, entitled "What Can I Do To Help Win The War?" The editor listed many things under seven, capitalized headings:

YOU CAN AWAKE from your lethargy...YOU CAN FOSTER CONFIDENCE in those at the helm of your government...YOU CAN STRENGTHEN MORALE...YOU CAN WORK. You can plant and cultivate...stand by your industry....YOU CAN LEARN new trades and arts...YOU CAN FIGHT...The battle line runs through every home, every farm, every factory, every office...You can fight selfishness, desire for self gain, softness, waste, disease...YOU CAN BUY DEFENSE STAMPS AND BONDS.[34]

In September 1942 the editor of the *Bedford Bulletin* urged citizens to salvage their excess scrap iron. Under the title of "Turn in Your Junk for War," the editor wrote:

There is hardly a home, farm or business place in Bedford County at which the owner cannot find from a few pounds up to hundreds of pounds of scrap metal....Every little bit helps....Do your part by turning in every piece of scrap iron you can find in order that our steel mills can keep operating at capacity.[35]

On June 15, 1944, the *Bulletin's* editor published an editorial titled "Back the Attack."

This invasion of the European Continent is the supreme crisis of the war. All that has gone before has been merely preliminary. The fate of America and all of Christian civilization hangs in the balance in this struggle between freedom and tyranny. What the world is to be for centuries to come is being decided now on the beaches and fields of Normandy. Our fighting men cannot win this battle alone. If we are to win this war, we must give them our increasing support. The invasion demands a new birth of patriotism. Our first and most urgent duty is to buy War Bonds. Hundreds of our young men from Bedford County will fight under a serious handicap if we fail to give them the supplies they need.[36]

On July 27, 1944, the *Bedford Bulletin* published the following editorial from the *Richmond Times-Dispatch* praising the record of the 116th Infantry Regiment.

> The 116th Virginia Infantry…has written a record of imperishable glory in Normandy. Not only did it break the German beach defenses at heavily fortified and most strongly held points of all, but it also took St. Lo last week….General Bradley's official tribute alone will give the 116th a place high on Virginia's scroll of honor….The whole Commonwealth is proud of their record, which is as brilliant as any in the AEF (Allied Expeditionary Force). We on the home front must prove ourselves worthy of these Virginia boys, many of whom died in the churning surf off the Norman coast or on the shell-swept approaches to St. Lo, so that we might live in liberty.[37]

Later in 1944, in connection with a fund drive for the USO and other organizations, the editor coaxed the people of Bedford to do more.

> Bedford County is not making a good showing in the War Fund Campaign….It is an extremely disagreeable thing to have to urge, coax, shame or intimidate a community into doing something that should require none of these to be done….We have more than 2,000 young men in the service, and that alone should be sufficient reason for supporting any cause looking to their welfare and comfort.[38]

In February 1945, the *Bedford Bulletin's* editor would chide some of the people for not salvaging paper.

> …A contribution can be made by every citizen of town and county by making it a chore of their daily life to save paper and paper products of all kinds and either take it to a junk dealer or turn it over to the county salvage committee. Hundreds of pounds of waste paper and paper boards and boxes are either destroyed in the home or hauled to the town dump every week, apparently

without any thought to its value for war purposes. Some may not know any better, but in most cases, we believe, no attempt is made at salvage because it involves some trouble in saving and making it ready for the salvage truck.

…The eternal column of smoke arising from the town dump is a continuing reflection upon the patriotism of the people of this town, because it rises from burning paper which is vitally needed for war purposes. It is just as necessary for our businessmen and householders to conserve paper as it is for our farm folks to cut pulpwood and haul it to the mills.[39]

Social Life

While people on the home front generally had less time to socialize because of war-related demands on their time, many still were able to find time to visit, participate in social clubs, play cards, shop, converse at local gathering places, and go to the movies.

The Movies

Going to the two theaters in Bedford, the Liberty and the Bridge, was a source of relaxation and pleasure. The theaters, which apparently shared a common owner, continued to operate throughout the war years, each theater showing a movie different from the other. On weekdays, there was an afternoon matinee and two evening showings. On Saturdays, the movies were shown continuously from 11:00 a.m. to 11:00 p.m. On Sundays, there were two matinees and one evening showing. Tuesday was bargain day, when an adult could buy a ticket for twenty cents and a child could get a ticket for fourteen cents.

In mid-November 1941, Roy Rogers came in person to the Liberty Theater. "Sergeant York," with Gary Cooper, was playing at the Bridge Theater at the time. As the war went on, movies with a war theme became increasingly popular, such as "Pin up Girl," with Betty Grable; "The Hitler Gang"; "Two Girls and a Sailor," with June Allyson and Gloria DeHaven; and "The Purple Heart," with Dana Andrews.[40]

Shopping

Shopping was another pastime. In the basement of Leggett's Department Store, a woman could buy a print dress for $1.00 and a slip for another $1.00.[41] A woman's suit or coat cost $29.50.[42] At the Raylass Department Store, a man could buy a dress shirt for $1.55, oxford shoes for $3.98, and a felt hat for $3.98.[43] A bottle of Pepsi-Cola was five cents.[44]

Wartime Humor

Jokes were also a way to relieve some of the pressure and tension during the war. Many of the jokes were about relations between the sexes. The *Bedford Bulletin* frequently used jokes to fill up extra space. Some examples follow:[45]

This corporal asks his buddy, "How did you find the ladies at the dance?" The private answered, "I just opened a door marked 'Ladies' and there they were."

"No," said the young lady to a girl friend upon returning from a date with a Navy man, "I don't know what his rank was, but I think he was the chief petting officer."

"Oh, for goodness sake, use both hands," cried the pretty girl in the auto. "I can't," replied the GI, "I have to steer with one!"

Said one old maid to her sister: "I can't understand why you go out with that young sailor." Sister: "Oh, it's just a platonic friend-ship—play for him and tonic for me."

First Parachute Jumper: "What a mess! We're going to land on that desert island and I'll bet it's full of wild men." Second ditto: "Cheer up, Bud. Where there's wild men there's bound to be wild women."

After the U.S. Government rationed the supply of rubber and declared "war time," moving clocks across the nation ahead one hour, a Bedford County resident recorded the following joke in a diary entry of February 13, 1942:

This may be off the record, but, Hitler, Mussolini and Roosevelt were in a conversation about how to get the country to produce more boy babies—Hitler: I pay each family $5 for each son that arrives. Mussolini: I pay each family $10 for a son. Roosevelt: I believe I have beat all of you in effectiveness and it costs nothing. I declared a rubber shortage and put the people to bed an hour earlier![46]

S/Sgt. John Schenk included the following jokes in letters he sent from England to his wife Ivylyn:

Did you hear about the Admiral in the Navy who broke his arm trying to make a WAVE in the washing machine?[47]

Did you hear about the little moron who threw his cow over the cliff to watch the Jersey Bounce?[48]

They say there was a little moron who wanted to join the "WACS"—she ate bullets so her hair would come out in bangs.[49]

Ivylyn Schenk sent the following joke to her husband:

Hitler asked a soldier what his last wish would be if he were to be killed by a Russian plane. The soldier replied, "That you would be with me, sir."[50]

Assisting Returning Veterans

Late in the war and shortly after the end of the war, various groups and organizations in Bedford began to plan how best to assist returning veterans.

In October 1944 a post-war employment committee was set up in the Bedford community to help returning veterans secure their old jobs or new jobs. The county agricultural committee committed itself to provide the county agent a list of farms for sale in the county, names of farmers needing tenants and share croppers, and farmers needing full and part time employees.[51]

In June 1945 the local chapter of the Red Cross—specifically its camp and hospital committee—met to discuss how to help meet the needs of returning wounded veterans.[52]

In October 1945 the local draft board was designated as an official Veterans Information Center, with the objective of assisting veterans in reestablishing themselves in civilian life.[53]

End of the War Victory Celebration

On August 15, 1945, as news of the Japanese surrender was broadcast on the radio, Bedford citizens were said to have "swarmed" up town to celebrate. The *Bedford Bulletin* reported:

The people of Bedford rejoiced over Japan's surrender Tuesday night as crowds gathered in the streets immediately following the President's announcement. The wailing of the blackout siren was followed by a spontaneous blowing of car horns and ringing of bells as people drove through the streets for hours. Factory whistles blew intermittently until far into the night. Well after the majority of the crowd had retired to their homes, a lone victory serenador was heard wandering about the streets singing lustily: "Happy Days Are Here Again." He repeated the song over and over, pausing now and again like a town crier to yell with a ringing cheer: "The war is over."

About 8:00 p.m. the Bedford Firemen's Band started playing in front of the fire station and the crowd gathered around and joined in singing "God Bless America" and "The Star Spangled Banner."

Last night the V-J Day program...was held. Beginning at 7 o'clock a parade of servicemen in uniform, veterans of World War II, the Virginia State Guard, Boy and Girl Scouts,

American Legion and Auxiliary, Veterans of Foreign Wars and
Auxiliary and just plain citizens, led by the Bedford Firemen's
Band, formed at the courthouse and marched to the high school
auditorium where everyone joined in a program of music and
religious services.[54]

Additionally, the *Bedford Democrat* reported that:

A "snake line" of boys and girls followed the procession over
Bridge and Main streets to the courthouse and back celebrating
the climax of a great struggle…Occasionally a soldier or sailor
would meet another service brother and embrace him with the
comment of "isn't this grand," or "we knew we could do it," or
"well, this means we can stay here."[55]

The war was over.

Chapter 12

Communicating with Loved Ones

Communicating with loved ones was extremely important for both those away in the military and those at home in Bedford. Receiving a letter was often the highlight of the day. Conversely, when no letter arrived, concerns increased and morale fell. Despite the demands of everyday life, be it in the service or home in Bedford, many—especially spouses—tried to write to loved ones nearly every day or several times a week. Others wrote less frequently, and some seldom wrote.

Mail was the preferred, or at least the most used, mode of communication. The telephone and telegrams appear to have been used infrequently.

At least two women in Bedford—Ivylyn Jordan Schenk Hardy and Eleanor Payne Yowell—have saved the letters they exchanged during the war with their respective husbands, S/Sgt. John B. Schenk and 1st Lt. William A. Yowell, Jr. These letters, despite the Army's censorship of the letters written by the men, provide valuable insights into the war at a personal level, both at home and overseas. Mrs. Yowell has published excerpts from her husband's and her letters under the title *Flying High: World War II Letters to and from U.S. Army Air Force Bases and the Home Front.*

In addition to sending letters, some parents and spouses arranged to have Bedford newspapers mailed to their loved ones to keep them informed of developments back home. People on the home front mailed loved ones packages filled with things to eat and other requested items, and those in the service sometimes mailed home packages with small gifts or souvenirs.

Telephone and Telegrams

Long distance telephone calls and telegrams appear generally to have been reserved for special occasions and while the service personnel were in the United States. There were some exceptions.

The federal government and the telephone industry asked people to restrict long-distance telephone calls so as to keep the lines open for official communication. For example, in July 1942, the Chesapeake and Potomac Telephone Company ran an advertisement in the *Bedford Democrat* asking people not to make calls to the Washington, D.C., area unless absolutely necessary, to limit the number and length of any calls, and to restrict calls to the hours of 12-2 p.m., 5-7 p.m., and 10 p.m. to 9 a.m.[1]

William Yowell called his future bride, Eleanor Payne, in Bedford from his U.S. Army Air Forces base in South Carolina on her birthday in March 1943, and she sent him a telegram on his birthday a month later.[2] After they were married and Lieutenant Yowell was stationed in England, they wrote letters to each other every few days. In June 1944 Eleanor wrote her husband that she had wanted to send him a congratulatory telegram when he was promoted but had found it too expensive.[3]

John Schenk and his wife Ivylyn wrote letters to each other almost every day. They seldom sent telegrams or made phone calls. During the twenty months John was stationed in England, he sent Ivylyn eight telegrams, some on special occasions such as her birthday, Christmas, and New Years. Ivylyn sent at least one telegram to her husband.[4] She has said that her husband called her one time from England.[5]

Cpl. Bernard W. Saunders, when he landed in California in 1945 after being held by the Japanese as a prisoner of war for three-and-a-half years, tried unsuccessfully to phone his parents' home in Bedford. He finally was able to complete a call to his father at his job in Blue Ridge, Virginia.[6]

When S/Sgt. Earl Newcomb of Company A landed in Massachusetts in June 1945 on his way home from Europe where he had been since October 1942, he sent his wife, Elva, in Bedford a short but sweet telegram, reading, "I'm over here from over there and will be with you soon. Love, Earl." He was able later to call and make arrangements to meet her.[7]

Telegrams took on an ominous aura during the war, as the War and Navy Departments used them to inform families of the death, loss, or wounding of loved ones.

Mail

There were at least four types of mail—regular mail, Soldier's Letters, Air Mail, and V-Mail ("V" for "Victory").[8]

Stamps for regular mail cost two cents apiece early in the war and three cents after March 1944. Service personnel could write the word "Free" in the upper right-hand corner of the envelope and avoid postage.

The U.S. Army provided its service personnel blue envelopes, each with the words "Soldier's Letter" printed on it. Postage was free unless the soldier wanted it to be sent via Air Mail. On the blue envelopes, the following was printed: "This letter must not be used for money or valuables; cannot be registered; and will not be censored by company or regimental censors, but by the Chief Military Censor." Below this and above a signature line for the soldier, the following was printed: "I certify that the inclosed (sic) letter or letters were written by me, refer only to personal or family matters, and do not refer to military or other matters forbidden by censorship regulations."

Air Mail appears to have traveled faster, but soldiers as well as civilians apparently had to pay six cents postage to send a half-ounce letter overseas via Air Mail.

V-Mail

In July 1942 the government announced a new type of mail, called "V-Mail." This was for use between service personnel stationed outside the continental United States and family and friends within the United States. A single sheet of form paper served as both letter and envelope. A person wishing to send a V-Mail letter had to obtain a letter sheet from postal authorities. The sheets were free, but for economy reasons, only three sheets could be obtained at one time or on any one day. The message was to be written on only one side of the form, with the address on the reverse. The letter could be typed or handwritten in ink or dark pencil. Nothing could be enclosed with the message. Letters sent by non-military personnel in the United States required a regular three-cent stamp for surface transportation and six cents worth of stamps for domestic air transportation. Service personnel could send V-Mail letters without paying postage. V-Mail letters were said to benefit from preferred sorting and handling. The government and the country were to benefit from the reduced weight and size of letters and the uniformity of dimensions of the correspondence.[9]

For at least part of the V-Mail, the Army and Navy set up stations in the United States and overseas to microfilm the V-Mail letters. Rolls of microfilm, instead of the letters, were then transported across the ocean. Once the microfilm reached shore, the microfilmed letters were enlarged and printed onto small but readable sheets of paper, 4.25-inches by 5-inches in measurement, which were enclosed in tan envelopes and distributed to the addressees. Authorities said V-Mail would provide a 98 percent savings in cargo space, space vitally needed for weapons and munitions.[10]

John Schenk wrote his wife from England that he preferred V-Mail:

> I hope you don't mind my writing V-Mail letters all the time but honestly dear I can't think of enough to write a regular letter and I think V-Mails are much the faster....[11]

William Yowell, on the other hand, wrote his wife that he much preferred to receive letters via airmail rather than V-Mail, even though V-Mail was faster.[12] He did not explain why he preferred airmail, but the reason may have had something to do with receiving an original, large letter, instead of a reduced-sized photocopy.

Censorship

An Office of Censorship was established within the U.S. Government during the war. This office asked newspaper editors and people at home not to publicize the names of ships and troop units to which American servicemen were assigned. The office posed no objection to mentioning publicly the country or ocean where a serviceman was posted.[13]

Letters written by those deployed overseas were subject to censorship to prevent military information from leaking to the enemy. Service personnel were instructed not to include in their correspondence any reference to military matters or other matters forbidden by censorship regulations. Censors operated at the unit level, such as Company A, and at higher levels, such as regimental headquarters and even up to the U.S. Army Chief Military Censor. The censors were supposed to read the servicemen's letters, have any forbidden material deleted, and then stamp the envelope to show that the correspondence had passed censorship, e.g., "Passed by Army Examiner #12459."

In the first days of Company A's deployment to Great Britain, Captain Fellers, the company commander, appears to have reviewed and censored his men's mail. Within a few days, however, Fellers began delegating this duty to a subordinate officer.[14]

Even after six months in England, however, Fellers still occasionally censored his men's mail, according to a letter to his mother.

> The outgoing mail has to be censored by one of the company officers, so once in a while it falls my lot to help with it and I could write a book on it. Those boys all have a technique on some of their phraseology to the girls they left back there. And from the local mail it seems that the same tactics work with the local lassies, too.[15]

Service personnel sometimes expressed frustration with the censorship rules, which prevented them from writing about the interesting things they were experiencing. Some also appeared intimidated from expressing intimate feelings because they knew a third party would be reviewing their letters. John Schenk expressed his frustration in letters to his wife.

> I hope you don't find this letter too boring. I could write about so many things but you understand that our letters are censored and we can't write about everything....[16]

> (New letter) My Darling Wife, All I can say is that I am still in Jolly England and very homesick for you....[17]

> (New letter) I have been sitting here for at least ten minutes trying to think of a good way to start a letter. If I could ever get a

good beginning to a letter the rest would be easy. My letters are probably very much alike but the things that are interesting are the things we can't write about....[18]

(New letter) I guess it looks funny to you but I am over here in a strange country where everything I see is new and should be of interest to you but we are forbid to write about them. When I get home I will take a whole day off and tell you all about everything. So you will have to be patient until then....It seems harder and harder each night to think of something to write.[19]

(New letter) Here I am trying again to write you with nothing to say. There are lots of things I could say to you in person but not on paper. I could tell you that I love you but you already know that....[20]

William Yowell wrote his wife:

I wish I could write you exactly what the situation is here, but they are so strict on what we can write it makes it impossible. If you get caught not adhering to their orders they can make it mighty tough for you....[21]

(New letter) There is very little that I can tell you about where I am or what I am doing. The English countryside is beautiful....Will try to send you some more pictures of the crew, but they are awfully strict here about what we can send out....[22]

(New letter) All mail is so strictly censored we have to be careful about what we write. As command pilot I have to censor the crew's mail as well as my own....[23]

(New letter) There is nothing I can say about missions now, but I am doing right well in cutting down the number left. Only wish they were all over now and I was on my way home....[24]

Cpl. Otho B. (Joe) Hawkins of Montvale, who was serving in the Army somewhere in Africa, sent the following poem home. Pfc. John Reynolds, serving in England, sent his family a similar poem, so the poem may have been one that was generally circulating among the troops.[25]

Dear family:

Can't write a thing, the censor's to blame,
Just say that I'm well and sign my name.
Can't say where we sailed from,
Can't mention the date
Can't even mention the meals I ate
Can't say where I'm going, don't know where I'll land,
Can't even inform you if met by a band.
Can't mention the weather,
Can't say if there is rain
All military secrets must secrets remain.
Can't have a flashlight to guide me at night,
Can't smoke a cigarette, except out of sight.
Can't keep a diary, for such is a sin,
Can't keep the envelopes your letters came in.
Can't say for sure now just what I can write
So I'll close this letter and say good night.
I'll send this letter to say I'm well,
Still grumbling and growling…
and fighting like H---

S/Sgt. Frank Draper of Company A expressed his views in the following poem he wrote in a small black notebook:[26]

Can't Say

I can't tell you from where I write
I can't tell you the day
I can't tell you for whom I fight
There's nothing I can say

I can't tell you the moon is brite
I can't say rain is falling
I have to write by candle lite
till I hear a bugle calling

I can't say what we're going to do
I can't say where we're going
I can't say much to interest you
So don't ask what we're doing

I can't say what we have to eat
I can't say whether it's good
I can't say how I have to sleep
On dirty ground or wood

I can't say when my day is thru
Or where I'd like to be
I can't say much at all to you
So just say a lot to me

Mail and the Impact on Morale—Overseas and at Home

Letters were a real boost to morale for the recipients, both overseas and at home. Conversely, not receiving mail was a depressing experience. Even for those who wrote their loved ones almost daily, there were gaps in delivery, as letters often accumulated and were delivered in bunches rather than daily, and occasionally were lost.

Taylor Fellers wrote his mother on March 27, 1943, after almost six months in England, thanking her for a letter and saying:

Nothing helps a soldier's morale like mail from home and his friends back there. I see in our paper here that quite a load of mail went down in one of our ships. But we can expect some of those things....Your letter today made me a bit homesick....[27]

William Yowell wrote his wife from England:

Surely was a fine day as I got three of your letters and one from your mother. This mail situation is funny. One of your letters was mailed the 7th and one the 17th. When I first got here I received 15 of your letters at one time! Another boy got 20 in one day.[28]

The impact on morale of receiving or not receiving letters is evident in the correspondence between John Schenk, training in Great Britain for the invasion of the European Continent, and his wife Ivylyn in Bedford. She wrote to him almost every day, and he wrote every day until his duties interfered. As the communications sergeant for Company A, John had access to a typewriter, which he used frequently for his letters. He wrote the following to his wife within two months of arriving in England:

(Almost a month after leaving the United States and arriving in England) Still no mail from the States. This is getting to be a terrible situation. Can't even hear from my wife for over a month. Anyway I hope you are not worrying too much....[29]

(Five days later) Today I am a very happy man. I just received six nice letters from you....[30]

(Three weeks later) We got a whole sack of mail and out of the whole lot there wasn't even one letter from you. I can't figure out what is happening to our mail....[31]

Sunday, four days, later was a morale-boosting day for Schenk. On that day, he received two letters from his wife in the morning and eight from her in the evening.[32] As time went by, the mail situation improved. Schenk greatly valued letters from his wife and was dismayed when her letters were delayed:

If it wasn't for letters from home I don't know what I would do....[33]

(New letter) Another day of this damn Army life is over and that means one day less before I see you. Every nite about this time I feel one of my moods coming on. Two letters came from you today....I don't know what I would do if it weren't for your letters....[34]

(New letter) No letters from home for the past two days. I guess they will all come at once. You have spoiled me by writing so often....[35]

(New letter) Again I find myself writing to you at three o'clock in the morning....No mail from you today but I shouldn't fuss because only yesterday I received four....[36]

(New letter) I can't figure out why you are not getting my mail. I have been writing just about every day and you should receive it on time. All of the V-Mail is flown across and the weather has a lot to do with when they can fly, and you know the weather in England isn't very pleasant at times....[37]

(New letter) Rainy England. Tis another rainy day in the E.T.O. (European Theater of Operations), but I can't complain because this past week has been unusually pretty. May be because no mail came from home is why I am so blue....Words seem to come hard today so I will have to close....[38]

The impact on morale can also be seen in the correspondence between William Yowell, who, between April and August 1944, was flying bombing missions from England against German targets on the continent, and his wife, Eleanor:

I have received all of your letters written up until April 11 and just can't tell you how much they meant to me....[39]

(New letter) Thought surely I would hear from you today, but again no letter. I'm not complaining because this mail situation is kind of poor. It doesn't come regularly and often piles up....[40]

(New letter) I know I am missing some of (your letters), because there have been periods of a week between some of them. I just hope it won't be very long before we can do away with this letter writing forever. It is awfully unsatisfactory, don't you think?[41]

The morale of those on the home front was also affected. Ivylyn Schenk wrote in mid-1943:

This is such a happy Monday morning. When I was getting breakfast a cable, sending your love and reassuring me of your safety, came. You are so perfectly marvelous to me, John. You're the best husband a girl could ever have. I don't blame all the girls for envying me. They have a lot to do in order to find anyone equal to <u>my husband</u>. Then, as I was teaching, a letter came. It was a blue letter, written March 16th...thank the Lord it was John's writing inside and that was, ah so, very welcome. It has been 12 days since I had a letter from you. But with both a cable and a letter today, I am very happy....[42]

(New letter) Your wife is really a happy girl today. Reason? Three typewritten V-mail letters![43]

Eleanor Yowell wrote the following during the period April-June 1944:

(New Letter) A nice long letter from you yesterday was the nicest possible thing that could have happened to me....[44]

(New Letter) Fortune certainly did smile on me today! I had three letters from you...and one was an extremely fat epistle! You don't know how glad I was to hear from you and to know that you have at last gotten my letters. So, it's England, the land of eternal mists and fogs?[45]

(New letter) What a grand and glorious day yesterday was—three nice fat letters from you! One was written May 31, one June 2, and one June 4. Do you realize that they are the only letters with the exception of two that I have received from you in a month? With the Invasion under way I realize the mail has been held up, and no one around here has gotten much. This is what has consoled me. It sure does sound like you have been taking a lot of rides on Buzz ("Buzztail" was the name of Lieutenant Yowell's bomber). They must be throwing it to you hot and heavy at this point. How many missions do you have now? And how often do you go on them? Don't know whether you can answer these questions, but it doesn't hurt to ask.[46]

(New letter) Yesterday was another red letter day for me, as I had two letters from you, one written June 5th and one June 8th. This makes six letters I've had this week! It's a lot better than hitting the jackpot and winning a bunch of quarters! From the way you write you must have been going on right many missions, and I know how tired you must be. You are under a physical and mental strain and nothing will make you more tired. Please try and relax as much as you can....[47]

Some people on the home front, especially wives in Bedford, tried to write every day or so, regardless of working at full-time jobs, volunteering, running the house, and engaging in social activities. Ivylyn Schenk sought to reassure her husband that she was writing him faithfully almost every day.

I have been noticing that the Army and Navy are insisting upon us homefolks writing to our men more! I feel that I'm not writing you enough. Are you getting a letter for almost every day? Sometimes I think you're not. I never skip a day unless I tell you....[48]

Eleanor Yowell wrote her husband the following:

Missing you like the dickens, but my days are busy ones and I have something to do every minute. That way I don't have time to sit and brood....[49]

(New letter) I haven't been writing you as much lately as I would like to, but the days are not long enough for everything I want and need to do....Later tonight. Got a letter from you, and it always does my heart so much good to hear from you. Your letters all sound cheerful, but I knew you would make the best of any situation....[50]

(New letter) And again I'm stealing Elks Home (where she worked and sometimes wrote letters to her husband) time, but it's for a good cause. After work yesterday I went by the Jacks and got 24 tomato plants, and then went home and planted them. Had to put the salve on Pam (her dog) and this takes an hour. Hurried through supper, bathed and changed to charge over to the library for surgical dressings. After that, Maria, Nora, Sarah and I played bridge....[51]

(New letter) From the way you write I know you haven't been getting half of my letters. Please don't have the idea that I am not writing, as for the last six weeks or longer I have been writing every other day and sometimes more. It was only back in May when all the chores piled up on me that I neglected writing you, and I have been sorry about it ever since....[52]

John Schenk expressed his appreciation to Ivylyn for her frequent writing and mentioned that others in his unit were not so fortunate.

I said to myself before I married you that beyond a doubt you were going to make the best wife in the world, and by golly I was right...a thousand...things that you do daily. Such as writing to me as often as you do. There are some husbands in this company that don't hear from their wives but once a week. I couldn't make it on that....[53]

Servicemen's Difficulty in Writing

The men and women in the service seem generally to have written fewer letters than their loved ones on the home front, given the military demands on their time and energy and the lack of quiet places to write. John Schenk's letters to his wife give an impression of the difficulties service personnel found in trying to write:

(Upon arrival in Britain) Sorry I couldn't keep up my continuous flow of mail. I would like to write you every day but I can see now that it will be impossible....[54]

(New letter) I just pick up the nearest thing at hand to write with and sometime I even write standing up. We don't have all the modern conveniences that we do in civilian life....[55]

(New letter) I started to write this letter last night but when I looked for the V-mail form it wasn't there so I had to wait until this a.m. These forms are pretty hard to get now....[56]

(New letter) At present I am sitting in a ditch by the telephone using the map board as a table trying to write you a letter....[57]

(New letter) This letter is being written under the most adverse conditions. I am using my knee as a table and a flash-light for a light. Just got back from seeing a show....[58]

(New letter) I feel ashamed of myself for not writing to you more than I do. I really want to write more often but things are moving so fast here in England that I hardly have time to take a deep breath....Please excuse the (typing) mistakes tonight cause I haven't had any sleep since yesterday morning. It is getting late...pleasant dreams.[59]

(New letter) Will try to write a few lines tonight if the noise ever dies down. All the boys in the hut are trying to talk at once. They will argue about anything....[60]

(New letter) It is raining and the tent is beginning to leak so I will have to close....(Author's note: Company A must have been on temporary maneuvers away from Ivybridge, where the men lived in rounded-roof, corrugated metal huts.)[61]

(New letter) I will try to write if I can think above all this noise (in the hut). The Yankees and the Rebels are at it again. The only regret I have is that my grandfather didn't kill a few more of the damn Yankees in 1861....[62]

(New letter) One of the boys in the hut got a fruit cake from home today and we are brewing a pot of coffee to go with the cake. Every nite we have coffee and cakes before we go to bed. I have a fine bunch of boys in my hut. They are all in my platoon and most are Southern boys. I have a bunch of Radio operators, Snipers, Clerks, Jeep drivers, Messengers and even Dog Robbers (Officers Orderlies to you) in my hut. Oh yes, Butch the mail orderly is also in the same hut. It is impossible to try to write a letter when they are all around so I have to go to the orderly room to do most of my writing....[63]

(New letter) Sunday...I find myself with a few extra moments to spare and I can think of nothing better to do than write to the sweetest girl in the world....I started writing this letter at one o'clock and here it is eight o'clock. Everytime I start to do anything of my own someone calls me. This Army life is hell on earth....[64]

(New letter) I will try to write you a letter if I can think above all the noise going on. They are having a party in the Mess hall and that happens to be next door....[65]

William Yowell answered his wife's question about having time to think, as follows:

About my having time to think, I do have too much at times and it isn't good for me. I try to keep occupied so I won't think too much, but at times it surely is hard....[66]

He wrote this just at the beginning of a three-month period in which he would fly thirty bombing missions over enemy territory. His letters reflect how physically and mentally draining these missions were:

Sorry I didn't write yesterday, but went on a mission and really was tired....[67]

In early June 1944, during a period of flying bombing missions over France in support of the invasion, Yowell wrote the following to his wife:

> We are all getting along fine except we stay right tired most of the time. Sorry for this short letter, but just wanted to let you know that I am OK. Kinda worn out, so will close and get some sack time.[68]

> (New letter) Surely hope you are getting my letters now, but as you have heard, all mail has been held up leaving here due to the Invasion. All of the boys have been getting letters from their wives saying they had not heard for some time....[69]

In mid-July, 1944, Yowell wrote:

> Have missed two days writing you, but I was too tired to write yesterday. Believe you understand....We are due another Oak Leaf Cluster to go on the Air Medal. As I wrote you, this represents a certain number of missions we have flown....[70]

Eleanor Yowell wrote her husband on July 18, 1944:

> How are you? And where are you? Had a letter from Judy today saying she had heard from Bud yesterday, and he told her you all were taking time out soon to pay a little visit to a 'flak happy' camp. You hadn't mentioned it, but I knew that every so often you all would go to a rest camp. Your letters always sound so chipper, but I know good and well you don't feel that way lots of times. I hope you can really relax and get a lot of good rest....[71]

On August 1, 1944, William Yowell reported:

> Had a right pleasant surprise yesterday. Am not at my base now, but we are now at a Red Cross Rest Home (which he later reported was at Southport, near Liverpool, England). It's not that there is anything wrong with us, but they have been sending

crews here when they get a certain number of missions. We will be here a week, and our time is our own to do exactly as we want. They have tennis courts, riding, golf, and also they tell us we can go swimming....It surely is a nice place from the looks of it so far, and I know it will do all of us a lot of good. They brought us up in a plane from the base. The only tough thing is we won't be able to get any of our mail until we get back to the base....[72]

The men in Company A, while they were on furlough, could not send letters to their loved ones back in the United States. As John Schenk explained it, "We have no way of getting our mail censored when away from our unit."[73]

Packages and Newspapers

While there were no restrictions on mailing packages within the United States, the U.S. Government placed restrictions on packages going to service personnel abroad, at least in the early part of the war. John Schenk reported in late January 1943:

Postal Services have put restrictions on the folks back home sending packages without written permission of our C.O. (Commanding Officer). If I ever need anything I will write and let you know and also send the proper papers....[74]

Under these restrictions, parcels could not weigh more than five pounds, be more than fifteen inches long, or exceed thirty-six inches in combined length and girth. Those in the United States wanting to mail packages overseas had to provide the post office with proof that the service person had requested the items and had the commanding officer's approval. As for magazines and newspapers, only those mailed by the publishers were forwarded to service personnel.[75]

Mothers, wives, and others in Bedford were able to send their loved ones packages filled with offerings of food and clothing or items the service personnel had requested. In spring 1943 Eleanor Yowell sent packages of cookies to her husband-to-be in South Carolina.[76]

She also sent him a large package for Christmas while he was in Tucson, Arizona, in 1943, but she reported that:

> Mr. Keeler said I had no business sending such a big package to the 'Red Eagle.' A lot of people aren't sending Christmas cards at all. The Post Office has requested them not to....[77] (She mailed the package on December 15, and he received it on December 31.)[78]

The restrictions on sending packages to armed forces personnel overseas appear to have been lifted in May 1943. A letter that month from John Schenk in England mentioned that the ban on packages from the United States had been lifted.[79]

Ivylyn Schenk sent her husband a pressure-cooked chicken in a sealed container, fruit cakes, a shaving kit, and a wallet and belt to replace ones ruined in amphibious training.[80]

For Christmas 1944, Mrs. J. B. Poindexter of the Goode community sent her son Thomas, a paratrooper serving in Luxembourg, a box of fried chicken, chittlings, and cake. Thomas wrote her a thank you letter saying he had eaten the food by a wood heater in a bombed-out barn and had enjoyed it. He asked her to send more chicken. In addition to the letter from her son, Mrs. Poindexter received a letter from one of Thomas's buddies, who wrote:

> Three of us helped Tom eat his Christmas box, and I'm wondering if it is asking too much to ask you to send us a fried chicken and cake. Tom would have us eat some of the 'chittlings,' but we liked the chicken best. If not too much to ask, we would appreciate a box.[81]

Eleanor Yowell sent her husband the one roll of film that she could get.[82] He advised her of other things he would like:

> As for my birthday, I would love to have a wedding ring. Also a pencil, some film, and send me all the air mail stationery you can, as it is very scarce over here. I really appreciate the Bedford paper....[83]

Some service personnel sent packages home, too, but relatively infrequently. These contained gifts, photographs, personal items they had acquired and wanted held for them, and collections of letters received from home that they wanted preserved. Although John Schenk complained at one point that he was not able to buy gifts in Britain because the purchaser needed a coupon and American soldiers could not get coupons, he was able to acquire a small, silver bracelet, which he had engraved and sent to his wife via a registered, air-mail letter. He also sent her linen handkerchiefs, some British coins, and an insignia of the Free French.[84]

Eleanor Yowell thanked her husband for sending her a cigarette case, bracelet and coins.[85]

John Schenk explained why he was sending home the letters he had received:

> I am going to put all my letters (from Ivylyn and others) in a package and send them home so we can have them to read over together. The way things are here we won't be able to keep them....[86]

William Yowell in spring 1943 sent his wife-to-be cigarettes and flashlight batteries from his base in South Carolina, and she asked him while he was in Tucson for pens and Hershey bars, which she could not get in Bedford. When he was stationed in England, she sent him a pencil, film, shampoo, and magazines. He requested air-mail stamps, which he had trouble getting. He mailed her his Air Medal, which he had received for flying six missions over enemy territory, and his Distinguished Flying Cross, which he received for flying thirty missions.[87]

Some families had copies of the local newspapers mailed to their loved ones in the service. The recipients did not seem to mind that the local news was dated by the time it reached them. They sometimes found uses other than reading for the newspaper.

Walker Ayres, serving in Belgium, wrote:

I enjoy the paper as it is my best source of hometown news. It usually takes from two to three months for it to reach me, but I never know the difference as it is all fresh news to me.[88]

Bennett H. Wheat, who fought in the Normandy Invasion and later in Germany, used the August 17, 1944, edition of the *Bedford Bulletin* to wrap a bayonet which he sent to his parents in Bedford. The newspaper reported this as proof that the men overseas received the newspapers that family members sent them.[89]

Poems

Several Bedford servicemen wrote poems, which they included in their letters home. Their loved ones often had the poems published in the *Bedford Bulletin*.

Capt. Dennis L. Arthur wrote the following poem for his mother for Mother's Day in May 1944:[90]

Mother's Day

On this lovely and beautiful day,
Everything so bright and gay;
May everyone stop long enough to
Remember that this is Mother's Day.

God bless all of the boys away
On this Mother's Day,
And God bless every Mother
On this beautiful Day.

And may everyone next Mother's Day
Sit at home and say,
Now I see what I was fighting for
Last Mother's Day.

P.S. Am I a poet? Love, Dennis

Frank Draper also wrote a poem for his mother for Mother's Day in 1944. He was killed the next month. The *Bedford Bulletin* printed the poem a year later in May 1945, noting that the author had been killed on D-Day:[91]

To Mother

Old Friends and New

I'm sitting here just thinking,
Of things I left behind.
A girl with brown eyes gleaming,
Of Mother so good and kind.

We miss our Mother's tender care,
We miss her apple pie,
She's the best one of them all we swear,
And we couldn't tell a lie.

Nothing compares to a loving mother,
To her kindness and concern,
Once she's gone, there is no other,
For her we'll always yearn.

When all the world is bright once more,
And full of smiling faces,
We can all go back to the old home shore,
Back to familiar places.

When all this strife is over,
After the peace is signed,
We'll forget the planes o'er Dover,
Forget the Nazi whine.

These humble lines I pen to her,
While far across the sea,
Wishing that I'd never stir,
From the land that's home to me.

So again your loving boy will say,
There's none so good and kind,
We'll meet again some happy day,
Far across the ocean's brine.

Cpl. Charles N. Overstreet, who was serving in the Southwest
Pacific, sent his wife, probably in May 1944, a poem written by an
unknown author and with no title. Mrs. Overstreet sent the poem to
the *Bedford Bulletin*, which printed it on June 1, 1944:[92]

So you're sick of the way the country's run,
And you're sick of the way the rationing's done,
And you're sick of standing around in a line,
You're sick you say, well, that's just fine!
So am I sick of the sun and the heat,
And I'm sick of the feel of my aching feet,
And I'm sick of the mud and the jingie flies,
And I'm sick of the trench when the night mush rise.
And I'm sick of the siren's wailing shriek,
And I'm sick of the groans of the wounded and weak,
And I'm sick of the sound of the bomber's dive,
And I'm sick of seeing the dead alive.
I'm sick of the roar and the noise and the din,
I'm sick of the taste of food from a can,
And I'm sick of the slaughter, I'm sick to my soul,
I'm sick of playing a killer's role.
And I'm sick of blood and of death and the smell,
And I'm even sick of myself, as well!
But I'm sicker still of Tyrant's Rule,
And conquered lands where the wild beasts drool,
But I'm cured damn quick, when I think of the day,
When all of this Hell will be out of the way;
When none of this mess will have been in vain,
And the lights of the world will blaze again.
And things will be as they were before,
And kids will laugh in the streets once more,
And the Axis flags will be dipped and furled,
And God looks down on a peaceful world.

Other Ways of Communicating—Prayers, Communing, Dreams, and Music

Many in Bedford and those in the armed forces prayed for one another. Churches in Bedford included service personnel in their prayers. On special occasions, such as D-Day, churches held special services.

Eleanor Yowell wrote her husband about those who were praying for him.

Aunt Dora, Aunt Jennie and Jeannette have all told me they pray for you every night. Doesn't that make you feel better? And I find myself praying for you at some of the oddest times.[93]

William Yowell responded:

It does make me feel so good to know that people are praying for me....[94]

Ivylyn and John Schenk prayed for one another. They also agreed on a unique way of praying or communing with one another. When they were apart during the war, they set a time—10:00 p.m.—when each would think of and pray for the other. John wrote:

Take good care of yourself darling and don't forget our prayer at 10:00 p.m. Good nite my dear. Love Always, John"[95]

(New letter) Guess I had better close and try to get a little sleep. In five minutes it will be 10:00 p.m. and we can be together for a few minutes....[96]

(Upon arrival in Britain) I am very safe but not so happy. You should be able to guess the reason for my not being happy. My happiest moments are our ten o'clock session....[97]

After John was deployed to England, he reminded Ivylyn that because of the time zone difference, she would have to think about him earlier in the day:

> Good night Dear, I will see you at 10:00 p.m. or 5:00 p.m. to you. Your Devoted Husband, John.[98]

Ivylyn also wrote about the evening time:

> Last night the moon was full. I couldn't help wishing for my sweetheart & praying you'd soon be here to love me and keep me from being lonely. You'll never be able to understand how very much that will mean to me....[99]

Couples sometimes wrote of dreaming about each other. John wrote Ivylyn from England:

> Bed time, so I will sleep and dream of you. Funny but I do quite often. Good night my sweet.[100]

> (New letter) Last night I had a dream that (I was) back home with you and we were getting ready to go on our second honeymoon. In fact for the last three nights I have dreamed about being home. I hope the saying about dreaming three nights in a row about the same thing is true....[101]

Music on the radio made couples sentimental, and they sometimes wrote each other about songs they had heard and asked if the other had also heard them and what they thought about them.

Letters Marked "Deceased" and "Return to Sender"

Letters also communicated sorrow, especially when letters were returned. When a serviceman was killed, any correspondence addressed to him was returned to the sender by military authorities. After John Schenk was killed on June 6, 1944, in the D-Day Invasion, at least twenty-four pieces of correspondence that Ivylyn had written and sent to him between May 21 and June 30, 1944, were returned to her, stamped "DECEASED" or "RETURN TO SENDER." John's name and Army postal address had been lined through or crossed out. While the dates of receipt of these returned letters were not recorded, it appears that Ivylyn Schenk received them after mid-July 1944, when the War Department sent the Schenk family a telegram informing them of John's death.[102]

Chapter 13

D-Day—Bedford's Special Tragedy

In the spring of 1944, both in Europe and in America, there was much anticipation of an Allied invasion of continental Western Europe by troops assembled in England. To keep the Germans from learning exactly where and when the invasion would take place, top Allied commanders kept the plans for the invasion a tightly-held secret. Many in Bedford knew that the men of Company A and other American units were in England, but they could only speculate about their mission. Even the servicemen who had been training in England since September 1942 did not know when or exactly where they would be landing.

Company A's Final Preparations in England

After over a year and a half in England, Company A was motivated and well-trained. John Barnes, a soldier from New York State, was sent to England in February 1944 and assigned as an individual replacement in Company A. Upon arriving at Ivybridge on a dark, rainy day, he and other replacements were taken into a brightly-lit building, where two of Company A's leaders—both from Bedford—greeted them. Barnes, in a memoir he has published on his service in Company A, has paraphrased this welcome:

> "My name is Wilkes. First Sergeant John Wilkes." A rusty-haired, burly man addressed us. "You men have been assigned to A Company. We have been in the ETO (European Theater of Operations) for 18 months and we are ready for combat." He stressed the word *ready*. "You men will be ready, too." He stressed the word *will*.
>
> The next man to address us was tall and leaner. He had the two silver bars. "My name is Captain Taylor Fellers," he drawled in a strong voice. "This company will be in the leading wave of

infantry in the invasion of Europe. You men will be part of a great force to end the war. Good luck!" That was it. No glad to have you join us. Not exactly a hearty welcome.[1]

In mid-May, Company A moved from Ivybridge to an assembly or staging area in preparation for the invasion. A fence surrounded the area, visitors were not allowed in, and the men were not allowed out. Sentries were posted to enforce the isolation.[2]

Up to this time, only about 200 men in the 29th Infantry Division had been informed of the area of the Normandy coast where the division would attack. By late May, all of the men in the division, including those in Company A, now sequestered, were briefed on the time and place for the invasion.[3]

Company A at this time had on its roster 220 men—nine officers and 211 enlisted men. On June 5, five enlisted men were absent, leaving a total of 215 officers and men present for duty.[4] The company had changed significantly in the nearly three-and-a-half years since it left Bedford for Fort Meade with a total of ninety-two men, all from the Bedford area. Now, of the 220 men in the company, only thirty-nine were from the Bedford community and had been with the unit since February 1941 when Company A left Bedford. (The thirty-nine included Allen Huddleston who was recuperating in England from a broken leg suffered in training, but not Andrew Coleman who was mortally ill.)

Many of the men from Bedford had been reassigned to other units as they were promoted or sought other types of service, and some had been released from the Army. Men from elsewhere in Virginia and from other states had joined Company A. Bedford men, still, however, provided much of the leadership of the company, including the company commander, the second in command, the company first sergeant, the supply sergeant, the mess sergeant, the communications sergeant, and many of the other non-commissioned officers in the three platoons.

On June 2 or 3, the men in Company A were moved by truck from the temporary staging area to the British port of Weymouth, located on the English Channel some seventy miles eastward from their base at

Ivybridge. There, the men boarded the British Ministry of War infantry landing ship *Empire Javelin* and settled in while waiting for Allied commanders to make the final decisions about starting the invasion.[5] (The *Empire Javelin* had been built months earlier in California. In late December 1944, a German submarine torpedoed and sank the ship in the English Channel, killing part of her crew.)[6]

Anticipation in Bedford

People in Bedford had been anticipating the invasion for months. They knew from the media that planning was underway for the invasion, and some Company A soldiers had hinted of the invasion in their letters home.

In mid-April 1944, the local defense coordinator, C. O. Updike, reported that ministers and other community leaders were preparing plans for church prayer and meditation services for the time of invasion. The day was to be known as "I Meeting Day," the "I" presumably standing for "Invasion." Church chimes and bells were to be rung on the morning of the invasion, and services were to be held in the evening at the Presbyterian and Washington Street Baptist Churches. Arrangements were also made for Big Island, in northern Bedford County.[7]

Two weeks later, the state coordinator for "I Meeting Day" reported that some people appeared to have misconceptions about this day. He reminded people that it was to be a day of prayer and suggestions on how to assist Allied soldiers, not a day of joy and celebration.[8] An editorial in the *Bedford Democrat* on May 25, 1944, spoke of widespread speculation as to the time of the invasion.[9]

Anticipation of the invasion grew towards the end of May and beginning of June. The media reported an increase in Allied bombing of French coastal areas and indicated that delays in mail coming from American service personnel in Britain could be attributed to transportation problems and pre-invasion censorship of the mail.[10]

On the afternoon of Saturday, June 3, Ivylyn Schenk was at home in Moneta, in southern Bedford County, listening to the radio. Over the radio came an announcement that excited her, if for only a few minutes. At 5:15 p.m. that day, she started a letter to her husband John, serving with Company A in England:

> My darling husband,
>   About an hour ago a program was interrupted with the announcement that Eisenhower's Headquarters announced an Allied landing on the coast of France. I was so excited that chill bumps goosed up all over me! I continued to listen and in a few minutes learned that it was all a mistake! I'm so disappointed! ...[11]

Despite all the Allied efforts to maintain secrecy about the invasion, a clerical error had led to several news agencies announcing on June 3 that Allied forces had landed in France. A twenty-two-year old British teletype operator, Joan Ellis, who was working for the London Bureau of the Associated Press after having served in the military, was practicing on what she thought was a disconnected teletype machine. There was a tape in the machine containing the message "Flash Eisenhower's headquarters announces Allied landings France." Despite all the censorship and safeguard procedures developed by the media and Allied authorities, at about 4:30 p.m. Eastern War Time, the operator somehow caused the message to be sent to New York and Latin America. In the two minutes before a follow-up "kill" message could be sent and received directing that the earlier message not be used, the erroneous report was spread widely throughout America. Some 450-500 radio stations in the United States, including those of the Central Broadcasting System and National Broadcasting System, broadcast the message, and announcements were made during sporting events. The *New York Times* reported the details of the foul-up the next day.[12]

Fortunately, the Germans appeared not to take this seriously. Berlin Radio reported on June 3 that "the invasion is nowhere near."[13]

Allied Plans for the Invasion of Normandy

The Invasion of Normandy was one of the largest military operations ever planned in the history of the world. The Allies assembled a force of 175,000 fighting men, 5,333 ships and other naval craft, and almost 11,000 aircraft.[14]

The Allied plans, known by the code name "Overlord" (sometimes "Neptune-Overlord," with "Neptune" applying to the amphibious portion of the plans), had divided the invasion area of the Normandy coast into five beach sections. These beaches were designated, from east to west, as Sword, Juno, Gold, Omaha, and Utah. Of the five landing areas, Omaha Beach would prove to be the most challenging for the Allies. Company A was assigned to the first wave of the attack on Omaha Beach.

German Defenses on the Normandy Coast

Defending the Normandy coast was the German Seventh Army, whose six divisions were deployed in the area of the five beaches where the Allies would land. The German Fifteenth Army had twenty-five additional divisions deployed to the northeast from the mouth of the Seine to the Pas de Calais opposite Dover.[15]

The Germans had stationed a single regiment of the static or vehicle-less 716th Division to defend Omaha Beach (the Germans had also stationed a single regiment at Utah Beach to the west). Shortly before the invasion, however, Allied intelligence learned that Germany's crack, mobile 352[d] Division had moved to the Omaha Beach area on training maneuvers. One regiment of the 352[d] reinforced the regiment of the 716th in the Omaha Beach area, while two other regiments of the 352[d] were deployed a few miles away.[16]

The Germans had built fortifications overlooking the beaches and placed obstacles in the water and on the beaches. General of the Army Omar Bradley, who had commanded the U.S. First Army in the invasion of Omaha and Utah Beaches (the British Second Army attacked the other three beaches), would later call Omaha Beach "truly an Atlantic Wall." He would write in his memoirs:

> The beach fortifications and terrain were formidable. There were three well-placed rows of underwater steel or concrete obstacles, most of them mined. At low tide—when we intended to land the assault forces—the beach itself was two hundred yards wide with no cover. Then came a low seawall. Beyond that were sand dunes and bluffs, slashed by five widely spaced draws which

we intended to use as exit roads from the beach. All the draws were heavily covered by enemy gun emplacements, and the area between the seawall and cliffs and dunes was sown with thousands of mines. In addition, the Germans had cleverly concealed concrete gun emplacements in the bluffs so as to enfilade almost the entire length of the beach.[17]

American Naval historian, Samuel E. Morison, would write of Omaha Beach:

Altogether, the Germans had provided the best imitation of hell for an invading force that American troops had encountered anywhere. Even the Japanese defenses of Tarawa, Peleliu, and Iwo Jima, are not to be compared to these.[18]

Allied Plans for Attacking Omaha Beach

Allied plans called for naval and aerial bombardment of the German positions on Omaha Beach before the troops landed. The Allies previously had not conducted any systematic bombardment of these positions, so as to avoid tipping off the Germans as to the location of the invasion. Navy ships were to open fire at 5:50 a.m. and continue to fire for thirty-five minutes. The battleship *Texas* and other ships were to fire on the German forces covering the beach exits toward Vierville-sur-Mer. At 6:00 a.m., 484 B-24s of the U.S. Eighth Army Air Force were to drop bombs on the German defenses. Allied troops were then to land at H-Hour, 6:30 a.m.[19]

The U.S. 29th Infantry Division, with its 116th and 115th Infantry Regiments, and the U.S. 1st Infantry Division were assigned to attack at Omaha Beach. The 116th Infantry Regimental Combat Team was assigned a portion of Omaha Beach, and this portion was divided into four sectors. The 2d Battalion of the 116th Infantry, with Companies E, F, and G, was assigned to attack in the three eastern most sectors, backed up by other units.[20]

Company A and Companies B, C, and D, all of the 1st Battalion of the 116th Infantry, were assigned to attack the fourth, western-most sector, designated as Dog Green Beach. These four companies were to attack as a column.[21]

Company A was to be the first wave of the attack against Dog Green Beach, the first ashore.[22] As D-Day veteran John Robert (Bob) Slaughter, a soldier in Company D, has put it, "Company A had the dubious honor of landing first at 6:30."[23] Six boats, loaded with most of the soldiers of Company A and lined up beside one another, were to assault the beach at H-Hour plus one minute (6:31 a.m.).[24]

Other units were to follow behind Company A. According to Slaughter, Company B was to land at 7:00, Company D at 7:10, and Company C, in reserve, at 7:20.[25] The official plan subsequently published by the War Department indicates that at H-Hour plus three minutes, 6:33 a.m., engineers and elements of the 2[d] Ranger Battalion were to land. At H+30 minutes, 7:00 a.m., the Headquarters Company of Company A, accompanied by most of Company B and an antiaircraft battery, were to land. Beginning at H+40 minutes and continuing to H+180/215 minutes, Companies D and C, other elements of the 2[d] Ranger and 5th Ranger Battalions, and additional engineer, antiaircraft, and chemical weapons units were scheduled to land.[26]

Company A Embarks for Normandy

On Sunday, June 4, Company A was aboard the *Empire Javelin* and ready to sail for Normandy. Around 5 p.m., the men learned that the attack had been postponed. General Eisenhower had delayed the invasion because of the likelihood of bad weather on the morning of Monday, June 5. The men tried to sleep aboard the ship on June 5.[27]

When the decision was subsequently made to proceed with the attack on June 6, preparations were made for the *Empire Javelin* to sail into the English Channel. The men were given last minute instructions. Each was also handed a piece of paper with the following message from General Eisenhower:

Soldiers, Sailors and Airmen of the Allied Expeditionary Force!
  You are about to embark upon the Great Crusade, toward which we have striven these many months. The eyes of the world are upon you. The hopes and prayers of liberty-loving people

everywhere march with you. In company with our brave Allies and brothers-in-arms on other Fronts, you will bring about the destruction of the German war machine, the elimination of Nazi tyranny over the oppressed peoples of Europe, and security for ourselves in a free world.

Your task will not be an easy one. Your enemy is well trained, well equipped and battle-hardened. He will fight savagely.

But this is the year 1944! Much has happened since the Nazi triumphs of 1940-41. The United Nations have inflicted upon the Germans great defeats, in open battle, man-to-man. Our air offensive has seriously reduced their strength in the air and their capacity to wage war on the ground. Our Home Fronts have given us an overwhelming superiority in weapons and muni-tions of war, and placed at our disposal great reserves of trained fighting men. The tide has turned! The free men of the world are marching together in victory!

I have full confidence in your courage, devotion to duty and skill in battle. We will accept nothing less than full victory!

Good Luck! And let us all beseech the blessing of Almighty God upon this great and noble undertaking.[28]

Each man carried equipment and arms weighing somewhere between sixty and one hundred pounds.[29]

T/Sgt. Frank Draper appears to have summarized the instructions for the early hours of D-Day in a small, black notebook. (His words are printed in the left column below; the author's interpretation is in the right column.)[30]

T/Sgt. Draper's text	Author's interpretation
H hr – 630	time to land on the beach
- 0145	earlier wake-up time, 1:45 a.m.
sleep in trousers & shirt	
gas mask, LB close by	have gas mask, life belt close by
Breakfast 2:30	eat breakfast at 2:30 a. m.
Ready to go 0400	get in landing craft at 4:00 a.m.
Hit water 4:30	landing craft lowered into water

6 Rings of bell – EM	(meaning unknown)
steady " –	(meaning unknown)
Hit before 12 disregard	(meaning unknown)
equip LB qm CANT	discard life belt, quartermaster
if possible	gear/canteen on beach perhaps

Anxiety Builds at Home with First Reports of the Invasion

On the morning of the actual invasion, Tuesday, June 6, American radio networks broadcast the first news of the Normandy Invasion around 5:00 a.m. Virginia time. All information at that hour came from German radio sources in Berlin, where it was midday. Not until three hours later was the news confirmed in London. The news was sparse.

Across America, people were said to have welcomed the news that the invasion had started, but with the realization that this was a critical point in the war against Germany. There were many reports of people dropping to their knees when they first heard the news. People later gathered in their places of worship to pray. On the night of June 6, President Roosevelt spoke on the radio and led the country in prayer. In all of this, there was reported to have been little rejoicing. People were said to have demonstrated a renewed determination to back their fighting men to the limit, in part by increasing their purchase of war bonds and offering to donate blood.[31]

The *Bedford Bulletin* sought to capture the feeling of people in Bedford upon hearing the news.

News of the invasion brought a feeling of uneasiness to hundreds of Bedford County homes for many of them have sons, husbands, and brothers in the Army in England. Old Company A of the National Guard has been in training there for nearly two years and probably was among the first landing forces, and hundreds of other Bedford County men will ultimately be thrown into the fight, and among them some casualties can be expected.[32]

As the news spread in Bedford on June 6, St. John's Episcopal Church and the Main Street Methodist Church opened their doors for those who wanted to pray. That evening, a union service of prayer was held at the Presbyterian Church, with ministers from several churches participating. Every seat on the main floor and in the gallery was filled, and many had to be turned away for lack of space.[33]

In the days that followed, the Bedford newspapers carried reports on the invasion, but there was no news of the involvement of men from Bedford. The following are extracts of news reports printed on June 8, 1944, in the *Bedford Bulletin*:

> Striking with the greatest seaborne forces in history, and protected from the air by thousands of bombing and fighter planes, the Allied army…landed at dawn on the sandy beaches between Le Harve and Cherbourg. They had surprisingly little opposition from enemy land forces and practically no opposition from the German air force, but at points on the beach losses were quite heavy from concentrated machine gun fire. A beachhead was quickly established, troops began pushing inland and within a few hours had gained a strong foothold.
>
> Landings from the sea were preceded by thousands of airborne troops, their mission being to seize strategic points and help protect those landing on the beach. The first phase of the invasion has gone better than the Allied command had dared hope for and losses have been far below what had been feared.
>
> Landing from the sea on an enemy coast is one of the most dangerous operations of war, and in this case it was on a coast supposed to be the strongest fortified in all history. The exact timing and power displayed reflects the long training given the men and the careful planning for the great event by Allied commanders.[34]

By mid-June, the Bedford community could read of progress in the invasion. The situation was reported to be improving, and General Eisenhower was said to have reported to President Roosevelt that more progress was being made than he had dared hoped at the beginning of the campaign. All reports indicated that the most critical stage of the invasion was over.[35]

Bedford citizens also could read, however, reports that the 29th Infantry Division was among the first to land on the Normandy coast and was operating on or near the base of the Cherbourg peninsula, which the Germans were fighting desperately to hold. While no one in Bedford appeared to have had direct news that Company A was fighting in Normandy, many seemed to accept that that was the case because its parent 29th Division was reported to be fighting there. Those in Bedford were said to have a mixture of anxiety and pride, a mixture of concern for their loved ones but pride that their sons, brothers, husbands, and friends had been chosen to be among the first to land on the French coast.[36]

As more detailed reports from personal observers were published, the anxiety in Bedford must have grown. One news report, published in the *Bedford Bulletin* on June 15, came from well-known war correspondent Ernie Pyle, who landed on the beach at Normandy the day after the invasion:

> Now that it is over, it seems to me a pure miracle we ever took the beach at all. For some it was easy, but in this special sector where I now am our troops faced such odds that our getting to the shore was like me whipping Joe Lewis down to a pulp....I want to tell you what opening the second front in this one sector entailed so you can know and appreciate and forever be humbly grateful to those both dead and alive who did it for you.
>
> Ashore facing us were more enemy troops than we had in our assault waves. The advantages were all theirs, the disadvantages all ours. The Germans were dug into positions they had been working on for months....
>
> A 100-foot bluff a couple of hundred yards back from the beach had great concrete gun emplacements built right into the hilltops. They opened to the sides instead of front, thus making it very hard for naval gunfire from the sea to reach them. They could shoot parallel with the beach and cover every foot of it for miles with artillery fire.
>
> Then they had hidden machine-gun nests on the forward slopes with cross fire taking in every inch of the beach....

Our only exits from the beach were several…valleys, each about 100 yards wide. The Germans made most of these into funnel-like traps, literally sowing their bottom sides with buried mines. They contained, too, barbed wire entanglements with mines attached to hidden ditches and machine-guns firing from slopes.

That is what was on shore. But our men had to go through a mass nearly as deadly before they even got ashore. Underwater obstacles were terrific…evil devices to catch our boats…masses of those great six-pronged spiders made of railroad iron…huge logs buried in the sand, pointing upward and outward, their tops just below the water. Attached to these logs were mines…they had floating mines…land mines buried in the sand…and…grass.

…the enemy had four men on shore for every three men we had approaching the shore. And yet we got on.

Our men at first simply could not get off the beach. They were utterly pinned down right at the water's edge by an inhuman wall of fire from the bluff. Our first waves were on that beach for hours instead of a few minutes before they could begin working inland….

The first crack in beach defense finally was accomplished by terrific and wonderful naval gunfire….destroyers ran right up into shallow water and had it out point blank with big guns in those concrete emplacements.

When the heavy fire stopped, our men were organized by their officers and pushed on inland….[37]

On June 22 the *Bedford Bulletin* printed another eyewitness report by a special correspondent with the *Baltimore News-Post* who, under relaxed censorship rules which permitted identification of specific units, wrote about the role of the 29th Division in the invasion.

…this (29th) division was among the first units to hit the beach. Since then it has been through some campaigns of the bitterest kind of fighting.

The division now occupies some forefront positions of the Allied line. And it has covered itself with glory….

Of the American divisions which hit the beach at "H-Hour," one was…the 29th.

It consisted largely of Virginians specially trained and outfitted for beach landings….

H-Hour boats approached the shore with suspicious care, but close in hell broke loose. Some landing boats were sunk as they were pulling down ramps for debarkation. Some men drowned. Some fell dead on the beaches. Others dug into the sand, huddled behind the low sea wall. They crawled forward and leaped forward.

They got forward. They got across the beach, up the cliff and captured Vierville and established a semi-circular defense line around it so no enemy troops could charge the beach while men and equipment poured in….

Later the 29th Division consolidated far inland. The men were already seasoned battle troops. Early trigger nervousness was all gone. The men are getting some rest. They need it. Some were on the move constantly for three days at a time….Now in Hitler's Europe, the division is fulfilling its motto (Twenty-nine, Let's Go).[38]

While the people of Bedford could read these general accounts in the newspaper and hear others on the radio, none had any specific information about Company A and other units with Bedford servicemen. They did not know for certain that their men were involved and, if they were, what was happening to them.

Across America in the days after the Allied invasion, the sale of war bonds increased, and the Red Cross reported a great rise in blood donors. In Bedford, the Red Cross reported that in the week after the invasion the number of women volunteers who showed up to help prepare surgical dressings tripled to thirty or forty women. By late July, however, the number of women volunteers was down to fifteen.[39]

Company A Hits the Beach

In landing at Normandy, Company A faced German obstacles and mines both in the water and on the beach, as well as German troops above and beyond the beach equipped with artillery, especially eighty-eight-millimeter guns, mortars, machine guns, rifles, and other weapons.

Allied naval and aerial bombardment had done little to soften up the German defenses in the particular sector where Company A was to land. Naval gunfire had been limited to thirty-five minutes of firing. Aerial bombardment was planned to follow, but the overcast weather appears to have significantly reduced the amount of aerial bombardment on target, either in terms of bombs not being dropped or not hitting the German defense positions.

As an example of the problems the Army Air Force had because of the poor flying weather, the author of a history of the American 384th Bomb Group, which was stationed in England and assigned to support the invasion, has reported that the bomber crews were disappointed that they could not have helped the ground forces more on D-Day. Because of the weather, few of the crews could see the Channel, and none had seen French soil. Many had been unable to drop their bombs because of the adverse weather. Some had bombed by instruments, and others had brought their bombs back to the base. Later in June, this unit was able to support the ground forces in Normandy by bombing bridges, airfields, and railroads, but on June 6 its assistance was limited.[40]

According to one source, 484 B-24s of the U.S. Eighth Army Air Force were to have bombed the German positions after the naval gunfire stopped, but the aircraft "missed the beach altogether and dropped their stuff on crops and cattle three miles inland."[41] Another source concluded that, "None of it (the aerial bombing)... hit the beaches at Omaha...(and) the 35 minutes of naval artillery firing at intelligence- and reconnaissance-generated targets didn't work either."[42]

On the positive side, the Allies had naval and air supremacy in the area of the Normandy Invasion. "No German aircraft interfered in any significant way with our operations at Utah and Omaha beaches on D-day. Nor did the German Navy," wrote General of the Army Bradley.[43]

Most of the men of Company A climbed into six boats, called "Landing Craft, Assault" or "LCAs," which were lowered into the sea by davits from the *Empire Javelin*. The LCAs were British-made and operated by British sailors.[44] (They were not the famous American "Higgins boats," named after their Louisiana designer and manufacturer, and used by other troops.) The cooks and perhaps a few others from Company A remained aboard the ship and were sent ashore about three days after D-Day.

One of the six landing craft carrying the men of Company A, LCA 911, sank some 500-2,000 yards from the shore.[45] Accounts as to the distance from shore and the cause of the sinking vary. George E. "Jimmy" Green, a British Royal Navy sub-lieutenant in charge of the group of landing craft for Company A, has indicated that the craft he was on, LCA 910, and LCA 911 collided as they came off the *Empire Javelin*, each sustaining damage but still able to float and operate on the water. Roy O. Stevens, a technical sergeant from Bedford, who was second in command of the men on this landing craft, is convinced the craft struck a German obstacle before it sank. He recalls the craft coming down off a wave and hitting something, punching a hole in the craft. He saw a hole about four inches round at the front of the boat and water pouring in.[46] Company A member John Barnes, who was also aboard the craft, has written that he neither heard a noise nor felt any impact before water flooded the landing craft, sinking it.[47]

A group of Rangers on another landing craft passed the foundering boat and saw "men jumping overboard and being dragged down by their loads."[48] Roy Stevens felt himself going under the water until a fellow Bedford soldier, Clyde Powers, saved his life by helping him stay up and then cutting off Stevens' pack with a knife.[49] All but one of the men (the radio operator) from the sunken craft were eventually rescued, after a harrowing experience of spending an hour or two in the cold water of the English Channel amid the turmoil of the D-Day landing. The survivors were picked up by naval craft and taken back to the *Empire Javelin*.

Aboard the *Empire Javelin*, the leader of the rescued men, Lt. Edward Gearing, placed Stevens in charge of the men and directed that they be taken back to England, reoutfitted, and returned to action. Four or five days later, the men, with fresh gear, were returned to Normandy. Lieutenant Gearing, instead of returning to England, was able to catch a ride directly to the Normandy beach, where he took command of the surviving elements of Companies A and B and organized them to fight over the following days.[50]

The other five landing craft carrying Company A soldiers continued toward the shore. Accounts vary about what happened to one of these landing craft, the one carrying the company commander, Captain Fellers. A U.S. Army historical account suggests that this craft was hit four times by mortar fire.[51] Author Stephen Ambrose, in his book *D-Day*, wrote that Captain Fellers and the men in this craft "were killed before the ramp went down." He went on to write that "It just vaporized. No one ever learned whether it was the result of hitting a mine or getting hit by an 88."[52] Sub-lieutenant Green, however, has said that he discharged Captain Fellers and the other men on the landing craft once the craft touched bottom about thirty yards from the shoreline. In one account, Green indicated he saw Fellers and the men make their way to the beach and lie down on an incline. In another, he said "I saw him (Captain Fellers) forming up, moving off (the waterline) and sort of getting organized."[53] Another account, one cited by Ambrose as a source for his statements above, reports that all thirty-two men in the group with Captain Fellers were killed, but it does not say whether they were in the boat or on the beach.[54] D-Day veteran J. R. Slaughter, who served in Company D and landed after Company A, has been reported as seeing Captain Fellers and his boat crew take a hit by an artillery shell, an explosion which "looked like it made Captain Fellers just evaporate into thin air."[55]

The other four landing craft discharged their troops in the surf or onto the beach. There, men had to contend with both the sea and the fire from German weapons. The Normandy beaches were relatively flat, and the tide had a wide range. On June 6, between 6:00 a.m. and 11:00 a.m., the tide would rise some twenty feet. By 9:00 a.m., the tide would be rising an inch a minute.[56] According to an official U.S. Army account, "At H+6 minutes (6:36 a.m.) the remaining craft grounded in water 4 to 6 feet deep, about 30 yards short of the outward band of obstacles. Starting off the craft…the men were enveloped in accurate and intense fire from automatic weapons…. "[57]

Official Accounts of Company A's Landing

The commanding officer of one of Company A's parent units, the 116th Infantry Regiment, Col. George Taylor, has been quoted as telling the officers of the 116th before the invasion began:

> The first six hours will be the toughest. That is the period when we will be weakest. But we've got to open the door. Somebody has to lead the way and if we fall, then the troops behind will do the job. They will just keep throwing men on the beaches until something breaks.[58]

An account by the Office of the Army's Chief of Military History reported:

> …The two right-flank companies (Company C of the 2[d] Ranger Battalion and Company A of the 116th Infantry) landed as scheduled in front of the Vierville draw. One craft foundered and one was hit four times by mortar fire. Men from the remaining craft struggled to shore. Intense small arms fire took toll of about two-thirds of Company A and more than half of the Ranger company before any reached the comparative shelter of the sea wall or base of the cliff….[59]

The commanding general of the 29th Infantry Division, Maj. Gen. Charles Gerhardt, with the assistance of seven survivors of Company A, wrote in an after-action report:

> …When the Company was still 5,000 yards out, the men saw the barrage from the rocket boats striking in the water about 1,000 yards to their right front. They saw nothing hit on their beach or anywhere near it. Company "A" came out on 6 assault boats. As they drew to within 700-800 yards of the beach, artillery and mortar fire began to fall among the boats. There had already been lost…one boat (which) foundered 1,000 yards out from shipping too much water…one man had drowned and the others had been picked up by Naval craft. At first the enemy shell fire was ineffective, but as the first boats drew to within 50 yards

of the sand, one was struck by an artillery shell and 2 men were mortally hit, the others taking to the water.

…What they saw was an absolutely unblemished beach, unpecked by artillery or bomb fire and wholly barren of shingle or any other cover. The first ramps were dropped at 6:36 in water that was waist deep to cover a man's head. As if this had been the signal for which the enemy waited, the ramps were instantly enveloped in a crossing of automatic fire which was accurate and in great volume. It came at the boats from both ends of the beach. Company "A" had planned to move in 3 files from each boat, center file going first, then flank files peeling off to the right and left. The first men tried it. They crumpled as they sprang from the ship, forward into the water. Then order was lost. It seemed to the men that the only way to get ashore with a chance for safety was to dive head-first into the water …A few had jumped off, trying to follow the S.O.P. (standing operating procedure), and had gone down into water over their heads. They were around the boat now, struggling with their equipment and trying to keep afloat. In one of the boats, a third of the men had become engaged in this struggle to save themselves from a quick drowning….many were lost before they had a chance to face the enemy. Some of them were hit in the water and wounded. Some drowned then. Others, wounded, dragged themselves ashore and upon finding the sands, lay quiet and gave themselves shots, only to be caught and drowned within a few minutes by the on-racing tide….But some men moved safely through the bullet fire to the sands, then found that they could not hold there; they went back into the water and used it as cover, only their heads sticking out above it. Others sought the cover of the underwater obstacles. Many were shot while doing so. Those who survived kept moving shoreward with the tide and in this way finally made their landing….They were in this tide-borne movement when Company "B" came in behind them. Others who had gotten into the sands and had burrowed in, remained in their holes until the tide caught up to them, then they, too, joined the men in the water.

Within 7 to 10 minutes after the ramps had dropped, Company "A" had become inert, leaderless and almost incapable of action. The Company was almost entirely bereft of officers. Lt. Edward

N. Gearing was back where the first boat had foundered. All the officers were dead except Lt. Elijah (sic—Elisha Ray) Nance who had been hit in the heel as he left the boat, and then again in the body as he reached the sands. Lt. Edward Tidrick was hit in the throat as he jumped from the ramp into the water. He went onto the sands and flopped down 15 feet from Pvt. Leo J. Nash. He raised up to give Nash an order…bleeding from the throat… "ADVANCE WITH THE WIRE CUTTERS!" It was futile. Nash had no wire cutters. In giving this order Tidrick (made) himself a target (for) just an instant. Nash saw machine-gun bullets cleave him from head to pelvis.

German machine-gunners along the cliff directly ahead were now firing straight down into the party. Capt. Taylor N. Fellers and Lt. Benjamin R. Kearfoot had come in with 30 men of Company "A" aboard L.C.A. No. 1015, but what happened to that boat team in detail will never be known. Every man was killed; most of them being found along the beach.

In those first 5 to 10 minutes when the men were fighting in the water, they dropped their weapons and even their helmets to save themselves from drowning, and learning by what they saw that their landing had deteriorated into a struggle for personal survival, every sergeant was either killed or wounded. It seemed to the others that enemy snipers had spotted their leaders and had directed their fire so as to exterminate them. A medical boat came in….The Germans machine-gunned every man in the section….Their bodies floated with the tide. By this time the leaderless infantrymen had foregone any attempt to get forward against the enemy and where men moved at all, their efforts were directed toward trying to save any of their comrades they could reach. The men in the water pushed wounded men ahead of them so as to get them ashore….Those who reached the sands crawled back and forth into the water, pulling men to land to save them from drowning, in many cases only to have them shot out of their hands or to be hit themselves….The weight of the infantry equipment handicapped all of this rescue work….(if) left unhelped…the wounded drowned because of it. The able-bodied who pulled them in stripped themselves of their equipment so as to move more freely in the water, then cut away the assault jackets and the equipment of the wounded, and dropped them in the water. Within 20 minutes of striking the beach, Company "A" ceased to be an assault company and became a forlorn little rescue party bent on survival and the saving of the lives of the other men. Orders were no longer being given by anyone; each man who remained sound, moved or not as he saw fit. The leading hand in the rescue work, by the account of all survivors, was a First Aid man, Tech.-5 Tom Breeding.

It was estimated by the men that one third of Company "A" hit the beach. One hour and 40 minutes after the landing, 8 men from the boat which had landed on the far right flank...worked up to the edge of the cliff. They saw no others from the company who had advanced as far....Two of the men of the Company had joined a group from the Second U.S. Rangers, who were assaulting over the cliff to the right...and fought with them throughout the day. Otherwise Company "A" 's contribution to the attack appears to have been a cipher. The few survivors stayed at the cliff bottom during the afternoon and joined the Battalion that night.[60]

In his memoirs, General of the Army Bradley described the Omaha Beach invasion as a "bloodbath" that went on for too long. After six hours, Americans held only ten yards of the beach. He credits the success in eventually breaking out across the beach to two Army leaders, personal gallantry of the men, and naval destroyers that moved in dangerously close to the beaches to provide fire support. The men moved beyond the beach to the seawall and bluffs after being rallied by Col. George A. Taylor, commander of the 116th Infantry, who shouted, "They're killing us here! Let's move inland and get killed," and Brig. Gen. Norman D. Cota, assistant commander of the 29th Infantry Division, who yelled, "Two kinds of people are staying on this beach, the dead and those who are going to die. Now let's get the hell out of here."[61]

While Company A and other brother units suffered devastating losses, overall, things went relatively better for the 116th Infantry Regimental Combat Team, and the unit went on that day to take Vierville-sur-Mer.[62]

Accounts by Company A Survivors from Bedford

Four Bedford men, all combat survivors of D-Day, have spoken of their experiences. The following remarks were first published either in the early 1980s or in 1994 on the occasion of the 50th anniversary of D-Day.[63]

Elisha Ray Nance, the only officer of Company A to survive the invasion and the war, although wounded on D-Day, has spoken of the company's eagerness for the invasion to begin and of what transpired during the invasion:

> We Bedford boys, we competed to be in the first wave. We wanted to be there. We wanted to be the first on the beach.

> …That's the spirit this outfit had. We had trained for so long we were hoping this would be the real thing. We'd been in the service for three years. We were professionals by then, only thing was that we hadn't been in combat yet.

> They were waiting for us. The minute the ramp went down, they opened up. We must have been torn up pretty badly. A good many men were killed on the ramp. (He saw four Bedford soldiers—John Reynolds, J. D. Clifton, John Wilkes, and John Schenk—hit by machine gun or sniper fire.)

> There was a kind of numbing shock. When our own aid man came, he'd been clipping first-aid packets off the dead, he told me that he'd seen Captain Feller's body. I was numbed.

Clyde Powers, who, along with Roy Stevens, survived the sinking of their boat offshore has said:

> I don't think most realized what they was getting into. We had no concept of what was going to happen.

G. E. Overstreet, who called D-Day the longest day of his life, provided the information for the following account:

When we got off the boat, the guy in front of me, he got killed. I had a flame-thrower and I dropped that, grabbed his rifle and took off. I got behind a tank and stayed there until it got hit. I took off for the beach. (As Overstreet struggled across the surf, he was shot in the abdomen.) I had to keep going. (With only cursory medical attention, Overstreet lay on the beach until 4:30 the next morning. While bodies washed ashore around him, he lay there 'scared to death.')

Roy Stevens, who survived the sinking of his boat, later found the grave of his twin brother Ray on the Normandy coast. Roy, who was subsequently wounded at St. Lo, has said:

I'm not bragging, but I think we were the finest, best trained men in the Army.

There was a challenge and some fascination. We were young, and maybe we didn't know fear, didn't know the danger....We were a proud outfit. Most anybody would have been proud to be in that outfit....

We was a crack outfit and we never got a chance to prove ourselves. That's kind of what got me. There was no cover, nothing that day, just manpower....

It was pure luck that I lived. It's not what you know, not how well you are trained. If that bullet or piece of shrapnel has your name on it, it's going to find you.

Ray would've done it again. He would've gone to preserve what we have here in this country....

I know they died for a reason, for a cause. The world is better off today because of what we did.

Other Bedford Men Serving on D-Day

About fifty men from Bedford County participated in the D-Day Invasion on June 6, 1944. They fought on the ground, on the sea, and in the air.

Most of the men involved in the invasion served with the U.S. Army. There were thirty-eight Bedford men present for duty in Company A alone. Others landed on Omaha Beach with Companies C and F of the 116th Infantry Regiment. Sgt. Boyd E. Wilson, who had served in Company A earlier, went ashore with the 1st Infantry Division, and there were men from Bedford in other divisions landing in Normandy.

At least two Bedford men served with elements of the U.S. Navy operating in the English Channel on D-Day. At least two or three others flew missions with the U.S. Army Air Forces in support of the invasion. Lt. William Yowell flew a bombing mission over Normandy on D-Day, and Lt. William Overstreet flew three missions over France that day in his P-51 Mustang fighter, dropping bombs when no German fighter aircraft were present.

More Bedford men would fight in Normandy in the days and weeks that followed, and more would serve in subsequent campaigns not only in France but also Belgium, the Netherlands, Luxembourg, and Germany.

(See Appendix B for details on Bedford men serving in the Invasion of Normandy and later battles in France.)

Number of Men Lost on D-Day

Company A's losses on D-Day, mostly in the first fifteen minutes of combat, were staggering. Accounts differ as to how many of the 215 men present for duty were lost. The *Bedford Bulletin* reported in 1994 that 93 percent of the men were killed, missing, or wounded.[64] (The 93 percent apparently included the men whose landing craft sank and who were later rescued.) Other reports indicate that somewhere between ninety-one and 102 men were killed or missing in action, with approximately fifty-four wounded, i.e., some 67-73 percent killed, missing, and wounded. The official morning reports for Company

A show present for duty 215 officers and men on June 5, 145 on June 6, and 126 on June 7—the last representing a loss of 42 percent compared to the number of men present for duty on June 5. The morning reports for June 6 and 7, however, were prepared under the most extenuating circumstances and appear to be incorrect in many respects; for example, they list only seven men from Bedford County as killed or missing.[65]

In any case, only a small portion of the men survived the first wave of the attack and were able to continue to fight on the beach and beyond on D-Day. About twenty-seven men in the landing craft that sank were rescued and returned to England for re-outfitting before being sent back to Normandy four days later.

In subsequent days, Company A, down to some fifty men, continued to fight toward St. Lo and Vire. Later in the war, gaining replacements, Company A fought toward Brest, France, and on into Germany.[66]

A year later, on June 6, 1945, after the German surrender, Company A, then in Spaden, Germany, observed the first anniversary of D-Day. John Barnes, who had served in Company A since February 1944, observed the tremendous turnover in personnel in Company A and reflected on the losses. He believed that as of June 1945 he was the only rifleman remaining in Company A who had first trained with the unit in England in spring 1944 and then gone on to fight with the unit throughout its engagements in France and Germany.[67]

Barnes has also reported that Company A clerk Gil Murdock claimed to have seen a total of over 1,100 different men listed on Company A morning reports, apparently over the extended period in which Company A was in combat.[68] If true, this would mean the loss of hundreds of men and a continuous effort to replace them in order to sustain a company of some 200 men in combat.

As for Company A's brother and parent units, they, too, suffered staggering losses on D-Day. Many men were killed in the other three companies of the 1st Battalion, including the commanders of Companies B and D, which followed Company A onto the beach.[69] The 116th Infantry Regiment had a planned strength (table of organization and equipment, or TOE) of 3,119 men and officers, and the 29th Infantry Division had a planned strength of 14,281.[70] On D-Day alone, the 116th Infantry sustained losses of more than 800 officers and men. For the entire war, the 29th Infantry Division, which received replacements for the dead and injured, suffered 20,668 casualties, which represents 130 percent of the division's planned total strength during the war. Some 4,839 officers and men died as a result of enemy action, 329 were missing in action, and 354 were prisoners of war. Some 15,146 received the Purple Heart medal for being wounded.[71]

The 116th Infantry Regiment received a citation for extraordinary heroism and outstanding performance for its actions in the Normandy Invasion. The citation concluded with the following:

> ...The successful assault and landing of the 116th made possible subsequent landings of other elements.
> Nor did the 116th stop when its beachhead had been attained. It pushed to the south and captured St. Clair-sur-Elle, Couvains, St. Andre De Liepine and Martinville in bitter hedgerow to hedgerow combat that enabled another infantry unit to capture St. Lo.[72]

General of the Army Bradley perhaps best summed up the invasion on Omaha Beach:

> Omaha Beach...was a nightmare. Even now it brings pain to recall what happened there on June 6, 1944. I have returned many times to honor the valiant men who died on that beach. They should never be forgotten. Nor should those who lived to carry the day by the slimmest of margins. Every man who set foot on Omaha Beach that day was a hero.[73]

Approximately 4,500 Allied service personnel lost their lives on the first day of the Normandy Invasion, June 6, 1944.[74] Many more would die or be wounded in the weeks and months of fighting that followed. Company A would be one of the hardest hit units in the invasion.

Bedford's Losses on D-Day

Of the thirty-eight men from Bedford County present for duty in Company A, nineteen were killed in action on June 6.

In addition to these nineteen, another man was killed on D-Day who had ties to Bedford County and Roanoke County. This man was Benjamin R. Hubbard. (Private First Class Hubbard, who served in Company F of the 116th Infantry Regiment, came from the Vinton area near the border between Bedford and Roanoke Counties. His induction records are recorded in Roanoke County, he is listed under both Roanoke and Bedford Counties in a book listing all Virginians killed in the war, and at the Bedford County Courthouse his name is on an honor roll inside the courthouse but not on a plaque outside memorializing Bedford men killed while serving with the 116th Infantry.) Counting Private First Class Hubbard raises to twenty the number of Bedford County men killed on D-Day.

These men were either directly killed in action, were reported missing in action and eventually officially declared killed in action, or wounded so severely that they would soon die of their wounds.[75] Many appear to have been killed by German fire in the first fifteen minutes of landing on Omaha Beach. Some likely died of drowning, perhaps after being wounded. Apart from the dead, others were wounded in action.

The remains of most of the dead were buried in Normandy. For some, burial in Normandy would be permanent; for others, their remains would be returned to Bedford a few years later. Remains of yet others washed out into the Channel or were otherwise never recovered and identified.

One of the nineteen Bedford men in Company A, T/Sgt. Frank Draper, was seriously wounded and then evacuated on one of the landing craft. Fellow Company A soldier John Barnes, who was rescued after his landing craft sank hundreds of yards off the beach, has reported that he saw the sergeant lying on the floor of a landing craft that was returning from the beach and that he lived only a few more minutes. (Barnes also reported seeing on the floor a second soldier, whom he could not identify and who was dead.)[76] Information attributed to Technical Sergeant Draper's mother indicates that he was wounded, could not get any medical aid for twelve hours, and was carried to a hospital in England where he was either dead on arrival or died soon after.[77] Frank Draper was buried temporarily in a cemetery in England until his remains were returned to Bedford in 1948.

No one in Bedford had heard from the men in Company A for weeks. It was not until July 10, 1944—five weeks after the June 6 invasion—that word first came to Bedford that a Bedford soldier in Company A, Captain Fellers, had been killed in the invasion. This first report was unofficial, coming in the form of a letter from an acquaintance of the soldier.[78] A week later, on July 16 and 17, the first official telegrams began to arrive in Bedford informing families of the deaths of their loved ones during the June 6 invasion, an event that by that time had taken place six weeks earlier.[79]

Chapter 14

The Aftermath—Bedford's Sacrifice

World War II, and especially D-Day, made a mark on Bedford—a mark likely never to be forgotten.

About one of every ten citizens in the county served in the armed forces during the war. Most everyone in the small community likely knew several young men who were serving. Often, they were relatives or friends.

Bedford men and women in the military, as well as their families, came to know well the meaning of sacrifice. Many spent not just months but years in the service. Some served more than four years. Most returned to Bedford. Many of the men returned wounded, and some had suffered for months or years as prisoners of war.

About 5 percent of the men who served paid the ultimate sacrifice, dying in service to their country. The remains of some of the dead were returned to Bedford for reinterment after the war, while the remains of others remained buried overseas or were never found.

Most families were fortunate enough to welcome their loved ones back home. Too many were not. Two particularly unfortunate families—the Hobacks and the Parkers—each lost two sons to the war. Many families had the bittersweet experience of losing one son while having other sons return.

The first Bedford County serviceman to lose his life in combat in the war, William H. Newton, the seaman, first class, lost in action on October 31, 1941, when a German submarine sank his ship, was killed even before America entered the war. It was almost another year before the next casualty was reported. Then casualties began to grow, increasing the community's grief. In January 1944, five Bedford men were killed in the Anzio Invasion. In the summer of 1944, grief turned to shock when the Bedford community learned of the loss of so many of its young men on a single day—June 6, D-Day. A year later, in the week of June 18-24, 1945, the last three Bedford men to lose their lives in combat in the war—Pfc. Thomas H. Byrd, Pvt. Herman Boyd, and Capt. Raymond O. Kidd—died in the Pacific on the islands of Okinawa and Ie Shima. Even after the firing stopped in August 1945, and before President Truman declared a cessation of hostilities at the end of 1946, several Bedford men were killed in accidents or died of natural causes while serving in the armed forces.

Bedford Learns of D-Day Losses

The Bedford community was slow to learn of the deaths of its servicemen on D-Day. Not until July 10, 1944—more than a month after June 6—did any news of even a single D-Day casualty arrive in Bedford, and this first news was in a condolence letter, not an official government communication.

The *Bedford Bulletin*, on the front page of its July 13 edition, reported that the family of Company A's commander, Capt. Taylor Fellers, had received on July 10 a letter from England from a Mrs. Lunscomb. Captain Fellers and Lt. Bill Williams, a fellow soldier from Lynchburg and Company B, had visited in Mrs. Lunscomb's home. In the letter, Mrs. Lunscomb offered her condolences, taking for granted that the Fellers family had already been notified of their son's death by the U.S. Government. Mrs. Lunscomb wrote that Lieutenant Williams, who had been wounded during the invasion and was in a hospital in England, had called her and then written her, telling her that Captain Fellers had been killed in action. Williams had not witnessed the death, but had talked to someone who had.

In reporting about this letter, the *Bedford Bulletin* offered the following observations: Since no official word had been received, there was still a chance that Captain Fellers had not been killed but was wounded too badly to send word home. While his parents were said to be convinced of his death, officials had warned that it was very risky to accept as final any reports sent home by men in battle since they could, during all the excitement and confusion, make mistakes. Mrs. Lunscomb's letter did not report the exact date of death, but her letter was dated June 29, and she reported that the death occurred some three weeks prior, which would place the date near the start of the invasion of France.[1]

It was actually mid-July, some forty days or almost six weeks after D-Day, before individual Bedford families, including the Fellers family, began receiving official notifications that their loved ones had been killed on June 6. These notifications, which were received beginning on Sunday, July 16, and Monday, July 17, were in the form of telegrams from the War Department addressed to the next of kin of the deceased, usually the serviceman's mother or wife. Notifications did not come all at once. Indeed, the family of one man killed on D-Day did not receive official notification until late September.[2]

Elizabeth Teass, who operated the Western Union telegram office in Jones (Green's) Drug Store, received the telegrams in Bedford, after they were relayed from nearby Roanoke. She has recalled starting out the morning of July 16 or 17 by typing "Good morning. Go ahead. Bedford." Back came the reply "We have casualties." She received nine such telegrams that day, seven reporting the deaths of Bedford servicemen in France on June 6 and two others reporting service deaths elsewhere. The telegrams came one after another, and she had to enlist Sheriff J. P. "Jim" Marshall, Harry Carder, who was associated with a local funeral home, and taxi service owner Roy Israel to help the regular delivery man, Frank Thomas, deliver all the telegrams, especially to families living outside the town.[3] More came the next day.

Only when the two weekly Bedford newspapers pulled together and published the reports of the individual casualties did the community begin to become aware of the magnitude of Bedford's D-Day losses. Even then the news was confusing and the number of casualties understated as reports came in piecemeal.

On July 20, the *Bedford Bulletin*, under a front-page headline reading "Nine Bedford Men Killed in Action," began its report as follows:

This has been a sad and anxious week for Bedford with many telegrams arriving announcing that Bedford men, most of them members of Company A, 116th Infantry, of the 29th Division, were killed or missing in action. Families who received word that their

men were only wounded considered themselves fortunate in view
of the darker news contained in some of the official telegrams
from the war department.[4]

The newspaper went on to report that eight Bedford County men
had been killed in the Normandy Invasion (M/Sgt. John L. Wilkes,
S/Sgt. John B. Schenk, Pfc. John Reynolds, Pvt. Bedford Hoback,
Pvt. Clifton G. Lee, T/Sgt. Frank Draper, Jr., Pfc. John Daniel Clifton,
and M/Sgt. John Wesley Dean). The *Bulletin* reported that Captain
Fellers was officially listed as missing in action, not killed. The ninth
man reported killed was Pvt. Hudson M. Lacy, who had earlier been
declared missing in action in Italy on January 26, 1944.[5]

The *Bedford Democrat*, on the same day, also reported significant losses to the Bedford community. Its front-page headline read
"Invasion Day Brings Deep Sorrow to Bedford Homes, Many Men
Reported Lost." According to the *Democrat*, families from the town
of Bedford and elsewhere in Bedford County had received messages
from the War Department between Sunday, July 16, and Wednesday,
July 19, that sixteen men from the Bedford community had been killed
or were missing in action and that several more were wounded since
the D-Day Invasion. Most were said to be from Company A.[6]

The *Democrat* indicated that the families of fourteen members of
Company A had been notified that their men had been either killed
or were missing in action since June 6. Seven were reported to have
been killed, and seven were reported as missing in action. The men
mentioned were S/Sgt. Leslie C. Abbott, Pfc. Wallace R. Carter, Pfc.
John D. Clifton, T/Sgt. Frank P. Draper, Jr., Pvt. Bedford T. Hoback,
Capt. Taylor N. Fellers, Pvt. Clifton G. Lee, S/Sgt. Earl L. Parker,
Pfc. Jack G. Powers, Pfc. John F. Reynolds, Cpl. Weldon Rosazza,
S/Sgt. John B. Schenk, M/Sgt. John L. Wilkes, and S/Sgt. Elmere P.
Wright. (Not included in this initial report on July 20 were five men
from Bedford and Company A who were later reported to have been
killed or missing in action on D-Day—Pfc. Nick N. Gillaspie, S/Sgt.
Raymond S. Hoback, T/Sgt. Ray O. Stevens, S/Sgt. Gordon H. White,
Jr., and Sgt. Grant C. Yopp.)

The *Democrat* reported that in addition to these fourteen men, one other man associated with Company A and Bedford had died of illness in the weeks after D-Day—Pfc. Andrew J. Coleman. It also reported that in fighting elsewhere in recent weeks three other Bedford community men had been killed in action and four wounded in action.[7]

Printed on the front page were pictures of five servicemen. Four were from Company A—M/Sgt. John L. Wilkes, reported killed on D-Day, and three reported missing in action on D-Day, including Capt. Taylor N. Fellers, Pfc. Wallace R. Carter, and Cpl. Weldon A. Rosazza. Also pictured was M/Sgt. John Wesley Dean, a member of Company F, killed on June 17 in France.[8]

One of the first families to receive official notification was that of Mr. and Mrs. John S. Hoback, who lived in the Center Point community, just northeast of the town of Bedford. The Hobacks received a telegram on Sunday, July 16, that their son Bedford had been killed in France on June 6. The next day they received word that their son Raymond was missing in action in France since June 6.[9]

Five other families of men in Company A received official word on July 17 that their loved ones had been killed in France on June 6 or were missing in action since that date. The parents of John Schenk and Frank Draper, and the wife of John Wilkes were informed that their loved ones had been killed. The wives of Taylor Fellers and Earl Parker were informed that their husbands were missing in action.[10]

On July 18, the parents of Jack Powers received notification that their son was missing in action in France. On July 19, the parents of John Clifton were notified that their son had been killed in action on June 6, and the parents of Elmere Wright and Wallace Carter were informed that their sons were missing in action.

On unreported dates during that week, the parents of John Reynolds and the sister of Clifton Lee received word that their loved ones had been killed in action on June 6, and the father of Leslie "Dickie" Abbott was informed that his son was missing in action since June 6.

Some of the men wounded in the invasion were reported to have been transferred to Army hospitals in England. Sgt. Robert Fizer, of

Company A, wrote his parents that on the first day of the invasion the transport ship on which he was riding had been sunk. He stated that, fortunately, all the 2,500 men on board except five were saved. The men were taken back to England and, after a few days of recuperation, were sent to join the attack in France.[11]

The newspaper reported some of the details of the service and death of Pfc. Andrew J. Coleman. Coleman had entered the service with Company A on February 3, 1941, deployed with it to Britain, become ill in February 1944 while training in Britain, and returned to the United States in May. He died in a military hospital in White Sulphur Springs, West Virginia, on July 16.[12]

As confusing as all of this reporting may have been, if one counted carefully, this July 20 edition of the *Bedford Democrat* informed the Bedford community that fifteen of its young men had been killed or were missing in action on D-Day.

The deaths of others killed on D-Day were reported later. While T/Sgt. Roy Stevens found his twin brother Ray's temporary grave in the Normandy Beach area just a few days after D-Day, the government did not the notify the Stevens family of Ray's death until September 23, three-and-a-half months after D-Day.[13]

As indicated previously, in the final analysis, it would be determined that nineteen Bedford County men from Company A were killed or missing in action on D-Day. Counting as a Bedford man Benjamin R. Hubbard, who served in Company F and had associations with Roanoke County as well as Bedford County, Bedford County's loss on D-Day was twenty of its young men.

The general impact on Bedford of the D-Day losses—although not the deep devastation felt by families of those killed—was captured in a letter Eleanor Yowell wrote on July 25, 1944, to her husband in England:

> I haven't written you about the boys from here who were lost in the Invasion. There were right many of them, way too many. John Schenk, a good friend of yours, Frank Draper, who was in school with me, and two Hoback brothers were among the lot. Capt. Fellers and Earl Parker are reported missing. You will read

it all in the *Bulletin.* Apparently…Company A, really was "cannon fodder," as they were in the lead assaults to hit those heavily fortified Normandy beaches.

The town has been in a state of shock once the telegrams started coming into Western Union. Because of its being located in Charlie Green's drugstore, the news spread like wildfire. I just hated to write you about it. The war is really hitting home now.[14]

Bedford's Sacrifice in the Normandy Invasion and Liberation of France

The Bedford community paid a great sacrifice in the Invasion of Normandy and the liberation of France. Much attention has been given to the Bedford community's loss of nineteen men in Company A on D-Day, but Bedford's total loss in France was more than twice that number.

At least forty-one Bedford County men were killed in action in the Normandy Campaign and later campaigns to liberate France. Twenty were killed on D-Day alone (nineteen from Company A plus Benjamin R. Hubbard, who was in Company F of the 116th Infantry and had ties to Roanoke County as well as Bedford County). An additional nine were killed in the overall Normandy Campaign, including fighting off the coast of Normandy. Twelve more Bedford County men were killed in later battles in France.

There is a memorial outside the Bedford County Courthouse that pays tribute by name to some of the Bedford County men in the 116th Infantry who were killed in France, but this memorial does not recognize many other Bedford men who fought and died there.

The memorial outside the courthouse consists of a large stone on which is mounted a bronze plaque with the names of twenty-three Bedford County men of the 116th Infantry Regiment, 29th Infantry Division, who gave their lives in the preparation for and the participation in the Normandy Invasion and later battles of World War II. (The names of the twenty-three are included in Appendix B.)

Of the twenty-three men whose names are on the plaque, twenty-one had served in Company A. The other two served in the 116th Infantry's Company C and Company F, which were based in other areas of southwest Virginia before the war. (Benjamin Hubbard of Company F of the 116th Infantry is not listed on this plaque, although he is listed on a plaque inside the courthouse.)

Of the twenty-one men in Company A listed, nineteen died in the D-Day Invasion. All nineteen probably died on June 6, and eighteen probably died on the beach or in the surf. One probably died after being wounded and evacuated from the beach. Most government information cites June 6 as the date of death for each of the nineteen.

(It is possible, but not likely, that two of the men may have died on June 7, instead of June 6. Frank Draper, who was mortally wounded on June 6 and evacuated from the beach by boat, died later on June 6, or possibly on June 7, at sea or en route to or at a hospital in England. Unlike the others, he was buried in England, until his remains were returned to Bedford.[15] Earl Parker appears to have been officially declared missing in action on June 6. Information believed to have been provided by his mother, however, lists his date of death as June 7.[16] The website for the American Battle Monuments Commission gives his date of death as June 7, 1945, which is clearly not the date he was reported as missing in action. For a man missing in action, such as Staff Sergeant Parker, the government declared him killed in action a year and a day after he had been reported missing in action, assuming no new information had developed. This could be the source of the June 7 date provided by his mother.)

Two other men in Company A listed on the plaque died in mid-July. One was the aforementioned Andrew J. Coleman, who had trained with Company A in England but died of illness in the United States, and the other was Sgt. Charles W. Fizer, who was killed in action on July 11 near St. Lo in Normandy.[17]

The two soldiers listed on the plaque under Companies F and C, M/Sgt. John W. Dean and Pvt. Joseph E. Parker, Jr., were killed in France on June 17 and August 27, respectively.

A summary of Bedford County's losses in the Normandy Invasion and later battles of France can be found in Appendix B.

Bedford's Comparative Loss on D-Day

As for the June 6 Normandy Invasion itself, Bedford County probably lost more men on D-Day, per capita, than any other community in America.

Similar statements have been distorted by some and challenged by others. Some statements incorrectly suggest that Bedford's D-Day losses came from only the town of Bedford. Some of these statements also mistakenly report a population for the town of 3,000, instead of the Census figure of nearly 4,000. In fact, about one-third of the Bedford men lost on D-Day came from the town, while about two-thirds came from other areas of Bedford County, which had a total population, including the town, of just under 30,000.

Still, a loss in one day's action of twenty servicemen from an American community of 30,000 was probably, on a per capita basis, a unique occurrence on D-Day, indeed in all of World War II. The circumstances themselves were unique. The mission for Company A—serving as the first wave of an assault landing from the sea—was one of the most dangerous of military operations. The enemy had been preparing its defenses for years, and enemy forces in the area where Company A landed, as contrasted to other areas of the Normandy beaches, had suffered little damage from Allied aerial and naval bombardment. Company A, originally a National Guard unit, still had a relatively high percentage of its men from Bedford. Similarly, of the divisions engaged in the June 6 D-Day Invasion, the 29th Infantry Division was the only original National Guard division and thus probably the only unit with a relatively high percentage of men from the same communities.

It is possible, of course, that a large community, say, New York City, may have lost more than twenty men in the June 6 invasion. It is also possible that some small community in America may have had a greater loss per capita on D-Day (say, perhaps, one man from a population of ten). This author has not come across any such claim. While this author knows of no official study regarding relative D-Day losses by American communities, he believes that, given (a) the unique circumstances in which Company A found itself during the invasion, (b) Bedford County's high loss on D-Day and small population, (c) the fact that other D-Day divisions recruited more broadly, and (d) the absence of claims from other communities, it is not only probable but highly likely that in losing twenty men, Bedford County lost more men on D-Day, per capita, than any other community in America.[18]

The Anzio Invasion and Bedford Men in the 83ᵈ Chemical Mortar Battalion

While many know of Bedford's sacrifice with Company A on D-Day in the Normandy Invasion, few may be aware of the community's loss of five men on January 26, 1944, in a unit participating in the Anzio Invasion.

In January 1944, Allied forces, in an attempt to break a stalemate in the fighting with German forces in Italy, launched an amphibious assault against the coastal resort area of Anzio, about thirty miles southeast of Rome. A U.S. Army Ranger task force with three Ranger units, a paratrooper unit, and two companies of the 83ᵈ Chemical Mortar Battalion attacked early in the morning of January 22.[19] The 83ᵈ was equipped with thirty-six 4.2-inch (or 107 millimeter) mortars, capable of firing white phosphorus rounds to make smoke screens and high explosive rounds to destroy the enemy.[20]

On the evening of January 26, Allied reinforcements were sent in by sea from Sicily. Two of the vessels in the American and British convoy were sunk by enemy mines or submarines. One was a British landing ship tank or truck, LST 422, and the other was an American landing craft infantry, LCI 32. According to unofficial reports, 600 men were aboard LST 422, including the Headquarters Company and Companies C and D of the 83ᵈ Chemical Mortar Battalion, along with large supplies of phosphorous and other explosive mortar rounds and gasoline. About twelve miles out from Anzio, a major explosion took place aboard LST 422, probably caused by a German mine. The explosion set off the volatile cargo and the ship was set ablaze. An order was given to abandon ship. Many of the men who had survived the initial explosion and the fire jumped into the cold water. Many drowned. Only some 170 of the 600 men survived.[21]

Five men from Bedford County were members of the 83ᵈ Chemical Mortar Battalion and perished on January 26, presumably on LST 422 and in the cold waters, or possibly on LCI 32.[22] James J. Dudley, technician, fifth grade, has been identified as a member of Company D. Three others from Bedford who were killed are T/5 Carlton A. Bennett, Pvt. Hudson M. Lacy, and Pvt. Charlie M. Sneed, Jr. The mother of the fifth man, T/5 Charles J. Gibbs, would later provide the Bedford County history committee a short account of her son's death. She had few details beyond the following, which the chaplain of her son's unit had written:

> If you have not heard the circumstances of the tragedy that befell our Battalion last January 26, you will be interested I am sure to receive what details I can give you. On that day a part of the Battalion was en route to the Anzio beachhead....The vessel on which the men were traveling on January 26 struck a mine a few miles out from Anzio. She was loaded with ammunition and gasoline and there was a fierce fire and explosions....Charles' body has not been recovered.[23]

The bodies of Carlton Bennett and Hudson Lacy were also not recovered, and their names, along with that of Charles Gibbs, are listed on the tablets of the missing at the Sicily-Rome American Cemetery in Nettuno, Italy. Two bodies were recovered. James Dudley is buried in the cemetery at Nettuno. The remains of Charlie Sneed were returned to Bedford and are buried in Oakwood Cemetery.[24]

American and British authorities did not publicize and perhaps even suppressed information about the loss of these two naval craft and the large number of men aboard. This event is not mentioned in the U.S. Army's history of World War II, a major book on the Anzio Invasion by a British news correspondent, and the *New York Times* coverage for that period.[25]

Bedford and the Malmedy Massacre

The Malmedy Massacre was yet another tragedy involving several Bedford County men. On December 17, 1944, near the Belgian town of Malmedy, a U.S. Army artillery observation battery, Battery B, part of the 285th Field Artillery Observation Battalion, found itself caught in the German counterattack at the outset of the Battle of the Bulge. Elements of a German SS Panzer Division attacked the battery, and the lightly-armed American unit surrendered. The Germans moved the men to a field near the road and then mowed them down, primarily with automatic weapons fire from three armored vehicles. German soldiers walked among the Americans lying on the ground and shot some of the men. Later, German armored vehicles driving by shot into the Americans. At least eighty-three, perhaps as many as eighty-six, Americans were killed.[26]

Three young men from Bedford were serving in Battery B that day. Two—Pfc. Warren Davis and Pfc. Richard B. Walker—were killed in the massacre. The third, S/Sgt. William H. Merriken, was hit twice in the back by the automatic weapons fire. Merriken lay quietly in the field. Another wounded American lying next to Merriken moved, made noise, and then flopped over partly atop Merriken. A German officer approached and shot the other American, the bullet continuing through and hitting Merriken in the leg. Merriken remained motionless. Miraculously, he was later able to escape from the field and, with the help of some Belgians, was rescued by American forces. (For more details, see the story of William Merriken in Part II of this book.)

Bedford's Broader World War II Sacrifice

Bedford's loss on D-Day should be kept in perspective and seen as part of a much broader sacrifice during World War II. While D-Day is Bedford's special tragedy, more than 98 percent of Bedford County servicemen were not involved in storming the Normandy beaches on D-Day, and seven times more Bedford County men died elsewhere during the war compared to those who died on Omaha Beach on June 6, 1944. Put another way, the twenty Bedford County men who died tragically on D-Day represent about one-half of 1 percent of all Bedford County servicemen in World War II and about 14 percent of those from the county who died while in military service. The loss on one day of twenty men from one community, nineteen serving in the same unit, must be seen as a great tragedy, but it represents only part of Bedford's sacrifice.

During the war, over 3,000 young men and women from Bedford County, including the town of Bedford, served in the armed forces. Thus, approximately 10 percent of the 30,000 citizens in Bedford County served in uniform.[27] (This is close to the 12 percent average for the entire nation, which had approximately sixteen million serving from a population of about 132 million.)[28]

The more than 3,000 men and women served in virtually every theater of operations. Bedford men fought, were wounded, and died on the ground, in the air, and at sea in all the major theaters of conflict. Some were captured and spent months as prisoners of war.

A total of at least 142 men from Bedford County were killed or died while serving in the armed forces between the fall of 1941 and December 31, 1946, when President Truman proclaimed the termination of hostilities.[29] At least 137 of these men were killed or died while serving in the armed forces prior to Japan's surrender in August 1945. The other five died from accidents or illness after Japan surrendered and prior to the President's proclamation on December 31, 1946. No Bedford servicewomen were reported to have died. (There were yet another twenty men who were killed or died during the war and who had some association with Bedford County but probably not enough to be considered "Bedford County men.") These figures do not include two Bedford County men who were discharged from the armed forces before they died of military-related causes. (One died from the effects of a military-training accident suffered before he was discharged. The other, Marvin B. Padgett, had served in the U.S. Army in the Philippines but left the military in 1938 and began working for an oil company in the Philippines. He was captured by the Japanese in 1942 and was killed when an Allied naval vessel unwittingly sank the Japanese ship that was transporting him and other prisoners away from the Philippines in October 1944.) (Specific information on those who were killed or died during the war is in Appendix A.) If these two men are counted, as they are on the memorial plaque inside the Bedford County Courthouse, then Bedford County lost 144 men serving in the military or from war-related causes during World War II. (The plaque inside the courthouse lists 135 names for World War II, compared to the 144 names this author lists in Appendix A, under categories A, B, and C.)

The great majority of Bedford County servicemen served in the Army, and the great majority of casualties came from the Army. Of the 137 who were killed or died prior to the Japanese surrender, 102 or almost 75 percent were Army soldiers. Fourteen of those who died served in the Army Air Forces, thirteen served in the Navy, and five were Marines. One served in the Royal Canadian Air Force. (None of the Bedford men serving in the Coast Guard were reported to have died.) The author did not discover the service of the remaining two who were killed.

Of the 137 men, at least 100 died as a result of combat, that is, they were killed in action, were initially reported as missing in action and later declared killed in action, or died of wounds received in action. Fifteen died in accidents, ten died of natural causes, one was lost in a storm at sea, another died from sickness while being held by the Japanese as a prisoner of war, and another was court-martialed and executed by the U.S. Army. The author has not been able to ascertain how the remaining nine men died.

Of the 100 who lost their lives in combat, the places they lost their lives and the number of them who lost their lives in those places follow:

Where Bedford Men Were Killed or Lost in Combat

Europe		80
France (total)		39
Omaha Beach	20	
Broader Normandy	7	
Broader France	12	
Off Normandy coast		2
Germany		16
Italy		7
Off coast of Anzio, Italy		5
Belgium		5
Luxembourg		3
Netherlands		1
Austria		1
N. Atlantic near Iceland		1

Mediterranean		3
North Africa		1
Pacific/Asia		16
South Pacific	5	
Okinawa/Ryukus	4	
Iwo Jima	2	
Philippines	1	
Guadalcanal/Solomons	1	
Bougainville/Solomons	1	
Ie Shima/Ryukus	1	
Wake Island	1	

Thus, of the 100 Bedford County men lost in combat, 80 percent (eighty men) died in Europe. Those killed in France and off the coast of Normandy alone represent 41 percent of all Bedford men killed in combat and 51 percent of those killed in Europe. Those killed in combat in the Pacific area represent 16 percent of Bedford's combat deaths, and those killed in the Mediterranean and North Africa areas represent 4 percent.

The servicemen who died from accidents or natural causes before Japan's surrender died in the United States (about twelve), Asia and Pacific area (five), England (two), Latin America (two), North Africa (one), Canada (one), and Germany (one). Of the five servicemen who died after Japan's surrender, three died in accidents (one each in the United States, Germany, and Japan), one died of illness in the United States, and the fifth died at home in Bedford County after he had been drinking and began to attack his family and his father shot and killed him.

Of the at least twenty-one Bedford County servicemen who were held as prisoners of war, one died in a Japanese POW camp in the Philippines. (Marvin B. Padgett, the former soldier who was a civilian when captured by the Japanese, also died while a prisoner.)

The soldier who was executed was from Bedford County near Vinton. Together with two fellow soldiers, he was court-martialed and convicted by U.S. Army authorities in France in October 1944 for raping a young French woman. He was sentenced to be hanged by the neck until dead, a sentence which the U.S. Army carried out in France in March 1945.[30]

Those who served in World War II, and especially those who died in the service of their country, have been honored and memorialized by the citizens of Bedford County, the topic of the last chapter.

Chapter 15

Honoring Veterans and War Dead

Bedford began taking steps to honor its servicemen and service-women during the war. After the war, the community found additional ways to honor and memorialize those who had served.

Newspaper Reports

As the deaths of servicemen became known and funeral and memorial services were planned, the two Bedford newspapers reported the news to the community. In more recent years, the *Bedford Bulletin* has published lengthy articles based on interviews with surviving veterans. The *News and Advance* of neighboring Lynchburg and the *Richmond Times-Dispatch* have both published special sections on Bedford's D-Day experience, and the *Roanoke Times* has written many related articles.[1]

Honor Rolls, Plaques, and Flags

During the war, factories, churches, businesses, and other organizations prepared honor rolls, plaques, and flags to honor servicemen and servicewomen from their organizations or the community at large. Plaques usually featured an honor roll which listed the names of those from the organization who were serving in the military. A star was usually affixed to the name of a man when he was killed or died. Few plaques listed the names of servicewomen. After the war, schools and government organizations established memorials to honor those who had died in service to their country.

Businesses, Industries, and Organizations

Jones (Green's) Drug Store was one of the first local entities, if not the very first, to honor Bedford's service personnel. In late summer

1942 the store invited parents and other loved ones to provide pictures of their servicemen for an honor roll exhibit in the store's windows. The *Bedford Democrat* reported that the response was splendid and that the resulting display had drawn much attention. The sponsors, however, were said to be disappointed that no pictures of "colored" soldiers had appeared; the sponsors let it be known that if such pictures were mailed to the store, they would be displayed, as "colored boys are fighting for the same common cause."[2]

In September of that year, the *Democrat* began printing lists of the names of the service personnel whose photographs had been sent to the drug store. In addition to the names, the newspaper printed the branch of service, the date of entry into service, and the military installation to which the service member had first been assigned. The title read "Men in Armed Services," but the name of at least one servicewoman was included.[3] In the list printed two weeks later, the assigned military installations were no longer provided.[4]

By October 8 the *Democrat* announced that it, in cooperation with the drug store, was compiling a list of all Bedford men (again, women were not mentioned) serving in any branch of the armed forces. Parents or next of kin were invited to fill out an eleven-line form and send the information to the drug store.[5] By December 10, the lists printed by the newspaper gave only the service person's name and branch of service.[6] This apparently was the last such list printed. Over the four-month period, the newspaper printed the names of approximately 580 servicemen and servicewomen, only a fraction of those serving.

The first business to honor its men was the Piedmont Label Company in downtown Bedford. In January 1943 the company erected a flagpole on its property and held a public ceremony the first day that it used the pole. Company representatives hoisted two flags—the American flag and a service flag with individual stars for the twenty men who had worked at the company before entering the armed forces. The company would later create a plaque with an honor roll for the men.[7]

In May 1943 the Hampton Looms of Virginia plant, the woolen mill, erected near the employees' entrance a large walnut and bronze plaque initially containing the names of thirty-three men who had worked at the plant before entering the military.[8] Sometime after the mill closed in 1972, the plaque, or an updated version, was moved to the Bedford City/County Museum, where it now is mounted on the wall. On the plaque, which pays "tribute to those who have left our midst to fight for our peace and freedom," are the names of seventy-two servicemen, three of whom—Frank Draper, Clifton Lee, and Martin Turpin—were killed in the war.

In late 1943 and early 1944 the Liberty Theater established an honor roll for all local service personnel whom a loved one or neighbor wished to honor by purchasing a war bond. In late February 1944 the *Bedford Bulletin* printed the names of 575 servicemen and servicewomen so honored.[9]

In June 1944 a memorial plaque was dedicated at the Firemen's Hall in honor of members of the fire company and the Bedford Firemen's Band who were serving in the armed forces.[10]

Churches

Many churches in the community constructed honor rolls to honor those service personnel affiliated with their individual churches. These honor rolls were usually displayed prominently inside the front entrances, and many still hang in Bedford churches.

Some churches, including at least two of the larger ones in Bedford, appear not to have prepared honor rolls, and one of the larger churches apparently had a scroll or plaque but no longer displays it.[11]

Some individuals were included on the rolls of more than one church, perhaps because their affiliation changed or because they and their family members attended different churches. For example, Joseph E. Parker, Jr., who was killed during the war, is listed on the honor rolls at both Main Street United Methodist Church and Salem United Methodist Church.

One of the first churches to develop an honor roll was the Bedford Methodist Church. In January 1943 the church announced its intention in the *Bedford Democrat*, where it published a list of forty-four of its men in service and asked readers to provide additional names if they knew any.[12] In May, the church announced that it had recently hung the honor plaque and that it intended to add six additional names.[13]

(More than sixty years later, in 2004, the Main Street Methodist Church displays near its front door an honor roll plaque dedicated in 1943 to ninety-four men who served in the war and a smaller plaque dedicated in 1947 to five men who gave their lives during the war.)

Other churches soon followed. In July 1943 St. John's Episcopal Church in Bedford dedicated an honor scroll with thirty names on it, and Flint Hill Baptist Church dedicated an honor roll to its members serving in the military.[14] In September of that year the Walnut Grove Church in Montvale dedicated a plaque and service flag in honor of thirty-six of its men.[15] The Bedford Christian Church in December 1943 unveiled a service plaque with at least thirty names.[16] The Shady Grove Church in February 1944 dedicated an honor roll plaque honoring the thirty-nine men and three women of the church and community serving in the armed forces.[17] The Quaker Baptist Church unveiled two service plaques in April 1944, one honoring ten men who had served in World War I and the other honoring thirty-two who were serving in World War II, including three women.[18] In the summer of that year the Leftwich Methodist Church in Huddleston dedicated an honor plaque and service roll to thirty-seven men and one woman.[19] In December 1944 the Ephesus Church of the Middle Bedford Methodist Charge dedicated an honor roll plaque to thirty servicemen who had been "connected in some way to the church in recent years."[20]

In June 1945 the Baptist Church in Bedford in a Sunday evening service dedicated a plaque honoring 104 of its servicemen, including six who had died.[21] This plaque, which was later extended to reflect a total of 110 men and eight dead, is displayed in the church's present building near the front door. The bell tower is also dedicated to the church's men and women who served in World War II.

The Bedford Christian Church building at the corner of Bridge Street and Bedford Avenue (the church is moving to a new location) had a display case in 2003 with the names of forty-eight of its men who served (up from the thirty names in December 1943), including five of the eight Dean brothers and four men who died while in the armed forces. The church also has two stained-glass windows memorializing two of the men killed in the war, John Dean and Frank Draper.

Among smaller churches in the county, the Salem United Methodist Church at Peaksville has a cloth banner and plaque with the names of its twenty World War II servicemen, including two who were killed. The banner and plaque were made by the church's Women's Society of Christian Service. The women made a blue star for each serviceman. Five of the young men were from the Karnes family, and three from the Parker family. When S/Sgt. Earl L. Parker and Pvt. Joseph E. Parker, Jr. were killed, the women covered two of the stars with gold cloth. A few years ago, the banner and plaque were framed to preserve them, and a dedication ceremony was held, attended by six men whose names are listed on the plaque, including William ("Billy") Parker, whose two brothers were killed in the war and who was, himself, a prisoner of war.

The Center Point United Methodist Church east of Bedford City has a banner made by its women's group, with six service stars, including two gold stars representing brothers Bedford and Raymond Hoback, who were killed on D-Day.

The Thaxton Baptist Church has a plaque dedicated to military veterans, at least eight probably from World War II.

Histories

In September 1943 the History Division of the Virginia Conservation Commission began a statewide project to collect war-related information. The commission sought to collect from each county and major city three types of information: (a) biographical sketches of Virginia men and women in the armed services who had died or were cited for bravery, (b) reactions of the civilian population to the war's events, and (c) news about local economic and social conditions during the war. The Virginia commission relied on local county or city committees to collect the information, including Bedford County's War History Committee, chaired by Mrs. George P. (Lula Jeter) Parker.[22]

In November 1943, in response to the commission's requests, Mrs. Parker formed in Bedford County a larger, more general committee, which included representatives of groups already collecting such information—the Daughters of the American Revolution, the United

Daughters of the Confederacy, the American Legion Auxiliary—as well as Mrs. Rosa Schenk, the county schools attendance officer.[23] Mrs. Parker's committee sought to collect information on all Bedford County men and women serving in the armed forces, not just those killed or cited for bravery.

By January 1944 Mrs. Rosa Schenk began using the Victory Corps of the local high schools to distribute military service questionnaires to families of men and women in the service. She worked with the supervisor of black schools, Mrs. Susie Gibson, to obtain information on Blacks in the service. The American Legion Auxiliary was asked to contact county men who had been discharged from the service.[24] The two local newspapers were asked to print sample copies of the questionnaire, properly filled out.[25]

Mrs. Parker's committee then assembled the completed questionnaires and had them bound in four separate books under the general title *Military Service Records, World War II.* These books are maintained in the office of the Clerk of the Circuit Court for Bedford County.

By 1945 the statewide organization evolved into the Virginia World War II History Commission. This commission asked local history committees to gather information on service personnel who had been killed or died during the war. The Bedford County War History Committee, in turn, asked relatives, usually mothers, of those killed to write about their loved ones and how they died. The relatives based their reports on information provided by the government, unit commanders, chaplains, and servicemen who had served with their loved ones.

By January 1946 Mrs. Parker had received questionnaires from the families of eighty-eight Bedford County men who had been killed or died in service. Mrs. Parker indicated that twenty-five or more additional questionnaires had not yet been received, indicating that a total of about 113 questionnaires had been distributed to Bedford County families known to have lost loved ones in the war. The number would increase before the book was published.[26]

The Virginia commission, using the basic information from the local history committees, collated and refined the information and prepared the book *Gold Star Honor Roll of Virginians in World War II*. This book, released in 1947, listed by county and major city the names of Virginia service personnel who lost their lives during the war. The section on Bedford County lists the names of 135 men.

War Memorials

Following the erection of plaques and flags by local factories and churches, the Bedford community at large began to discuss creating some type of "war memorial." The *Bedford Democrat* raised the issue in August 1944, suggesting that a committee be formed to plan a building that would serve both as a living memorial and as a community-use structure. The newspaper suggested that a tablet in memory of those who had served in both World War I and II be displayed in a conspicuous place at the facility.[27]

In April 1945, at the suggestion of the local American Legion post, the Bedford County Board of Supervisors voted to invest $10,000 in war bonds to be set aside for use at some future date in the erection of a war memorial to Bedford County veterans of World War II and all prior wars. The board indicated that it would decide on the type of memorial at a later date. Board members were appointed to a committee to work with citizens groups. J. Moorman Johnson, who served as chairman of the local draft board, was named chairman of the committee.[28]

In August 1945 Mrs. Parker raised the subject in a letter published in the *Bedford Democrat*.[29] A month later the local post of the Veterans of Foreign Wars (VFW) passed a resolution calling on the chairman of the Bedford County board of supervisors to form a War Memorial Commission to plan a suitable memorial to those who had served in World War II. These veterans had in mind a community center building.[30]

Almost a year later, in July 1946, the VFW post appointed a committee to work on a memorial and invited other community organizations to send representatives to a meeting to "start the ball rolling."[31] A meeting was held at the courthouse late that month, attended by representatives of the VFW, VFW Auxiliary, American Legion, Lions Club, Rotary Club, County Board of Supervisors, Bedford

Town Council, Chamber of Commerce, Eastern Star, Daughters of the American Revolution, United Daughters of the Confederacy, War History Committee, American Association of University Women, Red Cross, Home Demonstration Clubs, Medical Association, Business and Professional Woman's Club, and the Tuberculosis Association.

Differing views were expressed about the type of memorial, ranging from some form of community use facility, such as a hospital, a hotel, an auditorium, or recreation park, to something only of sentimental value. Views also differed as to the source of funding, with some suggesting an appeal for federal funds, and others wanting only local community funding. The group decided to establish a central committee, led by Jesse T. Davidson of the War History Committee.[32]

The War Memorial Committee met again in late August and this time went on record as favoring construction of a hospital as the war memorial. No one suggested a monument-type of memorial.[33]

In the final analysis, no memorial building dedicated specifically and solely to veterans was constructed. A Bedford County Memorial Hospital was built in the 1950s. At a cornerstone-laying ceremony for the hospital, the key speaker referred to the fact that it was Armistice Day and said that the holiday was relevant "since it (the hospital) is to be a memorial to the loved ones and friends of the people of Bedford County, including those who so gallantly gave their lives for their country." The name "Memorial" may have had as much, if not more, to do with people donating money for the hospital in honor of their personal loved ones and having rooms named after them, as it did with memorializing veterans per se.[34]

Schools

After the war, several schools in the Bedford community erected plaques or tablets paying tribute to former students who served in the armed forces in the war and those who were killed or died during the conflict. In May 1945 the Huddleston High School Parent Teachers Association placed a marble tablet in the Huddleston High School building honoring 200 former students who served, including two who were missing in action.[35] The memorial is now displayed on the wall at Huddleston Elementary School, the high school having been closed.

In 1948 the Bedford High School Class of 1944 erected a tablet on a stone outside the old high school (now Bedford Middle School) honoring all former students who served in the war and naming nineteen who gave their lives. The tablet was unveiled in May of that year by Miss Mary Daniel Parker, the daughter of former student Earl L. Parker, who was killed on D-Day.[36]

Clubs

In 1946 the Big Island Garden Club planted an evergreen tree near the Big Island Baptist Church on Route 501, honoring the men and women from Bedford County who served in the war. A bronze tablet was erected near the tree in 1949 and dedicated in March 1950.[37] On June 7, 1949 the Ruritan Club of New London dedicated an athletic field at New London Academy in honor of seventeen alumni of that institution who served in World Wars I and II.[38]

Courthouse Memorials

On May 30, 1949 the first of two memorials was unveiled at the Bedford County Courthouse. The first memorial is a bronze, honor-roll plaque "in memory of the men of Bedford County whose lives were sacrificed in defense of their country" in World Wars I and II. The plaque lists thirty-nine men for World War I and 135 men for World War II. The plaque was mounted inside the Main Street entrance of the courthouse and was unveiled by Lucille Hoback Boggess, who had lost two brothers, Bedford and Raymond Hoback, in the D-Day Invasion. The principal speaker was A. G. Cummings, division superintendent of schools for Bedford County, former head of the county war bond effort, and former rationing registrar.[39]

Five years later, on June 6, 1954, the tenth anniversary of the D-Day Invasion, the second memorial was unveiled. Donated by the Parker-Hoback Post of the 29th Division Association, this memorial is a stone with a bronze plaque honoring twenty-three Bedford County men of the 116th Infantry Regiment, 29th Division, "who gave their lives in the preparation for and the participation in the Normandy Invasion and later battles of World War II."

The idea for this memorial was broached at the 1953 reunion of the 29th Division Association by Ray Nance, who had served in Company A.[40] Kenneth Crouch was instrumental in bringing the idea to fruition.

More than 5,000 people attended the dedication of this memorial in front of the Bedford County Courthouse, including at least sixteen men who had served in the 29th Infantry Division during World War II. The speaker was Maj. Gen. Charles H. Gerhardt, who had commanded the 29th Infantry Division from July 1943 until sometime after D-Day.[41] The stone, a gift from the government of France, came from the area of Verville-sur-Mer, the point on Omaha Beach where Company A of the 116th Infantry Regiment landed during the D-Day Invasion. The Naval Attaché of the French Embassy in Washington, an admiral, presented the stone to representatives of Bedford's Parker-Hoback Post 24. The stone and plaque were unveiled by Mrs. P. A. Fellers, mother of Captain Fellers, who had commanded Company A and was killed during the invasion.[42]

Two other memorials have been installed in front of the courthouse, in addition to the 116th Infantry stone and plaque, the monument to Confederate soldiers and sailors, and the monument to Revolutionary War soldiers. One is a stone and plaque that matches the one for the 116th Infantry; this was presented by the VFW and its VFW Auxiliary in honor of veterans of all foreign wars. The other, dedicated in May 1965, is a flagpole with a small stone and bronze plaque dedicated to "the memory of all Bedford County members of the Armed Forces who have made the supreme sacrifice for their country."

Memorial Highways

The Commonwealth of Virginia has named two highways in honor of the regiment and division in which Company A and other units from southwest Virginia fought. One is State Highway 460, which has been designated "The 116th Infantry Regiment Memorial Highway." It runs east-west through the center of Bedford County, connecting to Roanoke in the west and Lynchburg in the east. The other is State

Highway 29, which has been designated "The 29th Infantry Division Memorial Highway." This highway runs north and south just east of Bedford County.

National D-Day Memorial

The largest and most impressive memorial in Bedford County is the National D-Day Memorial. This memorial honors not just those from Bedford but all the men and women of the Allied forces who participated in the D-Day Invasion of Normandy.

The inspiration for this memorial actually came from Roanoke, specifically from three men associated with the newspaper *Roanoke Times and World-News* (now the *Roanoke Times*), most significantly, John Robert (Bob) Slaughter, a D-Day veteran from Roanoke who had retired as the newspaper's composing room foreman. [43]

In 1987 an artist for the newspaper, Steve Stinson, suggested that newspaper columnist Brian O'Neill write an article promoting the idea of a D-Day Memorial. O'Neill talked to Slaughter and wrote an article. When the article failed to stir any activity, Slaughter and Stinson contacted interested parties and organized a memorial committee.

Many people contributed their time, efforts, and money over the ensuing years of struggle to establish a memorial. In 1989 the group created a non-profit foundation dedicated to creating a national D-Day memorial. Slaughter became the foundation's chairman of the board. Over the next couple of years, the foundation members discussed possible sites in Roanoke with influential parties, but to no avail.

Slaughter then was invited to help escort President Clinton on a walk on Omaha Beach during the 1994 50th anniversary of D-Day. Slaughter returned to Roanoke with renewed enthusiasm and support from others for a memorial.

When the foundation was still unable to find a site for the memorial in Roanoke, it received a boost from Bedford. Lucille Hoback Boggess, then Commissioner of the Revenue in Bedford County, had lost two brothers on D-Day and had become a member of the foundation. She talked to G. Michael Shelton, then Mayor of the City of Bedford, about the possibility of finding a site in Bedford for the memorial. Shelton and the Bedford City Council consulted and then showed the foundation members several sites. Next, with council approval, Shelton and Boggess offered the foundation twenty acres of land owned by the city. The land was on a high hilltop, from which one could look down on the quaint downtown section of the City of Bedford to the north and look west and see the majestic Peaks of Otter. The site, moreover, was visible from the main east-west highway passing through Bedford and running to Roanoke and Lynchburg. The city also offered $250,000 toward construction of the memorial on this site.

The foundation welcomed Bedford's generosity and, in November 1994, chose the Bedford site as the location for the memorial. Foundation chairman Slaughter declared that "Bedford's 20 acres of pristine mountain-view meadowland will be ideally situated for a National D-Day memorial. I have never seen such community support for a project."[44]

The foundation members began working on plans for the site, including construction of a monument, amphitheater, and education center. In January 1996 the foundation hired a full-time executive director, Richard Burrow, who began raising money for the construction. Plans were announced for a $12 million memorial complex, with a monument and education center.[45]

Also in 1996, Congress designated the project the "National D-Day Memorial." A boost to funding came in October 1997, when Charles Shultz, a World War II veteran and creator of the "Peanuts" cartoon strip, pledged $1 million toward the memorial.

On November 11, 1997, 2,000 people attended a ground-breaking ceremony. During the construction process, ceremonies continued to be held at the site on special occasions, particularly around the June 6 anniversaries of D-Day, Memorial Day, and Veterans Day. Sculptures were unveiled in ceremonies in 1998 and 1999, and on Memorial Day 2000 some 5,000 people attended the dedication of the arch and Victory Plaza and unveiling of a sculpture. Active members of the Army National Guard's 116th Infantry Regiment participated in the ceremonies.[46]

A year later, on June 6, 2001, the foundation officially dedicated the monument in a ceremony that included veterans, President George W. Bush and other dignitaries, and some 21,000 other attendees.[47]

As construction progressed, the cost of the project increased significantly. From the original projected cost of $12.5 million for the memorial complex, the cost for the monument alone appears to have increased to approximately $25 million.[48]

Funds were raised from a variety of sources, including private donors, the Commonwealth of Virginia, and lending institutions. After the June 2001 dedication, problems surfaced involving funding for the memorial.

Richard Burrow, whose title had changed from executive director to president of the foundation, resigned. The directors of the foundation then announced that they had learned that the foundation was some $5 million in debt and asked for a governmental investigation. Many of the board members resigned so that new board members could address the financial issues.

Following an investigation, federal charges were brought against Burrow, including one charge each of mail, wire, bank, and loan application fraud. The charges were related to the methods he used to raise funds for the memorial. There were no charges that Burrow sought personal financial gain from any of his fund raising activities.[49]

In 2002 the architect and then the construction company sued the foundation for a total of almost $3 million for unreimbursed work on the memorial. The foundation filed for Chapter 11 bankruptcy protection so that it could continue to operate while working out a plan to repay its creditors. In June 2003 the foundation emerged from bankruptcy, having reached agreement on a plan to pay the architect, construction company, and other smaller creditors a total of just over $3.5 million.[50]

A federal trial of Burrow in December 2002 ended in a hung jury, with seven jurors voting to acquit and five voting to convict. The U.S. Attorney for the area announced his intent to seek a new indictment of Burrow, and in early January 2004, a new grand jury indicted Burrow on twelve counts of fraud and two counts of perjury, the latter related to his testimony in the earlier trial.[51]

While these legal proceedings have continued, the foundation has been successful in moving forward to raise new contributions, reduce its debt, and welcome visitors to the memorial. From late summer

2001, when the debt was $5.9 million, the foundation, by the end of 2003, was able to reduce the debt to just over $3 million, with about $500,000 being raised between June and December 2003 for debt reduction.[52]

All of these legal and financial issues aside, the purpose of the memorial is being served. Large numbers of visitors—an estimated 110,000 in 2003 alone—are arriving at the memorial to learn more about D-Day; pay tribute to all the Allied soldiers, sailors, and airmen who participated in the invasion; and remember and honor the some 4,500 Allied servicemen who laid down their lives on June 6, 1944.[53]

The monument features a triumphal stone arch, measuring forty-four feet and six inches high, surrounded by a plaza with the names of the five Normandy beaches inlaid in granite. The flags of Allied nations fly in front of the arch. Below the arch and plaza are circular concrete areas, a pool, and concrete walls symbolizing the English Channel and the beaches, cliffs, and fortifications at Normandy. The site is adorned by statuary which represents soldiers storming the beaches and scaling the cliffs of Normandy, pays tributes to the fallen, and symbolizes the appreciation and thanks of the people of France.

The foundation is researching the 4,500 or so Allied personnel who were killed on D-Day and plans to display all their names on bronze plaques that will be erected on the inside of the wall around the perimeter of the main circular area. The plaques are already being installed as donations come forward. Once the debt is paid, the foundation plans to complete a now partially-constructed English garden, finish two semi-circular areas symbolizing the important roles of Allied air and naval forces in the invasion, and build an educational building. The English garden, at the far end of the memorial, symbolizes the shield of the Supreme Headquarters Allied Expeditionary Force. Some believe that the educational building will become the heart of the memorial.

Memorial Services During and After the War

One of the first memorial services for any of the men killed in the D-Day Invasion was held in Normandy on July 28, 1944. It was organized by the 29th Infantry Division to honor its men killed in the invasion and thereafter. The service was held at a cemetery the division had established, and representatives from the division attended. A report on the memorial service, written by a war correspondent, was carried in the *Bedford Bulletin* on August 3, 1944.[54] Without identifying the town near the cemetery, apparently for security reasons, the article quoted from a wooden sign bearing the division's insignia:

> This cemetery was established June 11, 1944, by the Twenty-ninth Infantry Division, U.S. Army, as a final resting place for officers and men of that division who made the supreme sacrifice on battlefields in Normandy.
>
> We who carry on salute these comrades and other honored dead of the division who could not be buried here (a reference to those missing in action). . . .

The correspondent reported that an American flag flew atop a high flagpole mounted in the cemetery's open plaza. At the bottom of the flagpole was a wreath with an inscription reading: "To our liberators. Children of the town." On one side of the plaza was a wide field marked with white crosses. On the other side were open graves.

After remarks by division commander Major General Gerhardt and others, and after prayers, an honor guard fired three volleys. A bugler blew taps, and "as the last low notes died there came from every man…the battle cry of the division: 'Twenty-ninth, let's go!'" After the ceremony, men walked among the crosses looking for graves of friends. As they exited the cemetery, they saw, near where they had entered, several litters with covered bodies, which had not been there before the ceremony.

In Bedford, memorial services were sometimes held shortly after a family was notified of the death of a loved one serving in the armed services. For example, a memorial service was held at St. John's Episcopal Church on September 10, 1944, for S/Sgt. John B. Schenk, who had been killed on June 6 but whose family had not learned of his death until July 17th.[55] On December 3, 1944, a memorial service was held at the Main Street Methodist Church for Pfc.

Robert A. Fizer, who had been wounded in France in mid-September 1944 and died of his wounds in October.[56]

Other memorial services were delayed until close to an anniversary of the death of the serviceman. As an example, a memorial and dedication service was held at the Nazareth Methodist Church near Goode on Sunday, June 10, 1945, in memory of Captain Fellers, who had been killed on June 6 a year earlier.[57]

Services were also held after the war, particularly in 1947 and 1948, when the remains of servicemen were returned to Bedford for burial.

More general memorial services were also held. The Bridge Street (now Bedford) Christian Church held a memorial service on August 27, 1944, in honor of four young soldiers who had been members of the church—M/Sgt. John W. Dean, T/Sgt. Frank P. Draper, Jr., Pvt. Clifton G. Lee, and Pfc. Andrew J. Coleman.[58]

On the afternoon of May 27, 1945, a Memorial Day service was held in the Bedford High School auditorium to pay special honor to all of Bedford County's World War II dead. At this service, the Bedford Firemen's Band played music, colors were presented and retired, the Pledge of Allegiance to the American Flag was recited, a salute was given to the Confederate Flag, invocations and speeches were made by local ministers, the roll was called of Bedford's honored dead, and Gold Star citations were presented to the next of kin of the deceased.[59]

Burials

The remains of many Bedford servicemen were buried in military cemeteries overseas. In the years after the war, the federal government contacted the next of kin and offered to bring the remains of their loved ones home to the United States for burial. Many of the remains were returned in 1947 and 1948. Some families chose to leave the remains of their loved ones in the overseas cemeteries, now maintained by the American Battle Monuments Commission.

The remains of most of those from Company A killed on D-Day were likely buried temporarily near where they were killed and subsequently moved to the military cemetery in Normandy established by the 29th Infantry Division.[60] (As mentioned previously, unlike others in Company A, Technical Sergeant Draper, who had been mortally wounded on D-Day and medically evacuated from Normandy, was buried in England, until his remains were returned to Bedford.)

The Hoback family, which lost two sons in the D-Day Invasion of Normandy, chose to leave their son Bedford buried in the military cemetery in Normandy, near where their son Raymond was reported missing in action, never to be seen again. The names of the Hoback brothers can be found among those memorialized at the Normandy American Cemetery, along with others of those in Company A.[61]

(According to the American Battle Monuments Commission, 405,399 American service personnel lost their lives during World War II. Of those who died overseas, the next of kin of 233,181 chose to have the remains of their loved ones returned to the United States for burial, while the next of kin of 93,242 chose burial in the commission's cemeteries overseas. The remains of 78,976 American service personnel missing in action were never recovered. The cemeteries include memorials to those missing in action.)[62]

In November 1947, Bedford learned that the remains of the first eight men to be returned to Bedford had arrived by ship in New York. Four of these men were from the town of Bedford and Company A, and the other four were from elsewhere in Bedford County and other units. A committee was organized, led by Col. John R. Boatwright, with representatives from the local posts of the American Legion and Veterans of Foreign Wars, plus 1st Lt. E. Ray Nance representing the National Guard. The committee developed a plan to have a six-man escort meet the first body and escort it to the funeral chapel where it would lie in state until 3 p.m. of the following day. After that, a National Guard honor guard, accompanied by an honorary procession of military, veterans, government, and civic organizations, including the Bedford Firemen's Band, would escort the body to the courthouse for a service memorializing all Bedford County men who died during World War II.[63]

Cemeteries

The remains of more than a dozen of those killed in the war are interred in Oakwood-Longwood-Greenwood Cemetery, located in the northwestern part of the City of Bedford. Remains of many other servicemen are buried elsewhere in the county, often in small church cemeteries or family cemeteries. (See Appendix A for available information on the burial sites of Bedford servicemen who died during the war.)

Quite a few are buried in Section 1 and 2 of Greenwood Cemetery, near the junction of Longwood Avenue and Walnut Street, near four, stately, old, oak trees. Some of these gravesites are marked with large family monuments, and the serviceman is buried next to relatives. Others have large headstones dedicated just to the serviceman, some inscribed with poems or information about the individual's service. Others have smaller headstones. Most of the gravesites of the servicemen include a flat, stone marker provided by the government, placed flush with the ground and providing the serviceman's name, home state, rank, unit, and war in which he served, and dates of birth and death, as well as a cross if a Christian.

Other Remembrances

The Bedford City/County Museum, located on Main Street in Bedford, has preserved files of World War II materials and collected several books on the war. It also displays World War II memorabilia. The Bedford Central Public Library has collected many local and other histories of the war. To the author's knowledge, the only World War II veteran from Bedford to have written about his wartime experiences and made copies available to the public is Bernard Saunders, a POW of the Japanese for over three years. A copy of Mr. Saunders' memoir is preserved in the library, along with a relatively extensive memoir by Bob Slaughter of Roanoke, one of the founders of the National D-Day Memorial Foundation, who has written of his experiences in the Normandy Invasion with Company D of the 116th Infantry Regiment. Two books published by former members of Company A who live in other states are also available at the library or museum.

On the evenings of May 27 and 28, 1994, the three Bedford County high schools and the Bedford Middle School presented a program of patriotic songs, dances, and vignettes commemorating D-Day and the sacrifice of Bedford County servicemen. The program was produced and directed by Nancy N. Johnson, a local drama enthusiast and supporter of veterans' recognition. Liberty High School students wrote and presented a short play entitled "Homefront."[64]

In the summers of 2000 and 2001, the Sedalia Center, a cultural arts center in north central Bedford County, presented a historical drama, titled *Bedford Goes to War: A Historical Drama of Bedford County in World War II*, written by the author of this book. Nancy Johnson also directed this presentation.

At least two songs about Bedford and D-Day have been written. "The Sons of Bedford" was written by Alan L. Barbee of Oakton, Virginia, and "Sons of Liberty" was written by Mike Pearrell, formerly of Bedford and later of Roanoke. Both were featured in the aforementioned historical drama.

Several television documentaries have been produced about Bedford's D-Day experience, including ones by Roanoke's Channel 7 (CBS affiliate); the regional Public Broadcasting Station, WBRA; and a French television company based in Normandy.

American Legion Post 54 in Bedford has organized many ceremonial programs of speeches, music, and prayers to honor veterans of D-Day, World War II, and all American wars.

The Rev. Jeff Clemmons, who worked for the Bedford school system as well as working as a minister before becoming a U.S. Army chaplain, in the late 1990s and early 2000s organized efforts to erect monuments and hold ceremonies in memory of fliers who died in military crashes in Bedford County during World War II. As part of his efforts to memorialize the five aviators killed in the 1943 B-25 crash on Sharp Top Mountain, Clemmons organized a ceremony at the Lynchburg Regional Airport in 2000 and arranged to have a memorial plaque erected at the crash site. Bedford's American Legion Post No. 54 is working on other memorials to airmen killed in Bedford County.

Several Bedford veterans and members of their families have visited memorials in France, including a monument to the 29th Infantry Division at Vierville and military cemeteries where American servicemen are buried.

Veterans and Their Families

Many of the veterans and loved ones of men who served in World War II have preserved memorabilia of the war, including letters, papers, photographs, medals, Bibles, newspaper clippings, and scrapbooks.

For many years, veterans and families associated with Company A of Bedford held reunions around the June 6 anniversary of D-Day.

The families of men killed on D-Day have kept many mementos. For example, Gamiel Draper still has the small diary or notebook his brother Frank carried. Lewis H. Wright kept the papers and photos of his brother Elmere and then entrusted them to close friends Donnie and Nancy Slusher. Lucille Hoback Boggess has the Bible belonging to her brother Raymond Hoback, the Bible found on Omaha Beach. The family of Taylor Fellers has passed from generation-to-generation a ring that belonged to Fellers.[65] Captain Fellers' sister, Mrs. Bertie Woodford, now has and cherishes the Purple Heart Medal awarded posthumously to his family.

A few Bedford veterans stand out in terms of their dedication to explaining what they and their fellow soldiers experienced during World War II. Roy O. Stevens and E. Ray Nance have granted innumerable interviews about what happened to Company A in the Normandy Invasion. Others who served in Company A prior to D-Day have shared their experiences, including Pride Wingfield, and, before he died in December 2003, Boyd Earl Wilson. These veterans and others have frequently visited the National D-Day Memorial and talked to visitors.

Perhaps no one in Bedford has committed as much time and effort in researching and explaining his war experiences as has William H. Merriken. Merriken has corresponded and visited with fellow veterans, government agencies, and citizens in Belgium, and even traced his steps on December 17, 1944, to help research and explain the Malmedy Massacre and what happened to him and to his fellow soldiers, many of whom, including two from Bedford, did not survive. (Again, see the section on William Merriken in Part II of this book.)

Remembrances of the Dead and Missing by Loved Ones

Many mothers, wives, sisters, and others in the Bedford community wrote tributes and recollections about their loved ones killed in the war. Some wrote poems and had them published in the local newspapers, often on anniversaries of the deaths of the servicemen. Some mothers had the local newspapers publish letters they received from military comrades of their deceased sons. The Bedford County War History Committee, led by Mrs. Parker, asked mothers or next of kin to help fill out forms about their loved ones, including how they died. These forms were compiled into a book, *Military Records of Bedford County's Gold Star Men in World War II*, now maintained in the Office of the Clerk of the Circuit Court in the Bedford County Courthouse.

Mrs. Roy Reynolds, mother of Pfc. John F. Reynolds, whose son was killed in action in France on D-Day, wrote the following poetic tribute, which was published in the *Bedford Bulletin* three weeks after she learned of her son's death:

> You are gone dear Jack, but not forgotten
> And the voice we loved is stilled;
> There's a vacancy in our home,
> That never can be filled.
>
> Since you were so far away,
> Our hearts ache both night and day,
> But had we been with you at the end, dear,
> How different things would seem to us here.
>
> You were such a jolly, fun-loving boy
> And mother you never forgot.
> No one knows how I miss you;
> No one knows the tears I shed,

> But in God's dear home, you are so safe.
> No suffering, tears or care, but in God's time,
> I'll surely find you waiting over there.[66]

Kathleen Bradshaw, the sweetheart of Private Reynolds, wrote her own tribute:

> How sad I was that lonely day
> When I heard that you'd been called away;
> But though you are gone, you linger still
> In my memory, you always will.
>
> You are one of the unsung heroes,
> God called away on that day.
> One of the many soldier boys
> That left his home to stay.
>
> I can't forget your smiling face,
> Full of love, friendship and grace;
> God called you on that other shore,
> To rest with Him forever more.[67]

The mother of M/Sgt. John W. Dean, who was killed in action in France on June 17, had a letter from a friend of Sergeant Dean published in the *Bedford Bulletin*:

Dear Mrs. Dean,

Being one of John's best friends, and at his request some days before, it is with my deepest regards and sympathy that I write....

He requested that in the event that anything happened to him, that I would write you personally and tell you...that he was right in it with all the others at the beginning and made it through the toughest part of the invasion...but...luck...didn't hold out. I don't think I need to say any more, except that the boys that served under his leadership are proud to have done so...he was a good soldier, straight and true, stood up for those things that were right and was admired by the boys.

Master Sergeant John W. Dean was a good boy and in closing this I want to assure you that not only my own but the sympathy of all of us goes with it for you and your family for John's death.

Wishing you all the best, I am,

Very sincerely, Louis L. Milam[68]

Mrs. John Hoback, whose sons Bedford and Raymond were killed on D-Day in France, had the following letter, dated July 9, 1944, published in the *Bedford Bulletin*:

Dear Mr. and Mrs. Hoback:

…While walking along the beach D-Day plus 1, I came upon this Bible…Knowing that you no doubt would want the book returned, I am sending it knowing that most Bibles are a book to be cherished. I would have sent it sooner, but have been quite busy and thought it best if a short period of time elapsed before returning it.

You have by now received a letter from your son saying he is well. I sincerely hope so. I imagine what has happened is that your son dropped the book without any notice. Most everybody who landed on the beach D-Day lost something….

…The beach is now peaceful and quiet since the German guns have been silenced. The birds have begun their daily practice and all the flowers and trees are in bloom, especially the poppies and tulips which are very beautiful at this time of the year.

With best wishes, Private H. W. Crayton.[69]

The family of T/Sgt. Frank P. Draper, Jr., nicknamed "Juney" (for Junior), who was killed on D-Day in France, erected a large, vertical headstone at his gravesite in Bedford's Greenwood Cemetery. The headstone is inscribed with the following poem:

> Our precious son from us is gone,
> His voice we loved is still,
> His place is vacant in our home
> Which never can be filled.
> We loved you, Juney, dearly loved you,

> But God loved you best.
> He took you home to heaven
> Where all is peace and rest.
> Our loss is heaven's gain.
> > Father, Mother, Brothers and Sister

The family of Pfc. John W. Allen, who was killed in September 1944 in Europe, buried their son in Greenwood Cemetery with a monument inscribed:

> Sleep on Dear Son
> and take your rest,
> our hearts are broken,
> but God knows best.
> > Mother, Father, and Sisters

The questionnaires which Mrs. Parker and her committee collected from the loved ones of men who had been killed or died in the war contain many moving accounts. Della Danner, the mother of Joseph S. Danner, wrote one of the most detailed accounts of how her son died in the crash of his bomber. This account can be found in Part II of this book.

The family of Sgt. Willie R. Martin, in their completed questionnaire, quoted a letter from Sergeant Martin's commanding officer:

...The end came suddenly and without suffering and he was buried in an American Military Cemetery in Eastern France...a Chaplain of the Protestant Faith officiated....Willie proved himself a splendid soldier and his outstanding character resulted in his being held in high regard by all members of the command. His loss will be deeply felt by his many friends. Willie's personal effects will be sent to you....Please accept my own personal sympathy and feel free to call on me for any additional information you may desire.[70]

The father of Sgt. Wilson G. Newman quoted from a War Department letter giving an account of why Sergeant Newman was awarded the Silver Star posthumously:

> For gallantry in action on 16 September 1944...Leading his heavy machine gun squad in an attack against strong enemy positions, Sergeant Newman, until mortally wounded, repeatedly exposed himself to direct enemy fire in order to direct the fire of his guns. His untiring devotion to duty and great personal courage enabled his men to deliver accurate supporting fire which greatly assisted the infantrymen in reaching their objective....[71]

The mother of Pvt. Thomas Cofer wrote:

> I only know he was killed by a sniper while on duty one night—he and another boy both were killed—a boy told me that. I have never heard from the government how he was killed.[72]

The mother of Pfc. George T. Miller wrote of her son's death on March 2, 1945, at age nineteen:

> The battle of Iwo Jima...was his first combat duty....He was hit by enemy shrapnel as his platoon was moving forward in the attack. A Navy hospital corpsman was present and able to be of immediate service but the end came swiftly, and he did not suffer.[73]

The mother of Pvt. Herbert O. Daniel, who was married and had two small children when he was inducted into the Marine Corps in June 1944, wrote:

> ...he died of wounds received on 12th of March, 1945. No indication was given as to how he received the wounds or whether he died on the same date. We have been notified that he was buried, Grave 640, Row #26, in the Third Marine Division Cemetery, Iwo Jima.[74] (After the war ended, Private Daniel's body was

returned to Bedford County and, with a memorial service, was buried at Horeb Methodist Church in Huddleston.)

Lucille Hoback Boggess, a sister of Bedford and Raymond Hoback, who were killed in France on D-Day, has on many occasions related how her family was informed of the deaths of her two brothers and how their deaths affected the family. The following is a paraphrased summary based on several individual accounts:

> It was Sunday, and our family was preparing for church. The Sheriff brought a telegram saying that Bedford had been killed. It was a great shock. More than twenty people came from church and tried to console us. The next day we kids were making home-made ice cream to help comfort our parents. A second telegram came saying Raymond was missing in action. This was devastating. For my parents, it was almost too much to lose two of their seven children. They never got over it. It took a lot of happiness out of the family, and there were lots of tears shed. Father would slip out the back door toward the barn, turning from the children so they wouldn't see him cry. My mother was never quite the same, and life never meant so much to her afterwards.[75]

Viola Nance was a bride at nineteen, a mother at twenty, and a widow at twenty-one when her husband, S/Sgt. Earl L. Parker, was killed on D-Day in France. A paraphrased summary of various of her accounts follows:

> I lived with my parents and our baby. I wrote Earl every day. I can still remember his dog tag number—20363625. I'll never forget that number. The telegram reporting that Earl was missing in action went to Earl's mother. Dr. Pete Rucker went by to check on her, and then he came to break the news to me. I later learned that Earl had been hit by a mortar shell and his body was washed back into the Channel. He was officially declared dead in 1945. Earl never got to see our child.[76]

To this writer, perhaps the most moving remembrance that has been written is one by Betty Allen Welch, the sister of Pfc. John W. Allen of the Thaxton area. For Memorial Day in 1994, nearly fifty years after her brother had been killed in France, she wrote the following tribute, which was published in the *Bedford Bulletin*:

> I remember a big brother I could look up to. He was the charming, handsome one in our family, with his blonde, wavy hair, big blue eyes and bright smile. I can see and hear him now walking through the house singing "San Antonio Rose."
>
> It's strange how memories return—in flash backs—scenes in which some of the smallest details are very clear.
>
> One Sunday morning in September 1944, I was dressing to go to Sunday School....My parents were in the kitchen, and suddenly I heard them crying out. When I went to the door, I saw them embracing as they wept. They held out their arms to me and showed me the "We regret to inform you" telegram. He had died on Sept. 10. On Oct. 16 he would have been 21 years of age—old enough to vote.
>
> No, my brother didn't storm the beach at Normandy. He was one of the countless American GIs who marched into Europe later to continue the struggle that changed the world forever. We received word that he was guarding a big gun when it happened. An enemy shell burst nearby and shrapnel hit him from the waist down.
>
> Then I remember the summer of 1948. One beautiful day, Daddy and I went to the train station in Bedford to claim his body. Two young soldiers had accompanied him. Nobody could have wished for a more honorable escort. Our "Golden Boy" had come home at last.[77]

Part II

Personal Experiences

Part II summarizes the personal experiences of the following:

Henry Chappelle and His Brothers

Henry Chappelle served during the war aboard a Navy tugboat, helping to salvage merchant ships and operating part of the time as a deep-sea diver and antiaircraft gunner. Five of his brothers also served, two in the Navy, two in the Army, and one in the Army Air Forces.[1]

Henry was one of eleven children of Mr. and Mrs. B. F. Chappelle. The family lived in the Lowry community of Bedford County before the parents moved to Roanoke. The father worked for the Norfolk and Western Railroad, where he was a fireman until he lost a leg in an accident. He later built steam engines in the shops in Roanoke.

Henry left home at age fourteen and moved in with a sister near his present home east of Bedford City. He found work at a supply company and then at Belding Heminway, the silk mill, where he worked in the spinning frames and dye department.

Twice Henry tried to enlist in the Navy; both times he was rejected because, at over six feet tall, he weighed only ninety-seven pounds. Finally, in March 1944, at age eighteen and with the help of a doctor at a Veterans hospital who brought his influence to bear, Henry was able to enlist successfully in the Navy. Arriving at the Great Lakes Naval Training Center near Chicago, he remembers stepping into a cardboard box, removing all of his clothes, dropping them into the box, and then preparing the box to be sent home by railway express. While standing there naked, he was issued Navy clothes. He was at the Great Lakes base for three weeks in March, when it was extremely windy and cold.

Henry applied for submarine warfare duty but was turned down because he did not have four months experience. He was sent to Camp Perry, Virginia, a Seabee base, for about sixteen weeks of "special forces" training. There he learned to use underwater explosives. Of the 900 men who took this training course, only nine were left at the end of the war, according to Henry. He was trained also to fire twenty- and forty-millimeter and fifty-caliber guns.

From Camp Perry he traveled to Norfolk and then sailed for eight days on a troop ship to Guantanamo, Cuba, where he and twenty-three others were dropped before the ship headed on to the Panama Canal. At Guantanamo, Henry was assigned to a tugboat, the USS *Montcalm*. The ship, with a complement of twelve officers and sixty-three men, had a mission of repairing and salvaging damaged American merchant ships. Men on the *Montcalm* would pump out a damaged ship and patch it up so it could sail again. Another mission was retrieving sensitive charts from sunken American ships before the Germans could get them. The *Montcalm* salvaged eighty-three ships in the two years Henry was aboard.

In Henry's opinion, serving on a Navy tugboat was the worst job in the Navy. The men were wet all the time, had to live with the foul odor of fuel oil, and slept twelve to a bunk area.

Henry started out as an apprentice seaman and was eventually promoted to seaman first class. He helped with maintenance of the *Montcalm*, served as a deep sea diver, and, when the men of the ship were called to general quarters, manned a twenty-millimeter antiaircraft gun on the bridge.

Trained aboard the *Montcalm* in deep sea diving by a chief petty officer who was a master diver, Henry suited up eighteen times and made nine dives. While the master diver went into the sunken vessels, Henry, as the second diver, worked outside the vessels. For being a diver, he received $5 a month in hazardous duty pay, added on to his regular pay of $83 a month as a seaman first class.

On one mission when the *Montcalm* had been ordered to salvage a ship off the Atlantic coast of Africa, a German fighter strafed the tugboat. Henry was manning his antiaircraft gun on the bridge. Assisting him as a loader of the gun was a young sailor named Bloom, who had replaced a man who lost both legs when caught between two ships. Two bullets fired by the German pilot penetrated the shield on the antiaircraft gun. Henry was grazed on the right ear and left collar. Bloom was hit five times and died in Henry's arms. Henry can still remember being soaked in Bloom's blood.

Henry was discharged from the Navy in April 1946. He married in 1957, has three children and two grandchildren, worked for fifty years as a plumber, and served as an assistant scoutmaster for ten years. He lives alone in eastern Bedford County, his wife Frances having died in 2000.

Brothers Alphonso and James also served in the Navy. John served in the Army Air Forces as a waist gunner on a B-25 Mitchell bomber. On John's twenty-fifth mission, his plane was shot down, and he was held as a prisoner of war in Germany for eighteen months. Thomas served in the Army Transportation Corps on an Army freighter in the South Pacific and on Tinian Island. Wilhelm ("Bill") was drafted into the Army during the occupation of Germany. A brother who was handicapped and four sisters did not serve.

Joseph S. Danner

Joseph S. Danner, who worked at a movie theater in Bedford during his high school years and in the months following graduation, joined the U.S. Army Air Forces. He earned a commission as a lieutenant, became a pilot of a B-26 Martin Marauder bomber, flew at least fifty missions over enemy-held territory in Europe, and, at age twenty-two, was killed when his plane crashed in England.[1]

Danner was born and raised in the town of Bedford. He was one of five children born to Albert V. Danner and Della V. Boblett Danner. As a part-time employee during his high school days and a full-time employee immediately after he graduated from Bedford High School, he worked for the Bedford Theater Corporation, which owned both theaters in Bedford. Danner worked at the Liberty Theater on West Main Street, where he performed a variety of tasks, including running the concessions counter.

Danner joined Company A of the National Guard. In October 1940, at age eighteen and just months after graduating from high school, he voluntarily enlisted in the Army, joining the U.S. Army Air Corps so that he could become a pilot. He loved airplanes, according to his sister Margaret, Mrs. R. G. Simpkins.

Danner trained at Langley Field in Virginia and then received training as a glider pilot at Stuttgart, Arkansas. On one occasion, he was commended for how he piloted a glider during a technical emergency, successfully avoiding a crash. In addition to flying gliders, he also was trained to fly P-38 Lightning and B-26 Martin Marauder bombers. He became a commissioned officer and eventually obtained the rank of first lieutenant.

In February 1943 he was given command of a B-26 and ordered to deploy to the United Kingdom. He and his co-pilot flew the bomber from Georgia to England. They were based at Bishop's Stortford, about twenty-five miles northwest of the center of London, as part of the 344th Bomb Group, 496th Squadron. He flew five bombing missions in support of the Normandy Invasion. Overall, he flew at least fifty missions over enemy-held territory. Wounded twice, he earned the Purple Heart, the Air Medal with ten Oak Leaf Clusters, and the Distinguished Flying Cross with one Silver and three Bronze Leaves.

On September 7, 1944, the *Bedford Bulletin* and *Bedford Democrat* ran front-page articles, with an accompanying photo, on Danner being promoted to first lieutenant and being awarded the Distinguished Flying Cross. Two weeks later, the newspapers announced that he had been killed.

On August 30, at age twenty-two, Danner was killed when his bomber crashed near his base in England. His mother received a telegram from the Army informing her of his death. His sister Margaret, who lived down the street from the Danner home, remembers that their father came with the telegram to break the news to her. Margaret had written to Joseph every day while he was in Europe, and Joseph had written to her often. Soon her letters to Joseph began being returned to her, with the word "deceased" written on the front of the envelope. She has kept some of the returned letters, the envelopes still sealed. The family received a sympathy letter from Gen. H. H. "Hap" Arnold, head of the U.S. Army Air Forces.

Joseph's mother later provided the following account of his death and burial service in England, apparently based on official information from the military:

On August 30, 1944, over Bishop's Stortford, England, the left wing of his plane caught fire at 3,000 feet. In an attempt to land, the plane struck a house, tearing off the roof, and then crashed into a field. All occupants were thrown clear of the wreckage. He lived only a few minutes. The cause of his death is listed as "simple fracture of the base of the skull"....He was buried September 21, 1944, in the Cambridge American Military Cemetery at Cambridge, England....He was granted full military honors, including a guard of honor firing three volleys from their rifles, a fly-over of Air Force planes, and the sounding of taps.[2]

Danner's remains were returned to Bedford in July 1948, and funeral services were held at the Danner home, conducted by three ministers. For the burial service at Greenwood Cemetery, there was a fly-over, and his grave was adorned with a floral wreath made in the shape of an airplane by Bedford florist and former U.S. Army Air Forces bombardier Harold Jarvis.

Joseph's brothers, Carl and Lewis Danner, served in the 29th Infantry Division as cooks. Carl, who became a sergeant, served in Company A with other men from Bedford. Lewis, a private, served in another company. They both participated in the Normandy Invasion. In honor of her sons serving in the military, Mrs. Danner hung a "mother's flag," with three stars, in the window of the family's home.

At the family gravesite in Greenwood Cemetery is a large head-stone with the family name "Danner" cut in large letters at the top. At the bottom is carved, "In Memory of Our Dear Son, 1st Lt. Joseph S. Danner, Oct. 4, 1921, Aug. 30, 1944, 344th Bomb Gp., 496th Sq. A.A.F., Lost in a Crash at Bishop's Stortford, Eng." In front of the headstone are markers for individual graves. Joseph is buried between his father, who died in 1949, and his mother, who died in 1985.

The Dean Family

The Dean family had seven sons—Ward, John, Bernard, Floyd, Orien, Lester, and Halsey—serve in the military in World War II, apparently more than any other family in Bedford County. (An eighth son, Herman, also joined the military, but this may have been after hostilities ended.)[1] The *Bedford Democrat* reported that "As far as it is known, no family in the state is entitled to hang more service stars in its windows than the Dean family of Bedford County."[2] For her contribution, Mrs. Dean was honored at a ceremony at the Hotel Roanoke. One son—John—was killed in action in France. Mary Burks Dean, the wife of Ward, helped manage the rationing system in Bedford during the war.

James Franklin "Frank" Dean and Pinkie C. (Creasey) Dean had thirteen children. In addition to the seven sons who served in the military during the war and the one younger son who joined the military around the end of the war, the family had a son who was a minister and did not serve, a son too young to serve, and three girls who did not serve.

The Deans lived on a farm in Bedford County until 1932, when they moved to a farm in Halifax County. In 1940 or 1941, they moved back to Bedford County, where they lived on a 160-acre farm a few miles south of the town of Bedford. There they raised tobacco, tomatoes, corn, wheat, and hay, as well as almost 1,000 chickens and twenty-four head of cattle. Some of the children went to high school in Halifax County when they lived there, and others later went to Moneta High School in Bedford County.

Four of the brothers—Floyd, Orien, Lester, and Halsey—joined the Navy. Ward, John, and Bernard joined the Army. Of the seven who served, the oldest six volunteered or enlisted; the youngest of those who served during the war, Bernard, was drafted. Herman, who was only fifteen years old in early 1944, was drafted into the Navy probably after the end of hostilities.

John Wesley Dean joined the National Guard while in high school in Halifax County. He served in Company F of the 116th Infantry

Regiment, based in South Boston, and rose to the rank of master sergeant. He was living at home in Halifax County when Company F was called to active duty in February 1941.

John landed with the 116th Infantry Regiment on D-Day. On June 17, 1944, while fighting in Normandy, he was killed in action. With his unit under fire, he was directing his men to stay down, when mortar fire hit him in the back of the head.

Ward Ashby Dean happened to be home on leave when his parents received the telegram notifying them of John's death. According to Ward, while the other sons would eventually return home safely, the Dean parents never got over the loss of John.

After the end of the war, in response to an offer from the government, the Dean family asked that John's remains be returned to Bedford. The remains were reinterred in Greenwood Cemetery, following an honor ceremony led by Bedford's National Guard Company A and attended by men from Company F as well as family and friends. The Dean parents and some of the Dean sons are now buried in a group of plots adjacent to John's.

Ward Dean enlisted in the Army in October 1941. When it appeared that he would be drafted, he volunteered so that he could have a choice of service. He wanted to serve in the infantry and thus enlisted in the Army. Before enlisting, he had been a student at Virginia Polytechnic Institute.

Ward was stationed at Camp Wheeler in Georgia when the Japanese bombed Pearl Harbor. He remembers men being positioned in trees, as lookouts for the Japanese, armed only with wooden guns. In July 1942 he was sent to officer's candidate school at Fort Hood, Texas, and received a commission in December of that year. He remained for a time at Fort Hood to help train recruits before being assigned to a tank destroyer company, either in Texas or Louisiana.

In March 1944 Ward returned to Bedford on a ten-day leave, married his girl friend, Mary W. Burks, and then returned to his unit.

After his tank unit was deactivated, he was sent in October 1944 to the Philippine Islands. His passage aboard a troop ship to the Philippines took twenty-nine days. There was not much for him to do in the Philippines, and in January 1945 he was returned to the United States and discharged, with the rank of captain.

In civilian life back home, Ward earned a degree in business at Lynchburg College and then worked as a parole and probation officer for the Commonwealth of Virginia, first in Lynchburg and then in Bedford. Ward stayed in the Army Reserves for a while and then joined the National Guard, serving in Company A of the 116th Infantry based in Bedford. He served as Commander of Company A for several years, beginning in 1951. He then served in the Army Reserves in Lynchburg, retiring in 1962 as a major.

Halsey Albert Dean entered the Navy and taught mathematics at a Navy school in Norfolk, Virginia, as a specialist teacher, first class.

Orien Franklin Dean served in the Seabees with a naval construction battalion, as a machinist's mate, third class. He was stationed in California for at least part of his service.

Lester Thomas Dean was a seaman, second class. At least part of the time, he was stationed in California.

Bernard Nelson Dean joined the Army and served as a tank driver in Lt. Gen. George S. Patton's Army in Europe. He returned home and was discharged during the war but later was recalled and sent back to Germany. He subsequently returned home again and pursued a civilian occupation.

Floyd Clarence Dean, a seaman, second class, served in Bainbridge, Maryland.

The Bedford Christian Church on North Bridge Street has mounted on a wall at the entrance to the sanctuary a glass-enclosed honor roll for its men who served in World War II, including five of the Dean sons—Bernard, John, Lester, Orien, and Ward. (Ward is also listed on the honor roll at the Main Street United Methodist Church.) On one side of the Christian Church's sanctuary is a large, stained-glass window, with a depiction of Jesus Christ in the middle and, at the bottom, a panel reading "In Loving Memory of John Wesley Dean by the Dean Family."

Mary W. Burks Dean, wife of Ward, graduated from Bedford High School in the early 1940s. After graduation, she volunteered for a time at Bedford County's War Price and Rationing Board, which was located in the courthouse. She went away to college for a period and returned to Bedford where she took a full-time job at the War Price and Rationing Board, helping issue rationing coupons. She worked at the board for two or three years.

Mary played trombone in the Bedford Firemen's Band and re-members that during the war years many of the band members were away in the service. Her two brothers served in the Navy. One was in Hawaii when the Japanese attacked Pearl Harbor. Mary met her husband-to-be while working at the War Price and Rationing Board. After she and Ward were married, she accompanied her husband back to Fort Hood. When Ward was ordered to the Philippines, Mary returned to Bedford and lived with her parents. A son was later born to the couple.

Kenneth Dooley

Kenneth Dooley landed on Omaha Beach on June 6. Unlike other D-Day veterans from Bedford who landed with the 29th Infantry Division, Dooley appears to be unique in that he landed with a field artillery battalion. While fighting in Germany in November 1944, he was wounded seriously in the arm. He spent fourteen months in hospitals.[1]

Dooley was raised in the Thaxton area of western Bedford County and attended Montvale High School. After leaving school, he worked at a shipyard in Newport News, Virginia, and then at the Belding Heminway plant in Bedford, where he operated a spinning machine.

In April 1943 Dooley went to the draft board to enlist, but a woman there told him to go home and look in his mailbox on the coming Monday. His draft notice was already in the mail. He passed his physical examination, was inducted into the Army in Richmond on May 1, and was sent to Camp Lee, south of Richmond.

Next, Private Dooley was sent to Fort Bragg, North Carolina, where he underwent thirteen weeks of artillery training as a loader for a 155-millimeter howitzer. He then went to Fort Meade, Maryland, where he was assigned as a replacement in the 186th Field Artillery Battalion, which was part of First Army, V Corps (the parent units of the 29th Infantry Division). Dooley returned to Bedford on leave and married; the marriage lasted about a year.

In 1944 Dooley deployed with his unit to New York City and then to England aboard the *Empress of Australia*. (This ship was later sunk by a kamikaze plane in the Pacific.) It took the ship about a week to cross the Atlantic as it zigzagged to avoid being attacked by German submarines. The ship landed at Liverpool and sat at the dock for two or three days before the men were allowed to debark. Dooley remembers listening to foghorns which blew frequently.

From Liverpool, Dooley's unit was deployed to a camp near the town of Bridgewater. The unit remained at this camp until the last week of May, when it deployed to an assembly area, called a "sausage." On the last day of May, the unit embarked on a ship to participate in the D-Day Invasion. The ship was anchored in the English Channel from May 31 to late on June 5, when it weighed anchor to participate in the invasion.

Dooley's unit landed on Omaha Beach late in the evening of June 6. There was still plenty of action in the area. The unit got off the beach, set up their guns, and began firing as soon as they could acquire targets. The howitzers had a range of up to fifteen miles and could fire antipersonnel rounds and armor-piercing rounds used against enemy armor and fortifications. Dooley, who was trained as a loader, eventually became the number one man on his howitzer, responsible for firing the weapon.

On June 14 and 16, Dooley wrote two letters to his mother, Mrs. Myrtle Dooley. She shared them with the *Bedford Bulletin*, which published them. (See Chapter 5 of this book.) Dooley closed one of his letters with the suggestion to "Go read the papers and you'll find where I am and what I'm doing." The people in Bedford actually had little idea what was happening to their loved ones in Europe.

In the ensuing months, Dooley's unit moved further into France and then into Belgium and Luxembourg.

On November 8, 1944, somewhere near the German border, Dooley was walking around just a few yards from his howitzer when a German sniper shot him in the right arm, shattering his elbow. Dooley made it back to his gun for protection and was treated by a medic who gave him a shot of morphine in his hand.

Dooley was taken to an aid station and eventually to a hospital in Paris. He spent the next fourteen months in hospitals in England and the United States and had several operations on his arm. From England, he traveled by ship to Boston and then took a train en route to a hospital in southern Georgia. Most of the time on the train he was in pajamas and a robe. When the train passed through Lynchburg, adjacent to Bedford County, Dooley had no money to make a call home.

At the hospital in Georgia, Dooley received physical therapy to straighten and limber his arm, which was curled up. As part of the treatment, the staff would dip his arm twice in hot wax, and then one nurse would hold his shoulder while another nurse grasped his hand and wrist and pulled them down to straighten the arm. The nurses would massage the waxed arm until the wax cracked and fell off. They also strapped his fingers together to straighten a couple of fingers which were curled.

Dooley would eventually be able to use his right arm, but the arm and hand would remain about 50 percent disabled. His "crazy bone" is rearranged so that it is no longer on the outside point of the elbow, and Dooley has no feeling in part of his hand. He has accidentally cut his hand and not known it until he saw it bleeding. Cold weather makes his arm hurt.

While still in the Army and convalescing, Dooley was able to come home to Bedford on leave. One day while walking down the street in Roanoke in uniform, a woman came up to him, grabbed him by the lapels, and shouted, "Why aren't you in camp. My son is in camp in the hot sun, having a hard time." Dooley was irate and had to restrain himself. He either doesn't remember or won't say what he said in response to the woman.

Dooley was discharged from the Army on January 28, 1946, and returned to Bedford. He went back to work at the silk mill, moved to a job at Rubatex, and then worked as a plumber. He married and began a family. He bought a backhoe, worked on water lines and septic tanks, and worked for a telephone company for ten years digging and driving grounding rods. He has worked on the security staff at the hospital in Bedford for more than ten years. He goes to the Veterans Administration hospital in Salem for medical care.

Dooley remarried, and he and his wife have three grown sons and grandchildren. Son Robbie Dooley, in 2000 and 2001, took a role in the Sedalia Center's production of the World War II historical drama *Bedford Goes to War* in part because the drama featured a letter written home by his father.

The Draper Brothers

The three sons of Frank Price Draper and Mary Draper served in the military during World War II. The eldest son, Frank P. Draper, Jr., served in the Army with Company A from Bedford. He died of wounds received on June 6, 1944, during the Invasion of Normandy. Middle son, Warren Gamiel Eugene Draper, served in the United States and in Europe in a military police unit of the 42[d] Infantry Division. Youngest son, David Samuel Lewis Draper, served in the Navy with the Seabees and was deployed to the Pacific Theater with a construction battalion.[1]

The Draper family lived on Railroad Avenue in the eastern part of the town of Bedford, about a quarter of a mile from the Rubatex factory. The three sons were born in nearly two-year intervals. There was one daughter, who was the youngest of the children. All three sons were athletes during their teenage years and played sports for Bedford High School, from which they graduated between 1936 and 1941.

Before and during the war, the father, Frank, Sr., who had worked earlier for ten years on the railroad, worked at Hampton Looms, the woolen mill. Mrs. Draper worked at the Rubatex plant. She also was instrumental in establishing the Church of God in Bedford.

Before the war, Frank, Jr., nicknamed "Juney" by the family, worked at Hampton Looms and was very active in the Christian Church on North Bridge Street. He was not married but had a girl friend. He joined Bedford's Company A of the National Guard and eventually worked his way up through the ranks to technical sergeant. He was mobilized into active duty with Company A in February 1941 and deployed with the unit to various bases in the United States and then in 1942 to England.

While training in England, Frank and three other Bedford soldiers in Company A played on a baseball team, which eventually won the European Theater of Operations baseball championship. Frank played center field. In the championship game, he got hits in three out of four times at bat and scored one run. He also found time to be best man at the wedding of a friend and fellow soldier from Virginia, Sgt. Hite Baker, who married a young English woman. (Baker was later killed in the war.)

Frank wrote poetry, including a poem about military censorship of the mail, a Mother's Day poem in 1944, and at least one poem written in a small, black notebook, perhaps shortly before he wrote notes that appear to be instructions for D-Day. (See Chapters 13 and 15.)

In the D-Day Invasion, Frank was mortally wounded. Reports indicate that he was evacuated from Omaha Beach on one of the landing craft and subsequently died of his wounds. It is not clear whether he died during the evacuation, as he was being taken to a hospital in England, or at the hospital. (See Chapter 13.) One soldier reported he died during the evacuation. Information provided by Frank's mother, contained in records at the Bedford County Courthouse, states that: "He was wounded, couldn't get any medical aid, was carried back to hospital in England, was dead on arrival at hospital or died soon after, twelve hours with no aid given him."[2]

Frank was buried in the U.S. Military Cemetery in Brookwood, England, while others in Company A killed on D-Day were buried in France. In 1948, at the Draper family's request, the U.S. Government returned Frank's remains to Bedford. On July 24, 1948, a funeral service was held at the Bedford Christian Church, followed by burial in Greenwood Cemetery, with former military compatriots serving as pallbearers.

Frank's death deeply affected the Draper family. Son Gamiel has said his mother was never the same afterward. A fellow worker at the Rubatex factory said Mrs. Draper never returned to the plant after her son's death, although Gamiel cannot confirm this.

Mrs. Draper wrote and had published in local newspapers several memorial tributes to Frank, including one in September 1944, on the anniversary of his twenty-sixth birthday. On Mother's Day 1945, she had published in the *Bedford Bulletin* a poem Frank had written for Mother's Day 1944. In addition to the large headstone erected at Frank's gravesite, the family memorialized Frank by donating and dedicating to him a stained glass window at the Bedford Christian Church, which he attended.

Warren Gamiel Eugene Draper was drafted into the Army in September 1944, while he was enrolled in a shipyard apprentice school in Newport News, Virginia. Earlier, in July 1944, while working at the shipyard, he had received a telegram from his aunt informing him of his brother Frank's death.

Gamiel had earlier met and married his wife, Fleda, in Newport News. By the time Gamiel was drafted, the couple had a two-week old son. Gamiel had earlier tried to enlist in the Navy in Richmond, but the Navy would not take him, saying he could do more good at the shipyard. During his time of service, Fleda remained in Newport News, took care of their son, and kept the books for her father's business.

Drafted as a private, Gamiel reported for ten weeks of basic training at Camp Crofts in Spartenburg, South Carolina. He was then sent to Camp Shanks, New York, and then boarded the USS *Brazil* with 5,000 other servicemen en route to La Havre, France. The trip took thirteen days as the ship zig-zagged across the Atlantic. From La Havre, the men were sent to a bivouac area and then assigned to various units. Gamiel was assigned to the 42d Infantry Division, the Rainbow Division, known by its distinctive rainbow patch. He would rise in rank to sergeant during his service.

Gamiel was assigned to a military police unit within the division. As the unit deployed forward into France, Germany, and Austria, Gamiel helped direct traffic and handle German prisoners of war. His unit had to move and process German prisoners and guard them in stockades. After the cessation of hostilities, he performed occupation duties in Austria for eight months, two months in Kitzbuhel and six months in Salzburg. Gamiel was in charge of security at the trial in Salzburg of three Yugoslav prisoners charged with shooting captured American airmen. The prisoners were tried, convicted, and hanged. Also during the occupation period, Gamiel helped run a stockade for American servicemen incarcerated under the U.S. Military Code of Justice.

In early 1946 Gamiel shipped out of Bremerhaven, Germany, for New York aboard the USS *George Washington*, a ship that had been captured from the Germans in World War I. He was sent to Fort Meade, Maryland, for a week or two of outprocessing and then was discharged from active duty. He took the bus to Newport News, where he was met at the bus station by his wife and toddler son, who had driven to the station in her father's pickup truck.

In 1947 Gamiel and his family moved to Bedford. He worked at an appliance store, which soon went out of business. After giving some thought to joining the state police, he decided to join the town of Bedford's police force. He served eighteen years with the Bedford police. Earlier, when being discharged from the military, he had signed up for the Army Reserves, and, during the Korean War in the early 1950s, he was recalled to active duty for a year, spending the time at Fort Meade.

Later he took a job at the Aerofin company in Lynchburg, helping to make heating coils and air conditioning units. For twenty-three years, he commuted to this job and held a second job painting buildings at the Rubatex factory in Bedford, normally working thirteen hours a day on the two jobs.

Gamiel and Fleda are retired, live in Bedford, have two sons and two daughters, and grandchildren.

David Samuel Lewis Draper was inducted into the Navy in August 1943 and served in the Seabees as a machinist's mate, first class, in a construction battalion in the Pacific Theater, including in New Guinea. After his service, he settled in New York for thirty-two years. He subsequently moved back to Bedford.

Taylor N. Fellers

Taylor Nicholas Fellers served as a captain and commander of Company A, 1st Battalion, 116th Infantry Regiment. He led Company A during the D-Day Invasion of Normandy and was killed on Omaha Beach on June 6, 1944.[1]

Fellers was born on June 10, 1914, and was raised on a farm in Bedford County's community of Goode, northeast of the town of Bedford. He was the oldest of six children born to Peter A. Fellers and Annie Leftwich Fellers. The children attended Cifax Grade School and Brooke Hill School, and all six graduated from New London Academy High School.

After his schooling, Fellers, in 1933, went to work for the Virginia Department of Highways. He worked there for eight years, rising to become principal highway foreman in charge of bridge work in Bedford County. He was highly respected in the department. The department's resident engineer for Bedford, after Fellers' death, paid tribute to him, saying he had been industrious, competent, thoroughly reliable, and one of the most valued employees in the Bedford residency.[2]

Sometime in the early1930s, Fellers joined Bedford's Company A, 116th Infantry, of the Virginia National Guard. He joined as a private and worked his way up through the enlisted ranks. He was enthusiastic about the military and enrolled in and graduated from Officers' Candidate School at Fort Benning, Georgia, receiving a commission as a second lieutenant. In 1940, as a second lieutenant, he was the third ranking man in Company A.[3]

While working at the highway department and serving in the National Guard, Fellers married Naomi Newman. The couple had no children.

When Company A was called up for active duty in February 1941, Fellers deployed with the unit to Fort Meade, Maryland. He occasionally came back to Bedford on leave or furlough. At some point, his wife accompanied him to Fort Meade and then to Camp Blanding, Florida, when Company A was deployed there in 1942.

In January 1942 he was promoted to captain and became the commander of Company A. He commanded Company A during its transatlantic passage in the fall of 1942 and its subsequent training in Great Britain.

His mother displayed in the window of the family home a "Mother's Flag" with four stars. One star was for Taylor; another was for son Royal, who served in the Navy; a third was for son Calvin, who served in the Army in Italy; and the fourth was for their daughter Bertie's husband, Clarence Higgenbotham, who served with the Army Corps of Engineers in England, France, and Germany.

On D-Day, June 6, 1944, Captain Fellers was in command of Company A. He was on one of the British landing craft with some thirty of his men. Some have written that the boat with Captain Fellers was destroyed by German fire before it reached the beach. Former British Royal Navy Sub-lieutenant George ("Jimmy") Green, who commanded the landing craft transporting Company A, avers that he saw Fellers and the men in his landing craft land on the beach. D-Day veteran John Robert ("Bob") Slaughter, who was in nearby Company D, has said that at the beach Fellers and his boat crew were hit by an artillery shell which "looked like it made Capt. Fellers just evaporate into thin air."[4]

Fellers was one of the nineteen men of Company A killed on D-Day. He was buried in a temporary grave near the beach. Fellow Company A soldier Roy Stevens visited the grave of Captain Fellers, as well as the grave of his brother, Ray Stevens, on June 10, 1944.[5] Some weeks later, Clarence Higgenbotham, Fellers' brother-in-law, visited the grave and placed flowers on it.

Although the Fellers family became suspicious when their letters to Taylor began to be returned, the family did not learn of his death until more than a month after D-Day, and the initial information was unofficial. On July 10, 1944, Taylor's mother received a letter from

England from a Mrs. Lunscomb, expressing sympathy in Taylor's death, about which she had heard from Bill Williams, a soldier from Lynchburg. Fellers and Williams had met Mrs. Lunscomb and visited in her home. The Fellers family did not receive official communication from the government until July 17, and this notice was that Taylor was missing in action in France since June 6. Not until the middle of September did the government inform the family that Taylor was considered to have been killed in action.

When the government offered the family the option of leaving Taylor buried in France or returning his remains to Bedford, the family chose to have the remains brought back to Bedford and buried in Greenwood Cemetery in an area where men from Company A and other units are buried.

On June 6, 1954, the 10th anniversary of D-Day, at a ceremony held at the Bedford County Courthouse, Taylor's mother was asked to unveil the memorial plaque mounted on a stone naming and honoring twenty-three men from Bedford County in the 116th Infantry Regiment, 29th Infantry Division, who died in the preparation for and conduct of the Normandy Invasion and later battles.

The wife of Captain Fellers remarried. She was later killed in an automobile accident. His sister, Mrs. Bertie Woodford, now has and cherishes his Purple Heart Medal, which was awarded posthumously.

Joseph E. Goode

Joseph E. Goode served in the U.S. Army Air Forces during World War II, attaining the rank of technical sergeant. He was first an airplane mechanic and later a flight engineer and gunner on a B-17 Flying Fortress bomber. He flew on thirty-five bombing missions against targets in Germany, including Berlin.[1]

Goode was born and raised in Bedford County. His family's farm was about ten miles south of the town of Bedford. He graduated from

Huddleston High School in southeast Bedford County in 1936 and worked on the farm until he enlisted in the U.S. Army Air Corps in January 1941 at the age of twenty-one. He thought that America would become involved in the war. He also thought that by enlisting his military experience would be better than if he were drafted.

His older brother, Austin Goode, served in Bedford's Company A of the National Guard but left that unit during the war and joined the 80th Division, which fought in Germany. The youngest brother, W. D. Goode, served as a navigator on a bomber in the U.S. Fifteenth Air Force in Italy. Austin now lives in Dillwyn, Virginia, and W. D. lives in Radford, Virginia.

After enlisting, Joe was sent to a number of bases in the United States for training and duty. He was first sent to Lowry Field in Denver for basic training. He then went to airplane mechanic's school for about eight weeks at Chanute Field in Illinois.

In the fall of 1943 he applied for pilot training. He was sent to Clemson College for a while. He took tests in Nashville, Tennessee, to qualify for training as a pilot, navigator, or bombardier. His scores were not high enough, and he was sent instead to gunnery school for six weeks at Tyndall Field near Panama City, Florida. He then went to a base near Alexandria, Louisiana, where he joined a B-17 crew and underwent two months of crew flight training.

Goode became a flight engineer and gunner. As flight engineer, he and the radio operator had to fly with the pilot, navigator, and bombardier as they trained in flying the B-17. After this training, the crew to which he was assigned was sent to Kearney, Nebraska, for equipment orientation.

The B-17s that Goode's crew flew later in combat were built by Boeing. They had four Wright engines, cruised at 187 miles per hour (mph), had a top speed of 287 mph at 25,000 feet, with a service ceiling of just over 35,000 feet, and could carry some 4,000 pounds of bombs.[2]

From Nebraska the crew traveled to New York City, where, in August 1944, they boarded the *Ile de France*, an oceanliner converted to carry troops, and sailed to Scotland, disembarking eleven days later. From Scotland, the crew traveled to the Midlands area of England near

Northampton and to an American air base at Grafton-Underwood, which became their operating base from September 1944 to March 1945.

Goode and his crew were assigned to the 544th Squadron, 384th Bomb Group, 41st Bombardment Wing, U.S. Eighth Air Force, based in England. To illustrate the size and strength of the Eighth Air Force, on the single day of December 24, 1944, while Goode was assigned to this unit, it sent over 21,000 American airmen in 2,034 heavy bombers and 936 fighters to bomb rail yards, communication centers, and airfields used by German forces. This was said to have been the greatest single force of airplanes ever dispatched.[3]

The 384th Bomb Group was particularly active against enemy targets on the European mainland between June 1943 and the end of April 1945, flying 316 missions, involving 9,348 aircraft sorties and 22,415 tons of bombs dropped on target. The bomb group lost in action 159 aircraft and more than 1,625 men, requiring continuing replacement. (Of the 1,625 men lost, 347 were killed in action, 270 were missing in action, 757 escaped from their aircraft but were taken as prisoners of war, 221 were able to escape or evade capture, and 30 were interned, but not as prisoners of war, or were repatriated.)[4]

In the 384th Bomb Group's first months of combat in the summer of 1943, German fighter aircraft as well as antiaircraft artillery posed significant threats to Allied bombers. In June 1943, nearly every seventh aircraft of the 384th that took to the air against the Germans failed to return. On one day alone, July 25, 1943, on a mission against Hamburg, Germany, the 384th lost seven of eighteen aircraft on the mission, including about seventy of 180 men aboard the planes. The subordinate 544th Squadron suffered extraordinarily. Six of the seven aircraft lost on July 25 came from the 544th, which saw only one of its planes return. By the end of July, the 544th, which began operations in England the month before with nine bomber crews, had lost more crews than it started with—eight original crews and four replacement crews.[5]

By the time Goode's crew joined the 544th Squadron of the 384th Bomb Group, the risks were still significant but the odds for survival were greater. In late 1943 a flying crewman in the 384th had only a 36 percent chance of completing a twenty-five-mission tour of duty. By 1945 his chances had jumped to 65 percent, even though a tour of duty had been increased to thirty-five missions.[6] In Goode's first month, September 1944, one in every sixty-one aircraft that took to the air failed to return, while by March 1945, the loss rate was down to one in 222 aircraft failing to return.[7]

Goode's crew flew thirty-five bombing missions against targets in Germany, in or near the Ruhr Valley, Cologne, Regansburg, and Berlin. Cologne was their most frequent target, and Berlin was their most distant. The crew flew missions about two or three times a week, with the frequency depending on the weather.

On a typical day when they were scheduled to fly a mission, the crew would be awakened around 4 a.m. They would be fed breakfast, which on a mission-day included real eggs, instead of powdered eggs, which many thought tasted like sawdust. The men would then attend a mission briefing and reach their aircraft between 6:00 and 7:00 a.m. If the weather were satisfactory, they would take off by 7:30 or 8:00 a.m.

A bomb group, such as the 384th, flew its thirty-six B-17s together as a unit. There could be three such bomb groups flying as a wing toward the same target. The aircraft flew together to defend against enemy fighter attacks and to coordinate the attack on the target.

The aircraft would take off individually, fly around in circles gaining altitude, and then, in mass formation, fly off toward their target.

As his plane took off on a bombing mission, Goode sat behind the pilots in the forward compartment and helped them with some of the switches and levers and advised them on any engine problems. As the plane approached the continental European landmass, he would climb into the turret on the top of the plane to look for enemy fighter aircraft and man twin fifty-caliber machine guns.

Goode and his crew, flying in the latter part of the war in the fall of 1944 and winter of 1944-45, never encountered any German fighter aircraft. Their biggest problem was antiaircraft artillery fire, commonly called "flak." The Germans would set the fusing of their antiaircraft artillery shells to explode at the altitude they expected the bombers to fly and then fire them into the suspected flight paths of the on-coming bombers. The shells often missed and did no damage, but they also often exploded near enough to a bomber to damage it and injure its crewmen, sometimes fatally. Occasionally a shell would make a direct hit on a bomber, with immediate fatal consequences. Pilots sought to avoid antiaircraft fire when possible, but flying in mass formation restricted their flexibility, and on the final run to target they had to fly straight ahead.

Although the pilots on Goode's plane did what they could to avoid antiaircraft fire, their plane was hit by flak on most missions, as were many other aircraft. Out of the ten men in Goode's original crew, two met with misfortune while flying on other aircraft. One was killed, and the other became a prisoner of war after bailing out of his aircraft.

The B-17s, loaded with bombs, would use about three-quarters of their fuel to gain altitude and reach their targets. One-quarter of the fuel was usually sufficient to get back to base after dropping their bombs.

Flying a bombing mission could be physically draining, given the long hours, the danger of flying over enemy territory, and the uncomfortable conditions aboard the aircraft. A round-trip mission to Berlin and back, the longest mission for Goode's crew, could involve over nine hours in the air. Counting pre-flight preparation, the time in flight, and the debriefing afterwards, the working day could be as long as sixteen hours.[8] The danger from antiaircraft artillery was great, as was the risk for some squadrons of enemy fighters. Flying in unpressurized and unheated bombers for hours at a time was uncomfortable. The men wore oxygen masks above 10,000 feet of altitude, and at 25,000 feet the temperature could reach some thirty to forty degrees below zero. The men wore suits that could be heated electrically by plugging them into the aircraft's electrical system.

Goode recalls three missions that were particularly out of the ordinary. On one, a gauge on the aircraft indicated an engine oil problem, and his plane had to turn back. The second extraordinary mission was one to Cologne. On this mission, the group had to make three runs at the target. On the first run, the lead plane was shot down, and the other planes had to circle around and regroup. On the second run, Goode is not certain what happened but thinks the lead plane might not have been able to pick out the target. The planes circled around once again. On the third run the planes dropped their bombs on the target.

The third and worst mission for the crew was their seventh, relatively early into their thirty-five missions. On this mission, the gas tanks on the left side of the plane were hit by flak. One engine on the left stopped, and because of the gasoline leak the crew had to shut down and feather the other left engine. The two right-side engines did not have sufficient power to pull the plane up. The pilot headed the plane toward an airfield in Brussels, which had been liberated in early September 1944.

Goode had to help drop the turret in the belly of the plane so the plane would have a flat bottom in case they had to crashland. Six of the crew took their emergency crash positions in the radio operator's compartment. The left wing of the plane hit a greenhouse, the plane crashlanded on some railroad tracks, and the plane broke apart in the middle. Miraculously, no one was seriously injured.

Some Belgians came to the crash site, and someone contacted American authorities. An American truck picked up the crew members and took them to an American base, after which they were flown back to England. After ten days of leave, the crew was given another B-17. They would go on to fly twenty-eight more missions. Goode earned the Air Medal with five Oak Leaf Clusters, among other medals.

After completing their quota of thirty-five missions, Goode and his crew were returned to the United States. They sailed on an American troop ship in a convoy, arriving in New York in late March 1945. Goode was given a thirty-day furlough, which he spent in Bedford. He was then sent by train to Santa Ana, California, for three weeks of recreation, after which he was sent to engine school at Chenute Field in Illinois and then to Montgomery, Alabama, where he was assigned to a B-29 Superfortress bomber, probably in preparation for deployment to the Pacific. He remained in Alabama until September 1945, when he was sent to Fort Meade, Maryland, and honorably discharged.

Goode returned to the family farm in Bedford. Using his veteran's GI Bill benefits, he enrolled in college at Virginia Polytechnic Institute and State University (now known as Virginia Tech) in Blacksburg, Virginia, receiving in three years a bachelor's degree in vocational education. He taught agriculture for one year at Climax in Pittsylvania County, Virginia. After the year of teaching, he returned to the family dairy farm in Bedford and farmed until 1980, when he retired. He helped on the farm until 1985, when he moved into town in Bedford.

Goode has been married twice, both wives dying of illness. He has no children. He has been a member of the American Legion since the late 1940s. He has also been a member of the Main Street Methodist Church, and at one time he was a deputy in the Grange organization. He has lived at the Elks National Home in Bedford since early 2002. Proud of his military service, Goode has hanging on the wall of his apartment a portrait of him in his uniform, painted by his second wife. He also has several books on the Air Force in his collection of books.

Martin Teaford Hatcher

Martin Teaford Hatcher served as a U.S. Navy combat pilot, commander of a squadron of Avenger torpedo bomber aircraft, and trainer of pilots during the war. He flew thirty-three combat missions and participated in many major actions in the Pacific.

Hatcher grew up in Bedford and graduated from Bedford High School. He then enrolled in the U.S. Naval Academy at Annapolis, Maryland, graduating in 1935. After becoming a commissioned officer, he went to flight school and became a Naval aviator.

During the war he first served as a pilot and squadron trainer at Pensacola, Florida. Then in July 1943 he deployed to the South Pacific, where he served as a pilot and unit commander, with the rank of Lieutenant Commander. He led a squadron of Grumman Avenger torpedo bomber aircraft, which were based on an aircraft carrier. The men in the air group to which he was assigned, Air Group 23, were nicknamed the "Sun Setters."

Flying a total of thirty-three combat missions, he and his squadron participated in attacks on the Japanese at Rabaul, Bougainville, Truk, Tarawa, the Gilbert and Marshall Islands, New Georgia, Munda,

Rendova, Palau, Buka, and Bonis. He and his aircraft attacked Japanese ships and airfields and shot down one Japanese Zero aircraft.

The *Bedford Democrat* on August 17, 1944, reported on Hatcher's accomplishments, quoting from a newspaper in Fort Lauderdale, Florida, which related one of the most significant missions of Hatcher and his squadron. This mission was against Japanese naval forces in the harbor at Rabaul, located at the northeastern tip of the island of New Britain, east of New Guinea and northeast of Australia.

> Word had come of the concentration (of Japanese ships), and it was thought likely that the Nippers were rendezvousing to attempt interfering with large-scale landings being carried out by American ground forces in the area. Those Jap ships had to be blasted out of there promptly and the little task group which included Commander Hatcher's squadron was elected because it was closer than anybody else to Rabaul.
>
> Multiply the number of AA (antiaircraft) guns on a single modern combat vessel by about fifty, then add the number of flak-throwers the Japs could be expected to have in one of their most important South Pacific naval bases, and then add to that the number of Nip fighter planes for air cover at a fortress like Rabaul—and you will have a rough idea of what Commander Hatcher and his squadron were ordered to skid into.
>
> Seven torpedo planes from Hatcher's squadron, including his own, went in. Two, literally enveloped in a geyser of shells and bullets, were promptly shot down. The others made their runs, released their torpedoes, and escaped the erupting volcano by a miracle they don't understand but for which they thank heaven. However, several of the returning planes were so riddled, they never flew again.
>
> Comdr. Hatcher got a direct hit on a Jap destroyer and saw an immense gush of flame erupt from it, but didn't wait around to see if it sank.[1]

Against the targets at Rabaul, Hatcher's and other torpedo bomber squadrons in their parent air group made more than sixty bombing runs and dropped almost 800,000 pounds of bombs and torpedoes. Together with accompanying fighter squadrons, the air group left three large Japanese warships in flames, destroyed or damaged forty smaller Japanese craft, and shot up fifty-five Japanese aircraft in the air and twenty-six on the ground.

After Rabaul, Hatcher and his unit did not get to attack Japanese Navy ships again, but they supported some of the main American offensives in the Pacific, as described below in the *Bedford Bulletin*:

> …they neutralized Buka and Bonis air fields while the Marines landed on Bougainville. They knocked out Nauru, while Tarawa fell, and Wotje and Taros during the taking of Kwajalein. Then they softened up Enrivetok so that it looked like a dump pile when it, too, was captured. The recent blows at Palau, Hollandia, and the devastating smash at Truk finished off the tour of duty.[2]

Hatcher also helped train Army Air Forces pilots on how to take off from an aircraft carrier, including bomber pilots who flew with Jimmy Doolittle in attacks on Tokyo and the Japanese mainland.

Hatcher was awarded the Distinguished Flying Cross and Air Medal. He returned to the United States in 1944 and became an aviation training officer at the U.S. Naval Air Station in Fort Lauderdale. Hatcher went on after the war to make the Navy a career.

The Hoback Family

Brothers Bedford T. Hoback and Raymond S. Hoback served in Bedford County's Company A of the National Guard, both as enlisted men and as non-commissioned officers. Both brothers were killed on D-Day in the invasion at Omaha Beach. The Hoback family was one of the first families in Bedford to be notified of the death of loved ones in the D-Day invasion. Lucille Hoback Boggess, a sister of the two brothers, has helped preserve the memory of her brothers and

Company A by giving many interviews and serving as a catalyst to have the National D-Day Memorial located in Bedford.[1]

John and Macie Hoback were the parents of seven children, including Bedford, Raymond, and Lucille. The family lived on a farm northeast of the town of Bedford in a community known as Center Point.

Bedford joined the active Army and served in Hawaii before returning to Bedford County. Raymond, who was six years younger than Bedford, went to work for the highway department after completing the eighth grade.[2]

In about 1939 Bedford and then Raymond joined Company A of the National Guard. By 1940 Bedford was a corporal, and Raymond a private first class.[3]

Both brothers were called up to active duty when Company A was federalized on February 3, 1941, and sent to Fort Meade, Maryland. By this time, they both had been promoted and given increased responsibilities. Bedford, with the rank of sergeant, was a platoon sergeant, and Raymond, with the rank of corporal, was a squad leader in a different platoon than his older brother's.[4]

Bedford has been described as having a wild streak and capricious personality, particularly when compared to the quiet, reserved Raymond. While the brothers were stationed at Fort Meade, Bedford returned home almost every weekend, whether he had permission or not, piling fellow soldiers into his station wagon for the trip at $2 a head.[5] By August 1941 Bedford had been reduced from sergeant to private.[6]

Bedford had a girl friend or fiancée, and she and five other women from Bedford traveled to Florida in September 1942 to see their loved ones in Company A before the unit deployed overseas. The women returned to Bedford County in Bedford Hoback's station wagon, driven by a brother of M/Sgt. John Wilkes of Company A.

Bedford and Raymond remained active in Company A through its training at various locations in the United States and subsequently in England. Raymond had severe nosebleeds and could have been discharged from the service, but he chose to remain in Company A with his older brother.[7]

By June 1944, Raymond had been promoted to staff sergeant. Bedford remained a private.[8]

On D-Day, both brothers were in the first wave to attack Omaha Beach. Bedford was killed in action. His sister Lucille believes he was killed by mortar fire. Raymond was declared missing in action, a status changed a year or so later to killed in action. Raymond's remains were never found. Lucille believes Raymond made it quite a distance up the beach before being wounded, as his Bible was found on the sand in a dry condition and returned to the family. She thinks the wounded were placed near the water to be evacuated by boat, and, in the chaos of the battle, the tide came in and washed him away.[9]

One D-Day veteran, Harold Baumgarten, has written: "I saw …Bedford Hoback, who received shell fragments in the face. The same explosion got me in the cheek of my face….It was reported that Raymond, wounded, drowned while lying at the water's edge, as the tide came in. His Bible, wrapped in plastic, is all that survived."[10]

On Sunday morning, July 16, 1944, more than five weeks after D-Day, the Hoback family learned of the death of Bedford. Lucille, fifteen-years old at the time, many years later described the event: "We were all getting ready for church when the first telegram came."[11] (Their church was the Centerpoint Methodist Church, a small country church right across the road from the Hoback's house.) "…the sheriff brought the telegram. He was a friend of my father's…."[12] Lucille described how her father walked out to meet Sheriff Jim Marshall. Lucille went out, too, but her father waved her back and soon called for her mother. The sheriff left, and soon her father called Lucille, her sister, and her third brother into the kitchen and had them sit at the table. Their mother was sobbing. Her father told the children that their brother Bedford had been killed in the war on D-Day. They all cried.[13]

Lucille has also described how the church members responded that Sunday morning. Someone had come to check on them when church was ready to begin and they had not arrived. The Hobacks were always present in the small, fifty-member congregation, and Mr. Hoback was church treasurer. Word filtered back to the church, and soon the pastor and some twenty-five people from the church came to the house to try to comfort the family. The formal church service was forgotten, and people began bringing food. At some point the Hoback parents left to go break the news to Bedford's fiancée.[14]

The next day, Monday, Lucille and her siblings were making ice cream in the basement to try to help make their parents feel better, when a second telegram arrived. It announced that Raymond was missing in action.[15]

Lucille has described the effect on her parents. "It just about killed my mother. She never was the same after that. Losing two sons was more than she could handle. She never wanted to have fun anymore."[16] Her father would walk out to the barn so the children wouldn't see him cry.[17]

A soldier from West Virginia, Pvt. H. W. Crayton, found Raymond's Bible in the sand on Omaha Beach and sent it to Mrs. Hoback with a note. Mrs. Hoback had given the Bible to Raymond for Christmas in 1938.[18]

Lucille has said that her mother always treasured that Bible. The Bible was then passed on to Lucille to treasure. This story surely was the inspiration for one of the bronze sculptures at the National D-Day Memorial in Bedford. The sculpture shows a young soldier dead on the beach, with his Bible lying on the sand beside him. Lucille has been quick to suggest that the sculpture does not represent her brother per se but all the soldiers who died on the beaches of Normandy.

When after the end of the war the government offered to bring home for burial the remains of the Hoback brothers, the family decided to leave Bedford buried in the American Military Cemetery at Normandy where there is also a memorial for men such as Raymond, who were killed at Normandy but whose remains were never recovered. Lucille has said, "My mother always said they left home together and served together and died together. She seemed to have more comfort with leaving them together."[19] The Parker family of Bedford County made a similar decision for their two sons killed in Europe, one of whom was also missing in action before finally being officially declared a year later as killed in action.

Lucille, for her own part, has done much to honor not only her two brothers but all the veterans of Company A and others who fought in the Normandy Invasion. She has done this both personally and in an official capacity. She has granted many interviews to journalists and authors, and she helped organize many annual reunions of Company A. She served for a number of years up to 2004 as a member of the Bedford County Board of Supervisors and chaired the board some of those years. In this capacity, she represented the county at many ceremonies related to veterans. She was a catalyst in having Bedford become the site of the National D-Day Memorial, and she served for several years on the board of directors of the National D-Day Memorial Foundation.

Willie J. Hobson

Willie J. Hobson, a black soldier from Bedford, served in the 366th Infantry Regiment and 92d Infantry Division. In the segregated U.S. Army of the early 1940s, these units were manned exclusively with Blacks, except for some white officers. Hobson fought against the Germans in North Africa, Italy, and Germany. While fighting in Italy, he was wounded in the leg and eye. As the war concluded in Europe, he was sent to the Philippines.[1]

Hobson was born and raised in Bedford County, in the area of Taylors Mountain, northwest of the town of Bedford. Following his schooling, he worked on a farm.

Hobson was drafted on April 8, 1941, at age twenty-three. He was sent to Fort Devens, Massachusetts, for basic training, which lasted about three months. He was trained as a rifleman on an M-1 rifle and qualified as a sharpshooter. It was at Fort Devens that he was assigned to the 366th Infantry. After his training he was sent to Ottawa, Canada, to guard a railroad bridge against possible sabotage.

In 1942 Hobson was sent on a troop ship to Casablanca, Morocco. The trip took twenty-eight days. He fought in North Africa on the front lines against the Germans for about a month.

His unit was subsequently deployed to Italy to fight the Germans there. The unit fought first in the Naples area for a couple of months and then was deployed to other areas of Italy, where they fought for a year or longer. Hobson was wounded in the leg and eye and was hospitalized for about a day.

From Italy his unit was deployed by train and foot to Germany, where they fought in the Berlin area.

As the fighting ended in Europe, Hobson and his unit were sent to Manila in the Philippines. They moved by ship, a distance of some 17,000 miles, which took forty-five days. They were in the Manila area for about three months, primarily guarding Japanese prisoners of war.

From Manila, Hobson was sent back to America via ship, a trip that took nineteen days. Landing in California, he took a five-day train ride back to the East Coast, where he was discharged on December 24, 1946. During his nearly five years of service, he had risen from private to technical sergeant.

During the war Hobson corresponded primarily with his sister. He helped write letters for some of the men in his unit who did not know how to write well.

Hobson returned to Bedford and worked at a number of jobs. He worked for three or four years at the Spar plant, which made finishes for the outsides of refrigerators. He did contract work for the railroad, worked at a sawmill, and worked at a brickyard, from which he eventually retired. He joined the Veterans of Foreign Wars and was active for a while but is no longer active. Hobson, who never married, lives in the City of Bedford.

Woodrow Wilson Hubbard

Woodrow W. Hubbard served in the U.S. Navy aboard a destroyer, the USS *Picking*, which, over the course of two years in 1944 and 1945, saw major action against the Japanese in the areas of the Aleutians and Kurile Islands, the Philippine Islands, and Okinawa.[1]

Hubbard was born in the Bedford County community of Moneta and went to school in the Flint Hill area. Following his schooling, he worked as a farmer and a truck driver. In 1942, he worked for the Virginia State Highway Department.

In 1943 he was drafted. He was married and had one child at the time. Inducted into the U.S. Navy on June 17, he was sent to the Naval Training Station in Sampson, New York. Following this training, he was assigned to the destroyer USS *Picking* (DD-685).

The *Picking* was commissioned at the Brooklyn Navy Yard on September 21, 1943. After a shakedown cruise, she steamed through the Panama Canal for the Pacific Ocean.

While deployed in the Pacific Ocean over the course of 1944 and 1945, remaining outside U.S. waters for two years and eight days, the *Picking* played a role in several of the major battles in the Pacific.[2]

From January to July 1944, the *Picking* operated in the general area of the Aleutian Islands. During this period she took part in five offensive operations that targeted Japanese shipping and installations in the Kurile Islands. In February 1944, the ship participated in the first naval surface bombardment of Japanese home waters, bombarding the Kurabusaki area of Paramushiru. In June, the *Picking* was involved in the first and second bombardment of Matsuwa To in the Kurile Islands. During intervals between these offensive operations, the ship performed escort duties, swept for Japanese submarines, searched for downed pilots, and trained.

On July 31, 1944, Hubbard wrote his wife in Bedford:

How long do the people back there think the war will last now? I believe it will be over by next year this time don't you, no one knows maybe sooner. That will be a happy day won't it. It can't come too quick for me. I hope little Boyd and Dan won't ever have nothing like this to go through....

Hubbard's guess for the end of the war was off by only two weeks, the Japanese surrendering a year later in mid-August 1945.

In August 1944 the *Picking* replenished in San Francisco and then steamed for the South Pacific.

In October the ship participated in the initial assault in the Leyte Gulf area for the liberation of the Philippine Islands. On October 20 the men of the *Picking* fired on three attacking Japanese planes; on October 24 they fired on another group of planes, downing one of the aircraft. In November the *Picking* assisted with the landing of American troops on Leyte Island and helped defend against attacking Japanese aircraft. On November 20 the American naval force was attacked by four kamikaze planes, and the *Picking* assisted in downing one.

In January 1945 the *Picking* participated in the invasion and occupation of Luzon in the Philippine Islands. On January 9, as the American force approached Lingayen Gulf off Luzon, it was fired upon by several Japanese aircraft, which the *Picking* helped drive off. In February the *Picking* assisted with the landing of troops in the San Narcisa area of Luzon, the bombardment and invasion of Mariveles, Bataan, Luzon, and Corregidor Island. The *Picking* fired the first U.S. Navy shell against enemy forces on Corregidor.

In March the ship was involved in the invasion of the Japanese Ryukyu Islands at Kerama Retto.

From March 26 to June 23 the *Picking* participated in the campaign for Okinawa. For a major portion of this period, from early April to early June, the ship participated in sixty-eight days of continuous naval fire support for ground force operations on Okinawa, while also helping to defend against Japanese forces from outside Okinawa, including suicide boats and aircraft. The men of the *Picking* fired over 15,000 rounds of five-inch ammunition against Japanese positions on Okinawa. During this campaign, the ship came under fire from Japanese artillery batteries on the shore and numerous attacks from Japanese fighters and torpedo attack bombers. On April 3 a torpedo launched from one plane narrowly missed the ship. On April 6 four Japanese planes attempted to attack the *Picking*, but the men drove off two with gunfire and downed the other two, one crashing 200 yards and the other 500 yards from the ship. The *Picking* was fired upon by shore batteries on April 5 and again on May 18, the latter when the ship went to the aid of the destroyer USS *Longshaw*, which had run aground on a shoal and come under fire from shore batteries. After helping to rescue men from the *Longshaw's* crew, the *Picking* was ordered to destroy by fire the *Longshaw*, which was beyond salvage.

In late June 1945 the *Picking* was ordered back to the United States for overhaul. She was put in mothballs for five years and then recommissioned for service in the Korean War.

Hubbard was discharged from the Navy in 1945 and returned to Bedford County. He went to work as a mechanic for the Kroger Grocery chain. He commuted from Bedford County to the Kroger facility in Salem, Virginia, a round trip of some sixty miles. He worked at Kroger for thirty years and never missed a day, with the exception of one day in 1967 when a major snow storm hit the area and the snow drifts were so high that the highway department had to bring in earth moving equipment to clear the roads. After he retired from Kroger, he worked at other jobs, such as school maintenance. He worked up to his mid-eighties, to give him something to do.

Hubbard and his wife, Edna Dillon Hubbard, have five children, as well as grandchildren. Hubbard has told his family stories of his days in the Navy. His son David remembers stories about his father's ship shooting down attacking Japanese aircraft and kamikaze fighter pilots in the battles of Leyte Gulf and Okinawa and of his father seeing dead pilots floating in the sea. David recently put together and presented his father a large, three-ring binder book filled with records and photos of his father and the USS *Picking* in World War II, some obtained over the internet.

David is representative of the first generation of descendants of the World War II veterans. In this small, history-rich Bedford community, many of these sons and daughters know the stories of Bedford and World War II. David's next door neighbor is a son of Bernard Saunders, a prisoner of war of the Japanese for three-and-a-half years. David works at Piedmont Label, where many of the Bedford men in World War II worked. A fellow coworker is the son of Billy Parker, who lost two brothers during the war (both of whom had worked at Piedmont Label) and who was himself a prisoner of war of the Germans.

Woodrow and Edna Hubbard still live in Bedford. Woodrow celebrated his ninetieth birthday in January 2004.

Allen M. Huddleston

Allen M. Huddleston joined Bedford's Company A of the National Guard and fought with the company in Europe. He missed the D-Day Invasion of Normandy on June 6, 1944, because of a training injury, which he says is probably why he lived to have a full life. After he rejoined the company, he was wounded in combat and spent months in the hospital and in rehabilitation.[1]

Huddleston was born and raised on a farm about three miles south of the town of Bedford along Route 122. He went to school in a one-room schoolhouse through the seventh grade and went on to graduate from Bedford High School, Class of 1936. Following graduation, he worked on the farm and as a soda jerk at both Ballard-Maupin and Lyles Drug Stores.

In January 1941, because he believed he would likely be inducted under the new draft law, Huddleston joined the local National Guard unit. Two weeks later, on February 3, Company A and Huddleston left Bedford for a year of active duty training. Huddleston remembers families and friends seeing the unit off at the train station when it left Bedford, but he does not remember the parade, party, and dance that the community held for the unit more than a week before its departure.

In April 1942, while stationed at Fort Meade, Maryland, Huddleston returned to Bedford on a three-day pass and married his sweetheart, Geraldine Gillaspie. Geraldine worked for a dentist in Bedford. The couple corresponded while separated during the war, but did not write every day.

In Company A, Huddleston became a machine gunner, trained on a thirty-caliber, air-cooled, machine gun. As a private, he earned $21 a month. He subsequently received promotions to private first class, sergeant, and staff sergeant. He became a section sergeant in the weapons platoon in charge of two machine gun squads.

Approximately ten days before D-Day, while Company A was engaged in man-to-man, unarmed combat training in England, fellow soldier Robert Goode threw Huddleston to the ground, breaking

Huddleston's right ankle. He was taken to a hospital, where his ankle was put into a cast. He was then sent to a rehabilitation facility, and he was at this facility on June 6 when Company A left England for the D-Day Invasion.

Huddleston rejoined Company A in mid-August 1944, at Brest, France. The unit was deployed by train to Paris and then was sent to the Dutch-German border. On September 30, 1944, during the unit's first day of combat near Aachen, Germany, Huddleston was hit in the right shoulder joint by shrapnel from a German eighty-eight-millimeter gun.

He was taken to an aid station, then to Belgium, and then to Paris, where, with his arm bandaged in a sling, he had to sit and sleep on a cot in an airport for three or four days waiting for the weather to clear so he could be flown to a hospital in England. The shrapnel had been removed, and Huddleston could pull back the dressing to see his wound, which to him looked like a piece of raw meat.

At the hospital in England, the doctors closed up the wound and placed his arm in a "Y" brace, which held his arm bent at a forty-five-degree angle up alongside his head. The brace was supported by wires which went under his stomach and up his back. The brace was uncomfortable, particularly when trying to lie down and sleep on the wires. It was very painful when the brace was finally removed. (In later years, Huddleston's injury would continue to hurt. For a while the injury didn't bother him too much. Over the last twenty-five years, however, he received cortisone shots infrequently and then took Vioxx, but he was taking neither by early 2002.)

From the hospital, Huddleston was sent to a rehabilitation facility in England, the same one where he had been sent after his ankle was broken. He left there in April 1945 and returned by ship to New York. He was sent to the Woodrow Wilson Rehabilitation Center in Staunton, Virginia, for a few days and then was issued a pass to go home. He took the bus to Roanoke, and his wife, whom he had called once back in the United States, met him at the Hotel Roanoke. He was not home for long until he was sent to Fort Story in Virginia Beach, Virginia, for relaxation for two or three weeks. He was discharged from the Army in late April 1945.

Huddleston returned to Bedford and took a job at the Alcoholic Beverage Commission store on Main Street. He and his wife then moved to Lexington, Virginia, where, with the help of funding from the GI Bill, he trained as a photographer in a portrait studio. He primarily shot yearbook photos for colleges in southwest Virginia. The Huddlestons returned to Bedford in 1949, and he owned and operated Bedford Photo on Main Street for over forty-five years until he retired in 1996. The Huddlestons raised three sons. Geraldine died in 1988. Huddleston has lived at the Elks National Home in Bedford since 2000.

Harold and Nina Jarvis

Harold Jarvis served in the Army Air Forces in World War II as a bombardier/navigator on a B-24 Liberator bomber. His plane was hit by flak over Austria and most of the crew bailed out over Hungary, where they were picked up by Soviet forces and later returned to American forces. His wife, Nina Cauthorn Jarvis, remained at home in Bedford with their young daughter.[1]

Harold and Nina, both natives of Bedford, had met in the second grade and were classmates through high school. Another classmate and life-long-friend-to-be was Charles "Pinkie" Yowell, who also would later join the Army Air Forces and become a B-24 and B-17 pilot.

Harold and Nina were married in 1937, the same year Nina completed her studies at Sweet Briar College in Amherst County, Virginia. Harold worked as a florist. Their daughter was born in 1939.

In 1942 Harold, who Nina says was born wanting to fly and was very patriotic, told Nina he wanted to join the U.S. Army Air Forces. He had gone to Parks Air College in St. Louis, Missouri, before the war. She told him to go ahead and enlist. His friend Pinkie Yowell had already enlisted.

Harold enlisted in July 1943 and was sent to Camden, South Carolina, as an air cadet enrolled in primary flight school. He was later assigned as a bombardier navigator.

While Harold was away during the war, Nina wrote him every day. He did not write as frequently. Nina volunteered with the Red Cross to prepare surgical dressings for the military.

In September 1944 Harold and the crew of their B-24 departed Savannah, Georgia, for Italy. Operating from a base at Foggia, Italy, the crew flew some thirty missions over Germany and Austria. Jarvis was promoted to lieutenant after the first five missions.

On March 15, 1945, Jarvis went on his thirty-second mission, but this time with a crew different from his regular crew. During an attack on oil refineries near Vienna, Austria, their plane ran into flak and three engines were knocked out. The pilot flew toward Soviet-occupied territory in Hungary and eventually ordered the men to jump from the damaged aircraft. Nine crew members parachuted to safety, but none saw a chute for the pilot. The survivors were picked up and turned over to Soviet military authorities, who held and questioned them for eleven days before returning them to American control.[2]

Nina received a telegram from the Army saying that Harold was missing in action. Two weeks later came a second telegram, saying that he had been returned to military control.

Jarvis was returned to Italy, where it was discovered that he had broken his foot during the jump. He was sent to the Isle of Capri for recuperation.

Jarvis was discharged in December 1945 and returned to Bedford. He brought his parachute back home and had a nightgown made from it for Nina. Parts of the parachute had holes in it, causing some to suspect that it had been sabotaged.

After the war, Harold and Nina operated a florist business in Bedford. In 1948, when the remains of 1st Lt. Joseph Danner, whose bomber had crashed in England in 1944, were returned for burial in Bedford, Harold made a floral arrangement in the shape of a bomber for the memorial service.

Early in the 1950s, the Jarvises sold their florist shop. Harold had stayed in the reserves and expected to be called back to active duty during the war in Korea, but he was not. He then started a landscaping business. He bought a Jeep for his business and soon picked up the nickname "Jeep." Nina began a career teaching school, which was to last twenty-six years. Two sons were born to the couple in the post-war years.

Harold died in 1993 at the age of seventy-eight. His Purple Heart and Air Medals are on display at the Virginia Military Institute Museum in Lexington, Virginia. Nina lives in Bedford in the home in which she was raised. Son Rob Jarvis narrated the World War II historical drama *Bedford Goes to War* when it was performed at the Sedalia Center in Bedford County in 2000 and 2001.

William H. Merriken

William Hite Merriken participated in the battles for Northern France, Ardennes, Rhineland, and Central Europe. He served in an Army field artillery observation battalion, eventually rising to the rank of battalion supply sergeant. In mid-December 1944, at the outset of the Battle of the Bulge, Merriken's unit was pulled back from Germany into the adjacent Ardennes area of eastern Belgium. Traveling as a convoy near the town of Malmedy, Merriken and some 120 men from his unit were attacked and then captured by lead elements of the German counterattack. The Germans, part of Hitler's private, elite troops, the Schutzstaffel or "SS," forced the Americans into a field and shot them down, in what has become known as the "Malmedy Massacre." At least eighty-three, perhaps eighty-six, Americans were killed. Most were killed while lined up in the field; some had been killed when the unit was first attacked, and others were killed trying to escape. Merriken was hit three times but miraculously escaped alive, although wounded. Two other men from Bedford were among the Americans killed.[1]

Merriken was born and raised in Bedford. He graduated from Bedford High School in 1940 and later graduated from National Business College in Roanoke.

In 1942 he tried to enlist in the Army Air Forces but was rejected because he did not weigh enough. In December 1942, at the age of twenty, he was drafted and inducted into the Army in mid-January 1943. He took basic training at Camp Lee, Virginia, and artillery training at Camp Grueber, Oklahoma. He went to Louisiana for maneuvers, what he has called "two months in the swamps." He then went to Fort Sill, Oklahoma, for three months of highly-technical artillery training.

He was assigned to the 285th Field Artillery. The subordinate unit to which he was assigned, Battery B, 285th Field Artillery Observation Battalion, was, in Merriken's words, a "sound and flash" unit, whose mission was to locate enemy artillery using visual techniques and sophisticated microphones placed in the ground.

When the unit was ordered to Europe, it traveled from Oklahoma by train through Canada and back down into New York. It sailed for Europe in August 1944. As their troop ship approached Scotland after having zig-zagged across the Atlantic for protection against German submarines, a nearby Allied tanker was blown up by a torpedo from a German submarine. Merriken's unit disembarked in Wales and subsequently was sent to continental Europe.

Serving with the First Army under Gen. Omar Bradley, Merriken's unit fought in Belgium, the Netherlands, Luxembourg, and Germany. In mid-December, the unit had been in the Hurtgen Forest area of western Germany when it was ordered to pull back to St. Vith in the Ardennes Forest area of eastern Belgium.

On December 16, 1944, German units began counterattacking westward in what became known as the Battle of the Bulge. On December 17 Merriken's unit, with some 120 men loaded on a thirty-truck convoy, was driving in Belgium along a country road toward St. Vith to link up with and support the 7th Armored Division. As the convoy approached an intersection near the village of Geremont, close to the town of Malmedy, it was attacked by lead elements of the German First Panzer Division, an SS division, which was advancing westward in a fifteen-mile-long column. After initially being fired upon, the Americans, armed with only pistols and small arms, pulled over and lay down in a ditch for cover. The Germans advanced with tanks and other armored vehicles. The American commander ordered his men to surrender.

The Germans herded the men into a field some sixty feet from the highway. At one point, a German tried to remove Merriken's Bedford High School ring, but the American's finger was too swollen from the cold. The Americans, their hands raised in the air, expected to be treated as prisoners of war and taken to the German rear lines. Instead, three German armored vehicles trained their machine guns on the Americans and opened fire. All the Americans fell—dead, wounded, or pretending to be dead. Merriken fell to the ground and was hit in the back by two bullets, one on either side of his backbone. The machine-gun fire lasted between five and ten minutes.[2]

The German armor column moved on down the road, with some vehicles firing on the Americans as they drove by. Five SS troopers remained in the field for nearly half an hour, moving among the fallen Americans and shooting survivors. Merriken has described his fortune: "What saved me, I think, was that I was lying with my face buried in my right arm…they weren't able to see my breath."[3]

At one point, an American lying to Merriken's left moved and made noise. Merriken urged him to be still, but the Germans saw him. The American flopped over, partly covering Merriken with his body. A German officer approached and shot the other American. The bullet passed through the other man and hit Merriken in the back of the right knee. Merriken has spoken of this particular time: "Somehow, I didn't flinch. For one thing, I was numb. For another, a sort of calm had come over me. I remember praying—not that I would be spared, but that someone would survive to tell the world about this."[4]

The Germans told some of the wounded that they would get medical treatment. When the wounded responded, the Germans shot them.[5]

After the Germans moved back, one of the Americans yelled for the survivors to run. A dozen or so ran for the back of the field. Merriken got up and moved across the field, his wounded leg feeling like lead. He encountered a single German soldier walking along a fence. The German aimed his pistol at Merriken, but it jammed, and the soldier ran off after two other Americans. "I think about that a lot," Merriken has said. "So many fortunate things happened to me—I guess it just wasn't my time."[6]

He made it into a woodshed, passed out for a while, and then hid there until dark. He was joined by another American, Charles Redding, who was uninjured. Redding and five other Americans had run to a nearby house, but the Germans saw them and set fire to the house. As five of the men ran out, the Germans shot them. Redding stayed in the house as long as he could and finally escaped after the Germans left.[7]

Merriken has described his time hiding in the shed: "My clothing was soaked with blood, my back hurt, and the cold was constant misery. We could hear moaning from the field and we could see flames from across the road, where a farmhouse was burning."[8]

During the nighttime, Merriken and Redding left the shed and moved to a thicket closer to the village of Geremont. In the morning, a farmer who was climbing over a fence spotted the men in the thicket and nodded his head toward a settlement. They moved toward the settlement and came upon a farmer milking a cow. This farmer took them into his kitchen. A woman in the house wanted to wash his wounds, but Merriken resisted, concerned that removing his shirt would open his wounds. The woman gave the men some coffee and soup. Merriken took a sip of the soup and passed out. He awoke in an upstairs attic, where the men passed the night. German forces continued to drive along the road, and at one point some Germans knocked on the door of the house but did not enter.

Redding, who spoke some French, wrote a note and asked the woman to take it to American lines. She stuffed the note in her bosom and left. Many years later Merriken learned that the woman went next door and arranged for a fifteen-year old boy to carry the note in his shoe back to American lines. The boy had to pick his way over mines planted along the road to get to the American forces. Two days after the massacre and after U.S. Army engineers had cleared a path through the mines along the road, the crew of an American ambulance drove into the "no-mans land" and rescued the two American soldiers. Merriken remembers that as he was being removed from the house on a stretcher the woman kissed him.

Of the 120 men in the American column, only thirty-five survived, while eighty-three to eighty-six were killed in the field, in the initial firing on the column, or after escaping. Two of the dead were from Bedford—Pfc. Warren Davis and Pfc. Richard B. Walker. The American Army identified and recovered the bodies and eventually buried them in an American cemetery in Belgium.

Merriken was treated overnight at a field hospital set up in a school in Malmedy. Then he was moved to a hospital in Verviers, Belgium, where the bullets were removed. Next he was moved to Paris for three days, and finally he was moved to a general military hospital in Wales. In all, he spent nearly four months in hospitals.

After being released from the hospital, he was given a week's leave and traveled to London. There, by chance, near a fountain, he ran into and had an emotional meeting with a fellow soldier from his unit who had also survived the Malmedy Massacre.

In April 1945 Merriken was returned to the continent and rejoined his unit. On one occasion, he returned to the site of the massacre and looked for the farmhouse and the Belgian family that had hidden him. He thought he might have found the house, but it was damaged and no one was around.[9]

Merriken performed occupation duties in Germany. He has said he carried a grudge against Germans during that period:

> …I made it pretty clear that I had no love for those people. Which was unfair of me, I know, but I was young and still mad. I lost good friends in that field.[10]

Some of the Germans involved in the Malmedy Massacre were tried for war crimes and condemned to death, but their sentences were commuted.[11]

Merriken returned to the United States in December 1945, and was discharged from the Army on January 1, 1946, at Fort Meade, Maryland.

When he returned to Bedford, he met with the families of the two Bedford men killed in the Malmedy Massacre. Before the war, back in Bedford, Merriken had known Warren Davis, primarily through his brothers, but had not known Richard Walker. Warren Davis is buried in the Henri-Chapelle American Cemetery in Belgium. Richard

Walker's remains were returned to Virginia and buried in a cemetery at Morgan's Baptist Church in southern Bedford County.

Merriken enrolled in the National Business College in Roanoke to complete work in the field of business administration. He joined his uncle in the plumbing and heating business, later sold this business, worked at Rubatex for a year, and then became an auditor for the Commonwealth of Virginia for sixteen years until he retired in 1985.

Merriken married Betty Roof in 1957. They have four daughters and six grandchildren and live in the City of Bedford.

In his retirement, Merriken has devoted considerable time and effort to researching the Malmedy Massacre and searching for those who helped him. He has attended many reunions of veterans of the 285th Field Artillery. After years of searching, in 1988 he was finally able to locate and meet up with Charles Redding, the man who had escaped with him. From his research on the Malmedy Massacre, he has become friends with others who share his interests, including Americans, a British retired major general, and many Belgians, some of whom are members of a society which assists American veterans. Merriken has obtained photographs of the site of the massacre from the United States National Archives and has had these enhanced with the assistance of Army personnel at Carlisle Barracks, Pennsylvania.

In May 1999 he and some of his friends traveled to Belgium, where they were hosted by Belgians living in the region where the massacre took place. The men visited the site of the massacre, the location of the shed where Merriken and Charles Redding hid, the house in which they found refuge, and the school in Malmedy, which served as a field hospital and where Merriken's wounds were first treated. Merriken even met the Belgian man, who at age fifteen, carried the note to American lines. Merriken and the others paid tribute at a cemetery where some of the American victims of the Malmedy Massacre are buried and at a monument that lists the names of those American comrades killed on that December day in 1944.

E. Ray Nance & Alpha M. Watson Nance

Elisha Ray Nance joined Company A of the National Guard in Bedford and advanced through the ranks to become executive officer of the company before D-Day. He was one of the few to survive the D-Day landing in Normandy, but he was wounded and spent six months in hospitals recuperating. Alpha Mae Watson served as an Army nurse during the war. She and Ray were married in 1944, while both were in the Army.[1]

Ray Nance grew up on a tobacco farm in Bedford County and graduated from Moneta High School. In 1933, he joined Bedford's Company A of the National Guard. He served as an enlisted soldier until 1940, when he was selected to attend a ten-day officer-training course and subsequently was promoted to second lieutenant.[2]

He was called up to active duty with Company A in February 1941 and helped lead the company through its training in the United States and, after October 1942, in England. While in England, he was sent for six weeks to a British intelligence school to train him to be an intelligence officer. He served in that capacity at the battalion level for a short period. He subsequently served in Company B of the 116th Infantry and then returned to Company A, where he became the executive officer, second in command to company commander Captain Fellers.[3]

On June 6, 1944, Nance landed on Omaha Beach about twenty minutes after the first elements of Company A. Coming ashore with others in Company A's headquarters platoon, he found little of Company A and a lot of German firing. In one interview, he described the situation he found:

> I never took command of the company. The company didn't exist....I went down (he was hit by enemy fire in the foot and hand). I don't know how I got across the beach. The first sergeant, the radio operator, and the foot messenger were killed beside me. The re-con (reconnaissance) unit got in front of me and I yelled at them to scatter, and a mortar shell landed on top of them....There

wasn't anybody in front of me. There wasn't anybody left behind me. I was alone in France.[4]

Nance was rescued and evacuated to a hospital in England. In October 1944 he was returned to the United States and recuperated at the Woodrow Wilson Hospital in Staunton, Virginia. He believes he may have been one of the first men of Company A to return home.

He went back to Bedford on leave in mid-November and on November 26 married Alpha Mae Watson, a lieutenant in the Army Nurses Corps from the Moneta community of Bedford County, whom he had known and dated previously. They were married on a Sunday evening in her home in Moneta, both dressed in their military uniforms.[5]

After a period of limited duty and then full duty in 1945, Nance was discharged from the service in mid-December 1945.[6] The Nances returned to Bedford to live. He has expressed some unease about how he was perceived:

> I wondered what the people thought. There he is and there they are. He's here and my son is over there dead. I never did find out.[7]

He became a rural mail carrier. One of the families on his route was the Stevens family. Twin brothers Ray and Roy Stevens also had served in Company A, and Ray had been killed on D-Day. Nance has said that Mrs. Stevens would sometimes come out to meet him while he was delivering the mail and ask him, "What happened over there? Where is my Ray?"[8]

Also after the war, Nance helped establish a new National Guard Company A in Bedford. He commanded the company and participated in memorial services in 1947 and 1948 when the remains of some of the Company A casualties were returned to Bedford for burial. He joined the Army Reserves and retired as a major. He was active in the local chapter of the Veterans of Foreign Wars and has attended reunions of veterans of the 29th Infantry Division and Company A. At a veterans meeting in 1953, he proposed that a memorial stone be placed outside the Bedford County Courthouse honoring men from

Bedford who died while serving in the 116th Infantry Regiment, 29th Infantry Division, during the Normandy Invasion. With others, including Kenneth Crouch of Bedford, he helped bring the idea to fruition, and the memorial was unveiled on June 6, 1954, the tenth anniversary of D-Day.[9]

Alpha Mae Watson graduated from Moneta High School and nursing school at Jefferson Hospital in nearby Roanoke, Virginia. She entered the Army Nurse Corps in November 1943. She had the rank of lieutenant and served primarily at Camp Lee, where she was one of the head nurses. After her marriage to Ray Nance on November 26, 1944, she returned to duty at Camp Lee. As the war ended, she left the service and, with her husband, returned to live in Bedford County.

Earl R. Newcomb & Elva Z. M. Newcomb

Earl R. Newcomb served as the mess sergeant for Company A, 116th Infantry, before and during World War II. His wife, Elva Zimmerman Miller Newcomb, worked in Bedford at Hampton Looms before, during, and after the war.[1]

Earl Newcomb was born and raised in Bedford County, east of the town of Bedford. One of six children, he attended New London Academy, finishing high school in 1932. Afterwards he worked in two Civilian Conservation Corps (CCC) camps where he obtained experience in the kitchen. He first worked for twelve months at a CCC camp at Kelso, northwest of the town of Bedford, and then worked for over a year at a camp at Clarkstown in neighboring Campbell County. He later went to work at Rubatex in Bedford.

Newcomb joined Company A of the National Guard in the late 1930s, primarily to earn extra money. The National Guard paid $1 for an evening of drill, plus extra for two weeks training in the summer. He became a rifleman and private first class. Later he became the company's mess sergeant and attained the rank of staff sergeant. He had a brother who served in the Army.

After Company A had been called to active duty in February 1941 and sent to Fort Meade, Maryland, Newcomb came home on leave in June 1942 and married Elva Miller. Elva's first husband had been killed in an accident, and Earl and Elva would go on to raise Elva's three children. Earl returned to Company A shortly after the wedding.

When Company A deployed to Europe in the fall of 1942 on board the *Queen Mary*, Newcomb remembers being on deck when their ship sliced through and sank a British cruiser shortly before they got to Scotland.

As mess sergeant for Company A, Newcomb was assisted by four soldiers from Bedford County—brothers James and George Crouch, Carl Danner, and Kedrick Broughman—and by Bill Watson. These men fed Company A while they trained in England and fought on the continent. When in the field, they had trucks and a trailer on which they could cook. Company A soldiers had to eat K or C rations whenever Newcomb and his mess unit couldn't get to the men. Allen Huddleston, who was in Company A, remembers that Newcomb and his men were good cooks. Huddleston has said that some colonels and other officers outside Company A would come to Newcomb's mess to get a good meal.

For the invasion of France, Newcomb and his mess unit boarded a ship before D-Day and sat in the English Channel for about three days while combat and other higher priority units went ashore. Newcomb and the other cooks landed about three days after D-Day. When only eight men from Company A—none from Bedford—showed up to eat, Newcomb felt like he had lost many brothers.

Newcomb remained with Company A throughout the war in Europe. He returned home to America on June 13, 1945. From a military base in Massachusetts, he sent Elva a telegram, which read: "I'm over here from over there and will be with you soon. Love, Earl." He then called Elva to meet him at the train station in Lynchburg. He was given thirty days of leave and then was sent to Fort Meade, Maryland, and Camp Butler, North Carolina, from where he was discharged from the service in August 1945.

Resuming civilian status, Newcomb took a vacation and then went back to work at Rubatex. Before long he quit Rubatex and bought a farm of over 250 acres, where he raised cattle and hay.

Elva, a native of Bedford County, worked at Hampton Looms, the woolen mill, in Bedford for some thirty-six years, from September 1935 to 1971 or 1972. She was a "dresser," making warps for the weaving process.

Elva does not remember a large turnover of personnel at the woolen mill during the war. Some men joined the military, and some left to work in the arsenal at Radford, Virginia, but men over the draft cut-off age of thirty-eight remained at the mill. To the best of Elva's recollection, the Hampton Looms plant continued during the war to make mostly civilian products, although she remembers the plant did make olive green woolen blankets for the military.

During their marriage, Earl and Elva have lived in five different homes east of the town of Bedford. In 1977, they moved from their farm to their present home in the Bedford suburbs, where, as of 2004, they still live.

Russell J. Otey and Marie R. Otey

Russell J. Otey served in the U.S. Army Air Forces, where he was trained in and performed clerical work in the United States and rose to the rank of staff sergeant. He married Marie Rucker during the war. After the war, they returned to Bedford and southern Virginia, where they pursued their education and careers. Russell, who became an educator, was the first Black to be elected mayor of Bedford.[1]

Both Russell Otey and Marie Rucker were born and raised in Bedford County. Russell had moved to Washington, D.C. and was working at the Internal Revenue Service and taking night classes at Howard University when he received an induction notice from the Bedford County draft board. He returned to Bedford and was inducted into the U.S. Army, joining the Army Air Forces. He was first ordered to Fort Bragg, North Carolina, and then to boot camp at Jefferson

Barracks in Missouri. He next was sent to Seabring, Florida, and then to school in Atlanta, Georgia. After this Air Force schooling, he was sent to Orlando, Florida, where he completed his military service.

Russell had four brothers who also served in the military—Clark, Frank, Payton, and William. Marie's brother James Thurman Rucker served in the Navy.

Russell and Marie were married in Orlando in 1943. As Marie could not live on base with Russell, she rented a room in the home of a funeral director. She worked at a local pharmacy. At some point during the war, Marie returned to Bedford and worked in a beauty shop above Jones (Green's) Drugstore, in downtown Bedford. When government messages reporting the deaths of Bedford servicemen arrived at the Western Union office in the drugstore, she remembers that word soon spread to the beauty shop on the second floor.

After Russell was released from military service in the summer of 1945, the couple returned to Bedford and pursued their education. Russell used his GI Bill benefits to help finance his undergraduate education. He earned a bachelor of science degree in education at St. Paul College in Lawrenceville, Virginia, in 1950. Later in 1971, without the help of the GI Bill, Russell earned a master's degree at Lynchburg College. Marie went to nursing school and became a licensed practical nurse, working in Bedford.

Russell was a teacher and administrator in the Bedford County and Lynchburg City School Systems for twenty-five years. He was active in local and regional government. He served on the Bedford City Council from 1972-1980 and was elected mayor of Bedford for the term 1978-1980. He also served as vice chairman of the Central Virginia Planning Commission from 1972-1974.

Russell died in May 2000. Marie still lives in Bedford.

The Parker Brothers

Earl Lloyd Parker, Joseph Ernest ("Joe") Parker, Jr., and William Eugene ("Billy") Parker all fought in U.S. Army infantry units in Europe. Earl, a staff sergeant with Company A, 116th Infantry, and Joseph, a private, with Company C of the 116th, were killed in action. William, a private with the 80th Division, was captured by the Germans and held as a prisoner of war for seven-and-a-half months before being released.[1]

The three Parker brothers, sons of Mr. and Mrs. Joseph E. Parker, grew up, along with their two sisters, on the family farm northwest of the Bedford City limits, in the foothills of the Peaks of Otter. All of the children attended Bedford High School. Earl was a year older than Joe and two years older than Billy. The sisters were younger than Billy.

When called to active service, Earl and Joe worked at the Piedmont Label Company in the town of Bedford. Billy worked on the farm. Earl was a member of Bedford's Company A of the National Guard when that unit was activated in February 1941. Billy, who graduated from Bedford High School in 1937, was drafted on September 22, 1942. Joe, who had served in the National Guard but left it before the United States entered the war, was drafted in February 1944.

While fighting in Europe, each of the brothers, for a period of time, was declared missing in action. Earl was declared missing in action during the D-Day invasion of France on June 6, 1944; not until 1945 was he officially declared killed in action. Joe was first declared missing in action in France and, a week later, when his body was found, was declared killed in action on August 27, 1944, in Brest, France. Billy was first declared missing in action in France and about a month later was officially declared to be a prisoner of war of the Germans.

Earl's body was never recovered, a fate suffered by many other soldiers who fought to get ashore on the Normandy beach on D-Day. His name is included on a memorial in the Normandy American Cemetery, along with others whose remains were not recovered for burial. The American Battle Monuments Commission lists his date of death as June 7, 1945. This is the date, consistent with U.S. law, that he was officially declared killed in action—one year and a day after he was reported missing in action. He actually died on June 6, 1944.

Joe's remains are buried in the Brittany American Cemetery in France. When, a few years after the war, the government offered to return Joe's remains to Bedford, the Parker family chose to leave them in Europe, rather than have the remains of only one son returned.[2]

Of the three brothers, only Earl was married when he joined the Army. While Earl was in England preparing for the invasion, his wife Viola bore him a daughter, whom they named Mary Daniel Parker. Earl never got to see his daughter. Viola later remarried and is now deceased.

Billy, upon being drafted, was sent to Camp Forest, Tennessee, for basic training. From there, he was sent to Salina, Kansas, for further training and then Yuma, Arizona, for desert maneuvers. He assumed he would be deployed to North Africa. Instead, he was sent to Fort Dix, New Jersey, and then, on June 6, 1944, loaded aboard the *Queen Mary* for a five-day crossing to England. After two weeks in England, he was deployed to France, landing in Normandy.

Billy served in a combat infantry unit in the 80th Division in France as number four man on an eleven-man, 57-millimeter, anti-tank gun crew. His job was to help spread the trails used to stabilize the gun and to pass ammunition forward to the assistant gunner.

He was in combat from the end of June to September 15, 1944. Before daylight on September 15, while his unit was manning a roadblock after having crossed the Moselle River, the Germans counterattacked and overran the unit's position with tanks and infantry. Of the eleven men in his unit, one was killed and another injured. The Germans captured the remaining nine and lined them up against a German tank that Billy's unit had knocked out of action.

The Americans were then forced to walk back toward German lines, carrying a wounded German soldier on a door that the Germans had removed from a home to use as an improvised stretcher. To Billy, it felt like they had to carry the German some five miles before they were able to load him onto a truck. Then, until about midday, the Americans were ordered to walk with their hands held over their heads. After midday, they were allowed to lower their arms while they continued to walk. That night their captors locked them in a house and kept them under guard.

The next day, the Germans loaded the Americans on a truck and drove them toward the rear. They were locked in a local French jail the second night and the next day. They had been given nothing to eat or drink since their capture.

The following day Billy and other prisoners were loaded aboard French boxcars, sixty men to a car. The cars were dark, and the men still were given nothing to eat or drink. They traveled aboard the boxcars for five to six days, after which they arrived at a tent prison camp in Germany, where they stayed two or three days. Then they were loaded back into the boxcars. They were given a can of meat to be shared among six prisoners and a loaf of black bread to be shared among four. The men thought the food was to be one day's rations, but it was all the food they were given for the next seven days as they were moved by rail to Prison Camp 4B.

After two weeks at Camp 4B, they were shipped to Stalag 7A near Moosburg, Germany, twenty miles northeast of Munich. There were reportedly 175,000 prisoners of several nationalities, including American, English, French, Poles, Russians, Indians, and Senegalese. Billy remembers no military hierarchical organization among the prisoners.[3]

Billy and the men in his unit became separated during the transit. Only one other man from the unit of nine captured together stayed with him, and Billy is not sure what finally happened to him. Billy also has no idea what happened to the man in his unit who was injured.

Billy was kept at Stalag 7A for the rest of his confinement, except for the last couple of months when he and others slept in boxcars near where they were forced to work. The Germans made them work on the railroad system, filling bomb craters and laying new track. Asked how hard the work was, Billy smiled and said, "We didn't hurt ourselves."

Each morning of their captivity, Billy and his fellow prisoners were given a drink referred to as "coffee." They were not sure what it really was. Around noon they were given soup, made mostly of grass. In the evenings early in Billy's captivity, each prisoner was given a small potato a couple of inches in diameter, but the Germans soon stopped feeding them anything at night. Billy survived by stealing potatoes from boxcars. Many prisoners died of starvation or sickness.

On April 30, 1945, Billy and other prisoners were in an air raid shelter near where they were working in Munich when American forces took the city. The Americans captured their German guards. Billy and other prisoners took over an apartment building for nine days and lived on canned food they found in the basement.

Billy was shipped to LeHavre, France, where he stayed for two weeks. He was then loaded on a small ship, *The Argentina*, and taken to Boston. From there he was sent to Fort Meade, Maryland. He was given a sixty-day furlough and money to buy a bus ticket home. He had not been paid for the better part of a year. He called his family from Fort Meade to tell them he was coming home.

The entire time he was in Europe, Billy's mother wrote him every day. He received only one of her letters, and that was before his capture. He wrote letters home before his capture, but his family never received them. In prison camp, he had nothing to write on. His parents were first informed that Billy was missing in action in France as of September 15, 1944. Later, in November 1944, they were informed that he was a prisoner of war.[4]

Billy took a Greyhound bus from Fort Meade to the town of Bedford. His mother, father, sisters, aunts, uncles, and cousins were all there to meet him. When he got off the bus, it was, he said, "a mighty good feeling."

Not until the family returned home to the farm from town did Billy's mother tell him that his two brothers had been killed. His mother never got over the loss of her two sons. His father was more reserved in expressing his feelings.

After his sixty-day furlough Billy was sent to Miami, Florida, for two weeks at a recuperation center and then to Camp Lee, Virginia, where he was stationed from August to November, 1945, and then discharged from the service.

Billy returned to Bedford County and farmed for the rest of his life. He married, and he and his wife have two sons and a daughter. Billy and his sons live on separate properties along Parker Road, which Bedford County named in honor of Billy's brothers who were killed in the war. Billy's son Joe works at Piedmont Label Company, where his uncles worked before World War II.

In the post-war period, Billy has not participated in many veterans activities. He had gone to Bedford High School with Bernard Saunders, who was a prisoner of war of the Japanese, and the two men exchanged stories of their captivity. At the Salem United Methodist Church near the Peaks of Otter in Bedford County where Billy worships, he participated in a program to recognize men from that church who participated in World War II.

One of the activities Billy loves is hunting. He has killed twelve black bears and more deer than he can count. The heads of a bear and a deer are mounted in his den, symbols of his hunting prowess.

Bernard W. Saunders

Bernard W. Saunders, while serving with the U.S. Army Air Forces in the Philippine Islands, was captured and held as a prisoner of war of the Japanese. He survived the Bataan Death March and three-and-a-half years of harsh captivity by the Japanese. He returned to Bedford, became a businessman, raised a family, wrote a short memoir of his war experiences, and engaged in public service, serving on the city council and being elected mayor of Bedford for one term.[1]

Saunders was raised in Bedford and graduated from Bedford High School. He enlisted in May or June 1941, in the U.S. Army Air Corps, becoming a private and later being promoted to corporal. He was sent first to Bolling Field in Washington, D.C., for training, and then to Savannah Air Base in Savannah, Georgia. He was trained as a machine gunner on a bomber and was assigned to the 91st Bomb Squadron, 27th Bomb Group. He sailed from San Francisco, California, on November 1, 1941, for Manila in the Philippine Islands, arriving on November 20. He arrived before the aircraft for his unit arrived.[2]

Less than three weeks later, the Japanese attacked Pearl Harbor, bases in the Philippines, and other Allied targets in the Pacific. Japanese aircraft attacking the Philippines shortly after the attack on Pearl Harbor strafed Saunders' bivouac area. Saunders manned a machine gun and helped with antiaircraft guns at the airfield. While Allied forces downed some Japanese aircraft, the Japanese destroyed Clark and Nichols Fields. Saunders subsequently fought on the front lines for four months as part of the "Air Corps Provisional Infantry" used to help defend against the Japanese invading forces.

In early May 1942, after several months of resistance, the commander of the outnumbered Allied forces in the Philippines ordered his men to surrender. Instead of surrendering, Saunders and nine other men sneaked through Japanese lines into the hills in search of Filipino guerrilla forces. The men lived in the hills for ten days until they, too, had to surrender.

The Japanese forced Saunders and the others to join other Allied prisoners of war on what became known as the Bataan Death March. Saunders marched 120 miles in eight or ten days, as part of a group of 100 men, marching four abreast in twenty-five rows. He remembered only one ration of raw rice on the march. The prisoners on the Death March suffered from the tropical heat, were weak from malnutrition and illness, and were provided little if anything to eat and drink. Over 7,000 men—4,000 of whom were Filipinos—died of exhaustion, illness, or execution by the Japanese during the march.[3]

Of the ten men who had escaped to the hills before surrendering, only Saunders and one other survived the march, and the other man died in the first Japanese prison camp they reached. Saunders learned that it was wise to keep one's mouth closed and eyes open.

The Japanese moved Saunders from one Japanese camp to another in the Philippines. He was held first at Camp O'Donnell at Tarlac for a month and then moved to a prison camp at Cabanatuan. The camps were abominable, with little sanitation and nutrition. At one point, he had malaria, dysentery, and beri-beri, and was exhausted and nearly starved. He was moved to "St. Peter's Ward," where the dying were placed. The Japanese announced that anyone who could move could board trucks to go to another camp. Somehow, Saunders found the strength to crawl to one of the trucks, someone helped him on, and he was taken to another camp. Saunders later would say:

> I was at death's door many times and came face to face with the Maker more than once and made my peace with God on the battlefields, in the foxholes, on the prison ships, on the Death March, and in the prison camps.[4]

As American forces prepared to win back the Philippines, the Japanese moved Saunders and other prisoners to a prison in Manila and then loaded them on ships headed to Japan, the infamous "hell ships," so named because of the atrocious conditions aboard. Saunders has described the conditions, in which prisoners sucked on their own blood for moisture.

> We were stripped and had to stand most of the time, it was so crowded. We took turns sitting and standing. There was little water and no fresh air. I remember there was a Catholic priest among us who kept praying, 'Oh Mother Mary, Jesus, have mercy on us.'[5]

The trip took seventeen days. Many prisoners died on these ships during the passage to Japan, some from illness and others when Allied forces attacked the ships, the Allies being unaware that prisoners of war were aboard. Saunders was taken to the main Japanese island of Honshu and imprisoned in a camp near Osaka, southwest of Tokyo, where he had to mine minerals.

Saunders' parents back in Bedford knew little of his status. They received very few communications from or about Bernard after the Japanese attack of early December. They often shared what little they knew with the Bedford newspapers, and the newspapers printed short reports on Saunders' status on the front pages. At some point Bernard sent a telegram saying, "Safe, Don't be alarmed." He sent his parents a letter written before his capture, dated February 9, 1942, but they did not receive it until six months later. The letter read, in part:

I am well and getting along as well as can be expected and assure you that with my faith in God I will continue to be all right....

I wish I could be there for a while and let you know that I have still a smiling face....

...when you are inclined to think a little on the dark side of life, remember   I have God with me and He will take care of me.[6]

In April 1943, the Saunders family was notified by the War Department that Bernard was reported to be a prisoner of war of the Japanese government, held in the Philippines.[7] In December of that year, the family received from the Japanese Imperial Army three cards signed by Bernard, in which he said, "Hope to see you all soon," "May God bless you all," and "Please write."[8] In August 1944, they received a card from Bernard from Philippine Military Prison Camp No. 4, in which he asked them not to worry and said he was getting along fine and that his chin was still up.[9] The family subsequently learned that Bernard had first been interned for nearly two years in the Cabanatuan Camp No. 1 near Manila, then transferred to Philippine military prison camp No. 4, and later, before February 1945, moved to Osaka Camp in Japan.[10]

During his entire captivity, Saunders received only eight Red Cross parcels of food, a packet of thirty-nine letters from home, and later one more letter.[11]

On August 6, 1945, Saunders heard a rumble and felt the earth shake. American forces had dropped the first atomic bomb on Hiroshima, less than 200 miles west of Osaka, where Saunders was held. Then in mid-August, after America dropped the second atomic bomb, the Japanese guards informed the men that the war was over. American planes parachuted food, clothing, and medicine to the men. Saunders was taken to Yokohama and given medical care aboard an American hospital ship. He weighed less than 100 pounds.

He was sent back to the Philippines for thirty days. From Manila, he sent his family a telegram, saying he had been released and would be returning home before long. His family passed the message to the local newspapers, which printed the story.[12]

Saunders left Manila on September 10 and arrived in San Francisco on October 15. From San Francisco, he tried to telephone his home in Bedford County but could not get through. Finally he was able to call his father at work in Blue Ridge. He traveled east by train for seven days from San Francisco and was transported to the Woodrow Wilson Hospital in Staunton, Virginia, where he received medical rehabilitation attention. When he was discharged, he had gained weight and weighed 140 pounds.[13]

Released from the service, Saunders returned to Bedford, attended the National Business College in Roanoke, opened a clothing store with fellow veteran Roy Stevens, married and raised a family, and later co-founded the Coffee & Saunders Farm & Hardware store. His two sons later joined him in the business.

He was active in the Bedford community, serving on the Bedford City Council for sixteen years as well as serving as mayor. In 2001 the Keep Bedford Beautiful Commission posthumously named him Bedford's Outstanding Citizen.

He agreed to be interviewed frequently and spoke publicly of his wartime experiences. He appears to have been the only Bedford man to write his wartime memoirs and make them available publicly. Bernard Saunders died in 2001. His wife, Margaret, and two sons live in Bedford.

John B. Schenk & Ivylyn Schenk Hardy

John Burwell Schenk served in Bedford's Company A of the National Guard and advanced to become a staff sergeant with responsibilities for communications and the headquarters platoon. In August 1942 John returned home on furlough and married Ivylyn Camack Jordan. After a ten-day honeymoon, John returned to his unit, which, within the month, deployed to England. Ivylyn returned to teaching school in Bedford County. In addition to teaching her elementary-school classes, she contributed to the war effort by teaching pre-flight aeronautics to high school students and teaching gardening and food preservation to adults. She also kept a Victory Garden and helped monitor retail prices charged to consumers. She and John wrote each other almost every day for the twenty months he was in England. John was killed in the D-Day Invasion on June 6, 1944, at age twenty-seven.[1]

John was born in the town of Bedford. His mother died when he was a boy, leaving four children. His father remarried, and there were two daughters from that marriage. His stepmother, Rosa Schenk, worked for the local school system and was very active in community projects to support the war effort. John's brother, George W. Schenk, Jr., also served in the Army in World War II.

John graduated from Bedford High School in 1935. His parents sent him to Virginia Polytechnic Institute and State University (now Virginia Tech), but he did not like it there and came home after a few months. He subsequently attended and graduated from Phillips Business College in Lynchburg, Virginia, where he studied stenography, typing, and bookkeeping. He found a job as a clerk at Thomas' Hardware Store in Bedford. Mr. Thomas, who didn't want John to go off to the war, offered him a partnership when he returned. The Thomas family would later befriend Ivylyn as a member of the family.

John joined Bedford's Company A of the National Guard sometime before 1940. He trained with the unit before the war and, along with others in Company A, was called to active duty on February 3, 1941, soon deploying to Fort Meade, Maryland.

Ivylyn Camack Jordan was born and raised on a farm in Goochland County, west of Richmond, Virginia. She graduated from Longwood College in Farmville, Virginia, in 1938 and moved to Bedford to teach at Liberty Academy, a demonstration school for students in grades one through eight. She returned to Goochland County for a year and then moved to the Moneta community in southern Bedford County where she taught for five years, mostly at the first grade level, and helped with administration in a school complex that ranged from first grade to high school.

John and Ivylyn met in early 1941, shortly before John was deployed to Fort Meade. John and a friend saw Ivylyn walk by on a street in Bedford, and the friend asked if John knew Ivylyn. John replied, "No, but I certainly would like to." He asked her to go out the next evening. Their courtship continued despite John's being stationed at Fort Meade. He was able to come back to Bedford many weekends, getting rides from fellow Bedford soldiers who had cars. He also visited her in Goochland.

On August 14, 1942, John called Ivylyn and told her that Company A was being deployed to Florida and that they could be married on August 24. John traveled from Camp Blanding, Florida, for the wedding, and the couple spent a ten-day honeymoon at Arcadia near Natural Bridge and Lexington in western Virginia. On September 2, John left Arcadia to rejoin Company A, which soon deployed to Camp Kilmer, New Jersey, and then departed New York for Britain on September 27. From Arcadia, Ivylyn returned to Moneta, where she and her mother rented a house near the school where Ivylyn taught.

In addition to teaching her regular school classes in Moneta, Ivylyn taught classes related to the war effort, helped the government monitor prices, and participated in volunteer projects. As an addendum to the curricula at Moneta High School, she taught pre-flight aeronautics. Each of the eight students she taught went on to serve in one part or another of the Army Air Forces during the war. She worked for the Department of Agriculture under the Production Conservation Program, teaching local adult residents how to grow their own Victory Gardens and how to dry, pressure cook, and can foods. She worked part-time for the Federal Government's Office of Price Administration monitoring retail prices charged by local businesses. She grew a Victory Garden, helped Red Cross volunteers prepare surgical dressings, and helped host British sailors visiting Bedford while their ships were repaired in Norfolk.

Ivylyn wrote to John nearly every day while he was overseas, and he wrote almost as frequently to her. She also frequently sent him packages with food and other treats.

John wrote Ivylyn that he was in England but could not say exactly where. He wrote that he and fellow Bedford soldier Pride Wingfield had purchased bicycles so they could ride out into the country to buy fresh eggs rather than eat powdered eggs.

In January 1943, John wrote from England: "…This Army life isn't a bed of roses. It may turn out to be a bed of poppies in Flanders Field…."[2] In August 1943, he went on a furlough in southern England and went swimming in the English Channel, which he afterwards described in a letter as "cold as the dickens."[3] Ten months later he crossed the Channel as part of the first wave of the Normandy Invasion force.

John mentioned in one of his communications with Ivylyn from England that while on guard duty once he unwittingly walked up on British Prime Minister Sir Winston Churchill, Supreme Allied Commander Gen. Dwight D. Eisenhower, and Lt. Gen. George S. Patton, who were discussing what to do about the Slapton Sands area in Devon County, England, which was evacuated to provide a realistic practice area for Allied forces and which later was the site of a German naval attack on Allied forces practicing for the invasion.

By the spring of 1944, the pressure of the war and separation were taking an increasing toll on both John and Ivylyn. In mid-March, Ivylyn was awakened in the middle of the night by a dream in which she was telling God, "No, you can't take him. We haven't had our children yet. You can't let him die." She was subject to terrible headaches, and she had one after this dream and in early June, around the time of the June 6 D-Day Invasion of Normandy.

On May 8, 1944, less than a month before D-Day, John wrote to Ivylyn:

This damn long war is beginning to get on my nerves. Even my hair is turning grey. Will you love me when I come home with grey hair and shattered nerves…[4]

Ivylyn's letters to John were upbeat, positive, and encouraging, while sometimes revealing her concerns. To his letter of May 8, she responded on May 21:

You were asking if I'd love you if you had grey hair and shattered nerves. Why shouldn't I? I meant it when I said "for better or worse, thru thick and thin." I hope that I shall ever grow more capable of loving you and being your wife. When you need me

most I pray that I shall be ready and able to do the things you
want me to do....[5]

On June 3, she had reported her disappointment over the false report in the media that Allied forces had landed in France (see Chapter
13). On June 5, she wrote:

> It has been two weeks that I haven't had a letter from Johnny!
> What the heck are they doing to you? No one at Moneta has heard
> anything from England since I have. Seems whatever is happen-
> ing to one must be happening to all of you....Maybe there'll be a
> letter in the morning![6]

On June 11, she wrote:

> This morning's paper gave us Allied confirmation of the presence
> of your division in the Invasion and located your group as work-
> ing just east of the Vire River. Since the thrust toward Cherbourg,
> I suspect you're going that way now. But enough of what you are
> seeing, hearing, breathing and making!...[7]

On June 20, Ivylyn responded to a letter John had written on
May 29, about a week before D-Day, in which John said he and
other soldiers had been discussing the differences in how people in
America and England perceived the pending invasion. The soldiers
thought those in America believed it would be "quite a show." Ivylyn
described how Americans had actually reacted to D-Day on June 6:

> Dearest, I got a good letter today. It was written on May 29th
> and you were disgusted with the way you were thinking D-day
> would be here. I thought it was quietly and reverently observed.
> There were no celebrations, drunks or shouting. Instead the entire
> nation seemed to be praying. John, the majority of this country
> are pulling tooth and toenail for you—never forgetting your
> sacrifices and those of millions more like you. I'm not forgetting.
> Just praying....[8]

On June 22, she responded to a letter of May 27 from John. In that letter, he had written that his aunt should not worry about her son, John's cousin, in Europe, saying that: "All that will save us now is God, Luck, and a Foxhole. The latter must be plenty deep, too." Ivylyn wrote, referring to his letter:

> I suppose you realized then that the Invasion was near and that you'd be in it. Anyhow you said that God, luck and foxholes were all you could depend on. Darling, you forget that you have the prayers and good wishes of many loved ones here at home. They ought to help a lot! Anyhow, we're all leaving it up to God to do the best he can for you and us. We, and you, too, will do our best and so the result will have to be right no matter how gloomy it may seem....[9]

In a letter of July 7, she wrote:

> Well, you've been in France a month and still I have no letters, but I'm not bothered, specially since I read an article today containing an account of the hard day's battle your division had on D-Day. Also to discover that your group has, since that day, marched fourteen miles inland has made me realize how exceedingly busy you and the other boys have been. Please tell me what you can of the work you are doing. It is hard to picture what it's like! I saw and saved a nice article about the kind things Gen. Monty (British General Bernard Montgomery, head of Allied ground forces) said about the 29th Division....[10]

Ivylyn had continued to write letters to John, unaware that he had been killed on June 6. She did not learn of his death until July 17, more than five weeks after D-Day. On that day, a War Department telegram arrived in Bedford reporting John's death. It was delivered to John's parents. (When servicemen entered the military, they usually listed their mothers as next of kin, and many servicemen who married while in the military appear not to have filled out new next-of-kin forms.)

July 17 was a Monday, and school was out for the summer for Ivylyn. Unaware of the telegram, Ivylyn packed her car and drove to visit John's parents, who lived just west of the town of Bedford. She pulled up to the Schenk home, and, as she tells it, "Mother Schenk was on the porch. She came off the porch toward the car, and I could tell."

After learning of John's death, Ivylyn and her mother went back to Goochland County, their prior home, for about a week. Then they returned to their home in Moneta in Bedford County, where they had chickens and a garden to tend.

Insensitively, on July 29, the Army's Office of Dependency Benefits sent Ivylyn and her mother a form notifying them that their allotments from John's pay and allowances had been discontinued. The reason cited was "Soldier Ineligible."

John was initially buried above Omaha Beach in Normandy. His cousin, Calvin Schenk, was present when John's body was prepared for burial. The Schenk family held a memorial service for John on September 10 at St. John's Episcopal Church in Bedford. Later, when the American Cemetery at Normandy, St. Laurent-sur-Mer, France, was constructed, John's remains were reinterred there, in Plot I, Row 14, Grave 20.[11] Rather than have John's remains returned to the United States, the Schenk family chose to leave John buried in France, believing that he would want to be buried where he gave his life.

Ivylyn, who resumed teaching in Moneta in the fall of 1944, had questions about John's death. At some point, she communicated with Cecil Breeden, who had been a medic assisting Company A on D-Day and who had been one of the last to see John alive on Omaha Beach. (Breeden happened to come from Arcadia where John and Ivylyn had honeymooned.) Breeden told her that John had been wounded, and he, Breeden, had administered first aid. When Breeden advised him to go back to a boat to be evacuated, John responded, "Hell, no. I've seen enough of England."

In February 1945, Ivylyn wrote a letter filled with questions to Sgt. Ned Bowman, who had been one of John's closest friends in Company A until Bowman was transferred in July 1943. In responding, Bowman sought to reassure Ivylyn that John wanted to live for her and that John savored the exchange of letters with her. Bowman went on to say that he could not imagine anything more that she could have done "for your love was everything and I know he had all of that." Finally, Bowman suggested that, while John wanted more than anything to enjoy life with her, he would want her to find someone else in the future so she could live a full life of happiness.

Ivylyn completed the school year in Moneta in late spring 1945, and then moved back to the outskirts of the town of Bedford, where, in the fall, she began teaching again at Liberty Academy.

In 1946, at a dinner party arranged by a matchmaking neighbor, Ivylyn was introduced to Ralph Hardy. They began a courtship and were married in July 1946. Ralph lived just north of the town of Bedford on a farm that had been in his family since the early 1800s, and the newlywed couple settled there.

They worked at jobs away from the farm, raised a family, and found time to manage the farm. Ivylyn continued teaching and completed nearly thirty-five years of teaching in Bedford County schools before retiring. In 2003, Ivylyn and Ralph, who still live on the farm, celebrated fifty-seven years of marriage. They have a son and daughter, grandchildren, and a recent great-grandchild. The Hardys have been active in the community in such things as promoting hospice services in Bedford.

Ivylyn has done many things to preserve remembrances of her first husband, John, and honor him and his comrades in Company A. She has kept the letters John sent her. She also has the letters she sent him, which he had read, bundled up, and mailed back to her so they could read them in future years when he returned. Some of the letters are ones she wrote in spring 1944, which were returned with the envelope stamped "DECEASED." She has also kept his medals and other personal effects. She has John's Purple Heart, a rolled up certificate from President Roosevelt honoring John, and a pocket-size New Testament given to John by his stepmother, which was found in Normandy and returned to his stepmother. Other memorabilia include an approximately three inch blue shield symbolizing the Free French.

Ivylyn also has kept condolence notes, including one from one of her former preflight aeronautics students and one from one of her first grade students, Booker Goggin, who wrote in July 1944:

Dear Mrs. Schenk,
I am so sorry to hear about your husband. I wish I could come
to see you. Come to see me. I hope you will be my teacher next
fall.
With love,

Booker

Some of her students from her choral reading class did a choral
reading honoring John.

In later years, Ivylyn has attended Company A reunions, traveled
to England where John was stationed, and visited John's grave in
Normandy. On her first visit to his grave, her former college room-
mate accompanied her, and the American civilian in charge of the
cemetery stayed with her the entire time she was at the cemetery.

Ivylyn has been interviewed many times by people writing stories
about D-Day and Bedford for newspapers, magazines, and books. She
also appeared in a documentary produced by a French company from
Normandy. She is a strong supporter of the National D-Day Memorial
Foundation and has encouraged contributions to the memorial and
its education center, which she believes will become the heart of the
memorial complex.

Ivylyn and her daughter, Sue, who lives with her husband in a
separate house on the family farm, grow poppies from seeds from
every Allied country that fought in the D-Day Invasion.

The Stevens Family

Three sons of Mr. and Mrs. W. E. Stevens served in the Army. Twin
brothers Ray O. Stevens and Roy O. Stevens, at age nineteen, joined
Company A of the Virginia National Guard in January 1938. They each
advanced to leadership positions in Company A as non-commissioned
officers, achieving the rank of technical sergeant. The twins were in

the first wave during the D-Day Invasion on Omaha Beach. Ray was killed on D-Day. Roy survived but was seriously wounded later in the fighting in France. Younger brother Warren L. Stevens was inducted into the Army in March 1943 and served in Europe from November 1944 to December 1945.[1]

The Stevens twins came from a farm family with fourteen children, including one set of triplets. They lived west of the town of Bedford. Roy and Ray went to school in the small one-room, Fairview and Ross schoolhouses.[2]

In 1938, Ray took the single opening in Company A one week, and Roy took the next opening a week later. (Grant C. Yopp, a neighbor whose mother had died and who came to live with the Stevens family, joined Company A about the same time. Yopp was killed on D-Day.)

Roy has said the young men joined the National Guard because many of their buddies had joined, they could earn a dollar for each Monday evening drill, as well as additional money for two-week training sessions in the summer, and they got to wear uniforms.

On Monday evenings, Company A either listened to lectures indoors at the National Guard armory in the basement of the courthouse on Main Street or practiced tactics outdoors. They also practiced close-order drills. Each summer, usually in August, Company A deployed for two weeks training to a military installation in Ogdenburg, New York, or A. P. Hill Military Reservation, located between Richmond and Fredericksburg, Virginia.

In addition to helping out on the family farm, Ray and Roy had taken full time jobs around the time they turned eighteen. Roy began working at Bedford's Belding Heminway plant, the silk mill. Roy worked in what was called the "throwing department," where he added color to the fabrics. One of his sisters worked near him in the plant. Ray worked at a dry goods store. The two brothers pooled their resources and purchased a farm near their parents' property.

When Company A was called up in February 1941 for a year of active duty for training, Roy and Ray deployed with the unit to Fort Meade, Maryland. After America's entry into the war following Pearl Harbor, and the consequent extension of Company A on active duty for the duration of the war, the Stevens brothers went with

Company A when it deployed, sequentially, to the Eastern Shore, Florida, New Jersey, Scotland, England, and France.

In the early morning hours of June 6, 1944, Roy and Ray embarked from Weymouth, England, on board the English troopship *Empire Javelin* to participate in the Allied invasion of Normandy. The brothers had previously agreed to meet and shake hands at one of Company A's objectives on Omaha Beach, the town of Vierville-sur-Mer. Ray had a premonition that he would not survive the invasion, and on board the troopship he extended his hand to Roy. Roy didn't take his brother's hand, saying, "No, we agreed to meet at the crossroads at Vierville-sur-Mer, and that's what we're going to do." The brothers subsequently got into separate landing craft, never to see each other again. Roy has said that this incident has haunted him.

Roy believes that about 500 yards from the Normandy coast, the boat on which he was riding struck one of the steel obstacles the Germans had placed in the surf area, water gushed in, and the boat sank. Roy wasn't much of a swimmer, and the weight of his equipment pulled him down. If fellow Company A soldier Clyde Powers had not cut the pack off Roy's back, he probably would have drowned. Roy floated in his inflated "May West" life jacket, supported by another "May West" on a bangalore torpedo, which was to be used to blow holes through obstacles and fortifications on the beach. At one point, Roy bumped into one of the German steel obstacles lying underneath the water.

After floating in the water for some two hours, Roy and others were rescued by an Allied naval craft, which took them back out into the Channel to the transport ship from which they had disembarked. The transport ship then returned them to England, the men were reoutfitted, and four days later they were returned to the same sector of Omaha Beach where they had tried to land earlier.

Soon after they landed, the men found a temporary gravesite with crosses to which had been nailed dogtags belonging to some of the men of Company A. Roy found a grave belonging to his brother Ray, and Clyde Powers found a grave belonging to his brother Sgt. Jack G. Powers. They also found the graves of Capt. Taylor Fellers, M/Sgt. John Wilkes, and Cpl. Weldon A. ("Tony") Rosazza, all of Company A.

The Stevens family back in Bedford were not officially notified of Ray's death until September 23, three-and-a-half months after D-Day. He had not been heard of since June 6 and had not been listed as missing in action.[3]

Roy and Company A then fought south, down the Cherbourg Peninsula. On June 30 or July 1, Roy was wounded in action near St. Lo. Shrapnel from a German "Bouncing Betty," a booby trap which sprang to shoulder height and then exploded, tore through the left side of his neck and shoulder. Another Bedford comrade from Company A, Harold Wilkes, treated Roy's wound with sulfa powder to stop the bleeding.

Roy was taken back to a field hospital, where he was placed among the men not expected to survive. Lying there, Roy grabbed a nurse by her smock and held on. She told him that if he would let go she would see what she could do to get him help. Roy let go. The nurse was true to her word and arranged for him to be operated on, which saved his life. He was then returned to England, where he was hospitalized near London for three months.

At the end of the three months, Roy was sent to a facility in France (probably at Compiegne, northwest of Paris), where it became evident that he was not fit for combat service. He was then sent to Belgium and then back to France where he helped officers—recent graduates of officer candidate school at Fort Benning, Georgia—learn what to expect once they reached the front lines. During this period, Roy was able to spend two weeks of rest and recreation in Nice on France's Mediterranean coast. Around March 1945, Roy's brother Warren, who was fighting in Germany, was able to visit him in France.[4]

On July 30, 1945, Roy left France on a supply ship to return to America. He landed at Newport News and traveled via Greyhound Bus to Washington, D.C., en route home. He remembers trying to get a drink in Washington and the bartender refusing to serve him until he finally showed his discharge papers.

Roy had alerted his parents of his pending arrival. The Greyhound bus dropped Roy off on the highway near his family's farm west of Bedford City. He hiked the road across the mountain toward home. When he met his parents on the road, his mother hugged him and cried, and his father cried also. It was the first time Roy had ever seen his father cry.

When after the war the government offered to return Ray's remains to Bedford, the family accepted the offer, and in 1948 Ray was buried in Greenwood Cemetery. Roy attended many services that year for men whose remains were returned to Bedford.

Roy wrote a poem in honor of his brother Ray:

Twin Brother Farewell

I'll never forget that morning
It was, the sixth day of June
I said farewell to brother
Didn't think it would be so soon.

I had prayed for our future
That wonderful place called home
But a sinner's prayer wasn't answered
Now I'll have to go there alone.

We had talked of the landing
And our girls across the sea
But things have happened so different
There is nobody to talk but me.

We had come a long ways
Together, we have been
When we greeted farewell
I didn't think it was the end.

O' Brother, I think of you
All through the sleepless nights
Dear Lord, he took you from me
And I can't believe it was right.

This world is so unfriendly
To kill now is a sin

To walk that long narrow road
It can't be done without him.

Dear Mother, I know your worries
This is an awful fight
To lose my only twin brother
And suffer the rest of my life.

Now fellows take my warning
Believe it from start to end
If you ever have a twin Brother
Don't go to the battle with him.

On returning to civilian life, Roy worked full time on the farm for a year. During this time, he met Helen Cundiff. She was in a crowd watching him pitch pennies for prizes at a carnival in downtown Bedford. According to Roy, he paid more attention to Helen than to the pennies. His interest in Helen continued, and he eventually won himself a wife.

In the immediate years after the war, while continuing to farm part-time, Roy pursued other employment. He worked at Johnson's Cash Store, a dry goods store on Washington Street in downtown Bedford. In 1949 he went into the dry goods business himself with fellow veteran Bernard Saunders, establishing the Peoples Clothing Store. By 1953 Roy had gone to work at the Rubatex factory. In September of that year, he lost his left hand and forearm in an accident at the factory. He continued to work at Rubatex for the next twenty-eight years.

In 2004 Roy was still actively farming, raising hay and cattle. He and Helen have two daughters and sons-in-law, grandchildren, and great-grandchildren. Roy has been active in three veterans organizations. He meets monthly with the 29th Infantry Division Association, and for some fifty years he has been a member of the American Legion and the Veterans of Foreign Wars. In the 1990s he served as commander of the local American Legion post. He and Helen frequently visit the National D-Day Memorial and engage in other efforts to support programs there. He has granted innumerable interviews about D-Day and related events and frequently speaks to student groups.

Helen Cundiff Stevens is a native of the Huddleston area of Bedford County. She was attending National Business College in Roanoke when the United States went to war in December 1941.

In 1942 she took a job at the Belding Heminway textile mill in Bedford for a couple of months but then left Bedford for Newport News, Virginia. There she took a job at the Hampton Roads Port of Embarkation, working in the office typing up lists of cargo to be shipped to sustain the war effort. When her sister came to join her in Newport News but then decided to return to Bedford, Helen decided also to move back to Bedford. Frozen in her job, she had to appear before a four-person panel and convince them that she was homesick and promise to seek defense-related employment in the Bedford area.

In 1943 she found a job at Rubatex in Bedford, working in the shipping office. She has estimated that there were some 300 workers at Rubatex, mostly women, making gas masks, parts for pontoon bridges, insulation for military equipment, shoe soles, and other supplies for the war effort.

Helen remembers when Mrs. Frank P. Draper, Sr., working at Rubatex, received a telegram informing her that her son Frank had been killed. Helen believes Mrs. Draper never returned to the factory.

When the war ended, Helen continued to work at Rubatex for a while. After she married Roy and they had their first child in 1947, she quit working at Rubatex. In the 1950s, she returned to Rubatex and worked there in the personnel department until retiring in 1986.

The Turpin Brothers

Three Turpin brothers served as enlisted men in the U.S. Army during World War II. The oldest, William H. ("Bill") Turpin, served in the Pacific Theater of Operations, helping U.S. aircraft land on island runways. Charles W. ("Charlie") Turpin also served in the Pacific Theater, primarily driving trucks and serving as a transportation dispatcher. He participated in three campaigns—New Guinea, Leyte, and Luzon. James ("Jim") Turpin served in the 2[d] Division, landing in Normandy two days after D-Day. He was wounded at St. Lo but served to the end of the war. (A fourth brother, Richard, served in the Army after World War II.)[1]

The Turpin brothers came from a tenant farming family that lived in the Thaxton area, west of the town of Bedford. William Turpin, who was born in Bedford County, moved with the family to North Carolina as a young boy and returned to Bedford around age eleven. His father died when he was fifteen, and he began to work full time on the farm to support the family.

In 1938 William moved to Newport News to work at a shipyard. In 1942 he received an induction notice from the Bedford County draft board and returned to Bedford. He attempted to enlist voluntarily in Roanoke but was refused because he had already received an induction notice. He entered the Army in September 1942 and was sent to Camp Lee, Virginia, and then to Camp Edison, New Jersey, for basic training. Next, he was sent to Fort Monmouth, New Jersey, and then Tampa, Florida, for U.S. Army Signal Corps training. He was trained to help operate and support mobile radars, which were set up on island bases to guide aircraft to safe landings on runways constructed there. He was sent to Hawaii for much of 1943 and then was deployed with a fighter control squadron to several Pacific islands, including Eniwetok in the Marshall Islands, Saipan in the Marianas Islands, and Okinawa.

When William was released from the Army in January 1946, he returned to Bedford. He took a mechanics course under the GI Bill and joined Company A of the National Guard for two years in 1946-1947. He worked for many years at two furniture factories in Bedford and three years at the Belding Heminway plant. He is still active with an upholstery shop that he runs in the Thaxton area. He and his wife have been married for fifty-five years and have two children and six grandchildren.

Charles was six years old when the family moved to the Thaxton area from North Carolina. He went to Thaxton School. After his schooling he farmed and drove a truck. He remembers hauling coal in a truck from Blacksburg, Virginia, to schools in Bedford—a round trip of more than fifty miles—for $1 a trip. For two years, except during the winter months, he helped build the Blue Ridge Parkway along the northern and western borders of Bedford County. Working on the parkway six days a week, he would drive his 1932 Pontiac up to the work site and work twelve hours a day mixing concrete and doing masonry work, for which he was paid thirty cents an hour, with time and a half for over forty hours a week.

In December 1942, when he turned twenty-one years of age, Charles was drafted. He was sent first to Camp Crowder, Missouri, and then to Fort Lewis, Washington. He was tested with good skills in using the Morse Code and was placed in the U.S. Army Signal-Intelligence Branch. For most of his service in the Army, however, he was a truck driver and transportation dispatcher. After Fort Lewis, he was sent to Two Rock Ranch, California, which was built to look like a chicken ranch, but which really housed men working to intercept and read Japanese codes.

After five months at the ranch, Charles was sent via ship to the Hollandia area of Dutch New Guinea. He traveled aboard the USS *General John Pope*, a large troop transport ship which carried 15,000 Army troops and Seabees. The ship departed from San Francisco and made two stops on the twelve-day voyage to New Guinea. It had no escorts, as it could travel at about twenty-eight knots and outrun Japanese ships and submarines.

In New Guinea, Charles drove trucks transporting troops to fight the Japanese. After seven months in New Guinea, he was deployed to the island of Leyte in the Philippines, where he worked as a telegraph operator at a message center. After four or five months he was sent to the island of Luzon, where he was a full-time dispatcher and truck driver.

When the fighting ceased, Charles was returned via ship to San Diego, arriving on January 24, 1946. He was sent to Fort Bragg, North Carolina, where he was discharged.

Charles was the last of the three brothers to return home. From Fort Bragg, he took a bus to Roanoke. On arriving in Roanoke and finding that it would be three hours before a bus would leave for Bedford, Charles and another serviceman hired a cab, which cost them a total of $26 to get to their homes in Bedford County.

Returning to civilian life, Charles went to work at Rebo Manufacturing Company making skids or pallets. Then, under the GI Bill, he undertook training to be a machinist at Miller's Machinery in Bedford, where he stayed for four years. Next, for over thirty-two years, he worked at Rubatex, seven years as a machinist, nearly twice as long as a foreman, and finally as a maintenance supervisor. He retired from Rubatex in 1984.

Charles was married in 1950; his wife died in recent years. He and his wife attended Thaxton Baptist Church, where Charles has been a deacon for forty-eight years. As of 2003, he lived in Bedford County, on the western outskirts of Bedford City.

James, who is now deceased, served in the infantry with the 2[d] Division. He went ashore in Normandy on June 8 and shortly thereafter was wounded in the leg at St. Lo. While being transported in a Jeep to get medical treatment, the Jeep struck a mine. The next thing he remembered was waking up in a hospital in England. He drove a truck for the rest of the war and returned to Bedford after the war.

Dean Wilkerson

Dean Wilkerson served in the 1st Infantry Division in World War II as a private first class. He fought in Europe where he was wounded in the Battle of the Bulge.[1]

Wilkerson was born in Bedford County and raised on a farm at the foot of the Peaks of Otter. He graduated from Bedford High School in the class of 1942.

Wilkerson left Bedford and went to Baltimore, where he worked at the Martin Aircraft Corporation. Several other young men from Bedford also went to Baltimore to work, including Jack Hicks, Everett

Holdren, Howard Longwood, and Harold Kennedy, and many of them roomed together. In early 1943 Wilkerson was drafted and took his thirteen weeks of basic training at Camp Wheeler, Georgia. He was trained as a machine gunner on the thirty-caliber, water-cooled, heavy machine gun.

Assigned to the 18th Infantry Regiment, 1st Infantry Division, Wilkerson deployed with his unit to England and landed in France after D-Day. He fought in France, Belgium, and Germany. There was a high turnover rate of men in his unit due to injuries and deaths, and Wilkerson felt he did not know his fellow soldiers well.

Military clothing and food left much to be desired. At times, Wilkerson felt that his feet and other parts of his body were nearly frozen in the sub-zero temperatures. He had only leather shoes and no coat or gloves. He remembers being served stew that was frozen.

On one occasion, he was wounded in the face and lip. Then, on January 15, 1945, during the Battle of the Bulge, Wilkerson was wounded by shrapnel from a German, heavy-artillery round. He was knocked unconscious by the concussion from the explosion. He was hit in the knee and buttocks, but the most serious wound was to his left ankle, which was shattered. He regained consciousness in a hospital in Belgium and found himself in a cast up to his waist. His wounds required bone and skin grafts.

From January to November 1945, Wilkerson was in thirteen different hospitals in France, England, and the United States, where he underwent a series of operations and physical therapy. In France, he and other American patients for fun taught unwitting French nurses to use English swear words.

When he returned to the United States still in a cast up to his waist, he landed in New Jersey. From there he called his parents, who knew he had been wounded, but he was not given leave to return to Bedford. Instead, he was sent on a train loaded with wounded men to a hospital at Camp Carson, Colorado. The trip took nearly two weeks. Once at the hospital he could leave for only three days at a time. He eventually was permitted to return to Bedford for a thirty-day leave. When he requested an extension, the response read, "Report immediately."

Wilkerson was discharged from the Army in November 1945, weighing 115 pounds and with a left leg about two inches shorter than the right. (To compensate, he wears on his left leg a brace and a shoe that is built up about two inches. He has received medical care at the Veterans Hospital in Salem, Virginia.)

After his discharge, Wilkerson returned to Bedford and then went to Baltimore to resume his job at the Martin Aircraft Corporation. After two or three weeks at the Martin plant, he found he could not stand the noise, and he returned to Bedford.

In 1946 Wilkerson married a young woman he had courted in Bedford before entering the military and with whom he corresponded during the war. He entered business as a partner with his brother-in-law at Northside Supply and General Merchandise Company, which sold feed, seed, fertilizer, and meats and offered auto repairs and a barber and beauty shop. He retired in 1974.

Over the years, Wilkerson has been active in the Bedford community, serving on the Bedford County Planning Commission, Road Commission, and School Board and on the board of a local bank. He has also been a member of various service organizations.

John L. Wilkes & Bettie Wilkes Hooper

John Leo Wilkes served in Bedford's Company A and rose to the rank of master sergeant, the "top sergeant" in Company A. He fought and died in the June 6, 1944, invasion of Normandy. His wife, Bettie Krantz Wilkes (now Hooper), worked in Bedford at Belding Heminway, the silk mill, where she and others made material for parachutes used during the war.[1]

John Wilkes was born in Bedford County in 1919, one of eight children of Leotie and Mary Wilkes. After finishing school, he worked on the farm and for a while worked in phelspar mines in Bedford County. In the latter part of the 1930s, he joined Bedford's Company A of the National Guard.

John's brother Henry was drafted and served in the Army. Their sister Rubye, who, after her marriage, used the last name Wilkes-Archer, served as an Army nurse and spent thirty-eight months in the Pacific Theater. Her husband, Lieutenant Howard Archer, was wounded in Saipan.

Bettie Krantz was born and raised on a farm about five miles east of the town of Bedford. She is one of seven children. She first attended Krantz School, named after her father who had donated the land for the school, and then went to nearby New London Academy for high school.

She met John Wilkes at a basketball game at the Academy. Bettie and John were married on August 10, 1941, while John was on a week's furlough from Fort Meade, Maryland, where Company A had been sent when called up to active duty in February 1941. In the weeks and months after their wedding, while Company A was at Fort Meade, John tried to come back to Bedford on the weekends. On one occasion, Bettie and others from the Bedford area drove to Fort Meade to see their loved ones, staying in a post guesthouse.

Bettie got a job at the silk mill. She worked in the entering department, helping with the initial processing of the heavy, coarse, durable material used to make parachutes for the military. She lived with her sister and brother-in-law in a new apartment on Otey Street in Bedford. In addition to her work, she socialized in Bedford and remembers helping to prepare surgical dressings. One of her close friends was Viola Parker, whose husband Earl Parker also served in Company A.

When John and Company A deployed to Camp Blanding, Florida, in August 1942, John rented a small apartment nearby. Bettie decided to go to Florida for a week's vacation and told the office manager at the mill that she intended to stay in Florida as long as John was there. The manager asked her to write him a letter asking him to hold her job for her return.

In mid-September 1942, after Bettie had been in Florida for nearly a month with John, five other young women from Bedford arrived to see their husbands or boy friends. On September 22, the men of Company A were ordered to deploy to Camp Kilmer, New Jersey, from which they were to be transported to New York City to sail for Great Britain aboard the converted-troopship *Queen Mary.*

For their trip from Florida back to Bedford, the six young women were able to use the station wagon belonging to Bedford Hoback, a soldier in Company A and boy friend of one of the six women. There was a complication, however. Of the six women, only Viola Parker knew how to drive, and she was pregnant. John Wilkes arranged for his brother Henry to fly down to Florida and drive the six women and their luggage to Bedford.

Once home in Bedford, Bettie and Viola Parker decided to go to New Jersey or New York to try to see their husbands while the men were in that area. The two women traveled by train to New York City and checked into a hotel. They tried to call their husbands at Camp Kilmer but could not reach them. At the end of the day, they got on a train headed back to Bedford.

While John was in Britain, Bettie wrote him every day, and John tried to write as often as he could. From John's letters and some photos he sent her, Bettie knew he was in England but not exactly where. Sometime in late May 1944, John wrote that he would not be able to write for a while.

It was sometime in July that Bettie learned of her husband's death on June 6, D-Day. The first word was unofficial. She was walking downtown in Bedford with an unwrapped box that she planned to mail to John as soon as she picked up one more article to include. As she approached one of the drugstores, a woman acquaintance who corresponded with another man in Company A, called to her from across the street and walked over to join her. Bettie asked if the woman had received any mail recently. The woman replied that she had received a letter that very day and the letter reported that John had been killed.

Bettie doesn't remember much about what happened after this conversation, other than that she somehow walked back to her apartment and someone called for a doctor. Family members tried to convince her that if John had been killed, she would have been notified by the government.

After a week, she went back to work at the silk mill. On the morning of her return, she was working in one of the factory rooms with her sister. The sister saw a telegram delivery person coming, motioned him to go back, and told Bettie she was going to the bathroom. Unaware of what was happening, Bettie kept working. Soon everyone in Bettie's department left their posts. Bettie eventually got up to look for her sister, and her sister told her that they needed to go home. Mr. Horn, one of the men in the office, drove them home.

Back home, someone again called for a doctor. At that point, Bettie knew that John was dead. Eventually someone gave her the telegram from the War Department informing her of John's death. Later she received a confirmation letter from the government. Her recent letters to John began to be returned to her, stamped to indicate that the intended recipient was deceased.

Bettie returned to work for a while. She wrote a poem about John, which was published in one of the local newspapers.

She later moved from Bedford to Lynchburg. She remarried, and she and her second husband had four children and six grandchildren. As of 2004, Bettie, widowed for a second time, still lived in Lynchburg.

Bettie has preserved the letters and photos John sent her, as well as his Purple Heart Medal, and she has visited Normandy. She has agreed to be interviewed for many articles and books.

Boyd Earl Wilson

Boyd Earl Wilson joined Bedford's Company A of the National Guard before the war, was reassigned to the 1st Infantry Division during the war, participated in the Allied invasions in North Africa, Sicily, and Normandy, and fought in Germany to the end of the war. He later fought in the Korean War and served in the Army for twenty-six years, retiring as a master sergeant. After re-entering civilian life, he eventually moved back to Bedford.[1]

Wilson was born in West Virginia but grew up in Bedford and attended Bedford High School. At age eighteen, in September 1938, he joined Company A to give himself something to do and to earn $4 or more every month. He started as a private and was assigned as a rifleman. In civilian life, he worked at Rubatex, where he made rubber hoses for gas masks, each hose designed to run from the mouth area of the mask to a canister worn on the user's body.

When Company A was called to active duty in February 1941, Wilson went with the unit to Fort Meade, Maryland. He recalled that Company A was transported aboard two-and-a-half-ton trucks provided by the National Guard service company in Roanoke; others recall riding a train to Fort Meade. Most men in Company A may have traveled to Fort Meade by train, while some traveled by motor vehicle. Wilson recalled being trucked earlier in the war to North Carolina and then Camp Blanding, Florida, where the men received new equipment.

At some point in his training, either in the United States or in England, Wilson was hospitalized. When it was time to be discharged, he was transferred from Company A and the 29th Infantry Division to the 1st Infantry Division, which he said was full of "damn Yankees." He was a rifleman and later a squad leader and sergeant.

Wilson flew to England as part of an advance detachment to get the barracks ready for his unit. In England he and his unit seemed to be constantly on maneuvers, and Wilson believed the troops were burned out by these maneuvers. Most of the men lived in barracks, some lived in tents, and some of the officers may have lived in private houses.

When it came time for combat, Wilson participated in three Allied invasions. In the invasion and fighting in North Africa, he landed near Oran, Algeria, and fought against the Germans for about a year. After North Africa, he participated in the invasion of Sicily, where his landing craft was hit about 500 yards off shore, and he had to remove his pack and swim. For the D-Day Invasion of Normandy, he claimed to have been the first man onto Omaha Beach from the 1st Infantry Division. In the sector where he landed, the Germans did not fire a shot, primarily, he believed, because of fear of naval artillery. For him personally, the Normandy Invasion was the easiest, least risky of the three invasions. After D-Day, as his unit moved into France and Germany, he did not have to fire a shot until his unit engaged the Germans in Aachen.

Wilson's unit fought its way to Pilsen, Czechoslovakia, where they met the Russians coming from the other direction. He was stationed in Czechoslovakia for a year after the war, and then was moved to Nuremberg, Germany, where he helped patrol the city.

In 1952-53, Wilson fought in Korea as part of the 7th Infantry Division. Overall, he served in the Army for twenty-six years and achieved the rank of master sergeant.

After he retired, he worked for the Del Monte food company for eighteen years and lived in Crozet, Virginia, near Charlottesville. When he retired from Del Monte in 2000, Company A veterans Roy Stevens and Pride Wingfield told him of plans to build the National D-Day Memorial in Bedford and encouraged him to return to Bedford. He returned to Bedford with his wife, Shirley, (his first wife had died).

While living in Bedford, he visited the new National D-Day Memorial almost daily, where he was a volunteer and spoke to many visitors.

Wilson died in December 2003 at age eighty-three, leaving his wife, a daughter, two sons, two stepsons, a stepdaughter, five grand-children, nine step grandchildren, two great-grandchildren, and eleven step-great-grandchildren.

Pride Wingfield & Rebecca L. Wingfield

Pride Wingfield entered the military as part of Bedford's Company A of the National Guard. He was subsequently transferred and served in at least three other Army units. While on leave in Bedford during the war, Pride met his future wife, Rebecca Lockard. Rebecca helped prepare surgical dressings for the Red Cross during the war.[1]

Wingfield was born and raised in Bedford County. In 1939 he joined Company A and eventually became the company clerk. As a civilian, he worked as a clerk at the Piedmont Label Company.

After Company A was called to active duty in February 1941, Wingfield deployed with the company to Fort Meade, Maryland.

When Company F of the 116th Infantry needed a company clerk, Wingfield was transferred to that company. As the 116th Infantry and its parent 29th Infantry Division prepared to deploy to Europe, Wingfield was sent to New York City for two weeks as part of an advance detachment to prepare for the transatlantic crossing. During the crossing on the *Queen Mary*, Wingfield slept with his old unit, Company A, because it was assigned to the upper A Deck, while Company F was downstairs on E Deck.

In England, Wingfield was stationed at Tidworth Barracks and Ivybridge where the 116th Infantry was stationed.

In early 1943 he transferred into the Army Air Forces. He returned to the United States and was sent to Biloxi, Mississippi, for pilot training and the University of Missouri for navigator training. He was then, however, transferred back into the infantry and ordered to Camp Van Dorn, Mississippi, where he joined the 63[d] Infantry Division as a company clerk.

Wingfield happened to be home in Bedford on leave when Allied forces, including his former units, Companies A and F, invaded Normandy on June 6, 1944.

In November 1944 Wingfield and the 63[d] Infantry Division were shipped across the Atlantic to Marseilles, France, and then sent northward into the French interior. By this time German forces were no longer in the area. When the war ended in Europe in May 1945, Wingfield and his unit were in Germany. He returned to America and was discharged on October 4, 1945.

During the war, Rebecca and Pride had corresponded. In addition to preparing surgical dressings for the Red Cross, Rebecca took a Red Cross first aid course, and sold tickets at the Liberty Theater and later the Bridge Theater in Bedford. Following Pride's discharge, he and Rebecca were married on October 22, 1945. The couple has one son and in 2003 celebrated their fifty-eighth wedding anniversary.

After the war, Pride returned to work at the Piedmont Label Company, where he worked until his retirement in 1982, a total of forty-five years, including time for military service.

Mary Witt

Mary Witt served overseas as a professional American Red Cross worker during World War II. She served in England, in France immediately after D-Day, and in Japan after the war.

Witt graduated from Bedford High School, class of 1928. She graduated from Radford Teachers College and then taught for three years in a one-room schoolhouse near Hillsville, Virginia. Next she moved to Georgia where she was employed as a social worker in remote areas. She then studied child welfare at the University of Pennsylvania and medical social work at Tulane University, after which she became the state supervisor of child welfare in Georgia.

When the war began in Europe, Witt volunteered for overseas duty with the American Red Cross. She underwent many months of preparation at Fort Bragg and Camp Davis. In July 1942 she was sent to England as a field director with the American Red Cross. She was first stationed in Oxford, England. In November 1943, she was transferred to London, and later was made traveling supervisor for a number of Army and Navy hospitals in Wales, Scotland, North Ireland, and East Anglia. From Britain she wrote:

> It is surprising how our idea of values has changed. A hot dog, hamburger, ice cream, fresh egg, good soap, fresh fruit take the first place. Money isn't too important for you can't buy anything that you want but the little you buy is expensive. I suppose that the same situation is in the States now. Or so we hear from some of the new people who have come over.[1]

In June 1944, after the Normandy Invasion, she deployed to France and became a field supervisor of the American Red Cross hospital division in one of the major U.S. Army organizations fighting in France against the Germans.[2] (See her letter regarding this period in Chapter 5 of this book.)

Witt was commended for doing "a great job" by Army Lt. Gen. John C. H. Lee, the chief of supply for General Eisenhower's command. She was awarded the Bronze Star for her work.[3]

By May 1946 Witt was serving as a rehabilitation worker with the American Red Cross in Japan and was in charge of nine hospitals throughout Japan.[4]

William A. Yowell & Eleanor P. Yowell

William A. Yowell, Jr., served in World War II in the United States and in Europe as a command bomber pilot. He flew B-24 and B-17 bombers on combat missions over Belgium, France, Holland, and Germany. He and Eleanor Payne were married during the war before he deployed overseas. Eleanor worked during the day as a secretary and bookkeeper, and in the evenings she kept busy with her Victory Garden, preparing surgical dressings for the American Red Cross, and socializing with her lady friends.[1]

William, nicknamed "Billy," "Bill," and, because of his red hair, "Pinky," was born and raised in the town of Bedford and graduated from Bedford High School. He went to work at the Piedmont Label Company as a salesman. He played clarinet in the Bedford Firemen's Band. For three years before the war, he served in Bedford's Company A of the Virginia National Guard.[2]

Eleanor, nicknamed "Ella," was also born and raised in the town of Bedford. She, too, graduated from Bedford High School, three years after William. After graduation, she worked at a hospital as a bookkeeper, at a law office, and at the Bedford County Welfare Department. She then took a job as a stenographer with the U.S. Department of Labor in Washington, D.C. She was in Washington when she first heard of the Japanese attack on Pearl Harbor—a newsboy called out the news as she came out of a movie theater. She later moved to Philadelphia where she worked for the Securities and Exchange Commission.

Eleanor returned to Bedford in 1942. She volunteered at the War Price and Rationing Board in Bedford and then took a paid position with the Board as its executive secretary. She later took a job in the bookkeeping department at the Elks National Home in Bedford, staying there for the duration of the war.

William and Eleanor had known each other for years, but in 1942 their relationship became serious. They considered getting married that summer but decided to wait.

In May of that year, at age twenty-seven, William had volunteered for the Aviation Cadet program of the U.S. Army Air Forces. His younger brother Charlie volunteered at the same time but was rejected because of his eyesight.

William was accepted as an Aviation Cadet. During a ten-month training program, he was sent to five different U.S. Army Air Forces facilities in the United States. He first went to Nashville, Tennessee, for nearly two months of tests to see if he was qualified for flight training. Then he was assigned to Maxwell Field in Montgomery, Alabama, for pre-flight school. Next, he went to Camden, South Carolina, for primary training, including actual flying. Following this, he was sent to Shaw Field, Sumter, South Carolina, for basic training. Then he went to Moody Field in Valdosta, Georgia, for advanced training, which he successfully completed and thereby earned his pilot's wings and commission as a second lieutenant. Finally, after a ten-day home leave, he was ordered back to Maxwell Field for operational four-engine training.

Eleanor visited William at Maxwell Field for a weekend in February 1943. Her boss at the War Price and Rationing Board, where she was not a happy employee, was against her going. Soon after her return, she found a new job at the Elks National Home. In June, she visited William at Shaw Field in South Carolina.

In July, while in Georgia finishing his flight training, William wrote Eleanor to ask her to come to Georgia in late August to attend the ceremonies for his graduation from pilot school, to pin his pilot's wings on him, and to marry him in the post chapel. The wedding was delayed until September 25. The couple was married on that date in the post chapel at Maxwell Field, Alabama, where William had been reassigned for more training. The couple lived in Montgomery, Alabama, for the next month.

In late October, William was ordered to Salt Lake City, Utah, where he was to be assigned a bomber crew. Eleanor returned to Bedford and her job at the Elks Home.

William then was assigned to Davis-Monthan Field in Tucson, Arizona, and then to Alamogordo, New Mexico, for operational four-engine training. He wrote Eleanor that from New Mexico he would be leaving for overseas.

In late January 1944, Eleanor traveled by train to New Mexico, and she and William rented a room in a house in Alamogordo for nearly two months. On the weekends, they and other couples relaxed at the officers' club, rode horses in the desert, and traveled to El Paso and the White Mountains. The latter part of March, William was ordered to Morrison Field in West Palm Beach, Florida, in preparation for flying to England. Eleanor and some wives left New Mexico to go back to their homes. En route to their respective destinations, William and Eleanor ran into each other in Herrington, Kansas, where, because of a blizzard, they were able to spend several more days together.

From Florida, William and his crew flew to Brazil and then across the Atlantic to Africa, landing in Dakar and then flying to Marrakech in French Morocco. From Morocco, they flew out into the Atlantic and north along the western coast of Europe until they landed at Prestwick, Scotland. They then flew south to Lavenham in Suffolk County, England, located approximately fifty miles northeast of the center of London, arriving in mid-April.

William was stationed in Lavenham from April to late August 1944, where he and his crew were part of the 837th Bomb Squadron, 487th Bombardment Group, Eighth U.S. Air Force. He was promoted to first lieutenant.

Operating from Lavenham, between May and August, William and his crew flew thirty bombing missions against enemy targets in Belgium, France, Germany, and Holland. On these flights, antiaircraft artillery fire, or "flak," was a greater risk to the high-flying bombers than enemy fighter aircraft. On one mission, William's bomber returned with twenty holes in it caused by flak. For his service, William was awarded the Distinguished Flying Cross.

William came home to Bedford on a thirty-day leave in mid-September 1944, with orders to return to his unit in England. At the end of his leave, a medical check determined him unfit for combat duty. He was sent to an Army Air Force rest camp in North Carolina for thirty days. Eleanor resigned her job at the Elks Home and joined him. William was then assigned to an Army Air Base in Fort Myers, Florida, and was discharged from active service in August 1945. He chose to stay in the reserves.

Eleanor kept busy during the war years working at the Elks Home during the day. In the evenings, she returned home to take care of a dog she had acquired, tend to the Victory Garden she planted, fix some supper, and then usually play cards or go to a movie with lady friends, or go to the library to prepare surgical dressings for the Red Cross. She also helped entertain in Bedford homes two groups of British sailors who visited Bedford while their ships were being repaired and replenished in Norfolk.

At home in the evenings, and sometimes at the Elks Home when her boss was not looking, she wrote letters to William. She and William corresponded frequently.

After the war, William returned to Bedford and resumed his career at the Piedmont Label Company. They started a family and had two children. William's career at Piedmont Label was interrupted in the early 1950s when he was recalled to active duty during the Korean War. He served in the Air Force in Japan during that war. In all, he served over twenty-three years in the armed forces, in both active and reserve status.

In August 1970 William and Eleanor traveled to Lavenham, England, for a reunion of the 487th Bombardment Group.

William died in 1972, at age fifty-six, after battling aplastic anemia for some three years. As of 2004, Eleanor still lives in Bedford, where she gardens, exercises, and writes. In addition to her two children, she now has six grandchildren and four great-grandchildren.

In recent years, Eleanor decided to write a book based on the wartime correspondence between William and her during the period

November 1942 to September 1944. With advice and technical assistance from her daughter and others, she wrote and had published in 2001, her hard-cover book, *Flying High: World War II Letters to and from U.S. Army Air Force Bases and the Home Front*. In 2003 she began work on a second book about the Korean War period.

Author's Comment

My research on Bedford County's World War II experience began in 1999, after the Sedalia Center, a cultural arts center located in Bedford County, advertised a contest for an original, historical drama about Bedford County after the Civil War. Having an interest in writing and in military affairs, and having become aware of the importance of World War II to Bedford since moving in 1995 to southwest Virginia, I decided to try my hand at writing a historical drama focused on Bedford's experience in that war. My drama won the contest, and, in the summers of 2000 and 2001, the Sedalia Center, with the help of volunteer directors, artists, and actors, presented to the public the historical drama, *Bedford Goes to War.*

Inspired by the reaction to the drama, I decided in early 2002 to broaden and deepen my research and write a book. Part of my motivation was to provide a record of Bedford's contributions and sacrifices—a record more comprehensive, detailed, accessible, tangible, and permanent than previous accounts—in effect, to leave a legacy to the people of Bedford that is as permanent as a book can be.

I conducted my research mainly in four places—the Bedford Central Public Library, the Bedford City/County Museum, the office of the Bedford County Clerk of the Circuit Court, and, perhaps most importantly, the homes of Bedford County veterans of World War II or their surviving loved ones. At the library, I read on microfilm, for all of the war years, the editions of the *Bedford Bulletin* newspaper and, thanks to an interlibrary loan from the Library of Virginia, the *Bedford Democrat.* Also at the library, I researched the local history section in the library's Tharp Room and the library's collection of books on World War II. (I also occasionally used the Roanoke City and County Libraries.) At the museum in Bedford, I read through the archival collections on World War II and the book collection on the war, as well as perused the exhibits. In the clerk's office, I did intensive research on the military service of individuals. (I was fortunate in having done my basic research before the Commonwealth directed that many of the records be restricted in access.) In a welcome respite from poring through microfilm, books, and records, more than twenty-five Bedford veterans or their loved ones were kind enough to welcome me into their homes and share with me their stories, photographs, and other memorabilia.

I owe a great debt of gratitude to all the people who helped me with my research and collection of photographs. Many of these are listed in the acknowledgments section of this book, along with authors and publishers who permitted me to use material from their original work.

Some of the many humbling things I have learned in writing this book are that no one individual can know the whole story of what Bedford experienced during the war, that the whole story cannot be written in a single book, and that, try as one may, it is probably impossible to avoid mistakes. The best that one can do—that I was able to do—is to present a general picture, with some details that may represent what happened to others. I was able to interview fewer than twenty veterans and fifteen loved ones of veterans, yet I know there are many more World War II veterans and loved ones still living in Bedford. I regret that I could not include the stories of more veterans in this book.

One of my greatest pleasures in writing this book has been meeting some wonderful people in the Bedford community, especially the World War II veterans and loved ones of those living and deceased. I salute and thank you for your service and for sharing your stories with me.

Several organizations in Bedford, which do much to serve those in the immediate community and beyond, have come to have special meaning for me. In appreciation, I plan to donate a significant portion of any profits from the sale of this book to five of these—the National D-Day Memorial Foundation, the Bedford City/County Museum, the Bedford Public Library, Bedford's American Legion Post #54, and the Sedalia Center.

Finally, I hope you, the readers, find this book educational, moving, and entertaining. For the younger readers, I hope you learn something about what Bedford and this country experienced during the war. For the older readers, it is my hope that the book stirs some memories of loved ones and of what it was like to live during the war years, and that you, too, learn something new—of life overseas if you were at home during the war, or, for you veterans, of life on the home front while you were away.

I welcome any and all comments on this book, including correction of mistakes of fact or interpretation and suggestions for additional stories that might be incorporated in any future printing.

James W. Morrison

80 Chickadee Circle
Moneta, Virginia 24121-2342
Phone: 540-721-1991
E-mail: EZWriter@att.net

Spring 2004

Acknowledgments

Since 1999 when I began my research, many people in the Bedford community and beyond have offered encouragement, generously shared their experiences, suggested sources, and provided all types of research materials and photographs. I thank each of them, especially those named below.

Ivylyn Jordan Schenk Hardy and Eleanor Payne Yowell have been more than generous and kind in talking with me, sharing information and photos, and permitting me to quote extensively from the correspondence between them and their husbands from World War II. Their love for history and writing has been a source of inspiration, and visits with them have been occasions to savor.

Without the Sedalia Center and its 1999 historical drama contest, I probably would never have begun the research that led to the drama and this book, both titled, *Bedford Goes to War*. My appreciation goes to Annis and Bill McCabe and the Sedalia Center board for their encouragement; to Judy Wynn, Rebecca Mays, Karen Dempsey, Mary Bains, and other staff members and volunteers at Sedalia who helped with production of the drama in 2000-2001; to Nancy N. Johnson for directing the drama, and to all the actors, musicians, artists, technicians, assistants, and Company A color guards who helped with the drama.

Many veterans, relatives of veterans, and Bedford residents who lived on the home front during World War II kindly welcomed me into their homes and shared their experiences and the experiences of their loved ones. I met more than once with Roy O. and Helen C. Stevens, William H. Merriken, and Bernard W. and Margaret Saunders. Others with whom I met include Lucille Hoback Boggess, Henry Chappelle, Ward A. and Mary Burks Dean, Kenneth Dooley, Warren Gamiel E. Draper, Joseph E. Goode, Willie J. Hobson, Bettie Krantz Wilkes Hooper, David Hubbard, Allen M. Huddleston, Nina Cauthorn Jarvis, Catherine and Rebecca Karnes, Ethlyn "Patsy" Graves Melton, Earl R. and Elva Z. M. Newcomb, Marie Rucker Otey, Virginia Foutz Pizzati and her son Roger Pizzati, William E. "Billy" Parker, Margaret

Danner Simpkins, Elizabeth Teass, Charles W. and William H. Turpin, Betty Allen Welch, Dean Wilkerson, Boyd E. Wilson, Pride and Rebecca L. Wingfield, and Bertie Fellers Woodford.

The staff and volunteers at the Bedford City/County Museum were always friendly and helpful. Many thanks to Ellen A. Wandrei, director, and staff members Louise Bonds, Bernice Sizemore, Ruth Farrar, and Elizabeth Evans. Volunteer Annie Pollard went above and beyond the call of duty in providing both information and copies of old photographs. I appreciate being able to use some of the Museum's photos in this book.

At the Bedford Public Library, I want to acknowledge directors Thomas Hehman and Peggy Bias, the staffs at the Bedford Central and Moneta/Smith Mountain Lake Libraries, and particularly the Bedford Central reference staff, including, over the years, Bernadette Brennan, Marcy Sallette, Rosey Clark, Tammy Key, Sharon Amstutz, Apryl Houghton, Cindy Perdue, and Gwen Wells. Bedford is indeed fortunate in having a wonderful public library system and a dedicated staff of public servants.

In the office of the Clerk of the Bedford County Circuit Court, Clerk Carol Black and assistants Karen O. Glover, Diane Luhrs, and, in 1999, Angelia Newby were very helpful, as was Rebecca Mahone in the Roanoke County Clerk's office.

At the National D-Day Memorial Foundation, Carol Tuckwiller was most helpful in suggesting ways to research military records and providing substantive comments. Joe Banner provided superb photographs and offered valuable suggestions.

The National Park Service, particularly Peter Givens, Gene Parker, and Randy Sutton, readily answered questions about the Peaks of Otter and the Blue Ridge Parkway.

Eric V. Voelz at the U.S. National Archives and Records Administration and Heidi Myers at the U.S. Department of the Navy Library were very responsive and helpful in answering specific military-related questions. Tom Goehner at the American Red Cross Museum provided information on surgical dressings.

Several individuals provided assistance. The Rev. Paul Greer, pastor for the Salem and Center Point United Methodist Churches, kindly opened these churches so I could see and photograph the honor rolls and memorials to the servicemen of World War II. The Rev. John Bain showed me the memorials in the Bedford Christian Church. Robert F. Harris and Edna Hayden helped direct me to members of Bedford's Black community who served in World War II. Skip Tharp was gracious in providing photographs and information about funerals for some of the men killed in the war, as well as suggesting other people to contact. Susannah H. Martin was helpful in accessing some of the photographs, letters, and memorabilia of her mother, Ivylyn Hardy.

I wish to thank the following, in addition to Eleanor Yowell, for permitting me to quote from or draw on previously published work: Rebecca Jackson, the *Bedford Bulletin* and the *Bedford Democrat*; John J. Barnes, *Fragments of My Life with Company A, 116th Infantry Regiment*; and Peter Viemeister, *A History of Aviation: They Were There.*

My fellow writers and friends in the Valley Writers Chapter of the Virginia Writers Club and the Lake Writers group of the Smith Mountain Arts Council have been supportive in many ways. Rodney Franklin has been instrumental in compiling information on Bedford County women serving in World War II. I especially want to thank Becky Mushko for her suggestions, encouragement, and occasional, good-natured prodding.

Melinda Williams of Melinda's Computer Graphics in Rocky Mount has been both responsive and creative in designing the cover of the book and arranging the photographs.

Joyce Maddox at Warwick House Publishing has been immensely helpful in editing this book and overseeing its publication. It has been a joy working with her. Many thanks also to Amy Moore for a superb job in formatting this book for printing.

Finally, I want to thank the love of my life, my wife, Edie, for all of her encouragement, care, and support over the course of the five years it took to prepare the historical drama and then this book. Her support has extended all the way from providing coffee, to offering suggestions for research and book design, to proof reading and editorial and marketing advice. Most important was her love and moral support day in and day out. I also want to thank for their encouragement our children, Jim and Jennifer, our daughter-in-law, Cary, my mother, Margaret Derrick, my sister, Marilyn Osterhoff, and many friends too numerous to mention. I am blessed to have such a family and friends.

Appendix A

Bedford County Men Who Were Killed or Died While Serving in the Armed Forces in World War II

This appendix provides information on men from or associated with Bedford County who were killed or died while serving in the armed forces during World War II. (No Bedford servicewomen died in the war.) It also includes information on servicemen discharged from the armed forces before suffering war-related deaths and men with only limited association with Bedford County. There are four categories:

- Category A, the main category, includes the names of 137 men who lived in or had substantial associations with Bedford County and who were killed or died between the fall of 1941 and mid-August 1945, when the Japanese surrendered.

- Category B includes the names of five additional servicemen who lived in or had substantial associations with Bedford County and who died from accidents or illness after the Japanese surrender in mid-August 1945 and before December 31, 1946, when President Truman proclaimed the end of "hostilities."

- Category C includes the names of two Bedford County men who had been discharged from the military before suffering war-related deaths. One died of the effects of a military training accident that occurred prior to his discharge. The other left the Army in 1938 and several years later was captured by the Japanese and died while being transported to Japan.

- Category D includes the names of twenty servicemen who had only limited association with Bedford County, apparently not enough to be included under Bedford County in a master honor roll list of Virginians who were killed or died during the war (see below).

Determining who can be characterized as a "Bedford County Man" is a subjective task. Those who were born and raised in the county and continued to live and work there until they left for active military duty are clearly Bedford County men. The task is more subjective for men who were born and raised in Bedford but moved away before joining the military; those who moved to Bedford County from elsewhere; those who had associations with two or more counties, cities, or states—including those who lived in one area and worked in another; those with loved ones living in different areas; and those who lived in communities lying along the border between Bedford County and adjacent counties or cities.

Provided for each man under each of the four categories are, to the extent available, his last name; first name; middle name or initial; his last rank; his branch of service; how, where, and when he died or was reported missing; the military unit in which he served; the community in which he lived in Bedford County prior to military service or where his family lived; his occupation prior to military service; his race if Black (three men in Category A and one in Category B were identified by historical committees as Negro or "colored," and their names on earlier honor roll lists were marked with asterisks at the urging of black scholars who wanted Blacks identified; a fourth Black, John Augustus Peoples, Jr., has been added to Category A, but he was not on the historical honor roll lists; all others for which race is not mentioned were White); where he is buried, and, finally, in parentheses, the extent to which the man's name appears on four honor-roll lists prepared shortly after the war and delineated below.

The cemeteries and monuments overseas where some of the men are buried or, if missing, memorialized, are managed by the American Battle Monuments Commission (ABMC). Details can be found at www.abmc.gov.

The four earlier honor roll lists, indicated by numbers, are:

1 – Bronze plaque honor roll mounted on a wall inside the Bedford County Courthouse. This list of 135 names was prepared by the

Bedford County World War II History Committee. It reflects the Bedford County portion of list 4 below, which the committee helped prepare;

2 – Bedford's Gold Star Honor Roll, which is included in "Reports and Correspondence Concerning Bedford County in World War II," compiled by Mrs. George Parker, chair of the Bedford County World War II History Committee. This list, a copy of which is maintained at the Bedford Central Public Library, contains 109 names. The committee appears to have used in its research some of the detailed material from the *Military Records of Bedford County's Gold Star Men in World War II*, compiled by the Bedford County War History Committee and maintained in the office of the Clerk of the Circuit Court in the Bedford County Courthouse. This list, or an expanded list, was sent to the Virginia World War II History Commission, which then compiled a master list for all of Virginia; see list 4 below.

3 – Lists of names of deceased servicemen published as an honor roll in Bedford newspapers, with the assistance of the Bedford County World War II History Committee. The *Bedford Democrat* published an initial list on May 17, 1945, and updated the list in August and again in September 1945. The number of names on the list increased from eighty-six to 107 to 116.

4 – A list of 135 names for Bedford County found in the book *Gold Star Honor Roll of Virginians in the Second World War*, ed. by W. Edwin Hemphill, Virginia World War II History Commission, Charlottesville, Virginia, 1947. Copies of this book are available in the Bedford City/County Museum and the Bedford Central Public Library. The Bedford County portion is derived from list 2 above. This list, in the section for Bedford County, includes men associated only with Bedford County and also men associated with Bedford County and other counties or cities outside Bedford County. Compilers of this list, in deciding under which primary county or city to list a given name, used the address of the next-of-kin as the determining factor. When there was an association with two or more counties or cities, cross references were entered in each county or city. In addition to the 135 men listed under Bedford County, one additional man from

Bedford County is listed in a separate section on men who died after they had been discharged from the service but whose deaths resulted from service-connected causes.

The War and Navy Departments prepared lists of servicemen who died during the war and broke these down by counties, but these included only servicemen who died in connection with combat service or as a direct result of operations against enemy forces. These government lists served as a starting point in the preparation of expanded lists, which include all who were killed or died while in military service, regardless of cause.

Category A

Bedford County Men Who Were Killed
or Died Before Japan Surrender

Abbott, Leslie Cecil, Jr., staff sergeant, U.S. Army, killed in action in France on D-Day, June 6, 1944, member of Company A, 116th Infantry Regiment, 29th Infantry Division, lived in Goode community, family lived in Bedford, was a farmer, buried in Bedford's Oakwood Cemetery, (on lists 1, 2, 3, 4) (Note: List 2 and the entry in the *Military Records of Bedford County's Gold Star Men in World War II*, located at the Bedford Courthouse, incorrectly indicate that he was killed in Italy in January 1944).

Allen, John Walton, private first class, U.S. Army, killed in action in France, September 10, 1944, member of 121st Infantry Regiment, 8th Infantry Division, lived in Thaxton community, worked at aircraft plant in Baltimore, buried in Bedford's Greenwood Cemetery, (on lists 1, 2, 3, 4).

Anderson, Clyde H., staff sergeant, U.S. Army, died (likely killed in action) probably in France, August 2, 1944, member of 112th Infantry Regiment, 28th Infantry Division, buried in Brittany American Cemetery, St. James, France, (on lists 2, 3, 4), (listed in 4 under Bedford and Halifax Counties).

Anderson, Robert Henry, technical sergeant, U.S. Army Air Forces, killed accidentally in England, June 29, 1943, member of 7th

Station Complement Squadron, family lived in Thaxton community, worked for Pepsi-Cola, buried in Cambridge American Cemetery, England, (on lists 1, 2, 3, 4).

Anthony, Houston Gettle, private first class, U.S. Army, killed in action in France, July 11, 1944, father lived in Lynch Station community, (on lists 3, 4) (listed in 3 for Bedford County; listed in 4 for Campbell County only).

Arrington, Robert William, private first class, U.S. Army, killed in action in Germany, February 21, 1945, member of an anti-tank company in 29th Infantry Division, family lived in Montvale community, was a farmer, (on lists 1, 2, 3, 4).

Arthur, Onyx Bennett, private, U.S. Army, killed in action in North Africa or Sicily, July 19, 1943, family lived in Moneta/Huddleston communities, was a tractor driver, (on lists 1, 2, 3, 4)

Ballard, John C., Jr., private, U.S. Army, killed in action in Belgium, January 4, 1945, member of 502 Parachute Infantry Regiment, 101st Airborne Division, born and raised through elementary school in Bedford County, mother lived in Front Royal, grandmother lived in Bedford, buried in Henri-Chapelle American Cemetery, Belgium (on lists 1, 2, 3, 4), (listed in 4 under Warren and Bedford Counties).

Barton, Russell Armstrong, private, U.S. Army, killed in action in Italy, February 20, 1945, lived in Stewartsville community, mother lived in Goodview community, was a farmer, (on lists 1, 2, 3, 4).

Bennett, Carlton Alfred, technician, fourth grade, U.S. Army, killed in action probably off the coast of Anzio, Italy, January 26, 1944, member of 83d Chemical Mortar Battalion, family lived in Huddleston community, was a farmer and worked at Belding Heminway, listed on tablets of the missing at Sicily-Rome American Cemetery, Italy, (on lists 1, 2, 3, 4).

Bowyer, Ernest Alfred, private, U.S. Army, died November 29, 1944, of wounds received in action in Germany, served in 22d Infantry Regiment, lived in Thaxton community, was a farmer, buried in Shady Grove Church Cemetery in Thaxton, (on lists 1, 2, 3, 4), (listed in 4 under Bedford and Roanoke Counties).

Bowyer, Nelson June, sergeant, U.S. Army, died June 2 of wounds received in action on Okinawa, member of 184th Infantry Regiment,

7th Infantry Division, father lived in Bedford, buried at Honolulu Memorial, Hawaii, (on lists 1, 2, 3, 4), (listed in 4 under Bedford and Nottingham Counties).

Boyd, Herman, private, (branch of service not identified), killed in action on Okinawa, June 19, 1945, lived in Moneta/Radford Church area, graduated Moneta High School in 1944, (not on any of 4 lists)

Boyd, Wilbur W. (or William W.), flight officer, U.S. Army, father lived in Blue Ridge, (no other details), (on lists 1, 2, 3, 4) (listed in 4 under Botetourt and Bedford Counties)

Brown, Landon Larry (or Lowry), private first class, U.S. Army, killed in action in Germany, December 12, 1944, served in an artillery unit, family lived in Leesville community, graduated from Huddleston High School and later worked in Baltimore, Maryland, was a sheet metal worker, (on lists 1, 2, 3, 4) (listed in 4 under Campbell and Bedford Counties).

Burks, Lionel Lodowick, warrant officer second class, Royal Canadian Air Force, killed in plane accident in Nova Scotia, Canada, July 24, 1942, was born in Bedford and his mother lived in Bedford but his address was West Virginia, was a salesman, (on lists 1, 3, 4).

Burnette, Clarence O., private first class, U.S. Army, killed in action in Germany, March 27, 1945, lived in Bedford County, (on lists 2 and 3 for Bedford County; listed in 4 under Lynchburg City only), (wife's address listed in 2 as Route 1, Bedford, and in 4 as RFD 1, Lynchburg City).

Burnette, Floyd Allen, private first class, U.S. Army, killed in action in Germany, April 12, 1945, member of 661st Tank Destroyer Battalion, family lived in Forest community, buried in Netherlands American Cemetery, Netherlands, (on lists 1, 2, 3, 4).

Burnette, Mahlon Thomas, private, U.S. Army, killed in action in North Africa, May 11, 1943, member of 115th Infantry Regiment, 3[d] Infantry Division, born in Huddleston community, parents lived in Huddleston or near Lynchburg, enlisted in Roanoke, was a baker, buried in North Africa American Cemetery, Tunisia, (on lists 1, 2, 3, 4).

Byrd, Horace Allen, ensign, U.S. Navy, died of heart failure in Brooklyn, New York, July 7, 1945, mother lived in Moneta or

Lynchburg, (on lists 1, 2, 3, 4) (listed in 4 under Lynchburg City and Bedford County).

Byrd, Thomas Herman, private first class, U.S. Army, killed in action on Okinawa, June 18, 1945, member of 383^d Infantry Regiment, 96th Infantry Division, family lived in Moneta community, listed on wall at Honolulu Memorial, Hawaii (on lists 1, 2, 3, 4).

Canady, Everett Morris, private first class, U.S. Marine Corps, killed in action on Guadacanal, September 24, 1942, born in Goode community, family lived in Goode or Lowry community, he then lived in Roanoke, worked at Coca Cola plant, (on lists 1, 2, 3, 4) (name is spelled Canaday on lists 2 and 3).

Carter, Wallace R., private first class, U.S. Army, missing in action and later declared killed in action in France on D-Day, June 6, 1944, member of Company A, 116th Infantry Regiment, 29th Infantry Division, family lived in Bedford, was a poolroom worker, buried in Bedford's Greenwood Cemetery, (on lists 1, 2, 3, 4), (on list 3 date of death is incorrectly given as June 11, 1944)

Cheatham, Russell H., private, U.S. Army, (no other details), had connection to Bedford, wife lived in Lynchburg, (on lists 1, 2, 3, 4), (listed in 4 under Lynchburg City and Bedford County).

Clifton, John Daniel, private first class, U.S. Army, killed in action in France on D-Day, June 6, 1944, member of Company A, 116th Infantry Regiment, 29th Infantry Division, family lived in Bedford, buried in Bedford's Greenwood Cemetery, (on lists 1, 2, 3, 4).

Cofer, Thomas Edward, private, U.S. Army, killed in action in France, June 17, 1944, member of 234th Infantry Regiment, family from Forest community, was a farmer, (on lists 1, 2, 3, 4) (listed in 4 under Lynchburg City and Bedford County).

Coleman, Andrew Jackson, private first class, U.S. Army, died of sickness (nepkritis chronic parenchymatous) July 16, 1944, in Ashford Army Hospital in White Sulphur Springs, West Virginia, had served in and trained in England with Company A, 116th Infantry, 29th Infantry Division, before becoming ill and being returned to America, family lived in Bedford, was a carpenter, buried in Bedford's Oakwood Cemetery, (on lists 1, 3, 4).

Compton, Lloyd Grayson, second lieutenant, U.S. Army Air Forces, killed in accidental crash of a bomber aircraft, El Paso, Texas, November 4, 1942, graduated from White Sulphur Springs High School in West Virginia, parents lived in Bedford, (on lists 1, 2, 3, 4), (listed in 4 under Bedford and Rockingham Counties).

Coppedge, John Henry, chief electrician's mate, U.S. Navy, died of a heart attack September 9, 1944, born in Bedford County, resided in Portsmouth, Virginia, was a Navy career man, (on list 1).

Creasy, Herman Ray, private first class, U.S. Army, died of illness/cardiac failure or wounds received in foreign service in a hospital in Staunton, Virginia, May 28, 1945, family lived in Goodview community, was a farmer, (on lists 1, 2, 3, 4).

Daniel, Herbert Odell, private, U.S. Marine Corps, died March 12, 1945, of wounds received in action on Iwo Jima, parents lived in Huddleston or Leesville community of Bedford County, wife lived in Altavista, worked at Belding Heminway, buried in Horeb Methodist Church Cemetery in Huddleston community (on lists 1, 2, 3, 4), (listed in 4 under Campbell and Bedford Counties).

Danner, Joseph Samuel, first lieutenant, U.S. Army Air Forces, killed in accidental crash of bomber aircraft in England, near Bishop's Stortford, August 30, 1944, family lived in the town of Bedford, had worked at the Bridge Theater after graduating from high school, buried in Bedford's Greenwood Cemetery, (on lists 1, 2, 3, 4).

Davis, Warren, private first class, U.S. Army, killed in action in Belgium in Malmedy Massacre, December 17, 1944, served with Battery B, 285th Field Artillery Observation Battalion, family lived in Bedford County, was a farmer, buried in Henri-Chapelle American Cemetery, Belgium, (on lists 1, 2, 3, 4).

Dean, John Wesley, master sergeant, U.S. Army, killed in action in France, near St. Lo, June 17, 1944, member of Company F, 116th Infantry Regiment, 29th Infantry Division, born in Forest community, inducted into service with National Guard in South Boston, Halifax County, Virginia, resided in Paces, Virginia, when entered service, parents lived in Bedford County, was a farmer, buried in Bedford's Greenwood Cemetery, (on lists 1, 2, 3, 4), (listed in 4 under Bedford and Halifax Counties).

Dinkel, James Luck, private, U.S. Army, died of wounds received in action March 21, 1944, Bougainville or Solomon Islands, member of 182^d Infantry, Americal Division, family lived in Montvale community, was a farmer, buried in Bedford's Oakwood Cemetery, (on lists 1, 2, 3, 4).

Draper, Frank Price, Jr., technical sergeant, U.S. Army, died of wounds received in action in France on D-Day, June 6, 1944, (possibly died June 7), member of Company A, 116th Infantry Regiment, 29th Infantry Division, family lived in town of Bedford, had worked at Hampton Looms, buried in Bedford's Greenwood Cemetery, (on lists 1, 2, 3, 4).

Dudley, James Joseph, technician, fifth grade, U.S. Army, missing in action, then declared killed in action probably off the coast of Anzio, Italy, January 26, 1944, member of Company D, 83^d Chemical Mortar Battalion, raised in Flint Hill community, he and his wife lived in Huddleston community, employed as a clerk in Bedford before the war, buried in Sicily-Rome American Cemetery, Italy, (on lists 1, 2, 3, 4).

Duff, Albert Ashby, corporal, U.S. Army, killed in action in France, November 11, 1944, member of 37th Tank Battalion, 4th Armored Division, lived in Big Island community, mother lived in Waugh community, had worked at Rubatex, buried in Lorraine American Cemetery, France, (on lists 1, 2, 3, 4).

Ellis, Henry Clarence, private first class, U.S. Army, died of a fractured skull in Germany, June 4, 1945, (after hostilities had ended), parents lived in Hardy community, (on lists 1, 3, 4), (listed in 4 under Bedford and Franklin Counties).

English, Carlton Carter, private first class, U.S. Army, missing in action and later declared killed in action in Germany, November 16, 1944, member of 12th Infantry Regiment, 4th Infantry Division, his mother lived in Forest community, was a farmer, buried in Ardennes American Cemetery, Belgium, (on lists 1, 4).

Fariss, Jack Price, staff sergeant, U.S. Army Air Forces, declared missing in action in Germany, December 11, 1943, and then in June 1945 declared killed in action, served on a B-17 bomber, member of 568th Bomb Squadron, 390th Bomb Group, Heavy, born in Bedford

County, graduated Huddleston High School, mother lived in Bedford County, his address was Portsmouth, Virginia, when he entered the service, listed on tablets of missing at Netherlands American Cemetery, Netherlands, (on lists 1, 2, 3, 4).

Farley, Herman M., private, U.S. Army, died (probably killed in action in Italy) November 8, 1943, member of 30th Infantry Regiment, 3d Infantry Division, father lived in Bedford, (no other details), buried in Sicily-Rome American Cemetery, Italy, (on lists 1, 3, 4).

Fellers, Taylor Nicholas, captain, U.S. Army, killed in action in France on D-Day, June 6, 1944, commander of Company A, 116th Infantry Regiment, 29th Infantry Division, lived in Cifax/Goode community, worked as foreman for state highway department in Bedford residency, buried in Bedford's Greenwood Cemetery, (on lists 1, 2, 3, 4), (listed in 4 under Lynchburg City and Bedford County).

Fisher, Owen H., private first class, U.S. Army, killed in action in Germany, November 18, 1944, served with 29th Infantry Division, family lived in Bedford or Hardy, (on lists 1, 2, 3, 4).

Fizer, Charles William, private first class, U.S. Army, killed in action in France near St. Lo, July 11, 1944, served in Company A, 116th Infantry Regiment, 29th Infantry Division, family lived in Bedford, was a student, buried in Normandy American Cemetery, France, (on lists 1, 2, 3, 4).

Fizer, Robert Alvin, private first class, U.S. Army, died of wounds received in France, near Bisoncort, September 17, 1944, served in 320th Infantry Regiment, 35th Infantry Division, lived in town of Bedford, worked as usher at movie theater and at Piedmont Label, buried in Bedford's Oakwood Cemetery, (on lists 1, 2, 3, 4).

Franklin, John Cauthorn (or Cauthon), Jr., private, U.S. Army, missing in action then declared killed in action in Germany, in Hurtgen Forest near Geimeter, November 5, 1944, served in 109th Infantry Regiment, 28th Infantry Division, family lived in Bedford County, near Joppa Mill, worked at Rubatex, buried in Bedford's Greenwood Cemetery, (on lists 1, 4).

Frazier, John Willie (or William), private, U.S. Army, killed in action in Italy, near Cassino, February 12, 1944, lived in Bedford County near Joppa Mill, worked at Rubatex, buried in Mt. Olivet

Church Cemetery in Bunker Hill area of Bedford County, (on lists 1, 2, 3, 4).

Gibbs, Charles James, technician, fifth grade, U.S. Army, missing in action and later declared killed in action off the coast of Anzio, Italy, January 26, 1944, member of 83^d Chemical Mortar Battalion, family lived in Bedford County, was a teacher and farmer, listed on tablets of the missing at Sicily-Rome American Cemetery, Italy, (on lists 1, 2, 3, 4).

Gillaspie, Nick Napoleon, private first class, U.S. Army, missing in action later declared killed in action in France on D-Day, June 6, 1944, member of Company A, 116th Infantry Regiment, 29th Infantry Division, family lived in Bedford, was a farmer, buried in the Normandy American Cemetery, France, (on lists 1, 2, 3, 4).

Gipson, Roy Boxley, seaman first class, U.S. Navy, lost at sea in a tornado in the China Sea, December 18, 1944, family lived in Bedford, worked at Belding Heminway, listed on tablets of the missing at Manila American Cemetery, Philippines, (on lists 1, 2, 3, 4).

Goad, James Calvin, private, U.S. Army, killed in action in Luxembourg, December 29, 1944, member of 317th Infantry Regiment, 80th Infantry Division, born in Huddleston community, wife lived in Lynch Station or Altavista, worked at a mill, buried in Luxembourg American Cemetery, Luxembourg, (on lists 1, 2, 3, 4), (listed in 4 under Campbell and Bedford Counties).

Gray, Herbert O., staff sergeant, U.S. Army, missing in action on transport aircraft flight from Burma to India, June 15, 1944, later declared dead, born in Bedford, wife lived in Montvale, was a lineman, (on lists 1, 4), (listed in 4 under Roanoke City and Bedford County).

Grayson, Frank George, second lieutenant, U.S. Army, (no details on how, when, or where he died), mother lived in Lynchburg, (on lists 2, 3, 4), (listed in 4 under Lynchburg City and Bedford County).

Griffin, Francis W., colonel, U.S. Army, (no further details), (on lists 1, 4).

Hagerman, Samuel Nash, captain, U.S. Army, missing in action and then declared killed in action in Southwest Pacific, February 11, 1945, lived in Bellevue, wife lived in Norfolk City, listed on tablets of the missing at Manila American Cemetery, Philippines, (on lists 1, 4), (listed in 4 under Norfolk City and Bedford County).

Hartung, Paul Lawrence, private first class, U.S. Army, killed in action in Germany, March 19, 1945, member of 311th Infantry Regiment, 78th Infantry Division, mother lived in Bedford, father was manager of Rubatex plant in Bedford for one year before leaving in early 1945 for Toledo, Ohio, buried in Henri-Chapelle American Cemetery, Belgium, (on lists 1, 3, 4).

Hatfield, Norman Eldon, second lieutenant, U.S. Army Air Forces, killed in a plane crash in China or India, June 14, 1944, he and wife lived in Forest community, was a book salesman, (on lists 1, 3, 4).

Hawkins, Clarence Gibbs, technician, fifth grade, U.S. Army, killed in action in Italy, July 27, 1943, member of a paratrooper unit, family lived in Forest community, (on lists 1, 2, 3, 4).

Hawkins, Harry Davis, private, U.S. Marine Corps, killed in action on Okinawa, April 26, 1945, family lived in Montvale community, listed on wall at Honolulu Memorial, Hawaii, (on lists 1, 2, 3, 4).

Hoback, Bedford Turner, private, earlier staff sergeant, U.S. Army, killed in action in France on D-Day, June 6, 1944, member of Company A, 116th Infantry Regiment, 29th Infantry Division, family lived in Bedford County, worked at Rubatex, buried in the Normandy American Cemetery, France, (on lists 1, 2, 3, 4).

Hoback, Raymond Samuel, staff sergeant, U.S. Army, missing in action and later declared killed in action in France on D-Day, June 6, 1944, member of Company A, 116th Infantry Regiment, 29th Infantry Division, family lived in Bedford County, worked for state highway department, listed on tablets of the missing at Normandy American Cemetery, France, (on lists 1, 4).

Holdren, Edward Cooper, sergeant, U.S. Army Air Forces, missing in action and later declared killed in action in Germany near Engenhahn, March 17, 1945, (bailed out of aircraft and was executed on the ground by a German who was later tried for war crimes and hanged), was a crewman on a B-17 bomber, 849th Bomb Squadron, 490th Bomb Group, U.S. Eighth Air Force, born and raised in Bedford, graduated from Bedford High School, worked in aircraft plant in

Baltimore, buried in Rose family cemetery in Penicks community, (on list 1).

Holdren, Laurison, private, U.S. Army, died of sickness en route home from Australia, July 1, 1943, family lived in Thaxton community, worked at munitions plant in Radford, Virginia, (on lists 1, 2, 3, 4).

Holland, Oscar Lee, boatswain's mate, second class, U.S. Navy, missing in action and later declared killed in action off coast of Normandy, France, June 9, 1944, (ABMC gives date of death as June 10, 1945, a year and a day after he was missing in action), family lived in Montvale community, was a lineman, listed on the tablets of the missing at Normandy American Cemetery, France, (on lists 1, 2, 3, 4).

Hubbard, Benjamin Reed, private first class, U.S. Army, missing in action and later declared killed in action in France on D-Day, June 6, 1944, served in Company F, 116th Infantry Regiment, 29th Infantry Division, induction records are in Roanoke County, parents moved to Vinton area after having lived in Huddleston community of Bedford County, worked for Norfolk and Western Railroad, buried in Normandy American Cemetery, France, (on lists 1, 2, 3, 4), (listed in 4 under Roanoke and Bedford Counties), (list 3 and ABMC give date of death as June 6, 1944).

Huddleston, Ralph Daniel, (no details available), mother lived in Roanoke, (on lists 1, 2, 3, 4), (listed in 4 under Roanoke City and Bedford County).

Hudson, James, private first class, U.S. Army, (no details), mother lived in Goode community, (on lists 1, 3, 4). (May be James E. Hudson, member of 394th Infantry Regiment, 99th Infantry Division, who entered service from Virginia and died on December 18, 1944, and is buried in Henri-Chapelle American Cemetery, Belgium, according to ABMC.)

Jackson, John Moses, steward's mate, first class, U.S. Navy, missing in action and later declared killed in action in South Pacific, October 27, 1944, family from Bedford County, was a brick mason, listed on tablets of missing at Manila American Cemetery, Philippines, (on lists 1, 2, 3, 4), (on lists 1, 2, and 4 name is annotated with an asterisk denoting belonged to Negro race; on list 3 as "colored").

Johnson, Ellis O'Neal, private, U.S. Army, killed in action in Luxembourg or Belgium, December 23, 1944, member of 707th Tank Battalion, born in Bedford, mother lived in Vinton area, made home in Bowie, Maryland, buried in Luxembourg American Cemetery, Luxembourg, (on lists 1, 2, 3, 4), (listed in 4 under Roanoke and Bedford Counties).

Johnson, Robert Edward, chief boatswain's mate, U.S. Navy, missing in action from Manila area of the Philippines, later determined to have been a prisoner of war who died of sickness probably in Cabanatuan, Philippine Islands, October 3, 1942, was career Navy, parents lived in Bedford County, buried in Manila American Cemetery, Philippines, (on lists 1, 2, 3, 4).

Kidd, Raymond Oscar, captain, U.S. Army, killed in action on Ie Shima in the Pacific during a bombing raid, June 24, 1945, graduated from Bedford High School, parents lived in Bedford County, wife lived in Arkansas, had been a salesman, (on lists 1, 2, 3, 4).

Kingery, Ellis William, Jr., private, U.S. Army, killed in action in France, September 20, 1944, member of 10th Infantry Regiment, 5th Infantry Division, parents lived in Hardy community, had been employed in Baltimore, buried in Lorraine American Cemetery, France, (on lists 1, 3, 4), (listed in 4 under Bedford and Franklin Counties).

Lacy, Hudson Miller, private, U.S. Army, missing in action later declared killed in action probably off the coast of Anzio, Italy, January 26, 1944, member of 83[d] Chemical Mortar Battalion, born in Huddleston community, family lived in Huddleston, worked in Danville as a baker, on tablets of missing at Sicily-Rome American Cemetery, Italy, (on lists 1, 2, 3, 4).

Lee, Clifton Glenwood, private, U.S. Army, killed in action in France on D-Day, June 6, 1944, member of Company A, 116th Infantry Regiment, 29th Infantry Division, mother lived in Bedford, father lived in Botetourt County, worked at Hampton Looms, buried in Normandy American Cemetery, France, (on lists 1, 2, 3, 4), (listed in 4 under Botetourt, Bedford, and Roanoke Counties).

Light, Edward D., private first class, U.S. Army, died (likely killed in action) March 17, 1945, member of 345th Infantry Regiment, 87th Infantry Division, wife lived in Hardy community, buried in Luxembourg American Cemetery, Luxembourg, (on lists 1, 3, 4), (listed in 4 under Bedford and Roanoke Counties).

Lindsay, Oscar Charlie, gunner's mate, third class, U.S. Navy, killed in action probably in the English Channel, June 7, 1944, possibly June 6, born in Lynchburg, parents lived in Forest community, had been employed by Craddock-Terry Shoe Company, (many newspaper articles suggest he was killed in the Pacific Theater, but the book *Military Records of Bedford County's Gold Star Men in World War II* maintained at the Bedford County Courthouse includes a statement by his mother that the Chief of Naval Personnel had advised her that he was in the invasion of Normandy and was killed in the English Channel; ABMC records indicate he was buried in Cambridge American Cemetery, England, (on lists 1, 2, 3, 4).

Lipscomb, James Washington, private first class, U.S. Army, killed in action on Leyte, December 11, 1944, family lived in Lynch Station community, (on lists 1, 2, 3, 4), (listed in 4 under Campbell and Bedford Counties).

Mariels, William Gleason, corporal, U.S. Army, killed in action in France, near St. Lo, August 5, 1944, served in 111th Field Artillery Battalion, born in Bedford County, moved to Martinsville as small boy, mother was born in Bedford County and lived in Martinsville and Bedford, he is buried in Bedford's Oakwood Cemetery, (listed in 4 under Martinsville City only).

Martin, Edward William, private, U.S. Army, killed in action in France, June 12, 1944, served with 2[d] Infantry Division, born in Moneta, father lived in Moneta, worked at a Civilian Conservation Corps camp, (on lists 1 and 4 as Edward William Martin; on lists 2 and 3 as Brud Edd Martin—see *Bedford Bulletin*, July 27, 1944, p. 1).

Martin, Orie Thomas, private, U.S. Army, died of wounds received in action in Germany, November 28, 1944, family lived in Huddleston community, (on lists 1, 2, 3, 4).

Martin, Willie Rucker, sergeant, U.S. Army, killed in action in Alsace Lorraine area of France, February 21, 1945, family from

Huddleston community, had been a cabinet maker, (on lists 1, 2, 3, 4).

Meador, Joseph Bradley, private first class, U.S. Army, killed in action in Belgium, January 14, 1945, served in 119th Infantry Regiment, family from Moneta community, was a college student, buried in family cemetery near Moneta, (on lists 1, 2, 3, 4).

Meador, Rucker Price, private, U.S. Army, drowned in canoeing accident in Georgia, June 13, 1943, family from Moneta community, had worked at a sawmill, (on lists 1, 2, 3, 4).

Menefee, Clinton Kirkham, private first class, U.S. Army, killed in action in France, December 1 or 10, 1944, mother lived in Vinton or Portsmouth after having lived in Stewartsville community, worked at ammunition plant in Radford, Virginia, (on lists 1, 2, 3, 4), (listed in 4 under Roanoke and Bedford Counties).

Miller, George Thomas, private first class, U.S. Marine Corps, killed in action on Iwo Jima, March 2, 1945, family from Holcomb Rock community, worked as a telegraph operator, (on lists 1, 2, 3, 4).

Morgan, Wilford Taylor, private first class, U.S. Army, died in an accident in Tennessee, March 17, 1943, parents lived in Hardy community, (on lists 1, 2, 3, 4).

Murphy, Henry Albert, seaman first class, U.S. Navy, died August 21, 1942, (no other details), listed on the walls of the missing at Honolulu Memorial, Hawaii, (on lists 1, 2, 3, 4), (listed in 4 under Campbell and Bedford Counties and Lynchburg City).

Nance, Francis Dodd (Jack), private, U.S. Army, killed in action in Italy, October 2 or 3, 1944, from Burk's Hill area of Bedford County, wife lived in West Virginia, worked at Piedmont Label Company as a pressman, buried in Bluefield, West Virginia, (on lists 1, 2, 3, 4).

Nance, Robert Francis, sergeant, U.S. Army Air Forces, killed in action near Sicily, Italy, April 13, 1943, member of 353d Bomb Squadron, 301st Bomb Group, Heavy, family from Bedford, worked at Piedmont Label Company in the photography department, listed on tablets of the missing at North Africa American Cemetery, Tunisia, (on lists 1, 2, 3, 4).

Newman, Wilson Gray, sergeant, U.S. Army, killed in action in France or Germany, September 18, 1944, born in Montvale, mother lived in or near Vinton, father was formerly of Bedford County, had been a shoe salesman, (on lists 1, 2, 3, 4), (listed in 4 under Roanoke and Bedford Counties).

Newton, William Harding, seaman, third class, U.S. Navy, missing in action and later declared killed in action near Iceland, October 31, 1941, when a German submarine sank the destroyer USS *Reuben James* prior to America's entry into World War II, parents lived in Villamont and/or Blue Ridge communities, had been a student before joining the Navy in 1938, listed on tablets of the missing at Cambridge American Cemetery, England, (on lists 1, 2, 3, 4), (listed in 4 under Botetourt and Bedford Counties).

Nimmo, Ralph E., technician, fifth grade, U.S. Army, died of wounds received in action in Belgium, September 7, 1944, wife lived outside Roanoke City, (on lists 1, 2, 3, 4), (listed in 4 under Roanoke City and Bedford and Roanoke Counties).

North, William, private, U.S. Army, (no details on how, where and when he died), father lived in Forest community, (on lists 1, 4), (name on lists 1 and 4 annotated with an asterisk denoting belonged to the Negro race).

Obenshain, James Garrett, major, U.S. Marine Corps, missing in action then declared killed in action on Wake Island, June 22, 1943, born and attended school in Montvale community, lived in Florida and Kentucky, mother lived in Michigan, had been a stock manager, listed on walls of the missing at Honolulu Memorial, Hawaii, (on lists 1, 2, 3, 4).

Otey, Collins A., sergeant, U.S. Army, died of acute heart problems in Latin America, family from Thaxton community, had been an electrical engineer, (on lists 1, 2, 3, 4).

Overstreet, Otey Spencer, private first class, U.S. Army, killed in action in France, September 9, 1944, family from Thaxton or Montvale communities, had been a farmer, buried in Brittany American Cemetery, France, (on lists 1, 2, 3, 4).

Parker, Earl Lloyd, staff sergeant, U.S. Army, missing in action and later declared killed in action in France on D-Day, June 6, 1944, member of Company A, 116th Infantry Regiment, 29th Infantry Division, lived in Bedford County, had worked at Piedmont Label

Company as a pressman, listed on tablets of the missing at Normandy American Cemetery, France, (on lists 1, 2, 3, 4), (he was definitely declared missing in action on D-Day, June 6, 1944; list 3 is misleading in indicating he was killed on June 7, 1944, and the American Battle Monuments Commission website is misleading in giving his date of death as June 7, 1945, which is the date on which he was, by government policy, officially declared killed in action—one year and one day after he was listed as missing in action).

Parker, Joseph Ernest, Jr., private, U.S. Army, killed in action in France, August 27, 1944, served with Company C, 116th Infantry Regiment, 29th Infantry Division, he and wife had lived in Bedford County, had worked at Piedmont Label Company as a pressman, buried at Brittany American Cemetery, France, (on lists 1, 2, 3, 4).

Peoples, John Augustus, Jr., steward, third class, U.S. Navy, died of wounds received in action in the Pacific, October 27, 1944, home of record was Vinton, accredited to 6th Congressional District of Bedford County, lived in Bedford County and attended New Hope Baptist Church in Chamblissburg per friend Robert Bonds, buried at sea and listed on tablets at Manila American Cemetery, Philippines, (on list 4 under Roanoke County only—Peoples was black but his name is not marked with an asterisk).

Powers, Jack Gilbert, private first class, U.S. Army, killed in action in France on D-Day, June 6, 1944, member of Company A, 116th Infantry Regiment, 29th Infantry Division, family from Bedford, worked at Rubatex, buried in Normandy American Cemetery, France, (on lists 1, 2, 3, 4).

Price, Paul Lankford, second lieutenant, U.S. Army Air Forces, killed accidentally in Tunisia in North Africa, while taking a shower bath when a heating unit exploded, November 9, 1943, born in West Virginia, family from Goode community, (on lists 1, 2, 3, 4), (list 3 indicates, probably mistakenly, that he was killed in combat).

Reynolds, John Franklin, private first class, U.S. Army, killed in action in France on D-Day, June 6, 1944, member of Company A, 116th Infantry Regiment, 29th Infantry Division, family from Bedford County, had been a farmer, buried in Bedford's Greenwood Cemetery, (on lists 1, 2, 3, 4).

Roberts, Adderson Clay, first sergeant, U.S. Army, died of sickness at home, June 29, 1945, family from Lynch Station community, was a career soldier for twenty-six years, (on lists 1, 2, 3, 4), (listed in 4 under Campbell and Bedford Counties).

Robertson, William D., corporal, U.S. Army Air Forces, missing April 5, 1945, in China-Burma-India area and later declared dead, served with Air Transport Command and had flown eighteen missions "over the hump," father from Hardy community, listed on tablets of the missing at Manila American Cemetery, Philippines, (on lists 1, 4).

Rosazza, Weldon Antonio, corporal, U.S. Army, killed in action in France on D-Day, June 6, 1944, member of Company A, 116th Infantry Regiment, 29th Infantry Division, had lived in Bedford before family moved to Washington, D.C., was a grocery clerk, buried in Normandy American Cemetery, France, (on lists 1, 2, 3, 4).

Saunders, John Lee, Jr., no detailed information on rank and service, killed in a plane crash in Brazil, December 18, 1944, no information on where he lived or where he worked prior to entering the military, mother lived in Bedford County, (on lists 1, 2, 3, 4).

Schenk, John Burwell, staff sergeant, U.S. Army, killed in action in France on D-Day, June 6, 1944, member of Company A, 116th Infantry Regiment, 29th Infantry Division, family lived in Bedford County, was a clerk in a hardware store, buried in Normandy American Cemetery, France, (on lists 1, 2, 3, 4).

Shannon, James Byron, private first class, U.S. Army Air Forces, killed in an accidental plane crash near Hylton Village, Virginia, January 7, 1942, family from Forest community, was a student, (on lists 1, 2, 3, 4).

Sligh, William Lawrence, private first class, U.S. Army, missing in action in Germany, April 14, 1945, died April 21, 1945, of wounds received, born in Coleman Falls community, attended school in Big Island and maybe high school in Lynchburg, parents and wife lived in Madison Heights in Amherst County, had worked in construction trade, (on lists 1, 2, 3, 4), (listed in 4 under Amherst and Bedford Counties).

Smith, John Cleveland, private, U.S. Army, was court martialed, convicted, and executed by hanging by the U.S. Army in France, March 3, 1945, mother lived near Vinton, had been a farmer, (on lists 1, 4), (listed in 4 under Roanoke and Bedford Counties), (name on lists 1 and 4 annotated with an asterisk denoting member of Negro race).

Smith, Lloyd Brown, Jr., captain, U.S. Army Air Forces, missing in action and later declared killed in action off the coast of Sicily, July 6, 1943, member of 316th Fighter Squadron, 324th Fighter Group, from Montvale community, wife lived in South Carolina and he entered service from there, had been a student, listed on tablets of the missing at North Africa American Cemetery, Tunisia, (on lists 1, 4).

Sneed, Charlie Melvin (Pete), Jr., private, U.S. Army, killed in action probably off the coast of Anzio, Italy, January 26, 1944, served in 83[d] Chemical Mortar Battalion, may have lived in Montvale community for some time, wife lived in Bedford, was a gasoline station attendant, buried in Bedford's Oakwood Cemetery, (on lists 1, 2, 3, 4).

Spradlin, Elmo William, sergeant, U.S. Army, died of wounds received in action in France, October 5, 1944, member of 317th Infantry Regiment, 80th Infantry Division, parents lived in Bedford County, wife lived in Vinton, worked at Belding Heminway, buried in Lorraine American Cemetery, France, (on lists 1, 2, 3, 4), (listed in 4 under Roanoke and Bedford Counties).

Spradlin, Henry McCabe, private first class, U.S. Army, killed in action in Germany, November 19, 1944, wife lived in Vinton, father lived in Roanoke, worked at a weaving mill, (on lists 1, 2, 3, 4), (listed in 4 under Roanoke and Bedford Counties).

St. Clair, Joe R., private first class, U.S. Army, killed in action in or over Holland, October 22, 1944, served with paratroop unit, parents lived in Vinton area, (on lists 1, 2, 3, 4), (listed in 4 under Roanoke and Bedford Counties).

Staton, Gerald H., staff sergeant, U.S. Army, killed in action in Germany, February 20, 1945, member of 302[d] Infantry Regiment, 94th Infantry Division, graduated from high school in Big Island, wife lived in Lynchburg, buried in Luxembourg American Cemetery, Luxembourg, (on list 4), (listed in 4 under Lynchburg City only).

Stevens, Ray O., technical sergeant, U.S. Army, killed in action in France on D-Day, June 6, 1944, member of Company A, 116th Infantry Regiment, 29th Infantry Division, family from Bedford County, was a farmer, buried in Bedford's Greenwood Cemetery, (on lists 1, 2, 3, 4).

Thompson, Charles Edward, seaman, first class, U.S. Navy, drowned in Elizabeth River, July 12, 1942, family lived in Blue Ridge community, had been a railroad brakeman, (on lists 1, 2, 3, 4), (listed in 4 under Botetourt and Bedford Counties).

Turpin, Martin Parks, fireman, first class, U.S. Navy, died during brain tumor operation in Navy or government hospital on Guam Island in South Pacific, April 23, 1945, from Big Island community of Bedford County, worked at Hampton Looms, buried in Bedford's Greenwood Cemetery, (on lists 1, 2, 3, 4).

Vaughn, Clyde Everett, machinist's mate, second class, U.S. Navy, missing in action and later declared killed in action in the Pacific, October 24, 1944, born in Hickory Grove community, wife lived in Roanoke City, parents lived outside Roanoke and had formerly lived in Bedford County, worked at ammunition plant in Radford, Virginia, listed on tablets of the missing at Manila American Cemetery, Philippines, (on lists 1, 2, 3, 4), (listed in 4 under Roanoke City and Bedford and Roanoke Counties).

Walker, Richard Boyd, private first class, U.S. Army, killed in action in Belgium in the Malmedy Massacre, December 17, 1944, member of Battery B, 285th Field Artillery Observation Battalion, family lived in Bedford County, worked at Lane Company cedar furniture manufacturer, buried in Morgan's Baptist Church Cemetery in Bedford County, (on lists 1, 2, 3, 4).

Walker, Richard Perrow, captain, U.S. Army, died in Italy, October 16, 1944, of wounds received in action on October 9, member of 349th Infantry Regiment, 88th Infantry Division, from Coleman Falls community, wife lived in North Carolina, had farmed and worked at a sawmill, buried in Florence American Cemetery, Italy, (on lists 1, 2, 3, 4).

Ware, Robert Goodwin, first lieutenant, U.S. Army Air Forces, killed in action over Austria, near Bruck, on February 23, 1945, was a pilot in 485th Bomb Group, 828th Bomb Squadron, U.S. Fifteenth Air Force, born and raised in Bedford County, mother lived in Lynchburg, worked at a hotel, buried in Bedford's Oakwood Cemetery, (on lists 1, 4), (listed in 4 under Lynchburg City and Bedford County).

Watson, Gilbert O., staff sergeant, U.S. Army Air Forces, missing in action on flight between San Francisco and Hawaii, October 27, 1942, member of 370th Bomb Squadron, 307th Bomb Group, Heavy, from Moneta community, had been a farmer, listed on tablets of the missing at East Coast Memorial, New York City, (on lists 1, 3, 4).

Watson, Stephen Earl, staff sergeant, U.S. Army, died of natural causes (heart failure) in Aleutian Islands, Alaska, June 11, 1945, served in 880th Port Battalion Transport Company, graduated from New London Academy high school in New London community, father lived in Bedford, wife lived in North Carolina, had been a meat packer, employed in North Carolina, buried in Bedford's Oakwood Cemetery, (on lists 1, 2, 3, 4).

Webber, Harold C., master sergeant, U.S. Army, died of heart failure in a hospital in Georgia, July 12, 1945, mother lived in Vinton area, (on lists 1, 2, 3, 4), (listed in 4 under Roanoke and Bedford Counties).

Weeks, Julian Joseph, private, U.S. Army, killed in action in Germany, November 18, 1944, member of 116th Infantry Regiment, 29th Infantry Division, born in Bedford, mother lived in Bedford, lived in Blue Ridge community, wife lived in Roanoke, buried in Netherlands American Cemetery, Netherlands, (on lists 1, 2, 3, 4), (listed in 4 under Roanoke City and Bedford County).

White, Gordon Henry, Jr., staff sergeant, U.S. Army, killed in action in France on D-Day, June 6, 1944, member of Company A, 116th Infantry Regiment, 29th Infantry Division, family from Forest community, was a student, (lists 1, 2, 3, 4).

Wickham, George Clifton, staff sergeant, U.S. Army, killed in action in France, June 11, 1944, member of 12th Infantry Regiment, 4th Infantry Division, born and resided in Bedford, parents and wife lived outside Vinton—probably Stewartsville, worked at CCC camp, accepted for enlistment in Roanoke, (on lists 1, 2, 3, 4), (listed in 4 under Roanoke and Bedford Counties).

Wilkes, John Leo, master sergeant, U.S. Army, killed in action in France on D-Day, June 6, 1944, member of Company A, 116th Infantry Regiment, 29th Division, family lived in Bedford County, had been a farmer, buried in Bedford's Greenwood Cemetery, (on lists 1, 2, 3, 4).

Williams, James Perrow, Jr., second lieutenant, U.S. Army Air Forces, missing in action then declared killed in action in Mediterranean area, August 15, 1944, member of 87th Fighter Squadron, 79th Fighter Group, from Holcomb Rock community, had been a student, listed on tablets of the missing Rhone American Cemetery, France, (on lists 1, 2, 3, 4).

Witt, Royall K., private first class, U.S. Army, killed in action in France, September 15, 1944, mother lived in Bedford County, he lived in Roanoke City, (on lists 1, 2, 3, 4), (listed in 4 under Roanoke City and Roanoke and Bedford Counties).

Wright, Elmere Price, staff sergeant, U.S. Army, killed in action in France on D-Day, June 6, 1944, member of Company A, 116th Infantry Regiment, 29th Infantry Division, family from Bedford County, had been a professional baseball player, buried in Normandy American Cemetery, France, (on lists 1, 2, 3, 4), (on lists 1, 2, 3, 4, first name is spelled incorrectly "Elmer").

Wroten, David H., (also Worten), private first class, U.S. Army, died of wounds, (no further details), (on lists 1, 4).

Yopp, Grant Collins, sergeant, U.S. Army, killed in action in France on D-Day, June 6, 1944, member of Company A, 116th Infantry Regiment, 29th Infantry Division, from Bedford County, mother in Buena Vista, wife in New Orleans, farmer, buried in Normandy American Cemetery, France, (on lists 1, 2, 3, 4), (listed in 4 under Buena Vista City and Bedford County).

Young, John A. technician, fourth grade, U.S. Army, (no details provided), (on lists 1, 4).

Category B

Bedford County Men Who Died in Service After Japan
Surrendered and Before the End of 1946

Andrews, William McKendree, master sergeant, U.S. Army, according to his wife he was asphyxiated by gas at Fort Knox, Kentucky, March 31, 1946, born in the Evington community, (no other details), (on lists 1, 4), (listed in 4 under Orange and Bedford Counties).

Dooley, William Henry, private first class, U.S. Army, died in a motor accident in Germany, near Rittenberg, August 24, 1945, family from Thaxton community, farmer, buried in Old Glade Creek Church Cemetery near Webster, Virginia, (on lists 1, 4).

Johnston, Samuel Anderson, major, U.S. Army, died of heart attack in New Jersey, June 6, 1946, wife lived in Washington, D.C., he was a tobacconist, (on lists 1, 4).

Luck, Lee Buford, seaman second class, U.S. Navy, was home on leave in Montvale community when, after drinking and while armed with a knife, he began hitting his family and his father shot and killed him, December 14, 1945, farm laborer, buried in Bedford County, (on lists 1, 4).

Martin, John Henry, (no detailed information on rank), U.S. Army, was killed accidentally February 29, 1946, perhaps in Japan, when a truck ran over him, came from Moneta community and may have lived in Roanoke County, father lived in Roanoke City, laborer, (on lists 1, 4), (listed in 4 under Roanoke City and Bedford County), (name on lists 1 and 4 annotated with an asterisk denoting belonged to Negro race).

Category C

Men Who Had Been Discharged from the Military Before Suffering War-related Deaths

Brevo, Richard Jackson, civilian, had been discharged as a private, U.S. Army, died July 4, 1944, from effects of a military training accident in Texas in 1943, mother-in-law lived in Forest community, was a dairy farmer, (on lists 2, 3, 4), (listed in 4 under heading for "discharged personnel whose death resulted from service-connected causes").

Padgett, Marvin B., civilian, had been discharged from the U.S. Army in the Philippines in 1938 and had gone to work as a civilian for an oil company in Manila, was taken as a prisoner by the Japanese and was being transported by the Japanese by ship away from the Philippines when an Allied naval vessel in the China Sea unwittingly sank the Japanese transport ship carrying him and other prisoners, October 24, 1944, family from Bedford County, (on lists 1, 2, 3, 4).

Category D

Men Not Closely Associated with Bedford

Basham, Mac L., second lieutenant, U.S. Army, declared missing in action in France, August 26, 1944, and declared killed in action August 28, father lived in Roanoke City, parents formerly lived in Bedford County, (on list 4 under Roanoke City only).

Dowdy, John Thurman, Jr., motor machinist's mate, second class, U.S. Navy, missing in action or buried at sea, burned and died somewhere in the Pacific, November 14, 1944, parents from Leesville community, on tablets of the missing at Manila American Cemetery, Philippines, (listed in 4 under Campbell County only).

Dudding, Raymond E., Jr., seaman, first class, U.S. Navy, killed accidentally while on duty in South Pacific, September 27, 1945, parents lived in Blue Ridge area, (on list 4), (listed in 4 under Botetourt County only).

Elliette, Albert P., Jr., corporal, U.S. Army, killed in action in France, March 28, 1945, parents had lived in Bedford before moving to Louisiana, (not on any of 4 lists).

Foster, Jack, private, U.S. Marine Corps, killed in action in the Marshall Islands, home was Freeman, West Virginia, formerly worked at Rubatex in Bedford, (not on any lists).

Hackworth, John Sydney, Jr., corporal, U.S. Army Air Forces, killed in action in the Southwest Pacific, March 15, 1945, member of 823^d Bomb Squadron, 38th Bomb Group, Medium, parents were formerly of Bedford, wife lived in Lynchburg, listed on tablets of the missing at Manila American Cemetery, Philippines, (listed in 4 under Lynchburg City only).

Hackworth, Ralph L., sergeant, U.S. Army, died in European Theater, December 26, 1944, (no other details), (listed in 4 under Lynchburg City only).

Hicks, Miles R., private first class, U.S. Army, died of non-battle causes, April 1, 1945, member of 717th Railway Operating Battalion, buried in Ardennes American Cemetery, Belgium, (listed on War Department casualty list under Bedford County but in 4 under Hopewell City and Lynchburg City only).

Kelly, James Emory, private, U.S. Army, killed in action May 7, 1944, member of 135th Infantry Regiment, 34th Infantry Division, buried in Sicily-Rome American Cemetery, Italy, (listed in War Department casualty list under Bedford County but in 4 under Roanoke County-Salem only).

Nichols, Howard Luck, staff sergeant, U.S. Army, missing in action and later declared killed in action in France on D-Day, June 6, 1944, reported—but not confirmed—to be a member of Company A, 116th Infantry, 29th Infantry Division, father lived in Roanoke City, parents formerly of Bedford County, (on list 3), (listed in 4 under Roanoke City only, but death reported in *Bedford Bulletin*, August 3, 1944, p. 1).

O'Brien, James B. (or E.), technician, fifth grade, U.S. Army, died of wounds received in France, August 5, 1944, served in National

Guard with 29th Infantry Division, parents from Vinton Route 1, father lived in Salem, (on list 4), (listed in 4 under Roanoke County only, but death reported in *Bedford Bulletin*, August 31, 1944, p. 1).

Pace, Harold Robinson, private, U.S. Army, (no details on how, where, and when he died), missing in action then declared killed in action in the European Theater of Operations, mother lived in Vinton area, (listed in 4 under Roanoke County only, but death reported in *Bedford Bulletin*, April 12, 1945, p. 1).

Patteson (or Patterson), George R., private, U.S. Army, (no details on how, where, or when he died). The remains of a George R. Patterson, possibly from the Moneta community, were returned to Bedford for burial in November 1947 (see *Bedford Bulletin*, November 27, 1947, p. 1). The book *Gold Star Honor Roll of Virginians in the Second World War* lists only a George R. Patteson, whose sister was next of kin and lived in Richmond City, (listed in 4 under Richmond City and Buckingham County only).

Plybon, Benjamin M., private, U.S. Army, killed in action in France, July 6, 1944, parents had lived in Bedford but moved to Bassett, Virginia, (listed in 4 under Franklin and Henry Counties, but death reported in *Bedford Bulletin*, August 10, 1944, p. 1).

Pollard, George Washington, private first class, U.S. Army, killed in action in the Pacific Theater, formerly of Bedford, he and mother later lived in Brookneal, grandparents lived in Bedford, (listed in 4 under Campbell County only, but death reported in *Bedford Bulletin*, October 12, 1944, p. 1).

Rosazza, Jack, private, (branch of service not given), missing in action and later declared killed in action, December 9, 1944, (location not given), he and wife formerly of Bedford County, (death reported in *Bedford Bulletin*, February 1, 1945, p. 1).

Tucker, David Thomas, private first class, U.S. Army, died of wounds received in action in Luxembourg, March 8, 1945, father from Evington, Route 1, (listed in 4 under Campbell County only, but death reported in *Bedford Bulletin*, April 12, 1945, p. 1).

Viers, Thomas, technician, fifth grade, U.S. Army, died of non-battle causes, June 5, 1945, (listed on War Department casualty list under Bedford County but in 4 under Pulaski County only).

Wilson, John Alexander, captain, U.S. Army, killed in action (location not given), (listed on War Department casualty list under Bedford County but in 4 under King and Queen County only).

Wright, Charlie Maurice, private, U.S. Army, killed in action in France, September 1, 1944, from Blue Ridge Heights, mother lived in Vinton area, (listed in 4 under Roanoke County only, but death reported in *Bedford Bulletin*, October 5, 1944, p. 1).

Appendix B

Bedford County Men and the Invasion of Normandy and Later Battles in France

Many Bedford County men participated in the fighting in 1944 to liberate France and defeat the German forces deployed there. In the various campaigns fought in France, at least forty-one lost their lives, and many were wounded.

At least fifty-two men from Bedford County participated in the Normandy Campaign. About fifty boarded ships in England prior to D-Day to participate in the invasion. Most of these were Army soldiers, but at least two were sailors in the U.S. Navy. At least two and probably three or more airmen from Bedford, serving in the U.S. Army Air Forces, flew from England over Normandy on D-Day to bomb German defenses or provide fighter escort for the bombers. Several other Bedford soldiers, who may or may not have landed on D-Day, fought and died in Normandy after D-Day.

At least six sets of brothers from Bedford County participated in the D-Day Invasion. Joseph Danner probably flew a bombing mission, while brothers Carl and Lewis, both cooks, were deployed on ships in the English Channel waiting to land a couple of days after D-Day. George and James Crouch, cooks with Company A, were also deployed aboard ships waiting to land. Bedford and Raymond Hoback, in Company A, were both killed on D-Day. Earl Parker was killed on D-Day; Joseph Parker landed on D-Day and was killed on August 27. Jack Powers was killed on D-Day, while his brother Clyde survived. Ray Stevens was killed on D-Day, while his twin brother, Roy Stevens, was later wounded but survived.

Company A accounted for thirty-eight of the Bedford County men who boarded ships prior to D-Day. Thirty-two of these were to assault German forces on Omaha Beach at the outset of the attack on June 6. The other six, who were cooks and supply personnel, were scheduled to go ashore three days later.

Of the thirty-two, five were in a landing craft that sank 500-2,000 yards from the beach. They were rescued and returned to England and then redeployed to France four days later. Within a month after these five men arrived in France, one was killed in action and another seriously wounded in fighting near St. Lo.

Of the twenty-seven Bedford men in Company A who made it to Omaha Beach on June 6, nineteen were killed in action on that day. Sixteen were confirmed dead (their remains were recovered for burial). Three were reported missing in action (their remains were not recovered); after a year and a day, these three were declared killed in action. Five of the twenty-seven were wounded in action on D-Day. Only three of the twenty-seven men are believed to have survived June 6 without being wounded, and one of these three later was seriously wounded on June 11.

Two other Bedford men who had trained with Company A in England were not in the invasion force on D-Day. One had become seriously ill and was returned to the U.S., where he died in July. The other was undergoing rehabilitation from a broken ankle suffered during training; after he rejoined Company A later in the summer, he was seriously wounded in action in Germany on September 30.

Of the thirty-eight Bedford men with Company A on D-Day, approximately fourteen came from the town of Bedford and twenty-four came from elsewhere in Bedford County. Of the nineteen who were killed on D-Day, six were from the town and the others from elsewhere in the county. Thus, with about one-third of the Bedford County men in Company A coming from the town of Bedford and about two-thirds coming from other parts of Bedford County, and with roughly the same ratio for the number of Bedford community men killed on D-Day, it is important to focus on the broader jurisdiction of Bedford County when addressing Bedford's sacrifice on D-Day.

In addition to the nineteen men from Company A killed on D-Day, at least nine other Bedford County men were killed in action during the Normandy Campaign. Two were in the Navy and were killed in action in the English Channel off the coast of Normandy on June 7 and June 9. Two men from Bedford serving in Company F of the 116th Infantry Regiment were killed on June 6 and June 17, and an additional soldier from Company A was killed on July 11. The others were assigned to various Army units.

The man from Company F killed on June 6 was Pfc. Benjamin R. Hubbard. When Hubbard is added to the nineteen from Company A, this raises to twenty the number of Bedford County men killed on D-Day. Hubbard is listed on the honor roll inside the Bedford County Courthouse, but he is not listed on the stone outside naming those in the 116th Infantry from Bedford who died as part of the Normandy Invasion. He is listed under both Roanoke and Bedford Counties in the book *Gold Star Honor Roll of Virginians in the Second World War*. On his induction records, which are maintained in Roanoke County, his address is listed as Vinton. The Vinton post office delivers to parts of both Roanoke and Bedford Counties. The author was not able to ascertain exactly where Hubbard lived before he joined the military.

Twelve other Bedford County men were killed in action while fighting in France after the Normandy Campaign. Thus, with twenty men killed on D-Day, nine killed in follow-on fighting in Normandy and off the coast of Normandy, and twelve killed elsewhere in France, the Bedford community lost forty-one men during the battle for France.

I. D-Day and Normandy Campaign

A. Company A, 116th Infantry, 29th Infantry Division

1. Confirmed as killed in action on D-Day, June 6, 1944

Abbott, Leslie C., Jr., S/Sgt., from Goode community
Carter, Wallace R., Pfc., from town of Bedford
Clifton, John D., Pfc., from town of Bedford
Draper, Frank P., Jr., T/Sgt. (wounded June 6 and probably died that day), from town of Bedford
Fellers, Taylor N., Capt., from Cifax/Goode community
Hoback, Bedford T., Pvt., from Center Point community
Lee, Clifton G., Pvt., from town of Bedford
Powers, Jack G., Pfc., from town of Bedford

Reynolds, John F., Pfc., from Bedford County
Rosazza, Weldon A., Cpl., from town of Bedford but family
    moved to Washington, D.C.
Schenk, John B., S/Sgt., from Bedford County
Stevens, Ray O., T/Sgt., from Bedford County
White, Gordon H., Jr., S/Sgt., from Forest community
Wilkes, John L., M/Sgt., from Bedford County
Wright, Elmere P., S/Sgt., from Bedford County
Yopp, Grant, Sgt., from Bedford County

2. Reported initially as missing in action, later officially de-
    clared killed in action on June 6, 1944

    Gillaspie, Nick N., Pfc., from Bedford County
    Hoback, Raymond S., S/Sgt., from Center Point community
    Parker, Earl L., S/Sgt., from Bedford County

3. Wounded in action on June 6, 1944

    Goode, Robert L., Sgt., from Huddleston community
    Marsico, Robert E., S/Sgt., from town of Bedford
    Nance, Elisha Ray, 1st Lt., from Moneta community
    Overstreet, Glenwood E., Pvt., from town of Bedford
    Thurman, Anthony M., S/Sgt., from Bedford County

4. On landing craft which sank on June 6, returned to England
    before being sent to France four days later

    Edwards, Robert D., Jr., Pvt., from Bedford County
    Fizer, Charles W., Pfc., from Thaxton community and town
        of Bedford, (killed in France at St. Lo on July 11, 1944)
    Powers, Henry Clyde, Pvt., from town of Bedford
    Stevens, Roy O., T/Sgt., from Bedford County (wounded at
        St. Lo on June 30 or July 1, 1944)
    Wilkes, Harold E., Pvt., from town of Bedford

5. Landed in Normandy, June 6, 1944, and not wounded June 6

Bush, Frank William, Pfc., from town of Bedford, (wounded
on June 11)
Lancaster, James L., Pfc., from Bedford County
Watson, James W., Cpl., from Bedford County, (wounded on
June 9)

6. Landed in France after June 6, 1944

a. Landed Three days after D-Day

Broughman, Cedric C., Pfc., cook, from Bedford County
Crouch, George E., Pfc., cook, from Bedford County
Crouch, James H., Pfc., cook, from Bedford County
Danner, Carl E., Pfc., cook, from town of Bedford
Mitchell, Jack W., S/Sgt., supply sgt., from town of
Bedford
Newcomb, Earl R., S/Sgt., mess sgt., from Bedford County

b. Landed in France in August 1944

Huddleston, Allen M., S/Sgt., (delayed by broken ankle),
from Bedford County, wounded near Aachen, Germany,
September 30, 1944

7. Company A soldiers killed or died after D-Day

Fizer, Charles W., Pfc., (killed near St. Lo, July 11, 1944),
from Thaxton community and town of Bedford
Coleman, Andrew J., Pfc., (became ill in England, died in a
hospital in U.S., July 16, 1944), from town of Bedford

B. Bedford men in other units in Normandy Invasion

   1. Killed in action on D-Day, June 6, 1944

      Hubbard, Benjamin R., Pfc., Company F, 116th Infantry,
        29th Infantry Division, from Bedford County and maybe
        Vinton area of Roanoke County

   2. Killed in action in Normandy area after D-Day

      Lindsay, Oscar C., gunner's mate, third class (GM3c), U.S.
        Navy, killed in action off Normandy coast, June 7, 1944,
        from Bedford County
      Holland, Oscar L., boatswain's mate, second class (BM2c),
        U.S. Navy, missing in action and later declared killed in
        action off the coast of Normandy, France, June 9, 1944,
        from Montvale community
      Wickham, George C., S/Sgt., killed in action in France,
        June 11, member of 12th Infantry Regiment, 4th Infantry
        Division, from Bedford County and Roanoke County
      Martin, Edward William, Pvt., U.S. Army, killed in action in
        France, June 12, 1944, from Moneta community
      Dean, John W., M/Sgt., landed on D-Day, killed in action
        near St. Lo, June 17, 1944, member of Company F, 116th
        Infantry Regiment, 29th Infantry Division, from Bedford
        County
      Cofer, Thomas Edward, Pvt., U.S. Army, killed in action in
        France, June 17, 1944, member of 234th Infantry Regiment,
        from Forest community
      Anthony, Houston G., Pfc., U.S. Army, killed in action in
        France, July 11, 1944, from Lynch Station community
      Mariels, William G., Cpl., U.S. Army, killed in action near
        St. Lo, France, August 5, 1944, member of 111th Field
        Artillery Battalion, family from Bedford County

3. Landed in Normandy June 6, 1944, not wounded

Wilson, Boyd E., M/Sgt., U.S. Army, landed with 1st Infantry
Division

4. Landed in Normandy June 6, wounded on later date

Dooley, Kenneth, Pvt., U.S. Army, landed with 186th Field
Artillery Battalion, later wounded on November 8, 1944

5. Bedford airmen supporting D-Day Invasion

Danner, Joseph S., 1st Lt., B-26 pilot, 496th Squadron, 344th
Bomb Group, five missions in support of Normandy
Invasion, likely including one or more on D-Day, killed in
plane crash, August 30, 1944, from town of Bedford
Overstreet, William, 1st Lt., P-51 pilot, 357th Fighter Group,
flew three missions over France on D-Day, dropped bombs
when no German fighter aircraft were present, area of
residence not identified
Yowell, William A., Jr., 1st Lt., B-24 bomber pilot, bombed
German military installations in France on June 6, 7, and
8, 1944, had resided in town of Bedford

II.   Later campaigns in France after Normandy Campaign

A. Killed in action in France after Normandy Campaign

Allen, John W., Pfc., U.S. Army, killed in action in France,
September 10, 1944, member of 8th Infantry Division,
lived in Thaxton area
Anderson, Clyde H., S/Sgt., died—likely killed in action—in
Brittany area of France, August 2, 1944
Duff, Albert A., Capt., U.S. Army, killed in action probably
in the Lorraine area of France, member of 4th Armored
Division, lived in Bedford County

Fizer, Robert A., Pfc., U.S. Army, died of wounds received near Bisoncort, France, September 17, 1944, member of 35th Infantry Division, from town of Bedford

Kingery, Ellis W., Jr., Pvt., U.S. Army, killed in action probably in Lorraine area of France, September 20, 1944, member of 5th Infantry Division, from Hardy area

Martin, Willie R., Sgt., killed in action in Alsace Lorraine area of France, February 21, 1945, from Bedford County

Menefee, Clinton K., Pfc., U.S. Army, killed in action somewhere in France, December 1 or 10, 1944, mother had lived in Stewartsville area

Newman, Wilson G., Sgt., U.S. Army, killed in France or Germany, September 18, 1944, from Montvale area

Overstreet, Otey Spencer, Pfc., U.S. Army, killed in action probably in the Brittany area of France, September 9, 1944, from Thaxton or Montvale areas.

Parker, Joseph E., Jr., Pvt. U.S. Army, killed in action probably in Brittany area of France, August 27, 1944, member of Company C, 116th Infantry Regiment, 29th Infantry Division, from Bedford County

Spradlin, Elmo W., Sgt., U.S. Army, died of wounds received in Alsace Lorraine area of France, October 5, 1944, member of 80th Infantry Division, from Bedford County

Witt, Royall K., Pfc., U.S. Army, killed in action in France, September 15, 1944, mother was from Bedford County

B. Executed in France by the U.S. Army

Smith, John C., Pvt., U.S. Army, was court-martialed, convicted, and executed by hanging by the U.S. Army on March 3, 1945, was from Bedford County near Vinton

Bibliography

Manuscripts, Records, and Other Works Specific to the Bedford Community

Bedford Bulletin. This local newspaper is available on microfilm at the Bedford Central Public Library.

Bedford County Bicentennial, 1754-1954, Official Program. This program includes historical accounts related to World War II and is available at the Bedford Central Public Library.

"Bedford County, Virginia, History and Geographic Supplement" to the *Bedford County Bicentennial, 1754-1954, Official Program*. A copy is available at the Bedford Central Public Library.

Bedford Democrat. This former, local newspaper is available on microfilm maintained by the Library of Virginia in Richmond.

Douchez, Jean-Louis. *Bedford—The Wave of Glory*. Normandy, France: Atelier Cinemade Normandie, 2001. A copy of this documentary film, featuring interviews with people from Bedford County, is available at the Bedford Central Public Library.

Induction and Discharge Records, World War II, Bedford County. These records, maintained in the office of the Clerk of the Circuit Court at the Bedford County Courthouse, consist of a general index book and nine detailed books, which, despite the title, contain records ranging from World War II to recent years. The first five-and-a-half books, up to Book 6, page 258, contain records up to mid-August 1945. Subsequent pages and books contain records from the second half of August 1945 to the 1990s and perhaps beyond. Not included in these records are: (1) men who had joined the National Guard and were called to active duty as part of their National Guard unit and who were subsequently killed or died while in service; former Guardsmen who survived World War II and were discharged are included through their discharge records; (2) some men who had been born or had lived in Bedford County but who enlisted or were inducted outside Bedford County; (3) all women from Bedford County who enlisted in the armed forces in World War II. A book in another series, *Military Service Records* (Bedford County), *World War II, Volume IV*, also maintained in the office of the Clerk of the Court, lists women who served during World War II. In late October 2002, in keeping with new Virginia legislation, these records were removed from the public access area of the Clerk's office, and access to the records is now restricted and controlled by the Clerk.

Kershaw, Alex. *The Bedford Boys: One American Town's Ultimate D-Day Sacrifice.* Cambridge, Massachusetts: De Capo Press, 2003.

Lester, Dr. Nelle P. "Scrap Book of World War II." This scrapbook of photographs and captions of Bedford servicemen and servicewomen, cut from the *Bedford Bulletin* and *Bedford Democrat*, is available at the Bedford City/County Museum.

Military Records of Bedford County's Gold Star Men in World War II. These records provide information on Bedford County men who were killed or died during World War II. The records were compiled by the Bedford County War History Committee, Mrs. George P. Parker, chairman. The records indicate that the committee, which was appointed in April 1943 by the Virginia Conservation Commission, did intensive work collecting information on Bedford County service personnel until these personnel began returning from service. Discharges were recorded by office of Clerk of the Circuit Court of Bedford County. The Committee then ceased collecting information on all service personnel and collected only information on "Gold Star" men, those killed in action and those who died accidentally or of disease while in the service. These records are maintained in the Office of the Clerk of the Circuit Court at the Bedford County Courthouse

Military Service Records (for Bedford County, Virginia), *World War II, Volumes I-IV*. These volumes were compiled by the War History Committee of Bedford County, chairman Mrs. George P. Parker, as a permanent record for the Virginia Conservation Commission and were placed in the Bedford County Clerk of the Circuit Court Office as a memorial to the Bedford men and women in World War II. The volumes are arranged alphabetically for Caucasian males; at the back of Volume IV are sections on women and Blacks, arranged alphabetically.

"Montvale (Bedford County, Virginia) High School Homecoming Program Booklet, June 2, 2000." A copy of this program, which contains material on former students who served in World War II and later, is available in the Bedford City/County Museum.

Parker, Lula Jeter, and Richardson, Gates R. *The Military History of Bedford County, Virginia, 1754-1950*. Bedford, Virginia, 1951. This manuscript was compiled by Lula Jeter Parker (Mrs. George P. Parker). Gates R. Richardson wrote the chapter titled "Bedford County's Part in the Two World Wars" (pages 149-169). The manuscript is available at the Bedford Central Public Library.

Parker, Lula Jeter (compiler). "Reports and Correspondence Concerning Bedford County in World War II." This is a compilation of exchanges between Mrs. Parker, Chairman, Bedford County World War II History Committee, and the Virginia Conservation Commission and World War II History Commission. A copy is available at the Bedford Central Public Library.

Parker, Lula Jeter. "The Town of Bedford in Virginia." A copy of this manuscript is available at the Bedford Central Public Library.

Saunders, Bernard W. "War Memoirs." A copy of this manuscript is available at the Bedford Central Public Library.

Scott, Melvin M. "Bedford Soldiers in the Civil War." Lynchburg, Virginia: J.P. Bell Company, 1970. A copy of this paper, read before the Bedford Historical Society on May 29, 1970, is available at the Bedford Central Public Library.

2 Centuries of Bedford County School Days: A Bicentennial Publication Sponsored by the Bedford County School Board, and the Bedford County Principals' Association, September 1952. A copy is available at the Bedford City/County Museum.

Witt, Brian. "Compliance and Non-Compliance with Government Regulation During World War Two: the Case of Bedford, Virginia." A copy of this senior thesis, written in 2000 by Brian Witt, a student at Ferrum College, during an internship at the Bedford City-County Museum, is available at the museum.

Yowell, Eleanor Payne. *Flying High: World War II Letters to and from U.S. Army Air Force Bases and the Home Front*. Lynchburg, Virginia: Warwick House Publishing, 2001. This book contains a narrative and extracts from letters between Bedford natives Eleanor Yowell and her husband William Yowell. Copies are available for sale at the National D-Day Memorial Bookstore and the Bedford City/County Museum, and a copy is available at the Bedford Central Public Library.

Books, Manuscripts, Newspapers, and Video Containing References to Bedford County

Balkoski, Joseph. *Beyond the Beachhead: The 29th Infantry Division in Normandy*. Harrisburg, Pennsylvania: Stackpole Books, 1989. A copy of this book is available at the Bedford City/County Museum.

Barnes, John J. *Fragments of My Life with Company A, 116th Infantry Regiment: From Omaha Beach to the Elbe River*. Holland Patent, New York: JAM Publications, 2000. Copies of this book are available at the Bedford Central Public Library and the Bedford City/County Museum.

Baumgarten, Dr. Harold. *Eyewitness on Omaha Beach: A Story About D-Day, June 6, 1944*. Jacksonville, Florida: Halrit Publications Co., 1994. A copy of this book is available at the Bedford Central Public Library.

Bennett, Clifford T. (senior consultant). *Virginia: Adventures in Time and Place*. New York: Macmillan/McGraw-Hill, 1997.

"'D-Day,' 6 June 1944, Account of the 116th Infantry Regiment," notes prepared by the commanding general of the 29th Infantry Division. A copy of this manuscript is available at the Bedford City/County Museum.

Hemphill, W. Edwin (editor). *Gold Star Honor Roll of Virginians in the Second World War*. Charlottesville, Virginia: Virginia World War II History Commission, 1947. This book lists, alphabetically and by county, the names of Virginia service personnel who were killed or died during World War II. Copies are available at Bedford Central Public Library and the Bedford City/County Museum.

National D-Day Memorial Foundation. *Overlord Report* and other publications. The foundation is located in Bedford, Virginia.

News & Advance, Lynchburg, Virginia. This newspaper has published several articles and special reports on Bedford County's experience in World War II and on the National D-Day Memorial.

Historical and Pictorial Review, National Guard of the Commonwealth of Virginia, 1940. Baton Rouge, Louisiana: Army and Navy Publishing Company, 1940. A copy of this book, which contains short histories of Virginia National Guard units (including Bedford's Company A), unit photos, and lists of names of men photographed, is in the possession of Mr. and Mrs. Earl Newcomb of Bedford, and a copy is available in the Bedford City/County Museum.

Richmond Times-Dispatch, Richmond, Virginia. This newspaper has published several articles and special reports on Bedford County's experience in World War II and on the National D-Day Memorial.

Roanoke Times, Roanoke, Virginia. This newspaper has published several articles on Bedford County's experience in World War II and on the National D-Day Memorial.

Slaughter, John Robert. "Wartime Memories of J. Robert Slaughter and Selected Men of the 116th Infantry, 29th Division, 1941-1945." A copy of this manuscript is available at the Bedford Central Public Library.

U.S. War Department, Historical Division. "Omaha Beachhead (6 June-13 June 1944, American Forces in Action Series." Washington, D.C.: U.S. Government Printing Office, 1945, reprinted 1948. A copy of this document, undated, is available at the Bedford City/County Museum.

U.S. War Department. *World War II Honor List of Dead and Missing, State of Virginia.* Washington, D.C., 1946. An extract of this document with the list for Bedford County is available in the Bedford City/County Museum.

Viemeister, Peter. *A History of Aviation: They Were There*. Bedford, Virginia: Hamilton's, 1990. This book, available at Hamilton's, P. O. Box 932, Bedford, Virginia 24523, or at www.peterv.com, provides information on many American aviators.

WDBJ7 Television Station. "Stories of Heroes, Virginians at Normandy." Roanoke, Virginia, June 1994. A copy of this video is maintained at the Bedford Central Public Library.

General Books, Manuscripts, and Websites
on World War II and Other History

Ambrose, Stephen E. *Citizen Soldiers*. New York: Simon & Schuster, 1997.

Ambrose, Stephen E. *D-Day June 6, 1944: The Climatic Battle of World War II*. New York: Simon & Schuster, 1994.

American Battle Monuments Commission. Website www.abmc.gov. This website provides information on service personnel buried or memorialized in cemeteries and memorials operated by the commission.

Bailey, Ronald H. et al. *The Air War in Europe*. Alexandria, Virginia: Time-Life Books, World War II Collectors Edition, 1981.

Bauserman, John M. *The Malmedy Massacre*. Shippensburg, Pennsylvania: White Mane Books, 1995.

Bigelow, Barbara C. *World War II: Primary Sources*. Detroit, Michigan: UXL, the Gale Group, 2000.

Botting, Douglas, and the Editors of Time-Life Books. *The D-Day Invasion*. New York: Time-Life Books, 1978.

Bradley, James, with Powers, Ron. *Flags of Our Fathers*. New York: Bantam Books, 2000.

Bradley, Omar N. and Blair, Clay. *A General's Life: An Autobiography by General of the Army Omar N. Bradley and Clay Blair*. New York: Simon & Schuster, 1983.

Blumenson, Martin. *United States Army in World War II, The Mediterranean Theater of Operations, Salerno to Cassino*. Washington, D.C.: Office of the Chief of Military History, United States Army, 1969.

Casdorph, Paul D. *Let the Good Times Roll: Life at Home in America During WWII*. New York: Paragon House, 1989.

Carroll, Andrew (editor). *War Letters: Extraordinary Correspondence from American Wars*. New York: Scribner, 2001.

Cole, Hugh M. *U.S. Army in World War II, European Theater of Operations, The Ardennes: Battle of the Bulge*. Washington, D.C.: Office of the Chief of Military History, Department of the Army, 1965.

Dear, I. C. B. (general editor). *The Oxford Companion to World War II*. Oxford and New York: Oxford University Press, 1995.

83ᵈ Chemical Mortar Battalion-related sources. Websites relevant to Bedford County's loss of five men in this battalion are:
(1) www.100thww2.org/support/cm/cm.html,
(2) www:4point2.org/flwmemorials.htm, and
(3) www.msfb.com/news/FarmCountry/sept01/tragedy.html. This last site includes an article by Ed Blake, "World War II sea tragedy is finally laid to rest."

Ellis, John. *World War II: A Statistical Survey*. New York: Facts on File, 1993.

Ewing, Joseph H. *29 Let's Go!: A History of the 29ᵗʰ Infantry Division in World War II*. Washington, D.C.: Infantry Journal Press, 1994.

Feldman, George (editor). *World War II Almanac*. UXL, 2000.

Goralski, Robert. *World War II Almanac, 1931-1945: A Political and Military Record*. New York: Random House, 1985.

Hargrove, Hondon B. *Buffalo Soldiers in Italy: Black Americans in World War II*. Jefferson, North Carolina and London: McFarland & Co. Inc., 1985.

Harris, Mark, et al. *The Home Front: America During WWII*. New York: Putnam, 1984.

Harrison, Gordon A. *Cross-Channel Attack, The European Theater of Operations, United States Army in World War II*. Washington, D.C.: Office of the Chief of Military History, Department of the Army, 1951. A copy of this manuscript is available in the Bedford City/County Museum.

Heide, Robert, and Gilman, John. *Home Front America: Popular Culture of the World War II Era*. San Francisco, California: Chronicle Books, 1995.

Jordan, Shirley. *World War II: Moments in History*. Logan, Iowa: Perfection Learning Corp., 1999.

Kallen, Stuart A. *World War II: The War at Home*. San Diego, California: American War Library, Lucent Books, 1995.

Kirkland, William B., Jr. *Destroyers at Normandy: Naval Gunfire Support at Omaha Beach*. Washington, D.C.: Naval Historical Foundation, 1944. A copy of this book is available in the Bedford Central Public Library.

Krull, Kathleen. *V is for Victory*. New York: Apple Sap Books, Alfred A. Knopf, 1995

Lyons, Michael J. *World War II: A Short History*. Englewood, N.J.: Prentice Hall, 1989.

Morison, Samuel E. *History of United States Naval Operations in World War II, Volume II, Battle of the Atlantic, September 1939-May 1943*. Boston, Massachusetts: Little Brown & Company, 1947.

Morison, Samuel Eliot. *The Two-Ocean War: A Short History of the United States Navy in the Second World War*. New York: Ballantine Books, 1971.

New York Times, New York, New York.

O'Neill, William L. *World War II: A Student Companion*. New York, Oxford University Press, 1999.

Owens, Walter E. *as briefed...a family history of the 384th Bombardment Group*. This appears to be a self-published book released in 1946. A copy of this book is in the library of Joe Goode of Bedford, a veteran of the 384th.

Parrish, Thomas (editor). *The Simon and Schuster Encyclopedia of World War II*. New York: Simon and Schuster, 1978.

Peaslee, Budd J. *Heritage of Valor: The Eighth Air Force in World War II*. Philadelphia and New York: J. B. Lippincott Co., 1964.

Pratt, Julius W. *A History of United States Foreign Policy*. Englewood Cliffs, New Jersey: Prentice-Hall, Inc., 1961.

Ryan, Cornelius. *The Longest Day: June 6, 1944*. New York: Touchstone Book, Simon & Schuster, 1994.

Seal, Henry F., Jr. *History of the 116th Infantry Regiment, 29th Infantry Division, organized from the 1st, 2nd and 4th Infantry Regiments, Virginia National Guard at Camp McClellan, Anniston, Alabama, 4 October 1917*. This book, compiled and revised by Henry F. Seal, Jr., Member of Headquarters Company, 3d Battalion, 116th Infantry Regiment, World War II, may have been self-published. A copy is available at the Bedford City/County Museum.

"Shipping" Magazine, June 1994. An article related to D-Day, published in this magazine, is available in the Bedford City/County Museum.

Stein, R. Conrad. *The Home Front During World War II in American History.* Berkeley Heights, New Jersey: Enslow Publishers, Inc., 2003.

Sulzberger, C. L. *The American Heritage Picture History of World War II.* New York: Crown Publishers, Inc., 1966.

Time-Life Editors. *The Home Front, USA, World War II Series.* New York: Time-Life, 1978.

29 Let's Go!, 1917-1965. This book appears to have been printed by the 29th Infantry Division. A copy is available at the Bedford City/County Museum.

U.S. Census Bureau. Website www.census.gov.

U.S. Department of Defense. *Defense Almanac '94, Issue 5.* Washington, D.C.: U.S. Government Printing Office, 1994.

Vaughan-Thomas, Wynford. *Anzio.* New York: Holt, Rinehart and Winston, 1961.

Zeinert, Karen. *The Incredible Women of World War II.* Brookfield, Connecticut: The Millbrook Press, 1994.

Notes

Prologue

1. Roanoke Historical Society map of Bedford County, 1750-1868, at Bedford Central Public Library (hereafter called "Bedford Library").
2. Estimates of the square mileage of Bedford County vary. Bedford County's website, www.co.bedford.va.us/facts/profile.htm, indicates 764. A Virginia Department of Highways map of Bedford County, dated 1945, at the Bedford Library, shows 781. A 1997 Virginia Department of Transportation map for Bedford County shows 754.8 square miles of rural land and 6.8 square miles of City of Bedford land. Ranking of size among Virginia's counties is from *Virginia: Adventures in Time and Place* (Macmillan/McGraw-Hill, New York, 1997), p. 308.
3. *Bedford County, Virginia, History and Geographic Supplement* to the Bedford County Bicentennial Official Program, prepared by the Publications Committee of the Bedford County Education Association, original 1947, second edition, 1949, p. 16 (copy at the Bedford Library). See also the historical marker outside the Bedford County Courthouse on Main Street; the 1992 Bedford City Directory maintained in the Bedford Library; and a one-page "Historical Facts, City of Bedford," in the Bedford City/County Museum (hereafter called "Bedford Museum").
4. See www.census.gov/population/cencounts/VA199090.txt, website of the U.S Census Bureau, for "Virginia, Population of Counties by Decennial Census 1900 to 1990," compiled by Richard L. Forstall, Population Division, U.S. Bureau of the Census, Washington, D.C.
5. Maps of the county on the second-floor wall of the Bedford Library.
6. U.S. Census website, op. cit., for Bedford County population figures prior to 2000. For 2000 figures for county and city, see *The Roanoke Times*, December 7, 2002, p. B4, which reported adjusted figures released by the U.S. Census Bureau. For the population of the town of Bedford in 1940, see the 1945 Virginia Department of Highways map of Bedford County, op. cit., and *Bedford County, Virginia, History and Geography Supplement*, op. cit.
7. Lula Jeter Parker, "The Military History of Bedford County, 1754-1950," p. 42. A copy is available at the Bedford Library. See also the stone monument and plaque erected in 1931 in front of the Bedford County Courthouse on Main Street by the Daughters of the American Revolution. This plaque lists the names of the fifty-two men in the Bedford company and pays tribute to them and Captain Buford.
8. Parker, op. cit., pp. 65-69.
9. Parker, op. cit., pp. 69-70.

10. Melvin M. Scott, "Bedford Soldiers in the Civil War," paper read before the Bedford Historical Society, May 29, 1970, printed by J.P. Bell Company, Lynchburg, Virginia. A copy is available at the Bedford Library. See also Gates R. Richardson, "Bedford County's Part in the Two World Wars," pp. 83-145, in Parker, "The Military History of Bedford County, Virginia, 1754-1950," op. cit.

11. Parker, op. cit., p. 146.

12. Parker, op. cit., p. 160. Also, *Bedford County Bicentennial, 1754-1954, August 8-14, 1954, Official Program*, p. 91. A copy is available at the Bedford Library. The names of the thirty-nine men who died in service during World War I are included on a plaque on the wall of the Bedford County Courthouse.

13. Bicentennial Program, op. cit., p. 92. Number of Bedford County deaths in the Korean War is taken from a plaque on an inside wall of the Bedford County Courthouse.

14. Number of Bedford County deaths in the Vietnam War is taken from a plaque on an inside wall of the Bedford County Courthouse.

15. Several Bedford County men served during the Gulf War in 1990-1991, e.g., see *Bedford Bulletin*, March 13, 1991, p. 17C. The *Bedford Bulletin*, November 12, 2003, p. 9A, reported that Pfc. Benjamin Daniel, a graduate of Liberty High School in Bedford, was deployed to Iraq in April 2003 with the 4th Infantry Division. The *Bedford Bulletin*, November 26, 2003, p. 1, reported that Ray Perdue, another graduate of Liberty High School, served in Kuwait and Iraq in 2003. See *Roanoke Times*, March 5, 2004, p.1, and *Bedford Bulletin*, March 3, 2004, p. 1, for information of the 2004 activation of Company A.

16. *Virginia Guardpost*, "116th Infantry—a history of 'Stonewall' Brigade," Summer 1984, article by 116th Military History Detachment, (published by the Public Affairs Detachment, Virginia Army National Guard), pp. 6-7.

17. Henry F. Seal, *History of the 116th U.S. Infantry Regiment, 29th Infantry Division*. A copy is available at the Bedford Library.

18. *Historical and Pictorial Review, National Guard of the Commonwealth of Virginia, 1940*, p. 57. A copy is available at the Bedford Museum.

19. *Virginia Guardpost*, op. cit., 7.

20. Seal, op. cit., pp. 28-32.

21. Seal, ibid.; 29 *Let's Go!, 1917-1965*, probably published by the 29th Infantry Division, p. 26 (copy at Bedford Museum); *Bedford Democrat*, April 4, 1946, p.1; *Historical and Pictorial Review, National Guard of the Commonwealth of Virginia, 1940*, op. cit., pp. 72-73.

22. *Bedford Democrat*, July 25, 1946, p. 1. The six men who served in Company A during World War II and who enlisted in 1946 were T/Sgt. Roy O. Stevens, S/Sgt. Jack W. Mitchell, S/Sgt. Earl R. Newcomb, T/4 James H. Crouch, T/5 James A. Mitchell, and T/5 James W. Watson.

Part I – Bedford's Story

Chapter 1: Bedford Before the War

1. In the 1940 census, Bedford County had a population of 29,687. The population had stabilized at about 30,000 since the turn of the century. By 1950, it would fall slightly to 29,627. Whites in 1940 numbered 23,330 (79 percent), and Negroes 6,357 (21 percent). See the U.S. Census Bureau website, www.census.gov/population/cencounts/VA190090.txt, for the study "Virginia, Population of Counties by Decennial Census 1900 to 1990." For the 1940 Census population of the town of Bedford, see the 1945 Virginia Department of Highways map of Bedford County, a copy of which is located in the poster map collection in the Tharp Room at the Bedford Central Public Library; see also the "Bedford County Virginia History and Geography Supplement to the Bicentennial of the Bedford County Education Association," 1947, a copy of which is in the Bedford Library. The source of the number of families in the county—6,903—was the *Bedford Bulletin*, August 19, 1943, p. 1.

2. The number of schools in the county declined over time in the 1930s and 1940s as many small schools, including one-room schoolhouses, were closed. In 1931, there were 143 schools—101 for white students (of which eight were high schools), and forty-two for black students (including one high school). By 1941, there were still nine accredited high schools in the county. With the decline in numbers of schools over the years, by 1949, only forty-four schools remained—fifteen for Whites (eight high schools and seven elementary schools) and twenty-nine for Blacks (one high school and twenty-eight elementary schools). For sources, see: (a) the 1931 map of Bedford County listing the names and showing the locations of schools in the county; copies of this map are maintained in the history room of the Office of the Clerk of the Circuit Court in the Bedford County Courthouse and in the Bedford Library; (b) *2 Centuries of Bedford County School Days: A Bicentennial Publication Sponsored by the Bedford County School Board, and the Bedford County Principals' Association*, September 1952, p. 69, a copy of which is located in the Tharp Room of the Bedford Library; and (c) "Publication of the Bicentennial Committee of the Bedford County Education Association," a copy of which is maintained at the Bedford Museum.

3. *Bedford Democrat*, June 20, 1946, p.1. By 1945, the number of farms had shrunk to 3,506.

4. *Bedford Democrat*, January 30, 1941, p. 8.

5. In March 1961, the *Bedford Bulletin* bought the *Bedford Democrat,* and beginning on March 21 of that year, a single newspaper was printed, the *Bedford Bulletin-Democrat*. On August 1, 1984, the newspaper dropped the word "Democrat" and reverted to the name *The Bedford Bulletin*, explaining that the *Bedford Bulletin* "has always been listed as independent politically and having

the name 'Democrat' in the title is confusing to newcomers" and the double name was too long and cumbersome. See the *Bedford Bulletin*, August 1, 1984, p. 2A.

6. Charles E. Green, of Chatham, Virginia, purchased Jones Drug Store in Bedford in January 1941. James Jones apparently sold the store before entering the Navy. Throughout the war, newspaper advertisements referred to the store as "Jones Drug Store," and the advertisements often included a reference to Charles E. Green as the owner and manager or proprietor. Many people in the town, however, often referred to the store as "Green's Drug Store" e.g., see Eleanor Payne Yowell, *Flying High: World War II Letters to and from U.S. Army Air Force Bases and the Home Front* (Lynchburg, Virginia: Warwick House Publishing, 2001), pp. 119-120, letter of July 25, 1944, in which Mrs. Yowell refers to "Charlie Green's drugstore." The change of the name to "Green's Drug Store" was announced on October 11, 1945, in both a front page article and an advertisement in the *Bedford Bulletin*. In the advertisement, Mr. Green claimed he wanted to change the name in 1941 but could not do so for reasons related to the war. The front-page article suggested that Mr. Green, as a stranger or newcomer to Bedford, had wanted to retain the Jones name for the store. The paper reported that, after four years of having many of his customers—particularly those from the county—address him as "Mr. Jones," he wanted to recover his identity. See the *Bedford Bulletin*, October 11, 1945, pp. 1 and 5. See also "Memories of Lyle's Drug Store," by Marie Powers, printed in the *Bedford Bulletin*, July 3, 2002, p. 3A.

7. "Bedford County Bicentennial, 1754-1954, Official Program," op. cit., pp. 82-83.

8. "Bedford County, Virginia, History and Geography Supplement," op cit., p. 31.

9. *Historical and Pictorial Review, National Guard of the Commonwealth of Virginia, 1940*, op. cit., pp. 72-73. Only sixty-seven men are shown in the photographs, but eighty-five men are named on the roster.

10. *Richmond Times-Dispatch*, May 30, 1994, p. 1.

11. *Historical and Pictorial Review, National Guard*, op. cit., p. 73.

Chapter 2: Preparing for War, 1940-1941

1. Michael J. Lyons, *World War II: A Short History* (Prentice Hall, Englewood, New Jersey, 1989), p. 147.

2. See *Bedford Bulletin* and *Bedford Democrat* for first two weeks of September 1939.

3. William L. O'Neill, *World War II: A Student Companion* (New York: Oxford University Press, 1999), pp. 231, 232, 338.

4. *Bedford Bulletin*, September 12, 1940, p. 1.

5. *Bedford Bulletin*, September 19, 1940, p. 1; Thomas Parrish, editor, *The Simon and Schuster Encyclopedia of World War II* (New York: Simon and Schuster, 1978), p. 560.

6. *New York Times,* October 30, 1940, pp. 1 and 15.

7. *Bedford Bulletin*, October 17, 1940, p. 1. J. Moorman Johnson served as chairman of the Bedford County Selective Service Board, and S. D. Gills and Frank W. Burks were members. Dr. W. V. Rucker was physician, and W. R. Saunders was legal advisor. Judge A. H. Hopkins and W. P. Hurt were named as advisors.

8. Ibid.

9. *Bedford Bulletin,* September 19, 1940, p. 1.

10. *Bedford Bulletin*, October 24, 1940, p. 1, and *New York Times*, October 30, 1940, p. 15.

11. *Bedford Democrat*, September 13, 1945, p. 1; Stuart A. Kallen, *World War II: The War at Home* (San Diego, California: American War Library, Lucent Books, 1995), p. 20, and www.ida.net/users/lamar/worldwar2.html.

12. *Bedford Bulletin*, October 24, 1940, p. 1.

13. *Bedford Bulletin*, October 31, 1940, p. 1.

14. Ibid.; O'Neill, op. cit., p. 319; *New York Times*, October 30, 1940, pp. 1 and 15.

15. *Bedford Bulletin*, October 31, 1940, p. 1.

16. Kallen, op. cit., p. 23.

17. *Bedford Bulletin*, October 31, 1940, p. 1.

18. *Bedford Bulletin,* October 3, 1940, p. 1.

19. *Bedford Bulletin*, November 14, 1940, p. 1.

20. *Bedford Bulletin*, September 12, 1940, p. 1.

21. Ibid.

22. *Bedford Democrat*, January 23, 1941, p. 1.

23. Ibid.

24. *Bedford Democrat*, January 30, 1941, p. 1.

25. *Bedford Democrat*, February 13, 1941, p. 1. Another source, Seal, op. cit., states that Company A was officially mobilized on February 17, 19, and 20.

26. This list of February 3 is maintained in the archives on Company A at the Bedford Museum.

27. *Bedford Democrat*, February 6, 1941, p. 1.

28. *Bedford Democrat*, February 13, 1941, p. 1.

29. Ibid.

30. *Bedford Democrat*, February 6, 1941, p. 1.

31. *Bedford Democrat*, February 13, 1941, p. 1

32. Ibid.

33. *Bedford Democrat*, February 21, 1941, p. 1. (The date of publication printed at the top of each page was February 20, but the date should have been February 21, consistent with the newspaper's publication on Thursday. On the microfilm,

someone has typed in the date February 21 above the printed date February
20.)

34. Ibid.
35. *Bedford Bulletin*, February 21, 1941, p. 1.
36. Ibid.
37. This photograph of Company A has been used in many stories on Bedford in
    various publications. Years after the war, Allen Huddleston, a former soldier
    in Company A who later became a professional photographer, reproduced the
    photo, adding a headshot in the lower right corner of S/Sgt. Earl Newcomb,
    who had been absent when the photograph was taken.
38. Roster of Company A dated August 21, 1941. A copy of this roster is maintained
    in the archives of the Bedford Museum.
39. John R. Slaughter, *Wartime Memories of J. Robert Slaughter and Selected Men
    of the 116th Infantry, 29th Division, 1941-1945*, Chapter 1, p. 9. A copy of this
    manuscript is available at the Bedford Library.
40. *Bedford Democrat*, June 12, 1941, p. 1.
41. Julius W. Pratt, *A History of United States Foreign Policy* (Englewood Cliffs,
    New Jersey: Prentice-Hall, Inc., 1961), p. 639.
42. *Bedford Democrat*, September 11, 1941, p. 1, and September 18, 1941, p. 1.
43. C. L. Sulzberger, *The American Heritage Picture History of World War II*,
    (New York: Crown Publishers, Inc., 1966), p. 193.
44. *Bedford Bulletin*, November 6, 1941, p. 1; Samuel Eliot Morison, *The Two-
    Ocean War: A Short History of the United States Navy in the Second World War*
    (New York: Ballantine Books, 1972), p. 30.
45. *Bedford Bulletin*, October 23, 1941, p. 1.
46. *Bedford Bulletin*, October 30, 1941, p. 1.
47. *Bedford Bulletin*, November 6, 1941, p. 1 and November 13, 1941, p. 10;
    Morison, op. cit. p. 30; Sulzberger, op. cit., p. 193; *New York Times*, November
    1, 1941, p. 1, November 4, 1941, p. 1, and December 15, 1941, p. 17; Samuel
    E. Morison, *History of United States Naval Operations in World War II,
    Volume II, Battle of the Atlantic, September 1939-May 1943* (Boston: Little
    Brown & Company, 1947), p. 94. Source of number of casualties is *Dictionary
    of American Fighting Ships*, Department of the Navy, www.history.navy.mil/
    danfs. In December 1937, Japanese forces attacked and sank the U.S. river gun-
    boat *Panay* in the Yangtze River near Nanking, China. While many believed the
    Japanese attack was deliberate, the Japanese government quickly apologized
    and offered reparations. For further information on both ships, see above U.S.
    Navy website and www.ibiblio.org/hyperwar/USN/ships.
48. *Bedford Bulletin*, November 6, 1941, p. 1.
49. *Bedford Bulletin*, November 13, 1941, p. 10.
50. *Military Records of Bedford County's Gold Star Men in World War II*, com-
    piled by the Bedford County War History Committee, Mrs. George P. Parker,

Chairman. This book of records is maintained in the Office of the Clerk of the Circuit Court at the Bedford County Courthouse.

Chapter 3: Entering the War, 1941-1942

1. *Bedford Bulletin*, December 11, 1941, p. 6.
2. Ibid.
3. *Bedford Bulletin*, December 18, 1941, p. 1.
4. *Bedford Bulletin,* December 4, 1941, p. 1.
5. *Bedford Bulletin*, January 1, 1942, p. 1.
6. *Bedford Bulletin*, December 18, 1941, p. 1.
7. *Bedford Bulletin*, January 1, 1942, p. 1.
8. *Bedford Democrat*, February 5, 1942, p. 1.
9. Diary or journal of Ivylyn Jordan (Schenk Hardy), February 16, 1942.
10. *Bedford Democrat*, April 23, 1942, p. 1, and April 30, 1942, p. 1.
11. *Bedford Democrat*, July 9, 1942, p. 1.
12. *Bedford Democrat*, July 23, 1942, p. 1
13. Ibid., p. 5.
14. *Bedford Democrat*, September 3, 1942, p. 8.
15. *Bedford Democrat*, October 8, 1942, p. 7.
16. *Bedford Democrat*, November 25, 1942, p. 1.
17. *Bedford Democrat*, December 10, 1942, p. 1.
18. *Bedford Democrat*, December 17, 1942, p. 1.
19. *29 Let's Go!, 1917-1965*, op. cit., p. 28, and interviews with Roy O. Stevens, spring 1999 and January 30, 2002.
20. Joseph Balkoski, *Beyond the Beachhead: The 29th Infantry Division in Normandy* (Harrisburg, Pennsylvania: Stackpole Books, 1989), p. 28. See also *29 Let's Go!, 1917-1965*, op. cit., pp. 28-29.
21. S/Sgt. John B. Schenk, letter postmarked December 28, 1941, to Ivylyn Jordan (Schenk Hardy).
22. Balkoski, op. cit., p. 28.
23. John Schenk, letter postmarked January 26, 1942, to Ivylyn Jordan (Schenk Hardy). Allen Huddleston, who also served in Company A, has spoken of how nice the community was to the soldiers, e.g., in the author's interview with him on May 31, 2002.
24. *Bedford Democrat*, March 12, 1942, p. 1, and copy of an otherwise unidentified 1957 Congressional Record, PA4805, available at the Bedford Museum.
25. Balkoski, op. cit., pp. 32-33. These dates and deployments are consistent with letters from John Schenk to Ivylyn Jordan (Schenk Hardy).
26. Balkoski, op. cit., p. 33.
27. John Schenk, letter postmarked September 8, 1942, to his wife of less than three weeks, Ivylyn Jordan Schenk.
28. Balkoski, op. cit., pp. 33-36.

29. Thomas Parish, editor, *The Simon and Schuster Encyclopedia of World War II*, op. cit., p. 512, and Balkoski, op. cit., p. 36.

30. Balkoski, op. cit., p. 37.

31. Ibid.

32. See profiles in Part II of this book of Allen Huddleston and Earl Newcomb.

33. Balkoski, op. cit., p. 37.

34. Balkoski, op. cit., pp. 37-38.

35. John Schenk wrote letters to his wife saying he was in England but not specifying the area. M/Sgt. John Wilkes similarly informed his wife. Both men sent their wives photographs taken of the men in their base area.

Chapter 4: Serving Their Country, 1942-1945

1. U.S. Department of Defense, *Defense Almanac '94*, p. 47.

2. Robert Heide and John Gilman, *Home from America: Popular Culture of the World War II Era*, Chronicle Books, San Francisco, California, 1995, p. 52.

3. The author counted the number of men listed in the *Induction and Discharge Records, World War II, Bedford County,* as having been inducted and/or discharged during the World War II period. These records are located in the Office of the Clerk of the Circuit Court in the Bedford County Courthouse. As of October 2002, pursuant to legislation by the Virginia General Assembly, these records have been removed from access by the general public.

4. See note number 41 below in this chapter.

5. I. C. B. Dear, General Editor, *The Oxford Companion to World War II* (Oxford and New York: Oxford University Press, 1995), p. 5.

6. *Bedford Bulletin*, July 29, 1943, p. 1.

7. *Bedford Democrat*, March 11, 1943, p. 1.

8. *Bedford Democrat*, July 22, 1943, p. 1.

9. *Bedford Bulletin,* July 29, 1943, p. 1.

10. *Bedford Democrat*, August 5, 1943, p. 1.

11. *Bedford Bulletin,* April 20, 1944, p. 3.

12. Eleanor Payne Yowell, *Flying High: World War II Letters to and from U.S. Army Air Force Bases and the Home Front* (Warwick House Publishing, Lynchburg, Virginia, 2001), p. 63, (letter of April 3, 1944).

13. Associated Press, Washington, D.C., as carried in the *Bedford Bulletin*, February 22, 1943, p. 1.

14. *Bedford Democrat*, July 23, 1942, p. 5.

15. *Bedford Bulletin*, October 22, 1942, p. 6.

16. Associated Press, Washington, D.C., as carried in the *Bedford Bulletin*, February 22, 1943, p. 1.

17. O'Neill, op. cit., p. 10.

18. O'Neill, op. cit., pp. 7, 152-154.

19. O'Neill, op. cit., p. 10.

20. Hondon B. Hargrove, *Buffalo Soldiers in Italy: Black Americans in World War II* (Jefferson, North Carolina, and London, England: McFarland & Co., 1985), pp. vii and 4.

21. Dear, op. cit., pp. 5-6; O'Neill, op. cit., p. 11; Hargrove, op. cit., p. 47.

22. Dear, op. cit., pp. 5-6; O'Neill, op. cit., pp. 10-11.

23. Ibid.

24. The books *Induction and Discharge Records, World War II, Bedford County*, maintained in the Office of the Clerk of the Circuit Court, Bedford County, contain induction records for the World War II period (up to August 1945) for about 490 men whose racial identity is listed as Negro or "colored." The book, *Military Service Records, World War II, Volume IV, W-Z, Women*, compiled by the War History Committee of Bedford County, has a last section devoted to Negroes. This is an incomplete listing, as there are pages for only 112 Blacks in this section. The local newspapers periodically throughout the war reported the names of men sent for induction, identifying separately "whites" and "colored."

25. The sole black woman identified as having served is U.S. Army Pvt. Doris H. Reed. See the list referred to in note number 41 below.

26. *Bedford Democrat*, July 23, 1942, p. 1.

27. See *Induction and Discharge Records, World War II, Bedford County*, op. cit., and *Military Service Records, World War II, Volume IV, W-Z, Women*, op. cit.

28. *Bedford Bulletin*, October 14, 1943, p. 1.

29. See *Military Service Records, World War II, Volume IV, W-Z, Women*, op. cit.

30. Richardson, op. cit., pp. 163-164.

31. Ibid., pp. 162-163.

32. Karen Zeinert, *The Incredible Women of World War II* (Brookfield, Connecticut: The Millbrook Press, 1994), p. 54.

33. *Bedford Democrat*, July 23, 1942, p. 5.

34. *Bedford Bulletin*, October 22, 1942, p. 6.

35. *Bedford Democrat*, March 11, 1943, p. 1.

36. Dear, op. cit., p. 1266.

37. O'Neill, op. cit., pp. 362-363.

38. O'Neill, op. cit., pp. 249, 362-363.

39. O'Neill, op. cit., p. 362.

40. Ibid.

41. There is no single authoritative source for the number of Bedford County women who served in the war. The *Military Service Records* (for Bedford County), *World War II, Volume IV, W-Z, Women*, in the Office of the Clerk of the Circuit Court in the Bedford County Courthouse contain information on only thirty-six women. Rodney Franklin, who was born and raised in the Montvale area of Bedford County and now lives in Roanoke, has compiled and continues to develop an expanded list, which now has the names, service, rank, and date of entry into service of approximately fifty women from Bedford County.

42. *Bedford Bulletin*, May 4, 1944, p. 1.

43. See note 41 and Rodney Franklin's paper in the Bedford Museum.

44. Sources on Rubye V. Wilkes-Archer and other Bedford women in the service include the *Bedford Bulletin* and *Bedford Democrat* newspapers; *Military Service Records, World War II, Volume IV, W-Z, Women*, op. cit.; newspaper articles in the archives of the Bedford Museum; and the list compiled by Rodney Franklin, op. cit. For Wilkes-Archer's obituary and summary of military service, see the *Bedford Bulletin*, May 8, 1991, p. 14A.

45. Sources include the *Bedford Bulletin* and *Bedford Democrat*; newspaper clippings at the Bedford Museum; author's interviews; *Induction and Discharge Records, World War II, Bedford County*; *Military Service Records, Bedford County, Volumes I-IV*; and other sources.

46. Author's interview with Ward and Mary Dean, February 26, 2002. See the profile on the Deans in Part II of this book.

47. O'Neill, op. cit., pp. 320-322.

48. *Bedford Bulletin*, May 30, 2001, p. 1.

49. *Bedford Bulletin*, August 13, 1942, p. 1.

50. *Bedford Bulletin*, April 22, 1943, p. 1.

51. *Bedford Bulletin*, October 29, 1942, p. 1.

52. *Military Records of Bedford County's Gold Star Men in World War II*, op. cit.

53. *Lyons*, op. cit., p. 180.

54. *Bedford Bulletin*, April 29, 1943, p. 1.

55. *Bedford Bulletin*, May 11, 1944, p. 1.

56. Parrish, *The Simon and Schuster Encyclopedia of World War II*, op. cit., p. 507.

57. James Bradley with Ron Powers, *Flags of Our Fathers* (New York: Bantam Books, 2000), p. 138.

58. *Bedford Democrat*, February 3, 1944, p. 1.

59. *Bedford Democrat*, March 2, 1944, p. 1.

60. Ibid.

61. Ibid.

62. *Bedford Democrat*, November 9, 1944, p. 1.

63. *Bedford Democrat*, February 22, 1945, p. 1, and September 13, 1945, p. 1.

64. *Bedford Democrat*, June 3, 1945, p. 1.

65. *Bedford Bulletin*, May 24, 1945, p. 1.

66. Interview with Henry Chappelle and an undated newspaper clipping in the scrapbook of Mrs. Elva Newcomb.

67. *Bedford Democrat* and *Bedford Bulletin*, May 3, 1945, p. 1; *Bedford Bulletin*, August 9, 1945, p. 3.

68. *Bedford Democrat*, August 2, 1945, p. 1.

69. *Bedford Democrat*, June 14, 1945, p. 11, and May 31, 1945, p. 1, and undated newspaper clippings in the scrapbook of Mrs. Elva Newcomb.

70. *Bedford Bulletin*, April 12, 1945, p. 1.

71. *Bedford Bulletin*, September 7, 1944, p. 7.
72. *Bedford Bulletin*, December 7, 1944, p. 1.
73. *Bedford Bulletin*, December 14, 1944, p. 1.
74. *Bedford Bulletin*, January 18, 1945, p. 1.
75. *Bedford Democrat*, May 17, 1945, p. 1.
76. *Bedford Democrat*, May 31, 1945, p. 1.
77. *Bedford Democrat*, September 6, 1945, pp. 1 and 8.

Chapter 5: Life in the Military

1. Balkoski, op. cit., pp. 38-42.
2. John J. Barnes, *Fragments of My Life with Company A, 116ᵗʰ Infantry Regiment: From Omaha Beach to the Elbe River* (Holland Patent, New York: JAM Publications, 2000), p. 48. Barnes states that Ivybridge was the base for the entire 1ˢᵗ Battalion of the 116ᵗʰ Infantry Regiment.
3. See interview with Allen M. Huddleston. Bettie K.Wilkes Hooper has what appears to be a professional photograph of a group of Company A soldiers on the back of which is stamped the seal of a Liverpool photographer. It is not clear whether this photograph made it by the censors before D-Day or she obtained it later with her husband's effects.
4. Balkoski, op. cit., p. 57.
5. Brochure on Slapton Sands in possession of Ivylyn Hardy of Bedford.
6. Description of German boats is based on Dear (editor), *The Oxford Companion to World War II*, op. cit., p. 318. Information on the attack is from Balkoski, op. cit., p. 57.
7. Barnes, op. cit., p. 54.
8. Balkoski, op. cit., p. 60.
9. Dear (editor), *The Oxford Companion to World War II*, op. cit., p. 803.
10. John Schenk, air mail letter of July 11, 1943, to his wife.
11. William Yowell, letter to his wife of May 18, 1944, excerpted from *Flying High*, op. cit., pp. 77-78.
12. William Yowell, letter to his wife of May 22, 1944, excerpted from *Flying High*, op. cit., pp. 81-82.
13. John Schenk, air mail letter to his wife of July 11, 1943.
14. Barnes, op. cit., p. 51.
15. *Bedford Bulletin*, April 22, 1943, p. 1.
16. Barnes, op. cit., p. 51.
17. John Schenk, letters to his wife of April 3, May 19 and 20, June 3 and 4, July 10 and 19, and August 7, 1943.
18. William Yowell, letters written to his wife on the following dates and found on the following pages of Eleanor Yowell's book, *Flying High*: August 18 and 23, 1944, pp. 134 and 136; July 26, 1944, p. 121; May 23, 1944, pp. 82-83; June 29, 1944, p. 104; June 12, 1944, pp. 92-93; July 24, 1944, p. 118, and June 25, 1944, p. 101.

19. John Schenk, letter to his wife of August 7, 1943.

20. *Stars and Stripes*, September 30, 1943.

21. A V-Mail letter dated Nov. 28, 1943, from John Schenk to his wife reported that the wedding was to be the next Saturday. Sergeants Baker, Draper, and Schenk were all killed on D-Day.

22. John Schenk, letter to his wife of January 30, 1944.

23. According to the *Bedford Bulletin*, April 13, 1944, p. 1, the men in the Army Air Forces company in the Solomons were Pfc. Jennings J. Sumner, Leon P. Dooley, Cpl. Odell Ashwell, Cpl. Meredith Bennett, and Pfc. Isaac Hogan. Men from Bedford serving in the 366th Regiment included Jackson S. Carey, Leroy Carter, Clarence Lazenby, and Allen C. Wright, according to *Military Service Records* (for Bedford County), *World War II, Volume IV,* op. cit. Willie J. Hobson in an interview with the author stated that he also served in the 366th Regiment. The men in Battery B of the 285th Field Artillery Observation Battalion were S/Sgt. William Merriken, Pfc. Warren Davis, and Pfc. Richard B. Walker, the latter two of whom were killed in Belgium.

24. *Bedford Bulletin*, June 8, 1944, p. 1

25. *Bedford Bulletin,* April 5, 1945, p. 1

26. *Bedford Bulletin,* August 9, 1945, p. 2

27. *Bedford Bulletin*, June 8, 1944, p. 1.

28. *Bedford Bulletin*, June 1, 1944, p. 1.

29. *Bedford Bulletin*, July 8, 1943, p. 1.

30. *Bedford Bulletin*, January 18, 1945, p. 5.

31. *Bedford Bulletin*, July 6, 1944, p. 1.

32. *Bedford Bulletin*, July 27, 1944, p. 1.

33. *Bedford Bulletin*, September 7, 1944, p. 1.

34. *Bedford Bulletin*, October 26, 1944, p. 1.

35. *Bedford Bulletin*, October 19, 1944, p. 3.

36. *Bedford Bulletin*, November 30, 1944, p. 1.

37. *Bedford Bulletin,* February 8, 1945, p. 3.

38. *Bedford Bulletin,* February 1, 1945, p. 1.

39. *Bedford Bulletin,* April 20, 1944, p. 1.

40. *Bedford Bulletin,* November 30, 1944, p. 1.

41. *Bedford Bulletin,* July 22, 1943, p. 1.

Chapter 6: Home Front: Overview & Civil Defense

1. O'Neill, op. cit., p. 152.

2. *Bedford Bulletin*, October 3, 1940, pp. 1 and 5: October 24, 1940, p. 1, and *Bedford Democrat*, April 4, 1946, p. 1.

3. *Bedford Bulletin*, October 17, 1940, pp. 1 and 5.

4. Richardson, op. cit., p. 168.

5. *Bedford Democrat*, January 16, 1941, p. 1.

6. *Bedford Bulletin*, February 6, 1941, p. 1.

7. *Bedford Bulletin*, June 5, 1941, p. 1.
8. *Bedford Democrat*, September 4, 1941, p. 1.
9. *Bedford Democrat*, October 16, 1941, p. 1.
10. *Bedford Democrat*, February 12, 1942, p. 1, and the journal of Ivylyn Jordan (Schenk Hardy).
11. *Bedford Democrat*, January 14, 1943, p. 5.
12. *Bedford Democrat*, October 14, 1943, p. 1.
13. Richardson, op. cit., p. 169.
14. Kallen, op. cit., pp. 31-33.
15. *Bedford Democrat*, January 30, 1941, p. 1, February 20, 1941, p. 1, October 4, 1944, p. 1, and April 4, 1946, p. 1.
16. *Bedford Democrat*, February 13, 1941, p. 9.
17. *Bedford Democrat*, May 29, 1941, p. 1, and Richardson, op. cit., p. 162.
18. *Bedford Democrat*, December 11, 1941, p. 1.
19. Richardson, op. cit., p. 167.
20. *Bedford Democrat*, November 4, 1943, p. 5.
21. *Bedford Bulletin*, March 1, 1945, p. 3.
22. *Bedford Democrat*, June 5, 1941, p. 1; Richardson, op. cit., p. 166; *Bedford Bulletin*, June 1, 1944, p. 8.
23. *Bedford Democrat*, January 29, 1942, p. 1.
24. *Bedford Democrat*, February 5, 1942, p. 1.
25. *Bedford Democrat*, January 22, 1942, p. 1.
26. *Bedford Democrat*, February 5, 1942, p. 1.
27. *Bedford Democrat*, February 19, 1942, p. 1.
28. *Bedford Democrat*, May 14, 1942, p. 1.
29. Ibid.
30. Richardson, op. cit., p. 166.
31. *Bedford Democrat*, June 11, 1942, p. 1.
32. *Bedford Democrat*, June 18, 1942, p. 1.
33. *Bedford Democrat*, August 13, 1942, p. 1.
34. *Bedford Democrat*, September 24, 1942, p. 4.
35. *Bedford Democrat*, March 18, 1943, p. 1.
36. Yowell, op. cit., p. 1, (letter of March 18, 1943).
37. *Bedford Democrat*, April 29, 1943, p. 1.
38. *Bedford Democrat*, January 27, 1944, p. 1.

Chapter 7: Home Front: Restrictions on Consumers

1. Kallen, op. cit., p. 49.
2. Kallen, op. cit., pp. 47-49.
3. Kallen, op. cit., pp. 42-43; *Bedford Democrat*, February 18, 1943, p. 1.
4. Kallen, op. cit., pp. 42-43.

5. *Bedford Bulletin*, May 21, 1942, p. 1; October 29, 1942, p. 1; May 27, 1943, p. 1; October 14, 1943, p. 1; and March 9, 1944, p. 1. For an example of the types of coupons and stamps, see *Bedford Democrat*, May 20, 1943, p. 5.

6. *Bedford Democrat*, February 18, 1943, p. 1; *Bedford Bulletin*, August 31, 1944, p. 1. Weinberg's ownership of the theaters was reported in the *Bedford Bulletin* of September 14, 1939, p. 1.

7. *Bedford Democrat*, February 18, 1943, p. 1.

8. *Bedford Bulletin*, January 8, 1942, p. 3; *Bedford Democrat*, January 21, 1942, p. 3.

9. *Bedford Bulletin*, January 8, 1942, p. 3.

10. Ibid.

11. *Bedford Bulletin*, January 8, 1942, p. 1; *Bedford Democrat*, March 5, 1942, p. 1.

12. Kallen, op. cit., pp. 41-42.

13. *Bedford Democrat*, April 23, 1942, p. 1.

14. *Bedford Democrat*, March 5, 1942, p. 4, and April 30, 1942, p. 1.

15. *Bedford Bulletin*, May 21, 1942, p. 1; Robert Heide and John Gilman, *Home Front America: Popular Culture of the World War II Era*, Chronicle Books, San Francisco, California, 1995, pp. 56-57.

16. *Bedford Democrat*, April 30, 1942, p. 1.

17. *Bedford Democrat*, June 18, 1942, p. 1.

18. *Bedford Bulletin,* September 3, 1942, p. 1; *Bedford Democrat*, October 29, 1942, p. 1; *Bedford Bulletin*, October 8, 1942, p. 4.

19. *Bedford Bulletin*, September 24, 1942, p. 1, and October 8, 1942, p. 1.

20. *Bedford Bulletin,* June 25, 1942, p. 1; *Bedford Democrat*, September 17, 1942, p. 1.

21. *Bedford Democrat*, October 14, 1943, p. 1.

22. For example, see *Bedford Democrat*, March 11, 1943, p. 1.

23. *Bedford Democrat*, February 17, 1944, p. 1.

24. *Bedford Bulletin,* June 11, 1942, p. 1.

25. *Bedford Bulletin*, November 12, 1942, p. 1.

26. Kallen, op. cit., p. 41.

27. *Bedford Democrat*, June 3, 1943, p. 1.

28. *Bedford Bulletin,* September 17, 1942, p. 1, and O'Neill, op. cit., p. 274.

29. *Bedford Democrat*, January 14, 1943, p. 1, and Kallen, op. cit., pp. 47-49.

30. *Bedford Democrat*, February 4, 1943, p. 1.

31. *Bedford Bulletin*, June 10, 1943, p. 1.

32. *Bedford Bulletin*, May 20, 1943, p. 1.

33. *Bedford Bulletin*, June 23, 1943, p. 1.

34. *Bedford Bulletin,* July 22, 1943, p. 1.

35. *Bedford Democrat*, September 2, 1943, p. 1.

36. *Bedford Democrat*, February 11, 1943, p. 1.

37. *Bedford Democrat*, February 18, 1943, p. 1.

38. Barbara C. Bigelow, *World War II: Primary Sources*, edited by Christine Slavey, UXL, the Gale Group, Detroit, 2000, pp. 72-73.
39. Yowell, op. cit., p. 20.
40. Brian Witt, "Compliance and Non Compliance with Government Regulation During World War Two: The Case of Bedford County, Virginia," 2000. A copy of this senior thesis, written by Brian Witt, a student at Ferrum College, during an internship at the Bedford Museum, is available at the museum.
41. *Bedford Democrat*, August 19, 1943, p. 1, and *Bedford Bulletin*, August 19, 1943, p. 1.
42. *Bedford Bulletin,* January 13, 1944, p. 1.
43. *Bedford Democrat*, July 6, 1944, p. 3.
44. *Bedford Bulletin*, September 23, 1943, p. 1, and August 31, 1944, p. 1.
45. *Bedford Democrat*, June 7, 1945, p. 1.

Chapter 8: Home Front: Volunteer Activities

1. *Bedford Democrat*, February 19, 1942, p. 4, May 1, 1941, p. 1, and December 11, 1941, p. 1.
2. *Bedford Democrat*, April 12, 1945, p. 1.
3. *Bedford Democrat*, April 26, 1945, p. 1.
4. *Bedford Democrat*, January 29, 1942, p. 1
5. *Bedford Democrat*, July 23, 1942, p. 1.
6. *Bedford Democrat*, December 17, 1942, p. 1.
7. *Bedford Democrat*, July 23, 1942, p. 1, and February 18, 1943, p. 1.
8. *Bedford Democrat*, November 19, 1942, p. 1.
9. *Bedford Democrat*, March 11, 1943, p. 1.
10. *Bedford Democrat*, June 17, 1943, p. 1.
11. *Bedford Democrat*, October 15, 1942, p. 2.
12. *Bedford Bulletin*, June 5, 1941, p. 1, and November 20, 1941, p. 1.
13. *Bedford Democrat*, July 17, 1941, p. 1.
14. *Bedford Democrat*, January 29, 1942, p. 1.
15. *Bedford Democrat*, February 12, 1942, p. 1.
16. *Bedford Democrat*, March 26, 1942, p. 1.
17. *Bedford Democrat*, June 4, 1942, p. 1.
18. *Bedford Democrat*, June 19, 1942, p. 1, July 9, 1942, p. 1, and July 23, 1942, p. 1.
19. Ibid.
20. *Bedford Democrat*, July 23, 1942, p. 1.
21. Ibid.
22. *Bedford Democrat*, November 12, 1942, p. 1.
23. *Bedford Democrat*, January 28, 1943, p. 1, and February 11, 1943, p. 1.
24. *Bedford Democrat*, October 7, 1943, p. 1.
25. *Bedford Democrat*, March 9, 1944, p. 1.
26. *Bedford Democrat*, April 4, 1946, p. 1.

27. *Bedford Democrat*, March 12, 1942, p. 1, and *Bedford Bulletin*, April 22, 1943, p. 1.
28. *Bedford Democrat*, July 23, 1942, p. 1.
29. Ibid.
30. *Bedford Bulletin*, September 10, 1942, p. 1.
31. American Red Cross Publication 441, Specifications for U.S. Army Surgical Dressings, Revised November 1940, provided courtesy of the American Red Cross Museum. Also, author's interview with Mrs. Nina Jarvis, April 23, 2002.
32. *Bedford Democrat*, January 14, 1943, p. 1; March 11, 1943, p. 1; September 16, 1943, p. 1; and June 5, 1944, p. 1.
33. Author's interview with Mrs. Betty Wilkes Hooper, June 6, 2002.
34. *Bedford Democrat*, March 15, 1945, p. 1.
35. *Bedford Democrat*, June 3, 1943, p. 1.
36. *Bedford Bulletin*, August 24, 1944, p. 1.
37. *Bedford Democrat*, March 15, 1945, p. 1.
38. *Bedford Bulletin*, May 31, 1945, p. 1.
39. *Bedford Democrat*, March 6, 1942, p. 4, and September 2, 1943, p. 1, and Richardson, op. cit., p. 165.
40. Kallen, op. cit., pp. 43-45.
41. O'Neill, op. cit., p. 349.
42. Kallen, op. cit., pp. 43-45, and *Bedford Democrat*, February 15, 1945, p. 6.
43. *Bedford Democrat*, January 18, 1943, p. 1.
44. *Bedford Democrat*, February 12, 1942, p. 4.
45. *Bedford Democrat*, February 5, 1942, p. 1.
46. *Bedford Democrat*, February 19, 1942, p. 1.
47. *Bedford Democrat*, October 22, 1942, p. 1.
48. *Bedford Democrat*, March 11, 1943, p. 1.
49. *Bedford Democrat*, April 22, 1943, p. 1.
50. *Bedford Democrat*, May 13, 1943, p. 1.
51. *Bedford Bulletin*, July 22, 1943, p. 1.
52. *Bedford Democrat*, July 22, 1943, p. 1, and October 14, 1943, p. 1; *Bedford Bulletin*, July 22, 1943, p. 1.
53. *Bedford Bulletin,* May 25, 1944, p. 5; *Bedford Democrat*, June 22, 1944, p. 5.
54. Yowell, op. cit., letter of April 26, 1944, p. 70.
55. Yowell, op. cit., letter of April 27, 1944, p. 71.
56. Yowell, op. cit., letter of May 7, 1944, p. 74.
57. Yowell, op. cit., letter of May 16, 1944, p. 77.
58. Yowell, op. cit., letter of May 19, 1944, pp. 78-79.
59. Yowell, op. cit., letter of June 2, 1944, p. 86.
60. Yowell, op. cit., letter of June 29, 1944, p. 104.
61. Yowell, op. cit., letter of July 19, 1944, p. 115
62. Yowell, op. cit., letter of July 27, 1944, p. 122.

63. *Bedford Democrat*, February 15, 1945, p. 6.

Chapter 9: Home Front: Fund Raising

1. Richardson, op. cit., pp. 158-159.
2. *Bedford Democrat*, January 27, 1944, p. 1, and January 11, 1945, p. 1.
3. Statements about the cost to the United States of World War II vary, with estimates generally between $288 to $318 billion. See Louisiana State University website www.cw.lsu.edu/civil/other/stats/warcost.htm, and O'Neill, op. cit., pp. 111 and 354.
4. Kallen, op. cit., pp. 54-55; Kathleen Krull, *V is for Victory* (New York: Apple Sap Books, Alfred A. Knopf, 1995), p. 17; Richardson, op. cit., p. 158.
5. *Bedford Democrat*, March 21, 1946, p. 1.
6. *Bedford Democrat*, February 19, 1942, p. 1.
7. *Bedford Democrat*, September 17, 1942, p. 1.
8. *Bedford Democrat*, April 12, 1942, p. 1, and March 21, 1946, p. 1.
9. *Bedford Democrat*, September 17, 1942, p. 1, and October 15, 1942, p. 1.
10. *Bedford Democrat*, March 5, 1942, p. 1.
11. *Bedford Democrat*, April 2, 1942, p. 1.
12. *Bedford Democrat*, May 7, 1942, p. 1.
13. *Bedford Democrat*, May 28, 1942, p. 5, and September 10, 1942, p. 7; *Bedford Bulletin*, April 22, 1943, p. 3.
14. *Bedford Bulletin,* October 15, 1942, p. 1, and *Bedford Democrat*, October 29, 1942, p. 1.
15. *Bedford Democrat*, September 30, 1943, p. 1.
16. *Bedford Democrat*, December 17, 1942, p. 1, and December 24, 1942, p. 1.
17. *Bedford Democrat*, March 11, 1943, p. 1.
18. *Bedford Democrat*, March 18, 1943, p. 1.
19. *Bedford Democrat*, September 16, 1943, p. 1.
20. *Bedford Bulletin*, May 20, 1943, p. 1.
21. *Bedford Democrat*, May 13, 1943, p. 1.
22. *Bedford Democrat*, September 16, 1943, p. 1.
23. Ibid.
24. *Bedford Democrat*, September 23, 1943, p. 1.
25. *Bedford Democrat*, January 27, 1944, p. 1.
26. *Bedford Democrat*, February 10, 1944, p. 1.
27. *Bedford Democrat*, January 27, 1944, p. 1.
28. *Bedford Democrat*, February 3, 1944, p. 1.
29. *Bedford Democrat*, February 10, 1944, p. 8.
30. *Bedford Democrat*, March 9, 1944, p. 1.
31. *Bedford Democrat*, February 17, 1942, p. 1.
32. *Bedford Bulletin*, June 15, 1944, p. 1, and June 22, 1944, p. 1, and *Bedford Democrat*, June 15, 1944, p. 1.
33. *Bedford Bulletin*, November 23, 1944, p. 1.

34. *Bedford Bulletin*, November 30, 1944, p. 6.
35. *Bedford Democrat*, May 3, p. 1, and June 3, 1945, p. 1.
36. *Bedford Democrat*, May 3, 1945, p. 1.
37. *Bedford Democrat*, March 21, 1946, p. 1, and Richardson, op. cit., p. 159. On a per capita basis, Bedford County, with a 1940 population of 29,687 and $7,048,954 in bond sales, purchased $237 worth of bonds for each resident. The bonds, of course, were purchased not only by individuals but also by businesses and industries and even the county and town governments. By comparison, Virginia, as a state, with a 1940 population of 2,677,773 and total bond sales of $1,193,014,766, purchased $446 worth of bonds per capita. Bedford County, however, met its quota for bond sales, while Virginia, as a whole, did not meet its total quota of $1,774,434,477.
38. *Bedford Democrat*, March 21, 1946, p. 1.
39. *Bedford Democrat*, February 10, 1944, p. 1. See article by Bedford Red Cross Chairman O. A. Thomas.
40. *Bedford Bulletin*, December 18, 1941, p. 1.
41. *Bedford Bulletin*, January 8, 1942, pp. 1 and 6.
42. *Bedford Democrat,* March 9, 1944, p. 1.
43. *Bedford Democrat*, March 11, 1943, p. 1.
44. *Bedford Bulletin*, April 29, 1943, p. 1.
45. *Bedford Democrat*, February 10, 1944, p. 1, and Richardson, op. cit., p. 165.
46. For stories on the USO and the Virginia War Fund, see the *Bedford Democrat*, April 30, 1942, p. 1; June 11, 1942, p. 1; October 14, 1943, p. 1; October 5, 1944, p. 1; and September 27, 1945, p. 1; *Bedford Bulletin*, December 2, 1943, p. 1, and November 30, 1944, p. 1.

Chapter 10: Home Front: Bedford's Economy

1. O'Neill, op. cit, p. 156.
2. Richardson, op. cit., pp. 151-152.
3. Richardson, op. cit., p. 153.
4. Richardson, op. cit., pp. 153-154.
5. *Bedford Democrat*, January 30, 1941, p. 8.
6. *Bedford Bulletin*, May 24, 1945, p. 1.
7. Richardson, op. cit., pp. 153-154, *Bedford Democrat*, July 31, 1941, p. 1, and Lula Jeter Parker (Mrs. George P. Parker), "The Town of Bedford in Virginia," p. 18. A copy of the latter is available in the Bedford Library.
8. *Bedford County Bicentennial, 1754-1954, Official Program*, op. cit., p. 39.
9. Richardson, op. cit., p. 153.
10. *Bedford Democrat*, November 18, 1943, p. 1.
11. Ibid.
12. Richardson, op. cit., pp. 153-154.
13. Ibid.
14. *Bedford Democrat*, September 7, 1944, p. 4.

15. *Bedford Democrat*, September 12, 1946, p. 1
16. Ibid.
17. Author's interview with Ivylyn Schenk Hardy, June 12 and 18, 2002.
18. *2 Centuries of Bedford County School Days*, op. cit., p. 42.
19. Copies of many of the Bedford High School yearbooks from the 1930s and 1940s are maintained in the Tharp Room of the Bedford Library.
20. *Bedford Bulletin*, September 10, 1942, p. 1.
21. Richardson, op. cit., p. 164.
22. *Bedford Democrat*, July 15, 1943, p. 1; *Bedford Bulletin*, April 27, 1944, p. 1.
23. See Chapter 1, end note number 6, and *Bedford Democrat*, August 13, 1942, p.4.
24. *Bedford Democrat*, September 9, 1943, p. 7, and July 6, 1944, p. 3.
25. *Bedford Democrat*, November 2, 1944, p. 4.
26. *Bedford Democrat*, October 18, 1945, p. 1.

Chapter 11: Home Front: Miscellaneous

1. Mrs. George P. Parker (compiler), "Reports and Correspondence Concerning Bedford County in World War II," letter of May 1, 1943, p. 4 of book, and letter of reply dated May 28. This book is available in the Tharp Room of the Bedford Library.
2. *Bedford Bulletin,* April 20, 1944, p. 3.
3. This poem was printed in a Bedford newspaper, probably the *Bedford Democrat,* in November 1943. A copy of the newspaper clipping with this poem, not identified as to name or date of the newspaper, is in the World War II scrapbook of Mrs. Elva Newcomb.
4. Kallen, op. cit., p. 23, and *Bedford Bulletin*, December 2, 1943, p. 1.
5. *Bedford Democrat*, December 2, 1943, p. 1, and February 17, 1944, p. 1; *Bedford Bulletin*, December 2, 1943, p. 1, February 10, 1944, p. 1, and March 9, 1944, p. 6.
6. Ibid.
7. *Bedford Bulletin*, February 24, 1944, p. 4.
8. *Bedford Bulletin*, March 9, 1944, p. 6.
9. Ibid.
10. Ibid.
11. Ibid.
12. *Bedford Democrat, September 11, 1941, p. 1, and Bedford Bulletin*, April 29, 1943, p. 1, and May 6, 1943, p. 1, and interviews with Mrs. Nina Jarvis, Mrs. Ivylyn Schenk Hardy, and Mrs. Eleanor Yowell.
13. *Bedford Democrat*, July 16, 1942, p. 1, and July 22, 1943, p. 1.
14. *Bedford Bulletin*, April 5, 1945, p. 1; April 12, 1945, p. 1; and April 19, 1945, p. 1.
15. *Bedford Bulletin*, June 21, 1945, p. 1.

16. *Bedford Bulletin,* February 4, 1943, p. 1. The five crew members were: 2^d Lts. Paul M. Pitts, William McClure, George R. Beninga, and Hilary S. Blackwell, and Cpl. Peter J. Biscan. Parts of the plane still lie on the mountain. For further information and photos, see the website www.wp21.com/b25crash.

17. *Bedford Bulletin,* April 29, 1943, p. 1. The other instructor was said to be Wing Wong, a Chinese instructor from New York, and the other student was Clarence Copen, who lived in West Virginia.

18. *Bedford Democrat*, November 2, 1944, p. 1. The Navy released the names of the pilot, Lieutenant Frank Bingham, and the aeronautical engineer, Herbert V. Thaden, whose home was in Roanoke and who was married to a leading, pioneer, woman flyer, Louise Thaden.

19. *Bedford Democrat*, September 9, 1945, p. 1; *Bedford Bulletin*, September 20, 1945, p. 1, and September 27, 1945, p. 1. The pilot was identified as 1st Lt. Edward A. Clark.

20. The *Bedford Bulletin* and *Bedford Democrat* merged on March 21, 1961, to become the *Bedford Bulletin-Democrat*. The newspaper reverted to the name *The Bedford Bulletin,* and the *Bedford Democrat* ceased to exist.

21. For example, see the war bond advertisement in the *Bedford Democrat*, June 14, 1945, p. 6; the advertisement for saving tin in the *Bedford Democrat*, March 11, 1943, p. 8; and the advertisement on the number of tin cans needed to make military hardware, *Bedford Bulletin*, September 24, 1942, p. 4.

22. *Bedford Democrat*, June 4, 1942, p. 3.

23. *Bedford Democrat*, November 19, 1942, p. 3

24. *Bedford Democrat*, January 14, 1943, p. 3.

25. *Bedford Democrat*, June 4, 1942, p. 2.

26. *Bedford Democrat*, August 27, 1942, p. 7.

27. *Bedford Democrat*, January 28, 1943, p. 2.

28. *Bedford Democrat*, May 28, 1942, p. 7

29. *Bedford Democrat*, July 22, 1944, p. 3

30. *Bedford Democrat*, July 20 , 1944, p. 7

31. *Bedford Bulletin*, December 11, 1941, p. 6

32. *Bedford Bulletin*, December 18, 1941, p. 6.

33. Ibid.

34. *Bedford Democrat*, March 12, 1942, p. 1.

35. *Bedford Bulletin*, September 10, 1942, p. 6.

36. *Bedford Bulletin*, June 15, 1944, p. 6.

37. *Bedford Bulletin*, July 27, 1944, p. 6.

38. *Bedford Bulletin*, November 2, 1944, p. 1.

39. *Bedford Bulletin*, February 1, 1945, p. 6.

40. *Bedford Democrat*, July-August, 1944.

41. *Bedford Democrat*, July 20, 1944, p. 5.

42. *Bedford Democrat*, September 28, 1944, p. 8.

43. *Bedford Democrat*, September 28, 1944, p. 3.

44. *Bedford Democrat*, September 14, 1944, p. 5

45. These jokes were contained in various editions of the *Bedford Bulletin*; for example see, *Bedford Bulletin*, February 17, 1944, p. 6; June 15, 1944, p. 2; September 7, 1944, p. 6; and November 2, 1944, p. 3.

46. The author is respecting the wish of the correspondent who wished not to be identified.

47. John Schenk, letter to his wife, dated March 21, 1943.

48. John Schenk, letter to his wife, dated May 15, 1943.

49. John Schenk, letter to his wife, dated May 19, 1943.

50. Ivylyn Schenk (Hardy), letter to her husband John Schenk, dated June 12, 1943.

51. *Bedford Democrat*, October 26, 1944, p. 1.

52. *Bedford Democrat*, June 3, 1945, p. 1.

53. *Bedford Democrat*, October 4, 1945, p. 5.

54. *Bedford Bulletin,* August 16, 1945, p. 1.

55. *Bedford Democrat*, August 16, 1945, p. 1.

Chapter 12: Communicating with Loved Ones

1. *Bedford Democrat*, July 30, 1942, p. 3.

2. Yowell, op. cit., pp. 20-21.

3. Yowell, op. cit., p. 102.

4. Ivylyn Schenk Hardy has saved the telegrams she received from her first husband, John Schenk. She sent him at least one telegram, to which he referred in a letter to her dated September 24, 1943.

5. Author's interview with Ivylyn Schenk Hardy, August 6, 2002.

6. Bernard Saunders, *War Memoirs*, pp. 21-22. A copy of these unpublished memoirs is available at the Bedford Library.

7. Author's interview with Earl and Elva Newcomb, June 3, 2002.

8. Correspondence from early 1941 to mid-1944 between John Schenk and Ivylyn Jordan Schenk, who became his wife in August 1942, includes each of these types of letters, including only one "Soldier's Letter." Much of the information in Chapter 12 on types of correspondence is based on the Schenks' letters. The source of information on postage costs is the *Bedford Bulletin*, March 8, 1944, p. 1.

9. *Bedford Democrat*, July 23, 1942, p. 1; October 15, 1942, p. 6; and June 17, 1943, p. 1.

10. *Bedford Bulletin*, July 23, 1942, p. 1; Krull, op. cit., p. 42; author's interview with Ivylyn Schenk Hardy, August 6, 2002; and correspondence between Ivylyn Schenk Hardy and her first husband, John Schenk.

11. V-Mail letter from John Schenk to his wife, dated January 4, 1943.

12. Yowell, op. cit., p. 116, (letter dated July 21, 1944).

13. *Bedford Democrat*, January 7, 1943, p. 1.

14. Captain Fellers' name appeared as the censor on envelopes from John Schenk in the early days of Company A's deployment to England, but this soon changed and the names of the executive officer, Lt. E. Ray Nance, and others then began appearing.

15. *Bedford Bulletin*, April 22, 1943, p. 1.

16. John Schenk, letter dated October 8, 1942.

17. John Schenk, letter dated October 16, 1942.

18. John Schenk, V-Mail letter dated January 21, 1943.

19. John Schenk, V-Mail letter dated January 25, 1943.

20. John Schenk, V-Mail letter dated February 15, 1943.

21. Yowell, op. cit., p. 134, (letter dated August 20, 1944).

22. Yowell, op. cit., p. 68, (letter from William Yowell, April 23, 1944).

23. Yowell, op. cit., p. 77, (letter dated May 18, 1944).

24. Yowell, op. cit., p. 100, (letter dated June 25, 1944).

25. *Bedford Bulletin*, March 16, 1944, p. 7, and *News & Advance* (Lynchburg, Virginia), June 3, 2001, p. II-4.

26. Staff Sergeant Draper's poem is in a personal notebook, which is now in the possession of his brother Warren Gamiel Draper.

27. *Bedford Bulletin*, April 22, 1943, p. 1.

28. Yowell, op. cit., p. 82, (letter dated May 23, 1944).

29. John Schenk, letter postmarked October 29, 1942.

30. John Schenk, V-Mail letter dated November 3, 1942.

31. John Schenk, V-Mail letter dated November 24, 1942.

32. John Schenk, V-Mail letter dated November 28, 1942.

33. John Schenk, V-Mail letter dated January 4, 1943.

34. John Schenk, V-Mail letter dated January 19, 1943.

35. John Schenk, V-Mail letter dated January 24, 1943.

36. John Schenk, V-Mail letter dated February 1, 1943.

37. John Schenk, V-Mail letter dated March 12, 1943.

38. John Schenk, V-Mail letter dated August 28, 1943.

39. Yowell, op. cit., p. 68, (letter dated April 23, 1944).

40. Yowell, op. cit., p. 77, (letter dated May 18, 1944).

41. Yowell, op. cit., p. 107, (letter dated July 7, 1944).

42. Ivylyn Schenk, V-Mail letter to John Schenk, dated April 12, 1943.

43. Ivylyn Schenk, letter to John Schenk, dated July 28, 1943.

44. Yowell, op. cit., p. 69, (letter dated April 23, 1944).

45. Yowell, op. cit., p. 73, (letter dated May 2, 1944).

46. Yowell, op. cit., p. 97, (letter of June 20, 1944).

47. Yowell, op. cit., pp. 99-100, (letter of June 23, 1944).

48. Ivylyn Schenk, letter to John Schenk, dated December 26, 1943.

49. Yowell, op. cit., p. 79, (letter dated May 19, 1944).

50. Yowell, op. cit., p. 82, (letter dated May 23, 1944).

51. Yowell, op. cit., p. 83, (letter dated May 25, 1944).

52. Yowell, op. cit., p. 110, (letter dated July 12, 1944).
53. John Schenk, V-Mail letter dated February 21, 1944.
54. John Schenk, letter dated October 2, 1942.
55. John Schenk, V-Mail letter dated January 16, 1943.
56. John Schenk, V-Mail letter dated February 3, 1943.
57. John Schenk, V-Mail letter dated August 19, 1943.
58. John Schenk, V-Mail letter dated October 26, 1943.
59. John Schenk, V-Mail letter dated January 4, 1944.
60. John Schenk, V-Mail letter dated January 11, 1944.
61. John Schenk, V-Mail letter dated January 19, 1944.
62. John Schenk, V-Mail letter dated February 11, 1944. Schenk's unit, Company A, was originally filled with men from the Bedford area but men from northern states were added as time went by.
63. John Schenk, V-Mail letter dated March 2, 1944.
64. John Schenk, Air Mail letter dated April 23, 1944.
65. John Schenk, Air Mail letter dated May 22, 1943.
66. Yowell, op. cit., p. 79, (letter dated May 20, 1944).
67. Yowell, op. cit., p. 81, (letter dated May 22, 1944).
68. Yowell, op. cit., p. 89, (letter dated June 6, 1944).
69. Yowell, op. cit., p. 91, (letter dated June 8, 1944).
70. Yowell, op. cit., p. 112, (letter dated July 13, 1944).
71. Yowell, op. cit., p. 114, (letter dated July 18, 1944).
72. Yowell, op. cit., pp. 124-125, (letter dated August 1, 1944), and p. 127, (letter dated August 4, 1944).
73. John Schenk, V-Mail letter dated September 12, 1943.
74. John Schenk, V-Mail letter dated January 23, 1943.
75. *Bedford Democrat*, January 14, 1943, p. 1.
76. Yowell, op. cit., p. 21, (letter dated April 22, 1943).
77. Yowell, op. cit., p. 45, (letter dated December 15, 1943).
78. Yowell, op. cit., pp. 45 and 47, (letters dated December 15 and 31, 1943).
79. John Schenk, V-Mail letter dated May 19, 1943.
80. Ivylyn Schenk, letter to John Schenk, dated July 22, 1943, and interviews with Ivylyn Schenk, June 12 and 18, 2002.
81. *Bedford Bulletin*, February 22, 1945, p. 1, and April 12, 1945, p. 8.
82. Yowell, op. cit., p. 70, (letter dated April 25, 1944).
83. Yowell, op. cit., p. 68, (letter dated April 23, 1944).
84. John Schenk, V-Mail letters dated January 16, February 20, September 8 1943, and January 25, 1944.
85. Yowell, op. cit., p. 101, (letter dated June 26, 1944).
86. John Schenk, V-Mail letter dated January 1, 1943.
87. Yowell, op. cit., pp. 24, 44, 45, 81, 106, 107, and 136, (letters dated May 16, 1943, December 9, 1943, May 22, 1944, July 1, 1944, July 5, 1944, and August 25, 1944).

88. *Bedford Bulletin*, November 30, 1944, p. 1.
89. *Bedford Bulletin*, November 30, 1944, p. 1.
90. *Bedford Bulletin*, June 1, 1944, p. 2.
91. A copy of Staff Sergeant Draper's poem from the newspaper may be found in the Bedford Museum.
92. *Bedford Bulletin*, June 1, 1944, p. 2.
93. Yowell, op. cit., p. 105, (letter dated June 30, 1944).
94. Yowell, op. cit., p. 112, (letter dated July13, 1944).
95. John Schenk, letter dated September 4, 1942.
96. John Schenk, letter dated September 5, 1942.
97. John Schenk, letter dated October 2, 1942.
98. John Schenk, letter postmarked December 31, 1942.
99. Ivylyn Schenk, letter to John Schenk, dated May 21, 1943.
100. John Schenk, letter dated January 1, 1943.
101. John Schenk, V-Mail letter dated February 12, 1943.
102. John and Ivylyn Schenk correspondence.

Chapter 13: D-Day—Bedford's Special Tragedy

1. Barnes, op. cit., p. 49.
2. Ibid., p. 57.
3. Balkoski, op. cit., p. 61, and Barnes, op. cit., p. 57.
4. Morning reports for Company A, which provide unit totals but not rosters of men by name, are maintained by the National Archives and Records Administration. Carol Tuckwiller at the National D-Day Memorial Foundation provided courtesy copies to the author. According to John Barnes, *Fragments of My Life with Company A...*, op. cit., pp. 57 and 139, the normal strength of Company A was about 180-220 men; around D-Day, he believes 220 men were on the company's rolls. In his book, Barnes incorporated a roster of Company A for June 6, 1944, said to have been obtained in about 1984 by Robert Rowe, Captain, U.S. Navy, (Ret.), from official sources, including the National Archives. This roster lists 209 men, to which Barnes would add three more.
5. Barnes, op. cit., p. 60. According to Balkoski, p. 6, each of the 116th Infantry's three battalions were aboard separate transport ships--1st Battalion aboard the *Empire Javelin*, 2d Battalion aboard the *Thomas Jefferson*, and 3d Battalion aboard the *Charles Carroll*.
6. *Shipping Magazine*, June 1994, pp. 25-35. The *Empire Javelin* was an infantry landing ship with a gross tonnage of 7,177. It was built by the Consolidated Steel Corporation in Wilmington, California, in 1944. On December 28, 1944, it was torpedoed and sunk in the English Channel by the German submarine U-772. There were more than 1,400 troops aboard. The *Empire Javelin's* crew and escort boats saved all but six men, according to Samuel E. Morison, *The Atlantic Battle Won, May 1943-May 1945, Volume X, History of the United States Naval Operations in World War II*, (Boston: Little Brown and Company,

1956), p. 337. On December 30, 1944, U-772 was sunk in the English Channel south of Weymouth, England, by depth charges from a Canadian military aircraft, killing the crew of forty-eight; see website http://uboat.net/index/html.

7. *Bedford Democrat*, April 13, 1944, p. 1.

8. *Bedford Democrat*, April 27, 1944, p. 1.

9. *Bedford Democrat*, May 25, 1944, p. 2.

10. *New York Times,* June 3, 1944, p. 1.

11. Ivylyn Schenk letter of June 3, 1944, to her husband John Schenk. The letter would eventually be returned to her from England, its envelope marked "deceased."

12. *New York Times,* June 4, 1944, pp. 1 and 12.

13. *New York Times*, June 4, 1944, p. 1.

14. Stephen E. Ambrose, *D-Day June 6, 1944: The Climactic Battle of World War II* (New York: A Touchstone Book, Simon & Schuster, 1995), pp. 24-25.

15. Omar Bradley and Clay Blair, *A General's Life: An Autobiography by General of the Army Omar N. Bradley and Clay Blair* (New York: Simon & Schuster, 1983), pp. 244, 249, and 250, and Samuel Eliot Morison, *The Two-Ocean War: The Definitive Short History of the United States Navy in World War II* (New York: Ballantine Books, paperback edition, 1972), p. 333.

16. Morison, op. cit., p. 333.

17. Bradley and Blair, op. cit., p. 250.

18. Morison, op. cit., p. 337.

19. Ibid.

20. See the plan for phased attack by the 116th Regimental Combat Team, Historical Division, War Department, reproduced in Ambrose, *D-Day*, op. cit., pp. 122-123.

21. Ibid.

22. Ibid.

23. Slaughter, op. cit., Chapter 7.

24. Ambrose, op. cit., pp. 122-123.

25. Slaughter, op. cit., Chapter 7.

26. Ambrose, op. cit., pp. 122-123.

27. Barnes, op. cit., p. 60.

28. Ibid, p. 62, and Slaughter, Chapter 7. General Eisenhower's letter, on stationery of the Supreme Headquarters Allied Expeditionary Force, is quoted here from a reproduction printed in the Current News Special Edition published by the Department of Defense on June 6, 1994, a copy of which is maintained in the Bedford Museum.

29. D-Day veterans have given differing estimates of the weight of the equipment they carried. Roy Stevens has estimated sixty pounds, while E. Ray Nance has estimated seventy pounds (see *Bedford Bulletin*, June 8, 1994, pp. 1 and 3A). In their memoirs or books (see bibliography), John Robert Slaughter estimates sixty pounds (Chapter 4), John Barnes estimates seventy pounds (p. 62), and

Harold Baumgarten estimates one hundred pounds of equipment and weapons (p. 3).

30. S/Sgt. Draper's small, black notebook is in the possession of his brother, Warren Gamiel Eugene Draper.

31. *Bedford Bulletin*, June 8, 1944, p. 1.

32. Ibid.

33. Ibid.

34. Ibid.

35. *Bedford Bulletin*, June 15, 1944, p. 1.

36. Ibid.

37. *Bedford Bulletin*, June 15, 1944, p. 6.

38. *Bedford Bulletin*, June 22, 1944, p. 1.

39. *Bedford Bulletin*, June 22, 1944, p. 1, and July 27, 1944, p. 1.

40. Walter Owens, *as briefed...a family history of the 384th Bombardment Group*, (self-published, 1946), pp. 113 and 125. Cornelius Ryan, *The Longest Day* (New York: A Touchstone Book, Simon & Schuster, 1994), p. 199, reports that the crews of 329 Allied bombers assigned to drop their bombs on the German guns on Omaha Beach were unable to see the beach because of clouds, did not want to risk bombing Allied troops, and hence dropped their bombs three miles inland.

41. Morison, op. cit., p. 337.

42. William B. Kirkland, Jr., *Destroyers at Normandy: Naval Gunfire Support at Omaha Beach* (Washington, D.C.: Naval Historical Foundation, Washington, 1944), p. 26. A copy of this book is maintained in the Bedford Library.

43. Bradley and Blair, op. cit., p. 250.

44. Barnes, op. cit., pp. 62-63.

45. Roy Stevens estimates the landing craft sank 500 yards from shore, for example, see *Bedford Bulletin*, June 8, 1994, p. 1. Several other sources estimate the craft was 1,000 yards from shore when it sank; see Kirkland, op. cit., pp. 45-47; and " 'D-Day,' 6 June 1944, Account of the 116th Infantry Regiment," notes prepared by the commanding general and others, a copy of which is maintained at the Bedford Museum. Former Royal Navy Sub-lieutenant George Green has estimated the craft sank about a mile from the beach. John Barnes, who was in the craft with Roy Stevens, has estimated the boat sank 1,000-2,000 yards out; see Barnes, op. cit., p. 68;

46. Former Sub-lieutenant Green's account is in *Overlord Report*, the newsletter of the National D-Day Memorial Foundation, Issue 4, Summer 1999, p. 2. For Roy Stevens' account, see the *Bedford Bulletin*, June 8, 1994, p. 1, and his interview in the "D-Day Oral History Readings" for Company A, a copy of which is maintained in the Bedford Museum. Cornelius Ryan, *The Longest Day*, op. cit., p. 203, reports that many of the assault craft began to take on water as soon as they were lowered from the transport ships.

47. Barnes, op. cit., p. 65.

48. Kirkland, op. cit., pp. 45-47.
49. Author's interview with Roy O. Stevens, January 30, 2002, and *Bedford Bulletin*, June 8, 1994, p. 1.
50. Barnes, op. cit., p. 70.
51. Gordon A. Harrison, *Cross-Channel Attack, The European Theater of Operations, U.S. Army in World War II* (Washington, D.C.: Office of the Chief of Military History, Department of the Army, 1951). A copy of this document is in the Bedford Museum. Along these lines, Cornelius Ryan, *The Longest Day*, op. cit., p. 225, wrote about one of Company A's landing craft disintegrating in one blinding moment and the men being blown out of the craft. Ryan wrote that it was the craft bearing Lt. Gearing. Ryan's account appears incorrect. Lt. Gearing was aboard the landing craft that sank hundreds of yards from the shore. Gearing ordered that the men rescued from the sunken craft return to England to be reoutfitted and then returned to France; Gearing, himself, hitched a ride on a vessel directly to Omaha Beach and organized survivors in fighting the Germans.
52. Ambrose, op. cit., p. 126.
53. Alex Kershaw, *The Bedford Boys: One American Town's Ultimate D-Day Sacrifice* (Cambridge, Massachusetts: Da Capo Press, 2003), pp. 127-128, and *Overlord Report*, op. cit., Issue 4, Summer 1999, p. 2.
54. Balkoski, op. cit., p. 125.
55. Article from the *Los Angeles Times*, carried in the May 29, 1994, *Daily Press* (city not known). A copy of this article is available at the Bedford Museum.
56. Kirkland, op. cit., p. 20.
57. *Omaha Beachhead, American Forces in Active Service*, U.S. War Department, History Division, 1945, reprinted in 1984, pp. 45-47, quoted in Kirkland, op. cit. p. 29.
58. *Bedford Bulletin,* June 10, 1954, p. 4.
59. Harrison, op. cit., pp. 313-314.
60. "The 'D-Day' Account of the 116th Infantry Regiment," Company A section. This account was prepared by the 29th Infantry Division's commanding general and seven survivors of Company A, including Pfc. Gilbert G. Murdock, Pfc. Leo J. Nash, Private Grosser, and Cpl. M. Gurry. A copy of this account is available at the Bedford Museum.
61. Bradley and Blair, op. cit., p. 251.
62. Samuel E. Morison, *The Invasion of France and Germany, Volume XI, History of United States Naval Operations in World War II* (Boston: Atlantic Monthly Press, 1975), quoted in Kirkland, p. 48.
63. Elizabeth Daniel, "D-Day—a Virginia town's memories," *News & Advance* (Lynchburg, Virginia), repeated in *Virginia Guardpost*, summer 1984, published by the Public Affairs Detachment of the Virginia Army National Guard, and *Bedford Bulletin*, June 8, 1994, pp. 1 and 3A.
64. *Bedford Bulletin*, June 8, 1994, p. 1.

65. John Barnes, who has estimated that 212 men were on Company A's roster on D-Day, has also written that 102 men from Company A were killed in action on June 6 or shortly thereafter. See Barnes, op. cit., pp. 57, 69 and 139. J. Robert Slaughter's memoir, op. cit., contains a list compiled by Robert A. Rove, Captain, U.S. Navy (Ret.), which lists ninety-one men in Company A killed or missing in action on June 6, 1944. Copies of morning reports for Company A are maintained by the National Archives and Records Administration.
66. Barnes, op. cit., pp. 76-138.
67. Barnes, op. cit., p. 136. Barnes believes that the only men who were in Company A in June 1944 and remained with Company A or in associated units up to June 1945 were Mess Sergeant Earl Newcomb, Supply Sergeant Jack Mitchell, Gil Murdock who became the company clerk, George Roach who was back at regiment, Paul Turner, and himself. The author believes that four other men from Bedford County, who in addition to Earl Newcomb served as cooks during at least part of their service, were assigned to Company A from at least February 1941 to the end of the war. The four were Pfcs. Cedric Broughman, George Crouch, James Crouch, and Carl Danner.
68. Barnes, op. cit., p. 137.
69. Slaughter, op. cit., Chapter 8.
70. Balkoski, op. cit. p. 280.
71. Slaughter, op. cit., Chapter 12; losses for the 116th Infantry are from the U.S. Army unit citation of the 116th Infantry's heroism and performance on Omaha Beach. The 29th Infantry Division fought throughout the Western and Central European campaigns and was decorated and awarded campaign streamers for the battles of Normandy, Northern France, Rhineland, and Central Europe. It was deactivated at Camp Kilmer, New Jersey, on January 6, 1946. The division was reorganized and federally recognized at Roanoke, Virginia, on November 29, 1947. Its headquarters were moved to Staunton, Virginia, in March 1948. (For details see Seal, op. cit.)
72. *Bedford Democrat*, August 3, 1944, p. 1.
73. Bradley and Blair, op. cit., p. 249.
74. Author's interview with Ms. Carol Tuckwiller, Director of Research and Archives, National D-Day Memorial Foundation, Bedford, Virginia, January 13, 2004.
75. The names of the twenty Bedford men killed on D-Day are listed in Appendix B.
76. Barnes, op. cit. p. 66.
77. *Military Records of Bedford County's Gold Star Men in World War II*, op. cit.
78. *Bedford Bulletin*, July 13, 1944, p. 1.
79. *Bedford Bulletin,* July 20, 1944, p. 1.

Chapter 14: The Aftermath—Bedford's Sacrifice

1. *Bedford Bulletin*, July 13, 1944, p. 1.

2. See *Bedford Bulletin* and *Bedford Democrat* from mid-July to September 28, 1944.

3. Source is author's interview with Elizabeth Teass in 1999. Ms. Teass has granted several interviews, excerpts of which have been published in many publications, e.g., *Richmond Times-Dispatch*, May 28, 2000, p. 7. For an audio-visual interview, see *Bedford—The Wave of Glory*, a documentary film by Jean-Louis Douchez, Atelier Cinema de Normandie, 2001, a copy of which is maintained at the Bedford Library.

4. *Bedford Bulletin*, July 20, 1944, p. 1.

5. Ibid.

6. *Bedford Democrat,* July 20, 1944, p. 1. The Rosazza family was reported to be living in Washington, D.C.

7. *Bedford Democrat*, July 20, 1944, p. 1. M/Sgt. John Wesley Dean, one of seven brothers to serve in World War II, was reported killed in action in France on June 17. The parents of Pvt. Hudson M. Lacy of Huddleston were informed that their son was killed in action in the Mediterranean Theater of Operations. The parents of T/5 Charles J. Gibbs, who previously had been reported missing in action, were informed that their son had been killed in action in Italy on January 26. Pvt. William Bush, who entered the service with Company A, was reported seriously injured in France on June 11. Maj. Fred McManaway, Sgt. Glenwood E. Overstreet, and Pfc. W. L. Watson were each reported wounded in France at unspecified times during the invasion.

8. Ibid.

9. Author's interview with Lucille Hoback Boggess, May 1999.

10. *Bedford Bulletin*, July 20, 1944, pp. 1 and 8.

11. *Bedford Bulletin*, July 20, 1944, pp. 1 and 8, and August 3, 1944, p. 1.

12. *Bedford Bulletin*, July 20, 1944, p. 8.

13. *Bedford Bulletin*, September 28, 1944, p. 1.

14. Yowell, op. cit., pp. 119-120, (letter of July 25, 1944).

15. Company A soldier John Barnes, whose landing craft sank hundreds of yards off Omaha Beach and who was rescued by a landing craft returning from the beach, has reported seeing Technical Sergeant Draper lying wounded in another landing craft headed away from the beach and has written that Draper "would live only a few more minutes." See Barnes, op. cit., p. 66. Information believed to have been provided by Frank Draper's mother, however, indicates that he died either twelve hours after being wounded or being evacuated early in the morning of June 6 or twelve hours after arriving at a hospital in England, the latter possibly making the date of death June 7. The information attributed to Mrs. Draper and recorded in the *Military Records of Bedford County's Gold Star Men in World War II*, op. cit., stated that her son was "wounded and could get no medical aid, was carried to England to hospital but too late. He died within 12 hours."

16. Information on the tablets of the missing at the Normandy American Cemetery in France and the list in John Robert Slaughter's memoir, op. cit., lists Earl Parker's date of death as June 6, 1944. Information believed to have been provided by his mother in *Military Records of Bedford County's Gold Star Men in World War II*, gives June 7 as the date of his death. The latter may reflect the government's policy of declaring a missing service person as dead one year and one day after he or she was reported missing in action. Mrs. Parker may have written June 7, 1944.

17. *Bedford Bulletin*, July 20, 1944, p. 8 and *Bedford Democrat*, August 10, 1944, p. 1.

18. Statements to the effect that Bedford—Bedford County, the town of Bedford, or the Bedford community—lost more men on D-Day, per capita, than any other community in America have been made in the *New York Times*, *Washington Post*, *USA Today*, *Roanoke Times*, *News & Advance* (Lynchburg, Virginia), and *Bedford Bulletin*, among others. The National D-Day Memorial Foundation has included a similar statement in some of its publications. This author included such a statement in a historical drama about Bedford County in World War II. The *Roanoke Times*, in an article on July 2, 2002, challenged whether there was sufficient proof to make such statements. The initial source of this statement is uncertain. One of the first such statements was made by Gates R. Richardson, on page 169 of his chapter "Bedford County's Part in the Two World Wars," in *The Military History of Bedford County, 1754-1950*, op. cit. Richardson, writing about Bedford's loss in the war generally, not just on D-Day, wrote: "Bedford County suffered heavily in World War II. It has been pointed out that our losses in lives were on the average about twice those of other population groups of the same size for the county as a whole." In 1959, Cornelius Ryan in *The Longest Day: June 6, 1944*, op. cit., page 281, suggested that the town of Bedford with a population of 3,800 lost twenty-three men on D-Day. Ryan's statement is incorrect in its use of the number twenty-three (probably reflecting the number on the stone outside the Bedford Courthouse, a number broader than just D-Day casualties), and he suggested the men killed came from the town of Bedford, whereas approximately two-thirds of the men came from outside the town in the broader Bedford County, with a population of nearly 30,000. The *Bedford Bulletin* on June 8, 1994, page 1, reported that: "Before the day was over, more than 90 percent of the men in Company A were dead or wounded. Twenty-one of about 35 Bedford soldiers in the unit were killed, more deaths per capita than any other comparable community in the nation, according to the U.S. Department of Defense." The author has made inquiries but has not been able to identify any such Department of Defense source. The National D-Day Memorial Foundation has undertaken a major project to collect all the names of Allied service personnel who died on June 6 in the invasion. It might be possible to use the foundation's database to gather information on the residences of those killed and then factor in census data for the 1940s to try

to determine with some certainty whether or not the Bedford community lost more men on D-Day, per capita, than any other community in America, but this would be a major undertaking.

19. See www.4pointw.org/flwmemorials.htm, including Robert Brimm, "Rounds Away: Two years of Combat with the 83ᵈ Chemical Mortar Battalion."

20. See www.100th ww2.org/support/cm/cm.html.

21. See (a) website www.msfb.com/news/FarmCountry/sept01/tragedy.html for article by Ed Blake, "World War II sea tragedy is finally laid to rest," in *Mississippi Farm Country*, September 2001, Mississippi Farm Bureau Federation; and (b) note number 19 and 20 above.

22. See website for the American Battle Monuments Commission, www.abmc.gov., for World War II deaths, and *Military Records of Bedford County's Gold Star Men in World War II*, op. cit.

23. See *Military Records* cited in note 22 above.

24. See www.abmc.gov, and records at Carder Tharp Funeral Home and Crematory.

25. Martin Blumenson, *United States Army in World War II, The Mediterranean Theater of Operations, Salerno to Cassino*, (Washington, D.C.: Office of the Chief of Military History, United States Army, 1969). Also, Wynford Vaughan-Thomas, *Anzio* (New York: Holt, Rinehart and Winston, 1961). Also Ed Blake. "World War II sea tragedy is finally laid to rest," op. cit. Also the *New York Times*, January 26-31, 1944.

26. Author's interviews with William H. Merriken, a Malmedy Massacre survivor, in 1999 and on October 8, 2002. Sources differ on the number of Americans killed in the Malmedy Massacre. One source, Hugh M. Cole, *U.S. Army in World War II, European Theater of Operations, The Ardennes: Battle of the Bulge* (Washington, D.C.: Office of the Chief of Military History, Department of the Army, 1965), p. 261, states that at least eighty-six Americans were massacred at Malmedy. Another source, John M. Bauserman, *The Malmedy Massacre* (Shippensburg, Pennsylvania: White Mane Books, 1995), pp. 84, 109, 110, lists eighty-one American soldiers killed in the massacre. Bauserman believes that three other Americans whose bodies were found in the area belonged to a different unit and were killed either before or after the massacre of B Battery.

27. In the *Induction and Discharge Records, World War II, Bedford County*, maintained in the office of the Clerk of the Circuit Court at the Bedford County Courthouse, there are listed 2,958 men from Bedford County who enlisted or were inducted in the U.S. armed forces during the World War II period, up to mid-August 1945. Not included in this number are: (1) men who had joined the National Guard and were called to active duty as part of their National Guard unit and who were subsequently killed or died while in service; former Guardsmen who survived World War II and were discharged are included through their discharge records; (2) some men who had been born or had lived in Bedford County but who enlisted or were inducted outside Bedford County;

(3) all women from Bedford County who enlisted in the armed forces in World War II; *Military Service Records* (Bedford County), *World War II, Volume IV*, also maintained in the office of the Clerk of the Circuit Court, lists thirty-six women who served during World War II. The collection, *Induction and Discharge Records, World War II, Bedford County*, includes a general index book and nine detailed books, which, despite the title, contain records ranging from World War II into the 1990s and perhaps beyond. The first five-and-a-half books, up to Book 6, page 258, contain records up to mid-August 1945; subsequent pages and books contain records from the second half of August 1945 and into subsequent years. Late in 2002, the Clerk's office removed these ten books from general public access in response to legislation by the Virginia General Assembly to protect privacy. As to Bedford County's population, U.S. Census records indicate the population of Bedford County was 29,687 in 1940 and about the same in 1950. (In World War I, a much smaller proportion of Bedford's citizens served in the military--about one out of every thirty citizens; see Richardson, op. cit., p. 163.)

28. The U.S. Defense Department's *Defense Almanac, 1994*, page 47, indicates that 16,112,566 individuals served in the U.S. Army (including the U.S. Army Air Force), Navy, and Marine Corps from December 7, 1941 to December 31, 1946, when hostilities were officially terminated by presidential proclamation. The number of those serving only up to the time of cessation of hostilities in August 1945 would be smaller. The U.S. population in the 1940 U.S. Census was 132,164,569, and it rose in the ensuing years so that in 1950 it was 151,325,798. Using the figure of sixteen million serving and the 1940 population of 132 million, this would mean that about 12 percent of Americans served; however, counting only those who served up to August 1945 (when this author cut off counting the number of Bedford County men serving) and increasing the U.S. population by several million as the population probably increased in the early 1940s (Bedford County's population actually fell slightly during the 1940s), the percentage of Americans serving may have been closer to 10 or 11 percent, closer to Bedford's 10 percent.

29. For details on which this summary assessment is based, see Appendix A, "Bedford County Men Who Were Killed or Died While Serving in the Armed Forces in World War II." Trying to determine the number of Bedford County men who were killed or died during World War II is a difficult, uncertain task. There are a variety of sources, both official and unofficial. Variables include starting and ending dates for the time period considered (e.g., the end of hostilities in August 1945 or the presidential declaration terminating the war in December 1946), how one is or is not determined to be a Bedford County man (e.g., born, raised, and always lived in the county; moved to the county and lived there some amount of time; moved away but parents still living there, etc.), and the circumstances of death. A mid-1946 War Department report listed eighty men from Bedford as killed or died during the war, including forty-seven

killed in action, eight died of wounds, eighteen died of non-battle reasons, and seven a finding of death after being missing in action for a year; see *World War II Honor List of Dead and Missing, State of Virginia*, U.S. War Department, June 1946, an extract of which is maintained in the Bedford City/County Museum. This list excludes Navy and Marine Corps personnel. Other sources include many Army personnel not listed in this report.

30. In the *Military Records of Bedford County's Gold Star Men in World War II*, maintained in the Bedford County Office of the Clerk of the Circuit Court, the entry for John Cleveland Smith includes information attributed to his mother, Susie Smith, of Vinton, Virginia, to the effect that he was court-martialed and hanged by U.S. authorities on March 3, 1945, in England. The author requested and obtained further information from the U.S. Government, both the National Archives and Records Administration and the U.S. Army Judiciary. According to this official information, on the afternoon of September 2, 1944, Private Smith and two other U.S. Army soldiers serving in a quartermaster troop transport company, stopped at a French home in Le Noyer, Commune de Bure, Orne, France, and asked for something to drink. The family gave them cider, and the men stayed for half an hour. The three men returned late that night, knocked on the door for a long time until it was opened, pointed a rifle at the husband and his uncle, and then forced the wife—a mother of a 2 ½ year-old child—outside. While one of the men used the rifle to force the husband and his uncle to remain in the house, the second soldier restrained the woman, and the third raped her. The men then switched positions, each taking a turn raping the woman. Each of the three men was arraigned and tried before a general court-martial convened at Rambouillet, France, on October 18 and 19, 1944, and each was found guilty of violating the 92[d] Article of War, an article dealing with rape. They were convicted specifically of having carnal knowledge forcibly and feloniously, against her will, with a French female (whom this author has chosen not to name). Smith was sentenced to be hanged by the neck until dead, a sentence that was carried out on March 3, 1945, at Le Mele Sur Sartie, Orne, France, under the direction of the Commanding Officer of the American Loire Disciplinary Training Center. The other two men were probably executed similarly.

Chapter 15: Honoring Veterans & War Dead

1. See especially the *News & Advance* (Lynchburg, Virginia), June 3, 2001, and the *Richmond Times-Dispatch*, May 28, 2000.
2. *Bedford Democrat*, September 3, 1942, p. 1.
3. *Bedford Democrat*, September 10, 1942, p. 8.
4. *Bedford Democrat*, September 24, 1942, an interior page.
5. *Bedford Democrat*, October 8, 1942, p. 6.
6. *Bedford Democrat*, December 10, 1942, an interior page.
7. *Bedford Democrat*, January 7, 1943, p. 1.

8. *Bedford Democrat,* May 13, 1943, p. 1.

9. *Bedford Bulletin,* February 24, 1944, p. 7

10. *Bedford Bulletin,* June 22, 1944, p. 1.

11. The author could find no remembrances at two of the larger churches in Bedford City—the Roman Catholic and Presbyterian Churches. St. John's Episcopal Church was reported in July 1943 to have unveiled a scroll or plaque upon which were listed the names of thirty men in the congregation serving in the Armed Services, but this appears no longer to be displayed in the church. (See *Bedford Democrat* and *Bedford Bulletin* of July 15, 1943.)

12. *Bedford Democrat,* January 28, 1943, p. 1.

13. *Bedford Democrat,* May 13, 1943, p. 1.

14. *Bedford Democrat,* July 15, 1943, p. 1; *Bedford Bulletin,* July 29, 1943, p. 1.

15. *Bedford Democrat,* September 16, 1943, p. 1.

16. *Bedford Democrat,* December 2, 1943, p. 1.

17. *Bedford Bulletin,* February 24, 1944, p. 1.

18. *Bedford Democrat,* April 27, 1944, p. 1.

19. *Bedford Democrat,* August 31, 1944, p. 1.

20. *Bedford Bulletin,* December 7, 1944, p. 1.

21. *Bedford Bulletin,* June 21, 1945, p. 1.

22. *Bedford Democrat,* September 16, 1943, p. 1.

23. *Bedford Democrat,* November 25, 1943, p. 1.

24. *Bedford Democrat,* January 27, 1944, p. 1.

25. *Bedford Democrat,* February 17, 1944, p. 1.

26. *Bedford Democrat,* January 17, 1946, p. 1.

27. *Bedford Democrat,* August 6, 1944, repeated on February 1, 1945, p. 2.

28. *Bedford Bulletin,* April 26, 1945, p. 1.

29. The source is an undated clipping containing August 27-29, 1945, letters to the editor of the *Bedford Democrat,* maintained in the files of the Bedford Museum.

30. *Bedford Democrat,* September 13, 1945, p. 1.

31. *Bedford Democrat,* July 11, 1946, p. 1.

32. *Bedford Democrat,* August 1, 1946, p. 1.

33. *Bedford Democrat,* August 26, 1946, p. 1.

34. The principal speaker at the cornerstone laying ceremony was Charles E. Green, the proprietor of Green's Drug Store. The complete sentence, reported in a short article in the *Bedford Bulletin,* November 12, 1953, p. 1, was: "It is indeed fitting and proper that the laying of the cornerstone of Bedford Memorial Hospital should fall on Armistice Day, since it is to be a memorial to the loved ones and friends of the people of Bedford County, including those who so gallantly gave their lives for their country."

35. *Bedford County Bicentennial, 1754-1954, August 8-14, 1954, Official Program,* op. cit., pp. 91-92.

36. Ibid.

37. Ibid.

38. Ibid.

39. *Bedford County Bicentennial Official Program,* op. cit., p. 91. The list of men memorialized on this plaque, at least for World War II, was prepared by the Bedford County History Committee and reflects the Bedford portion of the list published in the *Gold Star Honor Roll of Virginians in the Second World War,* op. cit. The use of asterisks on the plaque to denote Blacks probably stemmed from work of the Virginia World War II History Commission, which worked with local county and city committees to compile the names of the World War II dead. In an introduction to the book listing those killed, the commission's author stated that asterisks were used to identify Negro personnel on their master list "upon the urgent request of Negro scholars who have pointed out that to do so would pave the paths of research for students of the Negro's part in the war effort." See W. Edwin Hemphill, editor, *Gold Star Honor Roll of Virginians in the Second World War,* Virginia World War II History Commission, Charlottesville, Virginia, 1947.

40. *Bedford County Bicentennial Official Program,* op. cit., p. 92, and *Bedford Bulletin,* June 3 and 10, 1954, p. 1.

41. Ibid.

42. Ibid.

43. *Roanoke Times,* June 6, 1998, pp. A1 and A6.

44. *Bedford Bulletin,* November 16, 1994, p. 1.

45. *Roanoke Times,* June 6, 1999, pp. E1, E4, and E5; April 15, 2001, pp. 1 and A6.

46. *This is Bedford,* March 28, 2001, pp. 40-41; undated Fact Sheet from National D-Day Memorial Foundation.

47. *Roanoke Times,* June 7, 2001, p. A10, and *Bedford Bulletin,* "Progress 2002," August 14, 2002, p. 6.

48. *Roanoke Times,* December 15, 2002, pp. B1 and B7, and January 13, 2004, pp. V1 and V3.

49. *Roanoke Times,* January 7, 2004, pp. 1 and 7, and January 13, 2004, pp. V1 and V3.

50. Ibid.

51. Ibid.

52. *Bedford Bulletin,* December 3, 2003, p. 2A, and *Roanoke Times,* January 13, 2004, pp. V1 and V3.

53. *Roanoke Times,* January 13, 2004, pp. V1 and V3.

54. *Bedford Bulletin,* August 3, 1944, p. 1.

55. *Bedford Bulletin,* September 14, 1944, p. 1.

56. *Bedford Bulletin,* November 30, 1944, p. 1.

57. *Bedford Democrat,* June 3, 1945, p. 1.

58. *Bedford Bulletin,* August 24, 1944, p. 1.

59. *Bedford Democrat,* May 24, 1945, p. 1.

60. *Bedford Democrat,* July 27, 1944, p. 4.

61. See http://americanwardead.com/listww.asp, a website of the American Battle Monuments Commission.

62. See http://www.abmc.gov, a website of the American Battle Monuments Commission. The website contains a list of 172,218 names of those buried in the commission's cemeteries, those missing in action, and those buried or lost at sea. It does not contain names of the 233,181 Americans whose remains were returned to the United States for burial.

63. *Bedford Bulletin*, November 27, 1947, p. 1. The four men from the town of Bedford and Company A were S/Sgt. Leslie C. Abbott, Pfc. John D. Clifton, Pfc. John F. Reynolds, and M/Sgt. John L. Wilkes. The others were Pfc. Houston G. Anthony of Lynch Station, Pvt. Ernest A. Bowyer of Thaxton, Pvt. Orie T. Martin of Huddleston, and Pvt. George R. Patterson of Moneta.

64. *Bedford Bulletin*, June 1, 1994, p. 1.

65. *News & Advance* (Lynchburg, Virginia), June 3, 2001, pp. II-1 to II-10.

66. *Bedford Bulletin*, August 10, 1944, p. 8.

67. *Bedford Bulletin*, August 24, 1944, p. 7.

68. *Bedford Bulletin*, August 10, 1944, p. 3.

69. The letter was published in the *Bedford Bulletin* shortly after it was received.

70. *Military Records of Bedford County's Gold Star Men in World War II*, op. cit.

71. Ibid.

72. Ibid.

73. Ibid.

74. Ibid. In 1948, Herbert Daniel's body was returned to Bedford, and a service and burial were conducted at Horeb Methodist Church in Huddleston.

75. This summary paraphrase is based on the author's interview with Lucille Hoback Boggess in 1999 and on accounts of other interviews published in newspapers. See for example, *Richmond Times-Dispatch*, May 28, 2000, pp. A1-A7, and *News & Advance* (Lynchburg, Virginia), June 3, 2001, pp. II-1 to II-10.

76. This summary paraphrase is based on accounts of several interviews published in newspapers. See for example, *Richmond Times-Dispatch*, May 28, 2000, pp. A1-A7, and *News & Advance* (Lynchburg, Virginia), June 3, 2001, pp. II-1 to II-10.

77. *Bedford Bulletin*, May 23, 1994, p.10A.

Part II – Personal Experiences

Chappelle
1. Most of the information is from the author's interview with Henry Chappelle, June 4, 2002.

Danner
1. Much of the information is from the author's interview with Mrs. R. G. (Margaret Danner) Simpkins, sister of Joseph S. Danner, on February 26, 2002.
2. See *Military Records of Bedford County's Gold Star Men in World War II*, op. cit.

Dean
1. Most of the information is from the author's interview with Ward A. Dean and Mary W. (Burks) Dean, February 26, 2002;
2. *Bedford Democrat*, February 10, 1944, p. 3. The Roanoke *World-News* reported that a couple in Roanoke also had seven sons serving (see undated article in the archives of the Bedford Museum).

Dooley
1. Most of the information is from the author's interview with Kenneth Dooley on April 24, 2002.

Draper
1. Much of the information is from the author's interview with Warren Gamiel Eugene Draper, May 31, 2002.
2. Sources about Frank Draper's death include Barnes, op. cit., p. 66; former British Naval officer George (Jimmy) Green; and *Military Records of Bedford County's Gold Star Men in World War II*. See the bibliography for details on these sources.

Fellers
1. Much of the information is from the author's interview with Mrs. Bertie Woodford, Captain Fellers' sister, February 15, 2002.
2. *Bedford Democrat*, August 17, 1944, p. 1.
3. *1940 Yearbook of the National Guard of the United States, Commonwealth of Virginia*. A copy of this book is in the Bedford Museum.
4. For sources, see Chapter 13.
5. Author's interview with Roy O. Stevens, February 2002.

Goode

1. Most of the information is from the author's interview with Joseph E. Goode, September 11 and 17, and October 7, 2002.
2. Parrish, (editor), op. cit., p. 41.
3. Owens, op. cit., p. 140.
4. Owens, op. cit., p. 154.
5. Owens, op. cit., pp. 31-34.
6. Owens, op. cit., p. 154.
7. Owens, op. cit., p. 210.
8. Owens, op. cit., p. 88.

Hatcher

1. *Bedford Democrat*, August 17, 1944, p. 1.
2. *Bedford Bulletin,* June 1, 1944, pp. 1 and 8.

Hoback

1. Most of the information is from the author's interview with Mrs. Lucille Hoback Boggess in 1999 and from various accounts in the media and military records.
2. *News & Advance* (Lynchburg, Virginia), June 3, 2001, p. II-6.
3. *1940 Yearbook of the National Guard of Virginia*, op. cit.
4. Roster of Company A on February 3, 1941, maintained in the files of the Bedford Museum.
5. *News & Advance* (Lynchburg, Virginia), June 3, 2001, p. II-6.
6. Roster of Company A, August 21, 1941, maintained in the files of the Bedford Museum.
7. *News & Advance* (Lynchburg, Virginia), June 3, 2001, p. II-6.
8. Slaughter, op. cit., list from official records of men killed on D-Day.
9. *Richmond Times-Dispatch*, May 30, 1994, p. A7; D-Day video, "Stories of Heroes, Virginians at Normandy," produced by Roanoke, Virginia, television station WDBJ7, June 1, 1994; and *USA Today*, April 28, 1994, p.1.
10. Slaughter, op. cit., Chapter 9, p. 2, notes by Dr. Harold Baumgarten.
11. *Richmond Times-Dispatch*, May 30, 1994, p. A7, and D-Day video, op. cit.
12. National Public Radio's "All Things Considered," June 6, 1994—transcript maintained in the Bedford Museum.
13. *Richmond Times-Dispatch*, May 28, 2000, p. A6.
14. *Richmond Times-Dispatch*, May 30, 1994, p. A7; D-Day video, op. cit.; and National Public Radio's "All Things Considered," June 6, 1994, op. cit.
15. National Public Radio's "All Things Considered," June 6, 1994, op. cit.
16. *USA Today*, April 28, 1994, p. 1.
17. *Washington Post*, June 2, 1944, p. 1.
18. *Richmond Times-Dispatch*, May 30, 1994, p. A7; D-Day video, op. cit.
19. Ibid.

Hobson
1. Most of the information is from the author's interview with Willie J. Hobson, October 7, 2002.

Hubbard
1. Interview with David Hubbard and review of the book he prepared for his father, Woodrow W. Hubbard, January 20, 2004.
2. Ship's History. www.USS-Picking.org/History.htm and www.nobadlie.com/picking.htm.

Huddleston
1. Most of the information is from the author's interview with Allen M. Huddleston, May 31, 2002.

Jarvis
1. Much of the information is from the author's interview with Nina Jarvis, April 23, 2002.
2. Viemeister, op. cit.

Merriken
1. Much of the information is from the author's interviews with William H. Merriken, spring 1999 and October 8, 2002.
2. *Bedford Bulletin* or *Bedford Democrat*, late August or early September, 1945. Copies of these newspaper articles are maintained in the files of the Bedford Museum.
3. *News & Advance* (Lynchburg, Virginia), December 16, 1984.
4. Ibid.
5. Ibid.
6. Ibid.
7. *Bedford Bulletin* or *Bedford Democrat*, late August or early September, 1945.
8. *News & Advance* (Lynchburg, Virginia), December 16, 1984.
9. Ibid.
10. Ibid.
11. Ibid.

Nance
1. As the author was not able to arrange an interview with Mr. Nance, this profile draws on reports largely found in newspapers.
2. *Bedford Bulletin*, June 7, 2000, p. 1.
3. Ibid.
4. *Washington Times*, June 5, 2000, p. 32.
5. *Bedford Bulletin*, November 30, 1944, p. 5.

6. *Richmond Times-Dispatch*, May 30, 1994, p. A-7; *Bedford Bulletin*, June 7, 2000, p. 1.
7. *Washington Times*, June 5, 2000, p. 32.
8. Ibid.
9. *Bedford Bulletin*, June 3 and 10, 1954, p. 1.

Newcomb
1. Most of the information is from the author's interview with the Newcombs, June 3, 2002.

Otey
1. Most of the information is from the author's interview with Marie R. Otey, January 14, 2004.

Parker
1. Much of the information is from the author's interview with William Eugene "Billy" Parker, February 2, 2002.
2. The gravesites of Earl and Joseph Parker are listed on the official website of the American Battle Monuments Commission at http://americanwardead.com/listww.asp.
3. Details about the POW camp at Moosburg are from Andrew Carroll (editor), *War Letters: Extraordinary Correspondence from American Wars* (New York: Scribner, 2001), pp. 277-279.
4. *Bedford Bulletin*, November 30, 1944, p. 1.

Saunders
1. Much of the information is from the author's interviews with Bernard W. Saunders in 1999 and his widow, Mrs. Margaret Saunders, on February 13, 2002, and from Bernard Saunders' "War Memoirs," a copy of which is maintained in the Bedford Library.
2. *Bedford Bulletin*, April 22, 1943.
3. Lyons, op. cit., pp. 165-166.
4. Bernard Saunders, "War Memoirs," op. cit.
5. *Bedford Bulletin*, May 31, 2000, pp. 1 and 2A.
6. *Bedford Democrat*, April 22, 1943, p. 1.
7. *Bedford Bulletin*, April 22, 1943, p. 1; also see folder "Misc.#1" in the Bedford Museum.
8. *Bedford Bulletin* and *Bedford Democrat*, December 16, 1943, p. 1.
9. *Bedford Democrat*, August 24, 1944, p. 1.
10. *Bedford Bulletin,* February 8, 1945, p. 1.
11. *Bedford Democrat*, December 6, 1945, pp. 1 and 12.
12. *Bedford Democrat*, September 20, 1945, p. 1.
13. *Bedford Democrat*, December 6, 1945, pp. 1 and 12.

Schenk

1. Much of the information is from the author's June 12 and 18, 2002, interviews with Ivylyn Schenk Hardy and some of Mrs. Hardy's letters, notes, and memorabilia.
2. Letter from John Schenk to Ivylyn Schenk, January 26, 1943.
3. Letter from John Schenk to Ivylyn Schenk, August 7, 1943.
4. Letter from Ivylyn Schenk to John Schenk, May 8, 1944.
5. Letter from Ivylyn Schenk to John Schenk, May 21, 1944.
6. Letter from Ivylyn Schenk to John Schenk, June 5, 1944.
7. Letter from Ivylyn Schenk to John Schenk, June 11, 1944.
8. Letter from Ivylyn Schenk to John Schenk, June 20, 1944.
9. Letter from Ivylyn Schenk to John Schenk, June 22, 1944.
10. Letter from Ivylyn Schenk to John Schenk, July 7, 1944.
11. Source of the grave number is the website of the American Battle Monuments Commission, http: //www:abmc.gov.

Stevens

1. Much of this information is from the author's interviews with Roy O. Stevens and Helen Cundiff Stevens in 1999 and on January 30, 2002.
2. *Bedford Bulletin*, June 8, 1994, p. 1.
3. *Bedford Bulletin*, September 28, 1944, p. 1.
4. *Bedford Bulletin*, April 5, 1945, p. 1.

Turpin

1. Most of the information is from the author's interviews with William Turpin on February 12, 2004, Charles Turpin on June 4, 2002, and Richard Turpin on July 16, 2002.

Wilkerson

1. All of the information is from the author's interview with Dean Wilkerson on April 23, 2002.

Wilkes

1. Most of the information is from the author's interview with Bettie Wilkes Hooper on June 6, 2002.

Wilson

1. Most of the information is from the author's interview with Boyd Wilson on April 23, 2002, and information shared at his funeral on January 2, 2004.

Wingfield

1. Most of the information is from the author's interview with Pride and Rebecca Wingfield on April 24, 2002.

Witt
1. *Bedford Bulletin*, April 13, 1944, p. 1.
2. *Bedford Bulletin,* October 19, 1944, p. 1
3. *Bedford Bulletin,* May 16, 1946, p. 1.
4. Ibid.

Yowell
1. Most of the information is from the author's interview with Eleanor Payne Yowell on April 2, 2002, and Mrs. Yowell's book, *Flying High: World War II Letters to and from U.S. Army Air Force Bases and the Home Front* (Lynchburg, Virginia: Warwick House Publishing, 2001).
2. Yowell, op. cit., pp. 134 and 136.

Index

C